FILM MUSIC: A HISTORY

P9-DFE-156

Film Music: A History explains the development of film music by considering large-scale aesthetic trends and structural developments alongside socioeconomic, technological, cultural, and philosophical circumstances.

The book's four large parts are given over to Music and the "Silent" Film (1894–1927), Music and the Early Sound Film (1894–1933), Music in the "Classical-Style" Hollywood Film (1933–1960), and Film Music in the Post-Classic Period (1958–2008). Whereas most treatments of the subject are simply chronicles of "great film scores" and their composers, this book offers a genuine history of film music in terms of societal changes and technological and economic developments within the film industry. Instead of celebrating film-music masterpieces, it deals—logically and thoroughly—with the complex "machine" whose smooth running allowed those occasional masterpieces to happen and whose periodic adjustments prompted the large-scale twists and turns in film music's path.

James Wierzbicki is a musicologist who teaches at the University of Michigan and serves as executive editor of the American Musicological Society's *Music of the United States of America* series of scholarly editions. His current research focuses on twentieth-century music in general and film music and electronic music in particular.

FILM MUSIC

A HISTORY

JAMES WIERZBICKI

NEW YORK AND LONDON

First published 2009
by Routledge
711 Third Avenue, New York, NY 10017

Simultaneously published in the UK
by Routledge
2 Park Square, Milton Park, Abingdon, Oxon OX14 4RN

*Routledge is an imprint of the Taylor & Francis Group,
an informa business*

Transferred to Digital Printing 2011

© 2009 Taylor & Francis

Typeset in Sabon by
Florence Production Ltd, Stoodleigh, Devon

Library of Congress Cataloging in Publication Data
  Wierzbicki, James Eugene.
  Film music: a history/James Wierzbicki.
  p. cm.
  1. Motion picture music—History and criticism. I. Title.
  ML2075.W54 2008
  781.5′4209—dc22   2008027811

ISBN10: 0–415–99198–6 (hbk)
ISBN10: 0–415–99199–4 (pbk)

ISBN13: 978–0–415–99198–8 (hbk)
ISBN13: 978–0–415–99199–5 (pbk)

TO EVA, AS PROMISED

CONTENTS

CONTENTS

LIST OF ILLUSTRATIONS

PREFACE

> [MGM music director Nat Finston] launched into a long exposition
> of his career at the studio, detailing the chaos in which he found the
> music department and the perfection of organization that now
> prevailed.
> "I tell you," he said, "it's running like a well-oiled machine."
> The phrase appealed to him, and he repeated, "Like a well-oiled
> machine. Every man a cog in the wheel."
>
> Oscar Levant, 1939[1]

Film music has attracted the attention of writers since before World War I, and it seems
that in recent years—as the study first of film and then of film music gained legitimacy
in academia—serious writing on film music has flourished.[2] Vast though the modern
literature is, however, it still lacks an English-language volume whose main purpose is
to tell the story of how this fascinating art form came to be and how, for better or worse,
it developed.[3] A few pioneering scholars have indeed plunged deep into the matter of
film music's growth, but their impressive work concentrates only on film's "silent"
period.[4] This crucial period lasted more than three decades and to a large extent set the
agenda for all that was to follow, yet it is typically given short shrift in most books that
purport to be comprehensive treatments of film music.[5]

It is to an extent understandable that most accounts of film music in essence begin ca.
1933, the year in which Max Steiner's contribution to RKO's *King Kong* became the
model for the so-called classical-style film score. It is understandable, too, that most
books on film music—whether their aim is to survey the broad field, to help readers gain
an appreciation of the art form in general, or to explain theoretically how film music
"works"—deal primarily with scores that, like Steiner's for *King Kong*, have already
achieved a certain amount of fame. To make a point, after all, one needs to offer
examples, and it makes sense that examples have long been drawn from a "masterwork"
repertoire that is not just familiar but also "officially" sanctioned. Not surprisingly, most
historical accounts of film music focus on the extraordinary, not on the quotidian
ordinariness against which the "special" examples stand so distinctly apart.

With *Film Music: A History*, I take a different approach.

First and foremost, I set out to write a book that is simply a history of film music. It
is tempting to write that this is a "simple" history of film music, but in fact no history
can be simple. A history involves more than a chronology, more than the orderly listing

xi

of occurrences along a timeline; along with an accurate recitation of facts, a history must include a "reading" of those facts. The historian's job is not merely to report data but to interpret it, to offer opinion on the relative significance of certain events, to explain that significance in terms of the events' relationships to what came both before and after. For unless these relationships are discussed, any attempt at history would be, as Tolstoy put it, just "a tissue of disconnected accidents."[6] The saga of film music contains many instances of the right person being in the right place at the right time, but its genuine accidents are few. In film music as in most other phenomena that developed over a period of time, nothing has ever come from nothing.

Secondly, I wanted to concentrate on film music's norms, not its wonderfully aberrant masterpieces. This is not to say that *Film Music: A History* is a celebration of mediocrity. Rather, it is simply an effort to explain the development of the film music that at various times was considered by both its practitioners and its audiences to be respectably normal. In emphasizing film music's "run of the mill," this book will pay considerable attention to "the mill" itself. You will discover, as the narrative unfolds, that the chronological points of demarcation separating one basic type of film music from another are not much different from those noted in other books. But you will also discover, I hope, that the points of demarcation are consistently explained here not in terms of evolutionary leaps in film music *per se* but in terms of systemic shifts in the film industry.

Finally, I sought to fill an obvious gap in the film-music literature.

As a multi-media commodity intended to appeal to a relatively large audience, film has a great deal in common with opera, and therefore some comments on opera historiography might help put the goals of *Film Music: A History* into perspective. Opera, to be sure, does not lack for a supportive literature. In 1947 Donald J. Grout estimated that "volumes almost beyond counting"[7] had already been devoted to the art form; by now the literature likely has multiplied tenfold. The deepest probes tend to be found in journal articles, and usually these are examinations of single works or single aspects of the output of a particular composer. Of the actual books that occupy library shelves, the vast majority are either surface-scratching guides to opera appreciation or monographs—some of them quite weighty—devoted to the lives and works of opera's most significant composers. Although a sizeable number of books claim to be histories of opera, most of these are histories not of opera but only of operatic music.[8] But a handful of recent monographs[9] and journal articles resulting from conferences[10] suggest that opera historiography is experiencing a change. These newer studies explore not just the artistic contexts in which opera has existed but also the various forces that caused—and still cause—opera to evolve; they deal with economic systems and political ideologies, with contemporaneous developments in literature and the visual arts, with stagecraft and theatrical architecture, with the sociological implications of entrepreneurship, patronage, audience behavior, and critical response.

Film composers, like their operatic counterparts, never penned their music in isolation. Almost from the start they worked not as independent operators but as members of large and complex teams, and typically their purely musical ideas have been tempered by numerous practical considerations. Almost from the start, too, film composers—like opera composers—served at the pleasure of whoever controlled a production's purse strings. In order to do their work at all, let alone do it well, they needed to fit in. To borrow the phrase quoted in the epigraph, film music's composers have almost always had to function like cogs in the wheels of a well-oiled machine.

Encouraged by recent opera historiography, I have attempted here what is likely the first industry-based view of the whole of film music. Instead of examining, or celebrating, film-music masterpieces, this book deals with "the machine" whose smooth running allowed film music's occasional masterpieces to happen and whose periodic technical-economic adjustments, or socio-philosophical retoolings, prompted the large-scale twists and turns in film music's path.

Framed by an introduction and an epilogue, the book's four large parts are given over to Music and the "Silent" Film (1894–1927), Music and the Early Sound Film (1894–1933), Music in the "Classical-Style" Hollywood Film (1933–60), and Film Music in the Post-Classic Period (1958–2008). Within each of these parts there are two or three chapters, occasionally labeled by what seem to be nice round dates but nevertheless always demarcated by specific socio-economic, technological, or cultural-philosophical developments. It should be taken for granted that the content of the chapters, not to mention that of the book's large parts, overlaps. After all, film music is closer to liquid than to anything solid. An historian can make an effort to sectionalize the material at hand, but the boundaries of *any* history almost by definition are porous, and invariably they are subject to splash-overs and leaks.

The "turning points" that mark the chapter breaks will surely be familiar to anyone who has steeped himself or herself in the monographs and journal articles that over the last forty years have contributed to what today amounts to a voluminous bibliography of cinematic history. For persons not acquainted with that rich literature, this book provides not just a synopsis but also many references to works that deal either generally or in meticulous detail with important developments in film's technologies, aesthetics, and socio-economic conditions. But offered here, in what likely stands in marked contrast to both the film histories and the already existing books on film music, is a consideration of precisely *how* changes in the industry caused changes in the music. Most of the books that deal historically with film music concentrate on "landmark" scores and fairly skim over the circumstances that prompted these scores' creation; likewise, it seems that most of the film histories deal more or less intensely with the various circumstances and then mention only in passing, if at all, that they somehow had an effect on music. This book attempts to bring these two points of view into agreement, to cross-focus a pair of monocular outlooks in a way that adds a much-needed perspective—a genuinely historical perspective—to the field of film-music studies.

Film Music: A History is not a theoretical text, although discussion of various theories of film music certainly figures into the narrative. Nor is it a guide to film-music appreciation, although I trust that any teachers or students using this book—regardless of previous familiarity with the topic—will gain here not just information but insight into how film music, in various contexts, works its wonders. The book of course refers often to compositional efforts that have generally been deemed noteworthy, yet the reader will find here no biographies of film-music practitioners,[11] no extensive anecdotes as to how this or that famous score came to be, no close analyses of "classic" scores either in terms of their purely musical content or vis-à-vis the functional relationship of their component cues to a film's visual or narrative elements.[12] *Film Music: A History* does not purport to be a complete account of film music from its distant origins to the present day, and sensible readers will know that such a thing would be not just nearly impossible but also rather pointless. This book is not *the* history of film music. Rather, as its title suggests, it is *a* history; offered not as a chronicle but as a narrative, it is just one scholar's interpretation of how film music once upon a time came to be and how it changed, for better or worse, into what it is today.

* * *

For several years at the University of Michigan, and before that at the University of California-Irvine, I have taught upper-level introductory surveys of film music's history and aesthetics. Always these classes have been open to the broad student population, and always the enrollment has been dominated by young persons for whom the study of music, in any shape or form, is quite adjunct to their professional goals. Year after year I have been impressed by how passionately students majoring in, say, European history or sociology or computer science approach the topic of film music. These students know full well that "the movies" play a role in society that goes far beyond mere entertainment, and they seem quite aware that the content of "the movies" involves not just dialogue and on-screen action but—to a large and potent extent—the accompanying music.

One of the great joys of teaching these classes has been to demonstrate that many of the concepts that apply to music in the current cinema in fact go back a long, long way. With few exceptions, my students have not been much familiar with films from Hollywood's so-called classical period, let alone with "silent" films; indeed, for many of them, an "old movie" was something from the 1970s. Yet these students eagerly grappled with music-related questions that must have confronted the exhibitors of the very first motion pictures, and just as eagerly they explored questions that arose as technology, over the decades, allowed films to gain in both length and sophistication. What the students discovered is that their own proposed answers to perennial film-music questions, or their suggestions as to how music *might* figure into radically new filmic trends, were often in keeping with the ways in which things actually played out.

As rewarding as it has been for me to watch students work through, for themselves, the various problems and possibilities faced over the years by film music, I have long been frustrated by my inability to provide them with a text that contained solid information about what was *really* going on at this or that moment of film-music history. I realized early on that the general readings on film-music technique and aesthetics needed to be supplemented with cold, hard facts. Prodded by my best students, who always wanted to know not just *how* things changed but *why* they changed, I began to gather information and to deliver it, in dribs and drabs, in lectures; eventually I had gathered enough information to warrant presentation in the format of a book.

This book, then, is addressed not just to fellow film-music scholars but also to bright students of the sort it has been my pleasure to teach, undergrads and graduate students alike, whose majors likely are neither music nor film studies. It is addressed as well to the instructors charged with guiding such students through the rich field of film music. Instructors, I imagine, will want to concentrate on what they feel to be film music's "landmarks"; knowing that this book deals with the shifting "geographies" from which the "landmark" examples clearly stand out, instructors, I hope, will find here much of what they need in order to shed historical light on their chosen syllabus items.

ACKNOWLEDGMENTS

One does not, of course, write books single-handedly. While the blood, sweat, and tears shed over the computer keyboard might indeed spew solely from the body of a lone beleaguered author, the encouragement to carry on comes from a wide variety of human sources without whose nourishment, as they say, the thing never could have happened.

For the very idea that I might attempt such a bold project as this, I owe hugely to once-upon-a-time Routledge acquisitions editor Richard Carlin; for the impetus to carry through with the project, I owe thanks to Carlin's successor, Constance Ditzel, to the anonymous reviewers who in the book's early stages provided useful critiques and helped clarify my direction, and to the various Routledge editors who under Ms. Ditzel's rigorous direction saw this project through to completion. I owe thanks, too, to the many scholars whose works are cited in both the footnotes and in the bibliography and to the many casual commentators—journalists as well as their interview subjects—whose names appear only in the footnotes.

On a more personal level, for the emotional sustenance I needed to write this book, I remain forever indebted to my ever-loyal friend Lois S. Price, to my father Eugene V. Wierzbicki, to my brother Michael J. Wierzbicki and his movie-loving wife and daughters, and to my own film-savvy daughters Helene and Eva.

For countless insights and specific advisements, I sincerely thank William H. Rosar, whose encyclopedic knowledge of film music is surely one of the richest resources that anyone writing on film music today can ever hope to tap. For moral support, especially when the going got tough, I thank my University of Michigan faculty colleagues Judith Becker, James Borders, Mark Clague, and Jason Geary. Because in numerous ways they reminded me that this was a path indeed worth pursuing, I remain indebted not just to Dan Blim, Bretton Dimick, Rebecca Fülöp, Nathan Platte, and other U of M musicology graduate students who expressed interest in a project that went far above and beyond their immediate concerns but to *all* the students who over the last several years persisted through my "Film Music" classes. But I am especially grateful—because she so often understood and cared about the things that really mattered—to the U of M's newly minted Ph.D. Rebecca Schwartz-Bishir.

1

INTRODUCTION

Everything in creation has its history, and only when we are
acquainted with that are we in a position to understand its real
nature.

Kurt London, 1936[1]

Composers of film music have sometimes been persons of genius, yet typically they
worked at the behest of directors or producers whose sensitivity to music may or may
not have been fine-tuned. Typically, too, film composers functioned in environments
where economic or technological conditions placed limitations not so much on the
composers' imaginations but on the extent to which the fruits of their imaginations could
be realized. And typically the music of film composers, in the multi-media hierarchy, has
played a secondary role; in most cases it was created as a response to a filmic "product"
that in essence was completed well before the composer was invited to participate.

Along with traditionally being secondary to overt narrative content, and thus more
responsive than instigative, film music has long been derivative. This is not to say that
composers of film music have lacked originality. On the contrary, film composers
discovered long ago that their music's forced subordination to film's narrative concerns
allowed them a freedom denied composers who sought to win audience favor solely in
the concert hall; as early as the 1930s, cutting-edge idioms lauded by sophisticated critics
yet irksome to the "average" listener easily found a place in film scores, largely because
the attention of the audience of a well-made film was almost never focused on the music.
But while the environment of cinema sometimes gave composers a stylistic free hand, it
often demanded—for the purposes of storytelling—clear references to music that not
only already existed but which, to film's large audience, was very familiar.

Doubtless this is why film music for so long had been considered by academics to be,
ipso facto, inferior to concert music.

The "Problem" with Film Music

The prejudice has lately abated, or its public voicing seems lately to have been muted.[2]
One suspects, though, that some hallowed halls of academe still echo with negative
ideas. Among them: Film music is motivated not by artistry but by market forces; film
music is derivative to the extreme, sometimes exemplifying downright plagiarism and
typically resorting to gimmicks and clichés; film music is a field for hacks, not for "real"

1

composers; the only decent film scores are the occasional efforts by composers whose principal work was for the concert hall, and the only Hollywood regulars worth mentioning are those who at least made an effort to write for that more prestigious venue.

Ironically, some of the prejudice against film music can be traced to composers who benefited from the film industry's largesse yet felt that film work was, if not exactly beneath their dignity, then at least a formidable obstacle to their "serious" musical pursuits. While it is not likely that George Antheil and Oscar Levant will ever be counted among America's major composers, their articulate and witty autobiographical writings from the 1940s were nonetheless influential.[3] What Antheil and Levant had to say about their participation in the film-music scene[4] during Hollywood's "golden age" was hardly positive, but even more damning were the widely read film-music critiques—some of them first published as newspaper articles and then anthologized in books—of Virgil Thomson.[5] In the years surrounding World War II, shortly after the Hollywood film and its accompanying score supposedly "reached a level of classical perfection,"[6] Thomson, Levant, and Antheil contributed significantly to a popular literature that denigrated music for narrative films. Readers were informed that "movie music . . . cannot possibly be up to the same standard" as symphonic music,[7] that "picture music" consisted of bits and pieces inserted "with no recognition of the character of the complete score,"[8] that almost all of commercial cinema's innocuous yet ear-pleasing "commentary music" was "both architecturally and emotionally insufficient, because music can't be neutral and sumptuous at the same time."[9] These writings were biased and often glib, yet their message proved to be unfortunately durable.

Recent articles in British and German journals have attributed the academic bias against film music to envy on the part of relatively ill-paid professors of composition and to snobbery on the part of idealistic musicologists who feel themselves charged with upholding the values of Western music's canon.[10] In a 1994 essay-review of several books on film music, James Buhler and David Neumeyer suggested that the bias at least in the United States had something to do with the fact that music for commercial films fairly flew in the face of the many young composers and music theorists who were educated at such prestigious schools as Yale and Princeton under the aegis of the GI Bill and then, in the 1950s, began to populate the faculties of public universities all across the country; these newly minted assistant professors were committed to the archly modernist ideology that held that "real" music should be autonomous and stylistically pure, and thus it seems hardly surprising that they would take a dim view of film scores that almost by definition are responsive, subordinate, and derivative.[11]

Yet it is *because* film music is derivative that it has such a rich semiotic content. Whereas the strict modernist/formalist point of view prefers that music's meaning be fully contained within the music itself,[12] the more open aesthetics of film music allows for self-contained expressive devices to co-exist comfortably with material whose meaning derives from associations quite independent of the music itself. Like the formalist composer, the film composer can easily make a "statement" whose emotive essence involves nothing more than the interplay of consonance and dissonance, or whose placement in a score's large-scale rhetorical scheme depends entirely on the relationship of the statement's content both to what has already been heard and to what is yet to come. Unlike the formalist composer, however, the film composer has always been free to mix purely musical niceties with whatever else might serve a film's dramatic needs. Limited

2

to "pure" music, the formalist composer perforce deals with matters of tension and release only in an abstract way. Not so restricted, the film composer has license to apply comparable psycho-musical dynamics to material that vis-à-vis a filmic narrative seems somehow concrete; in the film score, harmonic patterns whose expressive content might otherwise be ineffable gain enormous amounts of specificity when they are linked, however briefly, not just with musical "symbols" of place and time but with aural reminders—in the form of allusions, paraphrases, and even direct quotations—of how the film at hand relates to earlier films in a particular genre.

Similarly, it is *because* film music is typically subordinate to a film's primary content that it so often has such subtle power. With few exceptions, music is something added to a film only after all of the film's other elements—dialogue, imagery, narrative flow—have been decided upon and more or less permanently fixed in linear celluloid. Directors have occasionally re-edited scenes so that a play of images might better relate to especially potent shifts in the accompanying music, but over the long course of film's history such privileged consideration of music has been exceedingly rare. Most often film music has been composed subsequent to the completion of the film *per se*, and most often the composer of film music has been charged simply with enhancing the director's more or less carefully considered, and not likely to be altered, treatment of verbal-visual material. In filmic hierarchy the telling of the story has always reigned supreme, and film music has almost always been at the humble service of the storytelling. Quite apart from whatever formal agreements might have been struck by individual composers and the directors whose films they scored, the unwritten contracts between filmmakers and their audiences called for music to be in all ways dramatically effective but never so prominent that it drew attention to itself. Right from the start, it was expected that film music would "do the job" in so deft a manner that few in the audience would even notice it.

To be sure, not all who tried their hands at film scoring have been comfortable with the idea that music, in film, generally plays a subordinate role. The negative comments of American composers Antheil, Levant, and Thomson have already been noted. Alongside these could go the opinions of Ernest Irving, a "pioneer of British film music" who by the onset of World War II had conducted and/or composed scores for dozens of films[13] and who in 1943 chose curiously to bite the hand that long had fed him. The time had come, Irving wrote, for sophisticated listeners to "pertinently inquire why music of anything approaching first-class quality is never heard in a kinema."[14] Having been a practitioner, Irving clearly knew that film music had special obligations, including the obligation to avoid as much as possible the forefront of the audience's attention. But in his apostate screed he for all intents and purposes equated artistic worthiness with the extent to which musical ideas are indeed brought to the forefront. "If it is good concert music it is essentially bad film music," he concluded, "and the converse is usually true."[15]

Somewhat along the same lines, the German composer Hanns Eisler—in *Composing for the Films*, a book he allegedly co-authored with Theodor Adorno in 1947—observed bitterly that "one of the most widespread prejudices in the motion-picture industry is the premise that the spectator should not be conscious of the music."[16] Indeed, Eisler argued that it was largely because of this "often reiterated opinion of the wizards of the movie industry, in which many composers concur," that the bulk of Hollywood's film music was not just unobtrusive but banal.[17] But Eisler, even though he provided scores for no

3

less than eight Hollywood feature films,[18] surely counts as a theoretical outlier, and there are many reasons to agree with Roy M. Prendergast's opinion that *Composing for the Films* is a "testy and relatively valueless book."[19] To judge from autobiographies[20] and an almost countless number of interviews that have appeared in books[21] and fan-oriented magazines,[22] the vast majority of composers who have achieved even modest success in the industry have felt that their film music—clearly designed not for the concert hall but for the movie theater—is anything but banal. At the same time, it seems that most film composers have had no problem whatsoever with the fact that their music, vis-à-vis the filmic product as a whole, has remained largely in the background.

Apparently with this in mind, Claudia Gorbman used the phrase "unheard melodies" in the title of the 1987 study that is often cited as the trigger for the current wave of scholarly interest in film music.[23] Likewise, the title of a textbook from 1998 reminds us that film music is not just literally but effectively an "invisible art."[24] Implying that for music to be "unheard" or "invisible" in a filmic context is a good thing, another textbook title from the same year tells us that film music is "the soul of cinema."[25] Aaron Copland, a mainstream concert-hall composer who on several occasions made forays into Hollywood and who wrote about film music in his popular *What to Listen for in Music*,[26] expressed the same thought in less spiritual terms; he said that film music, in general, "is like a small lamp that you place beneath the screen to warm it."[27] And film director Federico Fellini, commenting on his numerous collaborations with composer Nino Rota, complimented Rota on being free of "the presumptions of so many composers, who want their music to be heard in the film. He knows that, in a film, music is something marginal and secondary, something that cannot occupy the foreground except in a few rare moments and ... must be content to support the rest of what's happening."[28]

*   *   *

That film music at least to a certain extent supports "the rest of what's happening" is self-evident. But exactly *how* film music performs this supportive function remains very much open to debate.

Discussion of how film music works—or how it ought to work—dates to before World War I, when columnists for various trade magazines regularly offered both criticism and practical advice to musicians who accompanied "silent" movies.[29] Discussion of a more intellectual sort transpired—sometimes quite interactively—in the pages of music-oriented British and American periodicals during the late 1930s[30] and then again in the years following World War II;[31] it was renewed in the 1980s by a wave of articles and books emanating not so much from musicologists as from scholars who trained in literary criticism and then moved into the new field of film/media studies.[32] And in recent years the intellectual discussion has accelerated markedly: it now takes place at academic conferences,[33] in new journals devoted specifically to film music,[34] and in established journals whose focus is musicology or film studies in general.[35]

The current discussion on how film music works, or how it *seems* to work in particular films or types of films, is fascinatingly complex. It draws its examples from more than a hundred years of international filmic repertoire. And it interweaves strands from a great many lines of argument.

4

Studying Film Music

As noted above, considerable research has focused on the function of music for the so-called silent film; although the relevant scholarship concentrates on facts gleaned from a small number of extant manuscript or printed musical sources and a large number of journalistic accounts, it includes vigorous speculation on the music's relationship to the narrative content of the on-screen imagery.

But it seems that relatively little formal thought has been given to the various ways in which music served film between the introduction of pre-recorded sound ca. 1927 and the establishment of the so-called classical-style Hollywood film ca. 1933. To be sure, plenty of work has been done on this transitional period of film history, but most of it concerns technology, distribution, and reception.[36] Music-related writing on the function of music in the pre-classical sound film is noticeably absent from the literature as a whole; with that in mind, the pertinent chapters in this book are quite large relative to the small amount of chronology they cover, and it is hoped that they will provide readers with not just helpful information but also a bit of theory.

There is neither a theoretical nor an informational lack regarding the role of music in the classical-style narrative film that blossomed between the mid 1930s and the decade following World War II. Authors have not stinted on telling the life stories of Hollywood composers active during this fertile period. Just as important, serious effort has been spent in explaining the various ways in which music serviced—and still services—films of this sort, that is, films in which the ultimate goal of the storytelling is to eliminate all traces of ambiguity. A neat account of the musical conventions of the classical-style film was offered by Gorbman in her *Unheard Melodies* and then embellished in book-length studies by Kathryn Kalinak, Caryl Flinn, and Royal S. Brown. But the codification began long before the classical-style film was even identified as such,[37] and it was the prime concern of writers who seriously addressed film music in the 1940s and '50s. These accounts are enlightening for anyone who seeks to understand how film music "works." But the archly unambiguous classical-style film, which is their focus, is of course not the only type of film that today's audience encounters.

For more than a half-century the filmic style that eschews narrative ambiguity has co-existed with styles in which ambiguity is in one way or another embraced, and certainly inversion of the classical-style's musical conventions is one way in which deliberate ambiguity has been achieved. Whereas music in the classical-style film typically holds to certain norms of sonority, since the 1950s numerous film scores have performed classical-style narrative functions not with orchestral/symphonic music but with music written idiomatically for such unconventional media as solo piano, electronic instruments, and jazz bands. Influenced by the French "New Wave" and the Italian "neo-realist" movement, many films from the second half of the twentieth century feature only what film theorists like to call "diegetic" music and which persons in the film industry have long termed "source" music—that is, music whose source is somehow contained within the film's narrative (diegesis) and which thus would actually be heard by the film's characters. Responsive to demographic shifts that began in the years following World War II, many films since the 1960s use only music—diegetic as well as extra-diegetic—that is not specially composed for the film but, rather, is drawn from a repertoire of popular songs that presumably would be familiar to most members of the film's relatively young target audience. Especially in recent decades, many films have freely mixed classical-style scoring with pre-existing music—ranging from vintage grand opera and pop standards to examples of whatever currently leads the Hit Parade—that is laden with personal "meaning" that varies widely from spectator to spectator.[38] In recent decades, too, films have blurred the diegetic/extra-diegetic boundary lines that in the classical-style film seem almost always to be perfectly clear.[39]

If one were to go right now to the local Cineplex and buy a ticket for whatever film is next showing, the music encountered could fall into *any* or *all* of the categories just described. The music might be entirely in the classical vein, for this type of music— orchestral in sound, symphonic in idiom, utterly unambiguous in its narrative function —had a resurgence in the mid 1970s and since then has remained favored by producers who seek to make "blockbuster" hits. On the other hand, the music might well be cryptic or vague, far more connotative than denotative, loaded not with obvious symbolism but with myriad suggestions for interpretation.

The average moviegoer has the luxury, paid for by the price of his or her ticket, of taking all this in stride. Music in contemporary cinema often defies categorization; from film to film, the music is simply what it is. Vis-à-vis the overall content of any new film that competes for box-office attention, the music either contributes successfully or it does not. And for most ticket-buyers, this is really all that matters.

For persons who seriously study film music, however, things are rather more complicated. Influenced as we might be by ideas resonating from poststructuralist and postmodern schools of thought, we can wonder if the "meaning" of composed scores for classical-style films is really so cut and dried as it once seemed to be. We can wonder, too, about the extent to which the narrative functions of modern compiled scores—so-called because they are compiled from snippets of pre-existing music—actually deviate from norms established long, long ago. If we follow the lead of a great many of today's literary critics and borrow ideas formulated by such (mostly French) theorists as Roland Barthes, Jacques Lacan, Michel Foucault, Jacques Derrida, Jean Baudrillard, Julia Kristeva, and Gilles Deleuze, we can wonder if we know anything at all—or if anything can ever be known—about how film music "works."

In the febrile uncertainty of the early twenty-first century, it is perhaps one of the few certainties regarding film music that for a very long time music has been lending audible structure to filmic narratives and embellishing those narratives with aural signals as to how various scenes are to be "read" by audience members. It also seems a certainty that since the heyday of "silent" movies music has fairly often been used to identify films' locales and time periods, to illustrate on-screen action, to limn the basic personality traits of characters central to filmic plots, to explore those same characters' innermost thoughts and feelings. Then as now, film music by and large has offered a "gloss" on whatever might be presented overtly to the audience in the form of action and words. Now as then, film music makes dramatic points not just with entirely original material but also with sonic symbols to which audience members can easily relate and clichés whose "meaning" derives from the conventions of earlier music-theatrical art forms.

What has changed over the last hundred years is the substance of film music and its applications to filmic narratives. What has remained constant is the desire of filmmakers to put music—in some form, in some way, to some extent—at the service of their projects.

* * *

How film music functions—in general—remains debatable. And still debatable, too, is how any particular composed score, or compilation of pre-existing music, supports "the rest of what's happening" in its assigned film.

Case studies, especially when they include solid facts based on archival research and examination of score-related documents, are without question valuable contributions to this on-going discussion. Also valuable—at least when they result from accurate observation and careful thought—are "textual" analyses based primarily on a critic's perception of music within a film. Whether positivistic or interpretive, whether mostly objective or mostly subjective, such work collectively serves as the foundation for the next generation of film-music theory.

It will be interesting to see where that new theory leads. Doubtless it will confirm certain elements of older theory regarding the composed underscore, but surely it will challenge at least a few underscore-related concepts that have long been accepted as gospel-like truth. Doubtless, too, the new theory will balance consideration of freshly composed music—which until recently has claimed the lion's share of thought—with consideration of the pre-existing music that in fact has figured importantly in film accompaniments since film's earliest days. Formulated for the most part by persons young enough to regard music for the classical-style film as something of a throwback, the new theory will likely be far more inclusive than any theory hitherto expressed. It is guaranteed to be richly speculative; one can hope that it will be based on solid scholarship, that it will be not just insightful but intellectually rigorous. However it plays out, the new round of film-music theory promises to be at the very least interesting, and thus it is something to which all concerned with film and its music can look forward with eager anticipation.

If this book in any way contributes to the construction of an up-to-date theory of film music, the author would be pleased indeed. Vis-à-vis film-music theory for the twenty-first century, however, anything this book has to offer must be considered a fortuitous side effect. How film music over the years has been *thought* to "work" will of course be dealt with in the pages that follow. But how film music actually *does* "work"—or apparently *did* "work" at various times in the past—is not a concern here. This book is neither a theoretical text nor a guide to film-music appreciation. As stated in the preface, it is simply a history.

The Idea of History

Reviewing a pair of books that purport to summarize the entire flow of European art music in the nineteenth and twentieth centuries, Richard Taruskin in 2005 caustically chastised the books' editors for offering just a mish-mash of data and opinion. "A random harvest is fine for a conference report," Taruskin wrote. "But a history must aspire not merely to juxtapose, but (however fallibly or provisionally) to propose connections between things."[40] Indeed, a history, according to the nearest-to-hand standard lexicon, is not just a "tale" or "story" but "a chronological record of significant events" that "often includ[es] an explanation of their causes."[41] The voluminous and venerable *Oxford English Dictionary*, in the two and a half columns it devotes to the word, offers definitions that range from a mere "relation of incidents (. . . true or imaginary)" and "a story represented dramatically" or a "pictorial representation of an event or series of events" to "a systematic account of . . . a set of natural phenomena" and "the whole train of events connected with a particular country, society, person, [or] thing."[42]

To relate the "whole train of events" associated with film music worldwide since the mid 1890s would be a task far beyond the abilities of this author, and it is hoped that readers will sympathize with the decisions here not just to summarize international developments but also—amidst discussions of music in the arguably parochial but nonetheless widely influential American film industry—to "cut to the chase"[43] as quickly as possible. It is hoped, too, that readers, after digesting the first half of the book, will understand that film music's logical "train of events" a half-century ago was effectively—perhaps permanently—derailed.

Film music's linear progression—a progression based on cause and effect, in which specific trends clearly grew out of existing situations and just as clearly led to whatever happened next—extends from the 1890s *only* until the years following World War II. In the 1950s Hollywood was beset by hitherto unimaginable financial difficulties and at the same time swayed by burgeoning postwar technologies, iconoclastic artistic innovations from abroad, and large-scale changes in the demographic makeup of its audience. When the dust settled, film music's step-by-step advance in effect had ground to a halt. Film music, of course, did not disappear, but from this point on its movement was no longer unidirectional. Indeed, it was as though not just Hollywood but the film industry worldwide experienced the equivalent of what evolutionary scientists call the "Cambrian explosion": just as the fossil record suggests that some 530 million years ago a great many new multi-celled creatures—the ancestors of modern animals—quite suddenly came into existence, so the record of cinema shows that in the late 1950s and early '60s there sprang up all the various modalities of modern film music.

The course of film music in the first half of the twentieth century can be divided into distinct periods that are stylistically/ideologically unique yet nonetheless connected by technological, legal, or socio-economic developments that represent points of transition. Regarded from up close, these periods and their catalysts seem to be fascinatingly diverse, yet regarded from a distance they appear to be links in a single chain. No single chain reaches from the 1950s to the present day. For the sake of sustaining the metaphor, it is tempting to say that numerous film-music chains—including a very strong one that can be traced back to film music's earliest decades—extend through the century's second half. Such an image, however, would be misleading. There are indeed numerous chains, but they overlap and tangle; they sometimes have links in common, and sometimes their links have been melded with links from other chains to form not just new strands of chain but entirely new alloys of material.

*　　*　　*

It was not film music but, rather, global politics that Francis Fukuyama had in mind when he proposed, first in a 1989 article and then in a 1992 book, that the end of the Cold War in effect marked "the end of history."[44]

Fukuyama's concept of history was based on the "dialectic" formula articulated early in the nineteenth century by the German philosopher Georg Hegel. According to Hegel, the dialectic involved a regular pattern of confrontation between "thesis" (an old thought) and "antithesis" (a new thought) in such a way that old and new combined (in "synthesis") to form the foundational "thesis" for the next generation of thinkers. The so-called Hegelian dialectic calls to mind the swing of a pendulum, propelled by momentum but resisted by gravity until the time comes when the movement perforce changes direction. Compatible with the "train of events" view of history, the Hegelian dialectic makes a great deal of sense. Indeed, most of what humankind has done over the last several millennia can be interpreted according to this model.

It remains for political scientists of the future, of course, to determine whether or not Fukuyama was correct in announcing that the cessation of ideological conflict between East and West, ca. 1989, indeed signaled "the end of history" in the Hegelian sense. Likewise, it remains for future commentators on film music to decide if the art form's linear progression really did reach an "end" at around the time the Cold War was just getting started. On this, surely, the jury is still out.

In the meantime, it might be suggested—somewhat strongly—that since the 1950s not only has the course of film music changed direction many times but, indeed, the very nature of its course has changed. What was once a clear-cut path is now a jumble of crisscrossing avenues; the art form's growth pattern, once resembling that of a shoot reaching for the sunlight, now calls to mind an underground rhizome of interconnected roots and buds and nodes. Coming as it does after a more or less uncomplicated thread of development, the loopy knot of styles and approaches that represents film music's last fifty years might at first seem a huge obstacle for one attempting to contemplate, let alone write, film music's history. But no matter how multi-directional film music's progression may have lately become, one can take comfort in the obvious fact that the entire progression has transpired over unidirectional time; one can take comfort, too, in the idea that—for all the diversity—there nevertheless still seem to be "connections between things."

Part 1

MUSIC AND
THE "SILENT" FILM
(1894–1927)

2

ORIGINS, 1894–1905

Imagine, if you will, a screen placed at the back of a vast room, as large as can be imagined. This screen is visible by a crowd. On the screen appears a photographic projection. So far, nothing new. But suddenly, the image—of either natural or reduced size, depending on the scene's dimensions—animates itself and comes to life.

It is a factory gate, which opens and releases a flood of workers, male and female, with bicycles, running dogs, and carriages—all swarming and milling about. It is life itself; it is movement captured on the spot.

La Poste, December 30, 1895[1]

It seems that almost everyone who has written on the history of film music has, indeed, imagined the occasion at which projected motion pictures were first displayed before a paying audience. And with these imaginings, indulged in for more than three quarters of a century, there has developed a film-music mythology.

Right from the start, we have been told again and again, music was integral to the filmic experience. The most often cited reasons for the allegedly necessary presence of music during showings of even the most primitive commercial films are the acoustical need to mask noise generated by the projector, the psychological need to lend "warmth" to images that might otherwise be interpreted as "disembodied" or "ghostly," and the theatrical need—stemming from precedents in high-brow opera as well as low-brow melodrama—to embellish action and expressions of emotion with affectively appropriate instrumental accompaniment. All of these explanations for the quick and easy birth of film music are credible only to a limited extent. Yet in the conjecture-rich popular literature on film music they tend to be treated as holy writ.

Primary-source research into the early decades of film music is a relatively recent phenomenon. Based on methodical examination of not just extant musical materials but also newspaper reportage and commentary in trade journals, the new scholarship fairly puts to rest the legend as to how and why film music came into being. Emphatically, the evidence shows that film music of the sort that we know from televised versions of silent movies did not emerge fully formed, like Athena from the head of Zeus, at the very first exhibitions. Indeed, evidence shows that this "typical" music for silent films resulted only after a period of evolution that was as quirky as it was contentious.

In his 1947 treatise on film music, Hanns Eisler, a German-born composer who enjoyed Hollywood's beneficence yet could hardly discuss Hollywood without revealing his Marxist sentiments, wrote:

> If there is such a thing as a historical phase of motion-picture music, it is marked by the transition of the industry from more or less important private capitalistic enterprises to highly concentrated and rationalized companies, which divide the market among themselves and control it, although they fondly imagine that they are obeying its laws.[2]

Politics aside, Eisler is quite right in suggesting that the standardization of film music could have occurred only after the standardization of the film industry. In the United States and elsewhere, the period 1894–1905 witnessed the creation of dozens of companies devoted to the production and exhibition of motion pictures. It was not until shortly before World War I, however, that the more successful of the American companies began to coalesce to form the cultural entity known as "Hollywood."

Before the establishment of Hollywood norms that soon grew internationally influential, commercial filmmaking was limited by nothing except the ambitions and resources of its practitioners. Precedents being nonexistent, the pioneers in the field experimented imaginatively and hopefully, and their "anything goes" attitude resulted in what Richard Crangle calls "a bricolage of narrative, technical, economic, presentational, and audience practices taken from here, there, and everywhere."[3] Judging from recent research, the "anything goes" attitude applied as well to whatever sounds might have been in the air when the earliest films were exhibited before an audience.

The First Motion Pictures

The eye-witness account quoted above was published in a Parisian newspaper two days after the brothers Auguste and Louis Lumière hosted the first public exhibition of motion pictures both filmed and projected by means of a device they called the Cinématographe. Momentous though the event was, neither the technology nor the theory that made it possible was new.

Since the early 1820s there had been discussions, mostly in England and France, of the optical phenomenon known as "persistence of vision," and the first scientific article on the topic was published in 1829 by Joseph Antoine Ferdinand Plateau. Putting his investigations to good use, in 1832 Plateau patented a toy whose sequence of slightly varied images seemed to blend into a single "moving" image when the disc on which they were painted was spun and viewed, in a mirror, through carefully spaced slits in the disc. In the same year that Plateau released his Phenakistiscope to the French market, the German scientist Simon Ritter von Stampfer perfected a similar disc-based device he called the Stroboskope; in 1834, in England, William Horner advanced the entertainment value of motion pictures considerably by inventing the Zoëtrope, a slitted metal drum to the interior of which could be affixed interchangeable strips of paper containing printed images of clowns juggling, horses jumping, and so on. Almost simultaneous with Horner's Zoëtrope, the Baron Franz von Uchatius in Germany hit upon the idea that motion-pictures could be experienced not just by looking through slits in a fast-spinning disc or drum but by viewing a screen on which a quick series of images was projected.

14

Uchatius's first experiments involved a cumbersome and perhaps dangerous set-up that involved a light source moving rapidly from one projector to another, but by 1853 he had developed a means by which images on a spinning translucent disc could be viewed on-screen by means of a single candle-powered projector.

These early motion-picture devices were all based on the principle—first formulated by Plateau—that exposure to a minimum of sixteen images per second was required in order for the human eye to perceive a series of still pictures as a single "moving" image, and all of them featured drawings. Photography did not enter the picture, so to speak, until 1872, when Eadweard Muybridge devised a multiple-camera technique that allowed him to capture in an instant a dozen views of a fast-moving subject. The British-born Muybridge conducted his experiments for the sake of helping California governor Leland Stanford win a bet regarding the in-stride hoof positions of a galloping horse, but he quickly realized that his sequential photographic images of an animal in motion were remarkably similar to the sequential drawings featured in the early motion-picture toys. For the next twenty years, Gerald Mast writes in *A Short History of the Movies*,

> Muybridge perfected his multiple-camera technique. He increased his battery of cameras from twelve to forty. He used faster, more sensitive film. He added white horizontal and vertical lines on a black background to increase the impression of motion. He shot motion sequences of horses and elephants and tigers, of nude ladies and jumping men and dancing couples. He mounted his photographs on a Phenakistiscope wheel and combined the wheel with the magic lantern for public projections of his work. He called his invention—really just a variation on Uchatius's Projecting Phenakistiscope—the Zoopraxiscope, another very fancy name for a not-so-fancy machine.[4]

Perhaps inspired by the results of Muybridge's multi-camera experiments, in 1882 the French physiologist Étienne-Jules Marey developed a method by which a single camera could record a series of pictures on a circular glass plate. Marey's original Chrono-photographe, which looked very much like a rifle, was able to capture a dozen images in one "shot." Eventually substituting rolls of paper film for the glass plate, by 1888 Marey was able to increase both the duration of a "shot" and the rate of exposure, but his photographs were intended for anatomical study, not motion-picture exhibition, and none of his "shots" lasted more than a few seconds.

In the late 1880s the motion picture as we know it awaited just two technological breakthroughs. One of these was the development of a medium, as pliant as paper yet much more durable, on which a relatively long sequence of images could be photographed in rapid succession through the lens of a single camera. The other, more problematic, was the perfection of a projector with a steady start-stop action that emulated the spaced viewing slits of the Zoëtrope; in order for the "persistence of vision" phenomenon to create the illusion of a single picture that *seemed* to move, the audience's eyes had to take in a fast-paced sequence of pictures that in fact moved not at all.

Since 1884 the American film and camera manufacturer George Eastman had been experimenting with film made of cellulose nitrate. Expecting that the product would be used only in his simple "snapshot" cameras, in 1889 Eastman began to sell celluloid filmstrips that featured on their edges perforations compatible with the sprockets on his cameras' frame-advancement wheels. One of Eastman's most important first customers

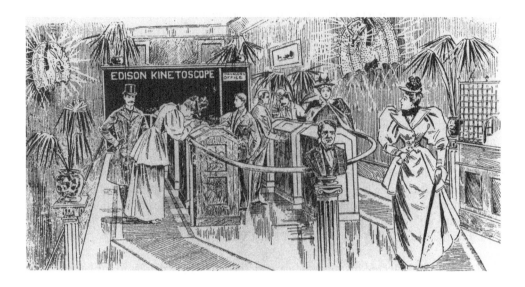

Figure 2.1 Edison Kinetoscope. © The Kobal Collection.

was the American inventor Thomas Alva Edison, who had long been striving for a visual equivalent of his 1877 phonograph. After assigning his best engineers to the project, by 1891 Edison was in a position to patent devices for both the capture and the playback of motion pictures, and over the next several years Edison's employees produced dozens of filmstrips intended for commercial exhibition. In keeping with his previous successes, Edison correctly anticipated a huge market for filmstrips made with his Kinetograph and compatible only with his Kinetoscope. On April 14, 1894, the first Kinetoscope parlor opened for business in New York City, and within months similar establishments sprang up in major cities all across North America and Europe.

Curiously, considering the public uses to which Edison's phonograph was being put, the Kinetoscope offered private entertainment viewable only when a customer—after paying a small fee—placed his or her eyes to a peephole. Even more curiously, considering the inventor's famous business acumen, the Kinetograph and Kinetoscope patents for which Edison applied limited protection to the United States. Elsewhere the equipment and its proprietary software were made available not for licensing but simply for purchase, and it did not take long for enterprising filmmakers in Europe to take advantage of the rich gift that Edison handed them.

* * *

Auguste and Louis Lumière had long been in the film business by the time they visited, late in 1894, a newly opened Kinetoscope salon in Paris. Their father, Antoine, was a Lyon-based photographer who operated not just a studio but also a plant for the manufacture of photographic plates and, eventually, celluloid film. As early as 1881 Louis Lumière—who like his older sibling had studied science at the Ecole de la Martinière—perfected an extremely fast "dry plate" based on gelatin emulsion, and

16

thanks to this invention the family prospered. By 1894 the factory had more than three hundred employees; annual sales of the Lumières' "blue label" photographic plates numbered about fifteen million.

Hardly unfamiliar with motion-picture technology, for several years the Lumière brothers had been conducting experiments of their own. Although up to this point it was primarily Auguste Lumière who had expended energy contemplating motion-picture equipment, apparently it was Louis Lumière who—after subjecting Edison's Kinetoscope to a reverse-engineering process—realized that all that was necessary to realize their mutual dreams was "adapting . . . the mechanism known by the name of 'presser foot' in the drive device of sewing machines."[5] Just as a few years before Edison had entrusted the execution of his motion-picture ideas to an employee (the English-born William Kennedy Laurie Dickson), so the Lumière brothers assigned the building of a prototype to their factory's head machinist (Charles Moisson). The prototype worked splendidly, and on February 13, 1895, the brothers jointly applied for a patent.

The Cinématographe differed in many respects from Edison's devices. Like the Edison machines, the Lumières' used rolls of 35-millimeter-wide celluloid film, but the Lumières' film featured the same high-speed emulsion as did their photographic plates, and thus the photographic images it captured were more sharply focused. Whereas film moved through the Edison devices at speeds as high as forty-eight frames per second, the Lumière brothers achieved what they felt were equally satisfactory results with a rate of only sixteen frames-per-second. The typical Edison motion picture was packaged in a fifty-foot loop that, for the one-time viewer, lasted approximately thirty seconds; packaged in reels up to a hundred feet in length, the Lumière films with their slower running speed could have durations of as much as three minutes. The Kinetograph and Kinetoscope were cumbersome, the one about the size of an automobile and the other about the size of a jukebox, and the film-advancement mechanisms of both were powered by electricity; the Cinématographe was contained in an easily portable box that could be mounted on a tripod, and its film was advanced by means of a hand-crank.

That the light-weight Cinématographe could not just record motion pictures but also display them gave it an obvious practical advantage over the bulky Kinetograph–Kinetoscope combination. But it was with its method of display—and the cultural ramifications thereof—that the Lumières' invention most soundly trumped Edison's. In line with a tradition that dates to the middle of the seventeenth century,[6] the Cinématographe in display mode used a lamp to project lens-magnified pictures onto a screen. To experience an Edison film in late 1895 was simply to view a peepshow; in marked contrast, to experience a Lumière film was to be part of an audience.

*　　*　　*

Presented on December 28, 1895, in the 100-seat Salon Indien below the Grand Café at 14 Boulevard des Capucines in Paris, the initial public showing of the Lumières' films attracted a meager crowd of only thirty-three persons. So impressive was this first exhibition, however, that "by the second day, lines of people stretched down the street," and soon "mobs of people numbering more than two thousand each day" sought admission.[7]

What the audience saw in the Salon Indien was a twenty-minute program of ten or so short films that included depictions of workers departing the Lumière factory, a baby

17

Figure 2.2 Poster for L'Arroseur Arrose/Cinématographe Lumière. © Bettmann/CORBIS.

being fed, a gardener squirted in the face by his own hose, a boy learning to ride a bicycle, a group of men playing cards, a pair of women apparently fighting, and a locomotive arriving at a railway station.[8] What the audience heard remains open to debate.

As Martin Marks points out in his landmark 1997 study of the use of music in the so-called silent film, "the presence of a pianist at this premiere has been asserted in many books."[9] There is no evidence, however, as to what music the pianist might have played or how his performance might have interfaced with the showings of the films. With justifiable caution, Marks writes that the pianist "*is said* to have improvised an accompaniment."[10] Whether that was indeed the case—or whether the pianist was engaged subsequent to the premiere for no other reason than, as some have suggested, "to drown out the sounds of the creaking machine"[11]—no one knows for sure.

To focus speculation on what might actually have transpired in the Salon Indien late in 1895, readers might do well to take the suggestion of the reviewer who is quoted at the head of this chapter. Imagine the situation. Imagine a public event in which the main attraction was the unprecedented exhibition of motion pictures excerpted from everyday life. Imagine the sounds that might have been part of such an event.

Doubtless at least some of us are old enough to recall an age that predates the advent—in the 1980s—of hand-held devices that captured not just moving images but also their concomitant sounds. Before the audio-sensitive tape-based camcorder, amateur collectors of motion pictures had access only to decidedly mute film-based cameras. After their film had been developed, camera-equipped persons typically summoned friends and relatives for in-home showings of the by and large unedited results. The showing of "home movies" before the 1980s required, at the very least, the setting up of a screen and the running, in a darkened room, of an electrically powered projector that generated both heat and a small amount of noise.

If memory serves correctly, the sonic aspect of the "home movie" ritual that I experienced repeatedly during my childhood involved much more than the clickety-clack of the projector. Whether the subject at hand was my own family's latest vacation in northern Wisconsin or a bachelorette aunt's once-in-a-lifetime visit to some exotic locale, the air was invariably abuzz with a mix of quasi-formal commentary and informal responses. Musical accompaniment for these showings of "home movies" could easily have been provided, for at the time both my grandfather and an uncle were professional musicians adept at improvising on the readily available keyboard instruments. Under the circumstances, however, musical accompaniments—however useful they might have been in masking the minimal noise of the projector—would hardly have been appropriate. The "home movies" offered entertainment aplenty, but it was entertainment of a spectacular, not a theatrical, sort, and it was self-contained entertainment that required no embellishment. Measured against the uninhibited and often vociferous audience reaction that was a crucial part of the "home movie" experience, accompanying music would have been an absurd encumbrance.

Perhaps it seems sacrilegious to liken the Lumières' trailblazing motion pictures of 1895 to the generic "home movie" of the 1950s, '60s, and '70s. But the content of these two classes of film, really, was not much different. Granted, the circumstances of the Lumières' "squirted gardener" and "fighting women" reels were doubtless contrived, but the other Lumière pieces—like the typical "home movie"—were just glimpses of real-life situations. With the exception of the "gardener" and "women" reels, the Lumière films did not even come close to telling stories; the films simply showed images of one sort or another that their makers—like the makers of "home movies"—felt might be of interest to viewers. In comparison with the television-numbed audiences for "home movies," of course, audiences for the virtually unprecedented Lumière films would have been immeasurably more interested in the imagery itself. Indeed, doubtless they would have been fascinated to the extreme by the mere fact that such imagery could even exist.

One has to wonder: In a room capable of accommodating a hundred persons, would it have been necessary to "mask" the noise of a hand-cranked projector whose mechanism was similar to that of a foot-powered sewing machine? Would patrons of the Lumière films have sat passively as life-size moving pictures—not just never-before-seen but for all intents and purposes never-before-imagined—played on a screen? Assuming the patrons responded favorably to what they witnessed, would their experience have been in any way enhanced by accompanying music? The iconoclastic questions might as well be asked: Would a musical accompaniment for the Lumière films have served any purpose at all?

Music and the Earliest Films

It is known that a paid pianist, whether he was present on the first day or not, participated in the history-making entertainments offered by the Lumière brothers in

Paris in December 1895.[12] It is also known that a performer on harmonium took part in the London premiere of the Lumière films, at the Polytechnic Institute on Regent Street, on February 20, 1896,[13] and that orchestras were involved in Lumière showings at London's Alhambra and Empire theaters over the next several months.[14] In the United States, an ensemble called Dr. Leo Sommer's Blue Hungarian Band was on the scene when the first projected motion pictures—not Cinématographe products but films run through an Edison-affiliated device called the Vitascope[15]—were displayed in New York at Koster & Bial's Music Hall on April 23, 1896.[16] An orchestra was present, too, when a Lumière program premiered in New York at Keith's Vaudeville House on June 28, 1896.[17]

All this is known. To the chagrin of scholars who have devoted entire careers to investigating the matter,[18] what is not known is precisely how these various musicians contributed to the earliest exhibitions of motion pictures. Film-music mythology has it that music purposefully accompanied the films and in so doing made cinema—almost from the moment of its birth—a multi-media art form. Common sense, however, suggests that music was merely an adjunct feature of public entertainments at which the unprecedented and much-publicized main attractions were entirely visual.

While it is certainly possible that a pianist performed *while* the Lumière brothers' films were being projected, it is just as possible—likely, considering the format of the event—that the pianist performed in the relatively long interludes during which one reel was exchanged for another and as the audience entered and exited the exhibition room. It also seems likely that music at these early film showings, especially those in larger venues, served a heraldic function. For example, in the case of the Vitascope premiere in New York, we have it from a witness that in advance of the program's first film "the band struck up a lively air," after which "there flashed upon the screen the life-size figures of two dancing girls who tripped and pirouetted and whirled an umbrella before them."[19] As Rick Altman points out, "the musical mode operative here is not accompaniment but fanfare. As it might have done for the entrance of an important vaudeville personality, the band is highlighting a featured performance by musically framing it."[20]

Granted, the idea that music's role in the earliest cinema was of a "framing" nature is conjecture. It is conjecture, however, supported not by wishful thinking but by an impressive lack of evidence to the contrary. If the performance of music had substantially contributed to the audience's experience of the Cinématographe and Vitascope films *per se*, surely this would have been remarked upon by at least some of the many persons who documented these extraordinary events. But the newspaper and diary accounts, if they allude at all to music, note only that musicians were on the scene and that music somehow added to an exhibition's festive atmosphere.

In his study of reasons why music might have been incorporated into early film exhibitions, Charles Berg notes that motion pictures devoid of musical accompaniment "were described in negative contexts as 'noiseless fleeting shadows,' 'cold and bare,' 'ghostly shadows,' 'lifeless and colourless,' 'unearthly,' and 'flat.'"[21] In order for critics to have made such observations, of course, they must have had experience with truly "silent" films, which seems to prove the point that at least some early films lacked accompaniment. But the accounts of these negative descriptions were penned long after cinema's birth,[22] and they smack of revisionist history.

More trustworthy is commentary from those who were actually on the scene. Upon first exposure to the results of the Cinématographe, the reviewer for *La Poste* concluded that "the beauty of the invention resides in the novelty and ingenuity of the apparatus."[23] Georges Méliès, a French illusionist who in 1895 was as savvy as anyone in all matters of show business, wrote of the Cinématographe premiere in Paris that he and his fellow audience members sat "open-mouthed, dumbfounded, astonished beyond words in the face of this spectacle."[24] Reflecting on his viewing of the Lumières' films at a fair in Nizhni-Novogrod early in 1896, the presumably highly observant Russian novelist/poet Maxim Gorky wrote:

> It all moves, breathes with life, and suddenly, having reached the edge of the screen, disappears one knows not where.
> This is all strangely silent. Everything takes place without your hearing the noise of the wheels, the sound of the footsteps or of speech. Not a sound, not a single note of the complex symphony which always accompanies the movement of a crowd. Without noise, the foliage, gray as cinder, is agitated by the wind and the gray silhouettes—of people condemned to a perpetual silence, cruelly punished by the privation of all the colors of life—these silhouettes glide [over the gray ground] in silence.[25]

It seems that what most impressed the Lumières' audience was the purely visual phenomenon of projected motion pictures and, for those mechanically inclined, the machinery that made such pictures possible. Writers on the history of film music have compiled litanies of statements that agree with the oft-quoted pronouncement of MGM producer Irving Thalberg that "there never was a silent film."[26] Yet there is no evidence to indicate that the earliest projected motion pictures were accompanied by music, and all the anecdotes from reliable sources suggest that these films were, indeed, silent.

* * *

Apparently mute at the outset, motion pictures did not remain silent for long. Music was being incorporated into public presentations of films within a year of the Cinématographe and Vitascope debuts. The purpose of this earliest filmic music, however, was not to set a mood or to illustrate action. Rather, the music's purpose was to lend a soupçon of credibility to on-screen imagery that was unimpeachably realistic.

With few exceptions, the first publicly exhibited motion pictures were recordings of real-life happenings. To enhance the audience's experience of these brief documentaries, film exhibitors (perhaps anticipating the "home-movie" ritual) often embellished the mechanically reproduced visual material with commentary from a lecturer. Less frequently, and usually only when films were exhibited in larger venues, the proceedings were enlivened with behind-the-scenes sound effects (a shaken metal sheet could replicate the sound of thunder, for example, and the stirring of dried peas could convince audience members that they were hearing waves break[27]). And sometimes these sound effects involved music.

A report on an August 1896 showing of Lumière films at Keith's Bijou in Philadelphia notes that the program featured "the reproduction of a parade of the Ninety-sixth Regiment French Cavalry." The reviewer remarks that "the wondrous realism" of "the

21

sham battle scene" was enhanced by "noise and battle din." Significantly, the reviewer also notes that at one point in the film "the soldiers march to the stirring tune of the 'Marseillaise.'"[28]

Self-explanatory in its title, one of the Lumière films included in a September 1896 program offered at Keith's Opera House in Providence, Rhode Island, was *Tearing Down a Wall*. A review of the presentation remarks on how the wall began to fall only after "a cry of 'look out' [was] given by [supernumeraries] in back of the stage" and how at the film's climax "the crash is heard as the bricks come tumbling down one after another."[29] Another film on the program was *The Charge of the Seventh French Cuirassiers*, during the showing of which the audience heard "the jingling of the troopers' accoutrements,"[30] "the clanking of sabers ... [,] and the ceaseless pattering of horses' hoofs."[31] Not surprisingly, the showing of *The Charge of the Seventh French Cuirassiers* also featured, at the appropriate moment, a bugle call.

A review of an 1899 film exhibition at the Regent Street Polytechnic in London enthused over "cutlass exercises (with audible hits), gun firing, yacht races, etc.," and it noted that "all the fakes possible, such as the boom of the guns, the swish of the water, and so on, are realistically maneuvered behind the scenes."[32] Along with the military and maritime images, the program offered a view of massed athletes moving to a "band accompaniment."

The band accompaniment, the bugle call, and the "Marseillaise" mentioned above represent early instances of what in later Hollywood parlance would be known as "source music." Most writers on film music today prefer the term "diegetic music" to describe music that exists within the filmic diegesis, or narrative, and which presumably is heard not just by the film's audience but also by its characters. Because it accommodates filmic situations in which there is no narrative *per se*, "source music" is perhaps a more useful term, for it suggests only that a source of the music is apparent— or at least implied— in the imagery. The on-screen soldiers at the Bijou marched to the strains of the "Marseillaise" played by a theater orchestra, yet audience members blessed with imaginations easily might have "heard" the music as issuing from an off-screen military band.

Source Music and Underscore

In addition to employing music as a sound effect whose actual source was suggested by the visual content of a film, exhibitors during cinema's earliest years occasionally found opportunities to embellish their audience's experience with music deemed appropriate because of its mimetic or symbolic value. (Mimetic music, usually in some rhythmic way, mimes or imitates action; symbolic music, because of listeners' familiarity with its cultural usage or lyric content, makes quick reference to non-musical situations.)

Along with the bugle call that enlivened the scene of the cavalry charge, for example, audience members at Keith's Opera House in September 1896 heard the orchestra play "a jig to which [a pair of] frogs kept time" during a Lumière film titled *The Aquarium*.[33] In October 1896, at the Olympia Music Hall in New York, members of the Republican Club watched a film titled *McKinley at Home* (produced by the newly launched Edison-affiliated Biograph company) while listening to a tenor's live rendition of the campaign song "I Want You, McKinley; Yes, I Do."[34] An 1897 showing in Philadelphia of the *Höritz Passion Play* was accompanied by both a lecture and "unseen organ music,"[35] and religious music for chorus and organ set the tone for a "Passion Play" film in New York in February 1898.[36] Although he did not cite a date, as early as 1899 the pioneering film historian Henry Hopwood recalled hearing an orchestra play "Rocked in the Cradle of the Deep" as he viewed a film of a wrecked ship.[37]

Writers who apply the term "diegetic" to music that somehow belongs to a filmic narrative have little choice but to employ a variation on the Greek-derived adjective when describing music that simply accompanies a film and is heard only by the film's audience. A common usage is "non-diegetic," with or without a hyphen, which denotes that the accompanying music is clearly *not* a part of the diegesis. But the negative prefix seems to imply, contrary to film-music reality, that diegetic music is somehow the norm. A better adjective—and one that will be used consistently throughout this book—is "extra-diegetic," which denotes only that the music is somehow apart from, or outside, the fictional world of the filmic narrative.

In any case, in traditional Hollywood parlance such music—whether mimetic, symbolic, or in some way emotionally affective—has long been called "underscore." The term derives from technological practice in the early years of the so-called sound film, when in the mixing booth a pre-recorded musical "score" was laid "under" the recorded tracks that contained sound effects and dialogue. But the concept of underscore long pre-dates the advent of the sound film. Indeed, it pre-dates the advent of film.

As many writers on film music have noted, the ancestry of underscore can be traced not just through the various types of "action music" that decorated nineteenth-century melodrama and pantomime[38] but all the way back—at the very least— to the non-sung, non-danced episodes of the earliest operas. When it was not illustrative of action or emotion, the primary function of pre-filmic manifestations of underscore was to establish in the minds of audience members a sense of mood and/or locale. Assuming an audience familiar with contemporary musical conventions, a deft opera composer could use melodic figurations or harmonic patterns to convince audience members—in an instant—that an about-to-unfold scene involved, say, a hero's tentative steps into a mythological underworld, a comic character's machinations in a stereotyped Spain, or a couple's romantic coming-together in a supposedly realistic Paris.[39]

The cinematic examples cited above represent early instances of mimetic and symbolic underscore. On at least three occasions before the wave of Lumière, Biograph, and Vitascope films swept Europe and the United States, however, music had been combined with filmic exhibitions at least in large part for the purpose of stirring an audience's emotions. And two of these occasions involved music composed specifically to support the films at hand.

Often quoted in books on film music is a passage, presumably referring to events in the mid 1890s, from the memoirs of the British exhibitor Cecil Hepworth:

> I always remember one little series which always went down very well indeed. It was called *The Storm* and consisted of half a dozen slides and one forty-foot film. My sister Effie was a very good pianist and she traveled with me on most of these jaunts. The sequence opened with a calm and peaceful picture of the sea and sky. Soft and gentle music (Schumann, I think). That changed to another seascape, though the clouds looked a little more interesting, and the music quickened a bit. At each change the inevitability of a coming gale became more insistent and the music more threatening; until the storm broke with an exciting

film of dashing waves bursting into the entrance of a cave, with wild music (by Jensen, I think).[40]

Whereas Hepworth's projections were accompanied by pre-existing piano music by the German composers Robert Schumann and Adolf Jensen, the "luminous pantomimes" that Émile Reynaud offered at Paris's Musée Grevin in November 1892 featured piano music written for the occasion by Gaston Paulin. Reynaud's program consisted of three hand-drawn animations—*Pauvre Pierrot, Clown et ses chiens*, and *Un bon Bock*—projected by means of his own Praxinoscope. Aptly titled *Pantomimes lumineuses*, Paulin's lightweight scores were published by G. Ducroitois; the cover and two pages of music are reproduced in the 1968 *Histoire comparée du cinéma* of Jacques Deslandes, who remarks on "how closely the composer has followed the 'cutting' of Reynaud's pantomime."[41]

The other early instance of music composed specifically to accompany the projection of moving pictures involves the November 1895 exhibition, at the Wintergarten Theater in Berlin, of films produced by Emil and Max Skladanowsky. Although the Skladanowsky brothers' Bioskop technology was awkward and ultimately impractical, it was viable enough to warrant not just a month-long engagement in Berlin but a tour, in the first half of 1896, to Amsterdam, Oslo, Copenhagen, and Stockholm. The Skladanowskys' programs included projected images of acrobatic acts, a juggler, various ethnic dances, and a boxing kangaroo; all of the scenes were supported by orchestral music, the hand-written parts for which are preserved in the Stiftung Deutsche Kinemathek in Berlin. While some of this music (dance pieces by Mikhail Glinka and Ernst Gillet) clearly pre-dates the Skladanowsky films, the bulk of it seems to have been written on commission by the German composers Hermann Krüger and F. Hoffmann. Precisely how this music was used in conjunction with the Bioskop films remains uncertain. After exhaustively examining the Skladanowsky materials, Marks concludes only that the compiler(s) of the music seem to have been guided by the principle that "each film in the program should be accompanied by a separate and generally suitable piece of music."[42]

In the minds of audience members, the orchestral accompaniments for the Skladanowsky brothers' pictures of a peasant dance, a Russian dance, and a "serpentine" dance might well have been perceived as source music generated by a within-the-film ensemble that somehow managed to elude the camera's gaze. The orchestral music for the other Skladanowsky pictures was probably heard as symbolic/mimetic, and likewise for the piano music that accompanied Reynaud's projections of animated depictions of *commedia dell'arte*'s Pierrot, a clown and his dogs, and the swigging of a good beer.

Hepworth's account of *The Storm*, on the other hand, suggests an altogether different use of music in conjunction with projected images. With a filmic sequence that featured only seascapes, it is doubtful that audience members would have assumed that any of the accompanying music somehow "belonged" to the scene. Responding to Hepworth's statement that the music that propelled the exhibition to its climax was possibly by Jensen, Marks suggests that the piece at hand might have been "Am Meeresstrand" ("At the Seacoast"), the eighth item in the composer's 1862 op. 8 *Romantische Studien*. Even if this were indeed the piece that Hepworth's sister played, it seems unlikely—since Jensen's music was hardly well-known in Victorian England—that audience members would have heard the music as symbolic of a seascape. Whatever music was played, it

24

is likely that the audience heard only "abstract" music that "begins softly and builds to 'wild' passionate climaxes"[43] and then linked this purely musical affect with the dynamics of the filmic imagery.

Narrative Film

Film music's evolution from "framing device" to quasi-realistic sound effect to evocative symbol to underscore was a natural one, but it would not occur until cinema itself evolved from a primarily exhibitionistic medium into one that was in essence dramatic.

The vast majority of films produced during cinema's first years were of the documentary sort. Of the 1,424 titles produced by the Lumière brothers between 1895 and 1907, barely a hundred feature actions that in one way or another were staged for the sake of the camera. Because of the limited lengths of the film reels or loops, the durations of early motion pictures were necessarily brief; the pioneering filmmakers could offer audiences little more than glimpses, and thus they concentrated on subjects that by virtue of their imagery alone were somehow spectacular. Most of the Lumières' films fall into the categories of maritime and military scenes, views of dances and festivals, miniature travelogues, and general panoramas. Likewise for the earliest films produced by the Lumière brothers' most serious French competitors (the studios founded, in 1896, by Charles Pathé and Léon Gaumont), by various English entrepreneurs (most notably Cecil Hepworth, G.A. Smith, and James Williamson), and—predating the Lumières' work—by Thomas Edison.

To be sure, even at cinema's dawn filmmakers were aware that the motion picture was capable of delivering more than objective views of the everyday world. Released in August 1895, one of Edison's most sensational early efforts was *The Execution of Mary, Queen of Scots*, a Kinetoscope film at the climactic moment of which (anticipating the "special effects" of modern horror movies) a disembodied head goes bouncing across the pavement. Sensational in a different way was Edison's 1896 *John Rice–May Irwin Kiss*; although the osculation of the Broadway actors named in the title amounts to nothing more than a quick smooch, the very idea of such a thing was enough to raise the hackles of prudish critics. As was obviously the case with Edison's *Kiss*, the Lumière brother's 1895 *L'Arroseur arrosée* (known in England as "The Sprayer Sprayed" and in the United States as "Tables Turned on the Gardener") and other of their "comic" films were contrived at least in terms of their action. In the films of Georges Méliès, contrivance involved not just action but imagery; by profession an illusionist, Méliès as early as 1896 was conjuring credible impressions of disappearances, levitations, transmutations, and the like by means of "trick camera" techniques.[44]

Edison labeled *The Execution of Mary, Queen of Scots* a "reeanactment," and the Lumière brothers—doubtless responding, at least for a while, to Edison's market-place success—applied a similar adjective to an 1897 film they called *Marat and Robespierre*. Like Méliès's cinematic magic tricks, Edison's and the Lumières' representations of historic scenes doubtless intrigued their initial audiences. Riveting though their portrayal of "events" must have been, however, these non-documentary early films were related only distantly to narrative drama.

The Execution of Mary, Queen of Scots gave its viewers a mere fifteen seconds of thrill; *John Rice–May Irwin Kiss* has a duration of eighteen seconds, and Edison's provocatively titled *The Interrupted Lovers* (1896) lasts only three seconds more.

Because their Cinématographe processed film at a slower speed, the early Lumière pictures in comparison to Edison's were longer, but only by a small margin. As late as 1898 the most temporally drawn-out film Méliès could offer was *Un homme de têtes*; the arguably complex scenario involves a man decapitating himself and generating a new head no less than four times, yet the whole of it takes place in less than a minute.[45]

Dismissive of the visual beauty of panoramas and the historic value of documentaries, in a 1933 *New York Times* essay L.H. Robbins recalled that in its earliest days cinema offered little more than "living pictures" in which "prizefighters pummeled and clinched, fat men were chased by bathing beauties, cross-eyed comedians were plastered with pies, and Catchem & Stuffem operated their sausage mill, dogs going in at the top and 'dogs' pouring out below, while the painted stage-set flapped in the breeze."[46] Echoing an apparently well-known idea that had been expressed in earlier "retrospective" articles, Robbins informed readers that the turning point in cinema's history occurred in 1903 with the release of Edison's *The Great Train Robbery*.

An announcement for a 1927 exhibit titled "Thirty Years of Motion Pictures" described *The Great Train Robbery* as a "pioneer feature."[47] Four years earlier, an announcement for an identically titled exhibit observed that it was with *The Great Train Robbery* that "the screen achieved its first real story."[48] More specific in its praise, a 1917 report on a seventieth birthday celebration for Edison noted that "the first long film telling a connected story was *The Great Train Robbery*," an entertainment that "created a veritable sensation in the movie world, which until then had seen only short films devoid of all pretense of plot."[49]

Sharing a bill with vaudeville entertainers Billy B. Van and Rose Beaumont, Cole and Johnson, Keno, Welch and Montrose, Mr. and Mrs. Jimmy Barry, Newell and Niblo, Colby and May, and William Cahill, *The Great Train Robbery* premiered at Hammerstein's Victoria Theatre in New York during the Christmas season of 1903.[50] It was not in fact the first extended film with a plot; in the previous year the Edison studio had issued *Jack and the Beanstalk*, a 625-foot reel whose duration was a bit more than ten minutes and whose fairy-tale story unfolded through nine different scenes. But *The Great Train Robbery* was longer—740 feet, almost twelve minutes, fourteen scenes—and presumably its content was more appealing to the adult audience whose responsiveness would help dictate the course of cinematic history. Enacted with a cast of forty and filmed in New Jersey under the direction of Edwin S. Porter, who for Edison earlier in 1903 supervised the narrative pictures *Uncle Tom's Cabin* and *The Life of an American Fireman*, this "faithful duplication of the genuine 'Hold Ups' made famous by various outlaw bands in the far West"[51] was indeed a thriller. More significant, it introduced editing devices—including "elliptical jump[s] in time" over which "the audience makes the connecting links that the director has purposely omitted"[52]—that remain fundamental to cinematic technique.

Frustratingly, there is no evidence as to how music might have figured into presentations of this prototypically modern film. Still, it is reasonable to assume that it was at least in some way musically enhanced. Like most films offered to the public after the turn of the twentieth century, the venue for *The Great Train Robbery* was the vaudeville theater.[53] Vaudeville music at the time would likely have been provided by a lone pianist or a small (three- to five-piece) orchestra; economic recession in the late 1890s forced many American vaudeville impresarios to dismiss the fairly large orchestras that up to this point had been standard, but it seems that by 1902 orchestras were starting to make a comeback. In any case, as Rick Altman reminds us, "we know that vaudeville theaters were never without music."[54]

The music that accompanied early showings of *The Great Train Robbery* may or may not have been reflective of the film's various situations or locales. At the start of Scene 11, when the action moves from a telegraph office to "the interior of a Dance Hall" with "a large number of men and women in a lively quadrille," did the music comparably change to something in a quasi-realistic dance style? At the end of the scene, when "the dance breaks up in confusion" and "the men secure their guns and hastily leave in pursuit of the outlaws," did the accompaniment modulate from "source music" to "underscore"? Considering the film's dramatic content, such effects certainly would have been appropriate. All that seems safe to say, however, is that there *probably* was music. It is hard to imagine that the average vaudeville audience of 1903—accustomed as it was to non-stop aural support for dancers and jugglers—would have tolerated, during a film showing, twelve minutes of silence.

*   *   *

The Great Train Robbery is a landmark because it stands out so clearly from contemporaneous films and because it represents the change in direction that cinema would quickly make. The turn from objective views of reality toward purposeful, artful narrative, of course, was not instantaneous. In a book written as an adjunct for a 1994 series on film produced by the Public Broadcasting System, John Belton explains that:

> early, pre-1906 cinema stresses "showing" rather than "telling." The majority of films made in this period are actualities, which outnumber fiction films until roughly 1906, when the percentage of story films begins to increase dramatically and actualities become less and less popular. The shift from one kind of cinema to the other takes place rapidly. By 1908, 96 percent of all American films tell stories.[55]

In a more recent assessment, film historian James Lastra differs only as to the date of what for cinema was in effect a sea change:

> After approximately 1907, narrative films dominated not only in sheer numbers but as the form around which the emerging industry grew. After that point as well, the heterogeneous and often boisterous field we call early cinema moved toward greater and greater formal and institutional unity.[56]

As the motion picture began to gain "institutional unity," so did it start to gain a consensus among producers and exhibitors as to how music should be employed in its service. Whereas film's first decade was a period of unfettered experimentation, its second decade was a period of consolidation not just of technology and content but also—importantly—of presentation.

Before the normative changes that followed in the wake of *The Great Train Robbery*, film's relationship with music took almost as many forms as did photographic and projection equipment. We have documentary evidence that during cinema's early years music heralded feature attractions, presented songs whose lyrics were illustrated on

27

screen, noisily attracted viewers to exhibition spaces, injected emotion into seascapes, embellished images with recognizable aural symbols, added touches of "reality" to glimpses of military pageants, helped set the scene for religious spectacles, and amusingly enlivened pictures of wriggling frogs. Music's other possible functions vis-à-vis early film—to cover the noise of projectors, to assuage fears of "ghostly" images, to sustain certain traditions of melodrama, to usher audiences in and out of screening rooms—are matters of conjecture, but they are within the realm of possibility, and so they might as well be included in what was clearly a very rich mix.

But these are all examples of music used in conjunction with film exhibitions. With few exceptions, they do not represent "film music" as the term is commonly understood today. Before music could become what one textbook author has aptly called "the soul of cinema,"[57] there first had to be—in the industrial, institutional sense—a cinema. A mature American cinema would develop by the time of World War I, but first the medium had to evolve through a chaotic period dominated by the so-called nickelodeon.

3

THE NICKELODEON,
1905–15

Most of the shows have musical accompaniments. The enterprising manager usually engages a human pianist with instructions to play Eliza-crossing-the-ice when the scene is shuddery, and fast ragtime in a comic kid chase. Where there is little competition, however, the manager merely presses the button and starts the automatic going, which is as apt as not to bellow out "I'd Rather Two-Step Than Waltz, Bill" just as the angel rises from the brave little hero-cripple's corpse.

The Saturday Evening Post, 1907[1]

The several years following the 1903 premiere of *The Great Train Robbery* represent the period during which the motion picture, as a cultural entity, evolved from what Tom Gunning has called an exhibitionistic "cinema of attraction" into a cinema devoted largely to the conveyance of narratives.[2] This is also the period during which the fledgling motion picture—after migrating from cafés and fairground tents to vaudeville houses where it shared the bill with a variety of entertainments—finally moved to a home of its own.

In the United States, the first more or less permanent venue devoted exclusively to the showing of motion pictures seems to have been the Electric Theater that Thomas H. Tally opened in Los Angeles in 1902. This was literally a store-front operation, i.e., an exhibition space set up in rented property that had previously been used as a retail outlet. Not so much following Tally's example as simply moving in the same direction, a handful of entrepreneurs in other American cities launched similar ventures. One of these had a name, based on the price of admission, that swept like wildfire through the public consciousness; opened in 1905 in Pittsburgh, the theater was called The Nickelodeon.[3]

The growth of the nickelodeon throughout the country over the next several years was nothing short of phenomenal. "Three years ago there was not a nickelodeon, or five-cent theatre devoted to moving-picture shows, in America," a writer for *The Saturday Evening Post* observed late in 1907. "Today there are between four and five thousand running and solvent, and the number is still increasing rapidly."[4] Just a few months before, a writer for *Harper's Weekly* estimated that during the 1906–7 theatrical season some two hundred nickelodeons opened in Manhattan alone.[5]

Figure 3.1 A Nickelodeon theater and penny arcade, ca. 1910. (Photo by American Stock/ Archive Photos/Getty Images.)

Along with speculating on the number of venues, these magazine reporters speculated as to the size of the nickelodeon audience. "Already statisticians have been estimating how many men, women, and children in the metropolis are being thrilled daily by them," wrote the reporter whose article focused solely on New York City. "A conservative figure puts it at 200,000, though if I were to accept the total of the showmen the estimate would be nearer half a million."[6] On the national level, wrote the other reporter, "over two million people on the average attend the nickelodeons every day of the year."[7]

Both of the magazine articles cited above suggest that, at least in the New York City area, the nickelodeons' seating capacity had something to do with the licenses under which the nickelodeons operated: whereas a venue capable of accommodating an audience of two hundred or more required a $500-per-year theater license, the articles state, a venue seating less than two hundred required only a $25-per-year "common show" license. Often repeated in books on film history, this information seems to be erroneous. According to an official report commissioned by the mayor of New York,

[W]here the entertainment consists of motion pictures coupled with vaudeville acts, a theatre or concert license, issued by the Police Department, is required

(Section 1472, 1473 of the city Charter). For this license, which is revocable only by the Supreme Court, a fee of $500 per annum is charged. Where the entertainment consists of motion pictures, songs and recitations not rendered on the stage, a so-called common show license granted by the Mayor is necessary (Section 307 of the Revised Ordinances). For this license, which is revocable, for cause, at the discretion of the Mayor, a charge of $25 per annum is made.

It will be seen therefore that the kind of license granted is determined not by the capacity of the hall nor by any other factor except the character of the performance. A fully equipped theatre could run moving pictures alone under a common show license.[8]

In any case, most of the nickelodeons—in New York and elsewhere—were small in comparison to the vaudeville houses where previously motion pictures "were used as chasers"[9] or "served merely as a 'turn.'"[10] A description of the typical "spectatorium" of 1907 as being "one story high, twenty-five feet wide and about seventy feet deep"[11] is probably not inaccurate.

In the United States, the rise of the nickelodeon had enormous societal impact. Whether nickelodeons were set up in "a narrow store or in a shack in the rear yard of a tenement,"[12] in a room that "last year or the year before was probably a second-hand

Figure 3.2 Edison's greatest marvel—The Vitascope. Courtesy of Library of Congress.

clothiers, a pawnshop or cigar store,"[13] or in some plusher and arguably more dignified space, their eponymous cost of admission contrasted strikingly with the price of tickets for "live" entertainments. Obviously, the nickelodeons' easy affordability was attractive to persons of limited means. At the same time, the subject matter of films displayed at nickelodeons was enticing to Americans who functioned on all economic levels, and the fact that stories were conveyed largely through action and pantomime meant that they were accessible to immigrants. The result was an unprecedented mixing, in the nickelodeon's semi-darkness, of audience members of diverse social classes and ethnic origins. Indeed, a columnist for *The Nation* remarked in 1908 that nickelodeon films, "devoid of high brow inclinations," represented "the first democratic art."[14]

The rise of the nickelodeon had a huge impact, as well, on the structure of the burgeoning American film industry. Well aware that the eclectic audience for motion pictures included rich and poor, young and old,[15] foreign-born and otherwise, film producers favored screenplays maximally packed with opportunities for visual excitement yet minimally complicated in terms of their narrative content. Aware, too, that patrons would return to the nickelodeon only if the bill-of-fare featured abundant variety, producers favored screenplays that could be executed in fairly short order. The profitable nickelodeon, historian Gerald Mast writes, "required a large number of films each week; about six films of one reel each (sixty minutes of film) made up a single program, and to keep the customers coming, programs had to change several times a week, if not daily."[16] Thus there arose a sophisticated system that allowed not only for the efficient manufacture of films but also for the efficient distribution of an abundance of films—for the most part rented, not purchased—to exhibitors all across the country.

It was not a system without conflict. In 1908 the nine leading American film producers—Biograph, Edison, Essanay, Lubin, Kalem, Méliès, Pathé, Selig, and Vitagraph[17]—banded together to form the Motion Picture Patents Company, a cartel whose members shared technological innovations, secured exclusive rights to the best film stock on the market, and made their films available only to exhibitors who agreed not to show films made by non-MPPC producers. Resistant to the monopoly, various theater owners opted to file suit against the MPPC and, more significant, to form production companies of their own. Fierce competition between MPPC members and the independent producers at first resulted only in an increase in the number of new films that were available each week. Eventually, the competition provoked a fundamental change in the nature of the American motion picture. Focused from the start on the nickelodeon, the MPPC companies were concerned with the manufacture and distribution of a huge number of relatively short films. The independent producers, who of necessity operated their own exhibition spaces, concentrated on fewer but longer films, and thus was born the multi-reel "feature."

With "movie companies [fighting] in the courts and . . . in the streets,"[18] the American film industry toward the end of the twentieth century's first decade was starting to get exciting. In part to support the burgeoning system and in part simply to cover the latest news, a number of trade journals sprang up: *Views and Film Index* began publication in 1906, followed in 1907 by *Moving Picture World*, in 1909 by *The Nickelodeon*, and in 1910 by *Moving Picture News*. And in the pages of these journals, as in the pages of periodicals issued by the production companies, the use of music in combination with film screenings did not go unnoticed.

Film-Music Columns

The *Saturday Evening Post* article quoted at the start of this chapter states that "most of the shows have musical accompaniment." But the other 1907 magazine article cited above, from *Harper's Weekly*, gives a different impression. Remarking that the statistician who gave him an attendance figure seems to have "left out the babies," the reporter notes that he counted an average of ten babes-in-arms at each of the dozen or so nickelodeons he had recently visited. One could hear the infants' cries, he writes, yet "they did not disturb the show, as there were no counter-sounds."[19]

In the first years of the nickelodeon, the presence of music—for better or worse—was clearly an option left to the discretion of the proprietors. As Rick Altman points out,

> Nickelodeon music was extremely varied, in location and source as well as type. Some theaters retained the older custom of exterior ballyhoo music, others moved their phonograph or automatic piano inside, at either the back or front of the projection space. Live accompaniment was sometimes featured, at first by a lone piano, then increasingly by a piano-trap drummer duo. In many theaters, accompaniment was live only at peak traffic hours, with mechanical noise provided early and late in the day. Still others concentrated their musical attention on illustrated songs, leaving the film to unreel in silence.[20]

Just as the symbiotic system comprising the manufacture, distribution, and exhibition of nickelodeon films gradually developed into a "three-part structure . . .[that], with some wrinkles, survives today,"[21] so did the use of music in the nickelodeon eventually develop into the norm associated with the classical-style Hollywood film. But the evolution of film-music practice was slower, and more chaotic, than that of the business model.

Columns offering suggestions as to how music might best accompany films did not start appearing in the trade journals until 1910.[22] In their early years these columns, as is the case with numerous contemporaneous newspaper accounts and retrospective anecdotes, were filled as much with condemnations of the film-music *status quo* as with practical advice for improvement.

Some of the criticism was directed at the indiscriminate presence or absence of music during film showings. Referring to "piano players who stop their work the very second the picture ends and sometimes quite a few seconds before it ends," for example, a 1912 editorial in *Moving Picture World* declared: "Nothing irritates and provokes an audience more than this widespread habit."[23] Citing the autobiography of a composer-conductor who figured importantly in the first decades of the sound film in England, where early film-music practice was not much different from its counterpart in the United States, Roger Manvell and John Huntley note that "Louis Levy . . . recollects how the little cinema orchestras round the period of 1912 were quite satisfied to play selections of light café music quite unrelated to the film on the screen—and, after a given period of the *William Tell Overture*, Rubinstein and Tchaikovsky, get up and leave the film and its audience to the deathly hush of silence."[24]

More often than not, however, the target of criticism was the use of music that seemed wholly inappropriate for the on-screen imagery. In 1909 a reporter for the *New York Dramatic Mirror* informed readers of his shock at having recently encountered "a pathetic scene showing a husband mourning his dead wife accompanied by the strains of 'No Wedding Bells for Me!' "[25] With comparable chagrin, a columnist for *Moving Picture World* observed in 1910 that when "a picture was shown some time ago containing a scene wherein Pharaoh's daughter discovers the infant Moses in the bulrushes," the pianist played "Oh, You Kid."[26] Regarding an incident that supposedly occurred in 1912, Max Winkler—an important figure in the eventual codification of music for the silent film—recalled that he and his fiancée visited

> one of the small movie houses that had begun to spring up all over town. The picture was one of the superb spectacles of the day. It was called *War Brides* and featured the exotic Nazimova in the role of a pregnant peasant woman. The ruling king of the mythical country where Nazimova was living with her family passed through her village. It was a pompous parade of uniforms and horses. As the king passed, Nazimova threw herself in front of him, her hands raised to heaven. She said—no, she didn't say anything but the title on the screen announced: "If you will not give us women the right to vote for or against war I shall not bear a child for such a country."
>
> The king just moved on. Nazimova drew a dagger and killed herself.
>
> The pianist so far had done all right. But I scarcely believed my ears when no sooner had Nazimova exhaled her last breath to the heart-breaking sobs of her people than the man began to play the old, frivolous favorite, "You Made Me What I Am Today."[27]

There may well have been humorous intent in these applications of light-weight music to dramatically heavy scenes. By 1912, the practice of satirizing a film through the use of musical puns or deliberately inappropriate music was apparently widespread enough to warrant a jargonistic label. But "funning" a picture, film historian James Lastra points out, "catered to particular audiences and their prejudices and/or drew attention to the musician's cleverness or stupidity," and they "did so to the detriment of the film, whose uniformly coherent address [because of the inappropriate music] was hopelessly fractured."[28] If jokes were indeed being perpetrated, they were not much appreciated by critics. "Bad judgment in the selection of music may ruin an exhibition as much as a good program may help it," declared one of them.[29] Musicians ought to be aware, chastised another, when they are "spoiling a tender scene with boisterous music or vice versa."[30]

One of the most interesting attacks on what was deemed to be the misuse of music in the service of film appeared in the January 21, 1911 issue of *Moving Picture World*. Aptly headlined "Jackass Music," the diatribe features illustrations by H.F. Hoffman that depict a female pianist blithely playing the popular song "Has Anybody Here Seen Kelly?" during a presumably somber death scene and then wandering off to the restroom, leaving a "Back in 15 Minutes" sign on her instrument, during what seems to be a climactic physical struggle between two of a film's main characters.[31] Convinced that in the nickelodeon such arguably idiotic events were far too common, author Louis Reeves Harrison strenuously suggests that improvements are in order:

> Ten thousand dollars a day is spent to produce the moving pictures and it would be impossible to say how much more to keep going the ten thousand

motion-picture theatres throughout the country. These pictures are not all masterpieces, many of them are very crude, but the whole art is in a primitive state, is constantly improving, and the exhibitions are kept alive by their production. People go every day to see the pictures, once in a while for the variety entertainment, and it is not only asinine but unbusinesslike to lower the grade of musical accompaniment when the lights are turned down. Inappropriate music may "do" for the unintelligent part of the audience, but what is the use of driving away the intelligent portion? Better music means better patronage and more of it, and superior patronage means a demand for superior photoplays. Suitable music is essential.[32]

Tellingly, Harrison argues his point for the improvement of film music not from the aesthetic perspective of audience members but from the economic perspective of film producers.

* * *

Whether prompted by their own artistic concerns or prodding from film producers, the trade journals' columnists offered plenty of general tips for how music might sensibly and sensitively accompany a film. That commercial film ca. 1910 was well on its way toward an institutional norm is reflected in the consistency of the suggestions. "From one publication to another and from one writer to another," Altman notes, "only the slightest variations appear."[33] Naturally, the columnists recommended that any music played during a film showing not be emotively inappropriate for the scene at hand. More significant, and reflective of the shift from the earlier "cinema of attraction" to the newer narrative cinema, they also emphasized the importance of musical continuity.

"The music should be arranged [so] that not a moment is lost in changing from one theme to another," declared a nickelodeon operator.[34] Similarly, one film-music columnist admonished that "a musician should never stop playing through the showing of a picture,"[35] and another suggested that film accompanists "try to make it a point to play your picture with just as few breaks as you possibly can."[36] The columnists repeatedly emphasized that adjusting the music to accommodate small-scale shifts of on-screen imagery was not only impractical but, for the audience, severely disruptive. "Pick out the theme of the picture and play to it," advised the author of a 1913 brochure on film accompaniment, and do not "change music any oftener than is absolutely necessary."[37]

The moments of necessary change, a columnist for *Moving Picture World* insisted, are the moments at which one large-scale scene is exchanged for another or when something in the action truly warrants a different kind of music. "Don't wait until you reach the end of the piece first," he cautioned, "and don't think you must always stop merely because you have reached the end of your number."[38] Arguing for uninterrupted accompaniment, the same writer offered a rationale based on historical precedent:

The moving picture drama (or photoplay) is simply a play in pantomime, and the accompanying music is essentially the same as that of a play given on the stage. There is this distinction, however. In the drama proper, music is only introduced at intervals to heighten the effect of certain scenes, while in the pantomime it is continuous, or nearly so.[39]

Historical-theoretical discussions of this sort were relatively few. Along with citing ridiculous examples of "jackass music" that ought not be emulated, most of the columns and editorials devoted to film music ca. 1910–15 simply got right to the point and advised film accompanists on how the job ought to be done. If the suggestions prompted dissenting opinions, these were not expressed in writing. Indeed, the contributors to the various trade journals seem to have been impressively like-minded. Their admonitions for thematic unity and musical continuity, for extreme discretion in the use of musical gestures that highlight on-screen details, for the avoidance of anything that might interrupt the flow of a filmic narrative—amount to a veritable rulebook for film accompaniment that more or less held sway throughout the entire twentieth century.

Along with general advice as to how music could most effectively be put to the service of narrative film, the trade journals from time to time offered suggestions as to how specific bits of music—or music of specific types—might be applied to specific films. But this idea did not originate in the film-music columns. Although the above-mentioned Max Winkler credited himself with being the first to prescribe music to coincide with on-screen events, by the time Winkler came on the scene the idea had already been in the air for three years.

Cue Sheets

The first "cue sheet" seems to have been published on September 15, 1909, in a promotional brochure called the *Edison Kinetogram*. A two-page section labeled "Incidental Music for Edison Pictures" offered suggestions as to how seven of the latest Edison films might be accompanied. Under each film title, a series of "music cues" recommended music that would either start or end at specific moments in the film. Cues for the shorter films tended to be identified simply as the starting points of various scenes. Typical of the lists, for example, were the music cues for *How the Landlord Collected His Rents*, a 230-foot reel that lasted three and a half minutes:

Scene 1—March, brisk.
      2—Irish jig.
      3—Begin with andante, finish with allegro.
      4—Popular air.
      5— "   "
      6—Andante with lively at finish.
      7—March (same as No. 1).
      8—Plaintive.
      9—Andante (use March of No. 1).[40]

For longer films, cues often took the form of brief descriptions of on-screen actions. The *Kinetogram* recommended that *Why Girls Leave Home*, a ten-minute film based on a popular 1905 melodrama, be accompanied thusly:

At opening, Popular air.
Till second scene, Pizzicato.

Till view of orchestra seats, Regular overture.
Till view of stage is shown, Waltz time.
Note—Knock at door till girl starts to leave home, Home Sweet Home.
Till audience applauds, Lively music.
Till Act 2, snow scene, Plaintive.
Till audience applauds, Lively music.
Till Act 3, bridge scene, Pizzicato.
Till gallery applauds, Lively music.
Till Act 4, heroine's home, Plaintive music.
Till hero bursts through window, Lively, work to climax.
Till next set, girl's return home, Waltz movement.[41]

And some of the *Kinetogram* suggestions—for example, the cues for a ten-minute film titled *The Ordeal*, based on Victor Hugo's *Les misérables*—combined descriptions of action with scenic divisions:

Scene 1—An andante.
2—An allegro changing to plaintive at end.
3—Plaintive.
4—Adagio or march changing at end to allegro strongly marked.
5—Andante to plaintive. Changing to march movement at end.
6—Lively, changing to plaintive at Fantine's arrest.
7—March with accents to accompany scene finishing with andante.
8—Andante.
9—Allegro, to march at arrest.
10—March, changing to andante at end.
11—Slow march, p.p.
12—Andante p.p. hurry at action of putting passport, etc., in fire.
13—March p., changing to f.f. at the entrance of Jean Valjean, the Mayor.
14—Andante to Javert's entrance, then a hurry till the Mayor tears off the piece of iron from the bed. Adagio to end.[42]

The above-cited examples from the September 15, 1909 issue of the *Edison Kinetogram* call for a wide variety of music, but they include just a single reference to a titled composition.[43] All the other suggested pieces, including "a hurry" recommended for the final scene of *The Ordeal*, are identified only by tempo or mood. Given such vague instructions, a film accompanist attempting to heed the advice of the published "Music Cues" might well have improvised the entire content of these passages. It is likely, though, that he or she would have based at least some of the improvisations on stock musical gestures from the repertoire of the still-popular melodrama.[44]

Improvisations would have had no place in an accompaniment for the filmic version of *Faust* that Edison released in December 1909. The suggestions for incidental music all make reference to the same-titled opera by Charles Gounod, and in its publicity materials the company calls attention to the fact that "we have gone to considerable trouble to specify the exact music from the opera" that makes up each of the seventeen cues.[45]

Not specified so precisely—and intermixed with passages that might well have required improvisation—are the operatic excerpts included in the cues for Edison's 1910 production of *Frankenstein*:

> At opening: Andante—"Then You'll Remember Me"
> Till Frankenstein's laboratory: Moderato—"Melody in F"
> Till monster is forming: Increasing agitato
> Till monster appears over bed: Dramatic music from "Der Freischütz"
> Till father and girl in sitting room: Moderato
> Till Frankenstein returns home: Andante—"Annie Laurie"
> Till monster enters Frankenstein's sitting room: Dramatic—"Der Freischütz"
> Till girl enters with teapot: Andante—"Annie Laurie"
> Till monster comes from behind curtain: Dramatic—"Der Freischütz"
> Till wedding guests are leaving: Bridal Chorus from "Lohengrin"
> Till monster appears: Dramatic—"Der Freischütz"
> Till Frankenstein enters: Agitato
> Till monster appears: Dramatic—"Der Freischütz"
> Till monster vanishes in mirror: Diminishing Agitato[46]

While the "Bridal Chorus" from Wagner's *Lohengrin* and the song "Annie Laurie" doubtless needed no additional identification, it is not clear what is meant by "dramatic music" from Carl Maria von Weber's *Der Freischütz*, but one can suppose that it somehow involved the frightfully tremulous diminished seventh chords that permeate the score and which within just a few years of the opera's premiere had been adapted as melodrama cliché.[47] One can suppose, too, that the reference to "Then You'll Remember Me" in the opening scene points to an aria from Michael Balfe's *The Bohemian Girl* and that the "Melody in F" indicated for the laboratory scene is the piano piece by Anton Rubinstein.[48] In any case, the cue sheet for this first filmic rendition of Mary Shelley's horror story remains remarkable for its mix of iconographic compositions with music— a "moderato" and several segments identified only as "agitato"—of a generic sort.

*　*　*

One of the first cue sheets offered not as a prescription from a production company but, rather, as a suggestion from a film-music practitioner appeared in Clarence E. Sinn's "Music for the Picture" column in *Moving Picture World* on September 23, 1911. The film under discussion was *Romeo and Juliet*, an ambitious two-reel picture (about twenty minutes in length) just released by the independent producer Edwin Thanhouser.

> Part I.
>   1.   Martenique Intermezzo (or Allegretto) till sub-title "Capulet and Montague, etc."
>   2.   Heroic till combat, then—
>   3.   Agitato till end of combat.
>   4.   Gavotte till "Romeo is Persuaded, etc."
>   5.   Allegretto (similar to No. 1) till "Romeo and Juliet Meet."
>   6.   Valse Lento till they form for dance.

7. Minuet slow and well marked till dancers exit, then:
8. La Cinquantine till "His Name is Romeo, etc.," then:
9. Valse Lento till "But Soft, What Light Through Yonder Window."
10. Intermezzo from "Cavalleria Rusticana" or something similar till "Romeo Entreats the Good Friar, etc."
11. Vesper Bells till "Juliet's Old Nurse Acts as Messenger."
12. Reverie (The Roses Honeymoon) till change of scene.
13. Gavotte till "Then Hie You Hence, etc."
14. Valse Lento till "Holy Church Incorporate." Then:
15. Religioso till garden scene, then:
16. Light pretty waltz movement or semi-sentimental.
    (I heard one pianist use "Oh, Promise Me" with good effect.)
17. Swell or change to sentimental for finish.

Part II.
1. Semi-mysterious till next scene.
2. Agitato at duel till they stop fighting, then
3. Short plaintive till second duel.
4. Agitato till end of scene.
5. Religioso all through scene. At change:
6. Pathetic till "Juliet's Father Not Knowing, etc."
7. Waltz movement till Juliet is alone with her father.
8. Reverie (The Harvest Moon) till Friar opens door for her.
9. Semi-religious till Juliet appears in the garden.
10. Reverie (Heart's Ease) till "Believing Juliet to be Dead."
11. Pathetic till "Paris, who Loved Juliet."
12. Pathetic (minor key—suggestive of funeral) till "Stop Thy Unhallowed Toil."
13. Agitato pp. Swell for combat. Then:
14. Plaintive till "The Friar Learns That His Letter to Romeo."
15. Mysterious till Juliet rises.
16. Plaintive till change of scene.
17. Mysterious till Friar enters the tomb.
18. Plaintive (minor key) till end.[49]

Here, too, the suggestions involve a mix of generic music and pre-exiting works that presumably would have been not just emotively effective in their slated scenes but also—at least for some audience members—recognized and thus perhaps meaningful in some symbolic way.[50] Of special interest in this cue sheet is the author's flexibility. For Part I, scene 10, Sinn recommends the intermezzo from Mascagni's opera *Cavalleria Rusticana* yet notes that "something similar" would do just as well, and in his comments for Part I, scene 16, he leavens his suggestion for a generic "pretty waltz" with a complimentary note about one of his colleague's specific choices.

Whereas Sinn in his "Music for the Picture" columns in *Moving Picture World* offered "musical suggestions," Ernst Luz—in his "The Musician and the Picture" columns that began appearing in *Moving Picture News* in 1912—offered "musical plots." Luz also opted for a different format. He included blank spaces in which precise timings could be filled in by a film accompanist, and in advance of his list of cues he provided a musico-dramatic "set-up":

MUSICAL PLOT No. 1
"Two Battles"—Vitagraph Release of August 17

SET-UP
No. 1. Slow Waltz (very legato).
No. 2. Dramatic (battle music, lengthy).
No. 3. Military March (any Von Blon march appropriate).
No. 4. Dramatic (battle music, short).
No. 5. Dirge or funeral chant (Funeral chant by Hauptman appropriate and effective).
No. 6. Sentimental (Traumerei or similar).
No. 7. Waltz (slow).

CUES
Play No. 1 until leader "In Africa"   (—— min.)
Play No. 2 until leader "Two Letters"   (—— min.)
Play No. 3 until soldiers go to the front   (—— min.)
Play No. 4 until Gordon walks among dead on battle field (—— min.) (Begin softly crescendo at battle.)
Play No. 5 until Gordon covers body of friend with flag (—— min.)
Play No. 6 until Army Club scene, crescendo while fiancee plays piano (—— min.)
Play No. 7 until end. Crescendo as they embrace (—— min.)

Note: Any good-bye song of mild temperament can be used for No. 1. No. 4 can be materially accentuated by a bugle call immediately after the third officer gives orders to Gordon.[51]

Like Sinn, Luz was open to a variety of means by which a desired end might be reached. For the military music in the film's third scene, Luz suggests that "any Von Blon march" would be appropriate.[52] Likewise, the set-ups for scenes 5 and 6 are not so much specifications for pre-existing music as recommendations that music affectively comparable to the named compositions be at hand. Vis-à-vis musical flexibility, Luz's addendum to the cue sheet is especially telling; along with pointing out an opportunity for "source music," the appended note emphasizes the idea that the set-up's recommended "slow waltz (very legato)" for the opening scene can easily be replaced with "any good-bye song of mild temperament."

The "musical plot" cited above is for a one-reel picture issued by Vitagraph. Following the lead of Edison, in 1912 the company began publishing "Music Suggestions" in its *Vitagraph Bulletin*. These resembled the trade-journal cue sheets of Sinn and Luz in content, but in format they tended to be much more prosaic:

During the scene between Tom and Mary, play "Since I Fell in Love With Mary" (Cahill). As the Miners are seen entombed, play "The Traumerie" (Schuman), and "Hearts and Flowers." As the Blind Miner leads the way, play

"Show Me the Way, Oh Father" (Rossiter). As he finds the men and they are rescued, play "Pilgrim's Chorus" (Tanhauser). As Mary and Tom are reunited in each other's arms, play "I Love the Name of Mary."[53]

The Vitagraph "music suggestions" were put together by Bert Ennis, who in a memoir reported that instead of actually watching the films he "simply scanned . . . the synopses of the current flicker, sat down at the typewriter, and with the aid of a good memory, plus the catalogues of [publishers] Remick, Feist, Von Tilzer, Ted Snyder, Witmark, etc., proceeded to cue the film."[54]

Original Scores and "Special Music"

Many books on the history of film music suggest that the first musical score composed specifically to accompany a narrative film—in other words, the first "original" film score—was the one that Camille Saint-Saëns concocted in 1908 on commission from the French production company Pathé and a Parisian organization called the Societé Film d'Art. Actually, the first "original" score might well have been an anonymous accompaniment for a film titled *Soldiers of the Cross*, made by the Salvation Army and first exhibited in Melbourne, Australia, in 1900.[55] Another candidate is the "beautiful and very original music" from "the harmonious pen of Herman Finck" that supported a London showing of *Marie Antoinette* in 1904.[56] It would be more accurate to say that Saint-Saëns's music for *L'Assassinat du Duc de Guise* is the first completely original film score by a composer who at the time was famous and who remains famous today.

When *L'Assassinat du Duc de Guise* premiered at Paris's Salle Charras on November 17, 1908, it shared the bill with *Le Secret de Myrto* and *L'Empreinte*, both of which were accompanied by original music by, respectively, Gaston Berardi and Fernand LeBorne. Whereas *L'Assassinat* was an eighteen-minute drama that realistically depicted the 1588 murder of Henry, Duke of Guise, by henchmen of France's King Henry III, *Le Secret de Myrto* was a relatively brief balletic portrayal of the mythological character Myrtle (danced on-screen by Regina Badet) and *L'Empreinte* ("The Impression") was a comparably brief series of tableaux featuring traditional French pantomime characters. Nowadays virtually nothing is known of Berardi and LeBorne, except that LeBorne served as conductor at the film showing.[57] Saint-Saëns, in marked contrast, easily retains a place in Western music's canon of "great composers." Indeed, Saint-Saëns was well on his way to becoming a "great composer" even at the time of his pioneering film score; by 1908—at age seventy-seven—he had to his credit twelve operas (including the 1877 *Samson et Dalila*), three symphonies (including the 1886 "Organ Symphony"), the novel *The Carnival of the Animals* (also from 1866),[58] and dozens of songs, choral works and pieces for solo piano and chamber ensemble, and he had been the recipient of honorary doctorates from both Oxford and Cambridge.

The scores of all three composers were published in piano reduction shortly after their premieres,[59] and an orchestral version of the Saint-Saëns music—for strings, piano, and harmonium—was published in 1908 as the composer's Op. 128.[60] How the music of Berardi and LeBorne might have interfaced with their visual stimuli remains a mystery, for the films are no longer extant. *L'Assassinat*, on the other hand, survives in both script and several versions of filmic print.[61]

In his 1997 book on film music, Russell Lack asserts that since "the manuscript reveals just one formal cue, . . . it therefore remains unclear exactly how the score was to have been synchronized in performance with the picture."[62] Forty years earlier, however, Roger Manvell and John Huntley confidently noted that Saint-Saëns's published score "consisted of an Introduction and five Tableaux, each part being carefully cued for the film."[63] Concurring, Martin Marks compares the music for *L'Assassinat* with Saint-Saëns's 1896 ballet *Javotte*, which contains "pantomimic segments in which the music changes frequently and is carefully cued," to the extent that "the music accompanying a scene in which the dancers mimic a conversation has cuing so precise that seven times the word 'Non!' is aligned with the second or third beat of a measure."[64] Marks concludes that "though the printed score [for *L'Assassinat*] contains only nine cues (for example, 'Entrée du page,' 'Entrée du Duc,' 'Départ du Duc,' etc.), study of the music in relationship to the film makes clear that it follows the action just as closely—with and without cues—as in portions of *Javotte*."[65]

Along with abundant instances in which a specific musical gesture is "cued" by an on-screen action, Saint-Saëns's score for *L'Assassinat* features demarcation points that correspond with the narrative's changes in time or locale. "Analogous to the film's use of [inter]titles," Marks writes, "each musical tableau is set apart from the others by a pause; and each begins with a clearly defined meter, tempo, theme, and key that contrast with those that precede and/or follow."[66] Royal S. Brown echoes this thought, and—focusing less on structure than on detail—he notes that "the climactic moments that back up the assassination remarkably foreshadow film-music tropes still in use."[67]

The foreshadowed tropes to which Brown refers, presumably, include not only precisely cued "hits" and "stingers" but also modulations and silences that seem to correspond to specific camera shots. These gestures are forward-looking, indeed. The use of meter, tempo, and the like to indicate shifts in narrative *topoi* was advocated by film-music columnists and authors of handbooks throughout the 1910s and 1920s, but mimetic detailing of the sort exhibited in the *L'Assassinat* score was generally discouraged. Not until the start of Hollywood's so-called classical period—in the mid-1930s, after the film industry had adjusted to the new sound technology—would such devices become the norm.

Perhaps because the light of its historical prescience shines with such brilliance, the score for *L'Assassinat* tends to get short shrift in terms of its musical quality. This is unfortunate, for Saint-Saëns's Op. 128 is a substantive composition that removed from its filmic context still generously rewards any listener's attention. Responding to the music alone, Brown observes that "in listening to the score, one often has the impression of an accompaniment for an unsung opera."[68] Apparently not even thinking of the score's theatrical applicability, a reviewer of the original presentation boldly declared that "Saint-Saëns has written for *L'Assassinat du Duc de Guise* a masterpiece of symphonic music."[69] Marks warns that "to praise a score in such terms is to imply that it can be appreciated like concert music, apart from its film—a dangerous claim for any film score, and one that often suggests the critic has missed the point."[70] But he adds that in the case of the *L'Assassinat* score, which has "sufficient intricacy, coherence, and expressive power to be compared . . . with the tone poems composed by Saint-Saëns thirty years before," the claim "for once . . . has some validity."[71]

For all its virtues, Saint-Saën's 1908 score for *L'Assassinat* had little immediate influence either in Europe or in the United States. Since the film united the talents of many prestigious French artists,[72] the Paris premiere was indeed a celebrated affair. But when *L'Assassinat* was presented in New York in February 1909, its length was drastically reduced and apparently its original music was nowhere to be heard.[73] Scores for three other Pathé/Societé Film d'Art productions—*L'Arlésienne*, which used the same-titled 1872 suite of incidental music by Georges Bizet, *Le Retour d'Ulysee*, with original music by Georges Hüe, and *L'Empreinte ou la Main Rouge*, with original music by LeBorne[74]—were likewise absent when the films were released in the United States, and by the middle of 1909 Pathé had ceased production of films with precisely tailored scores. Altman makes the point that, even though these scores failed to cross the Atlantic, "it was not lost on American producers and exhibitors that special music was an integral part of the European approach to prestige productions."[75] The timing was not right, however. As Marks points out, *L'Assassinat* was "a special film with a special score, and neither was suited to the nickelodeon-centered American film industry of 1909."[76]

*   *   *

It is interesting that both Altman and Marks, in the quotations immediately above, use the value-laden adjective "special" to describe the scores associated with Pathé's 1908–9 Societé Film d'Art productions. In the first case the word seems to mean "deluxe" or "high-class," and in the second case it seems to mean "highly unusual." But the term "special music"—meaning nothing more than music associated with a particular film—can be traced as far back as 1899, when Edison issued sheet music in conjunction with his release of *The Astor Tramp* and *Love and War*.

Precedent having been set, the term "special music" was used sporadically during the early nickelodeon period, and after the Edison experiments it appeared almost exclusively in conjunction with films based on operatic subjects. One of the first operatic films released simultaneous with an edited piano score adapted from the source was Méliès's 1904 *Faust et Marguerite*. In 1909 Edison issued its own version of *Faust*, with a piano score drawn from Gounod that publicity materials admonish "should be played according to the action of the film as indicated."[77] A few years earlier, however, Edison had similarly provided edited sheet music concomitant with its release of an adaptation of Wagner's *Parsifal*, and in 1907 Kalem offered a version of Franz Lehár's operetta *The Merry Widow* along with "a complete musical score synchronized with the picture."[78]

The idea of "special music" based on opera scores triggered a small wave of scores composed for and fitted to non-operatic films later in the nickelodeon period. Marks has identified more than a hundred American films released between 1910 and 1914 for which "special music" was composed.[79] Of this large handful of scores, only thirty-one are extant and are preserved in the Library of Congress, the New York Public Library, and the library at UCLA; the others are identified through references in *Moving Picture World* or the *Catalogue of Copyright Entries*. Most of the films on Marks's list are not accompanied by details; they are labeled simply as having "special piano music" or "special music." But a few stand out. A review of the 1912 *The Life of John Bunyan*, for example, bore the headline "Symphony Orchestra Interprets Pictures," and it notes that "Modest Altschuler, the conductor of the [Russian Symphony] orchestra, had specially composed, selected, and adapted music for the occasion."[80] The 1913 *Hiawatha* had

43

a score by John J. Braham that apparently called for eleven instruments.[81] And a review of the 1914 Italian-made *Cabiria* notes that "the specially written music was interpreted by an orchestra of fifty or more pieces."[82]

Among the composers of "special music" during the last years of the nickelodeon period, the most prolific seems to have been Walter Cleveland Simon, who between November 1911 and May 1913 composed most of the approximately two dozen scores issued simultaneously with Kalem films. The score for Simon's debut effort, the three-reel *Arrah-Na-Pogue*, was offered in arrangements for both piano and four-piece ensemble, but everything else was written only for solo piano. The music was deliberately simple, so that "any pianist can play it,"[83] and the scores typically made generous use of reference-rich material from the public domain. In keeping with the advice of the contemporary film-music columnists, affect in Simon's music tended to change only with scenic shifts; in most cases, the notated point of synchronization was not a filmic action but, rather, an on-screen title that indicated a new dramatic *topos*.

Emphasizing the fact that so many of them are made up of repeatable short segments, Altman writes that in terms of structure Simon's "numbers" are "similar to familiar melodrama music and to the many generic film accompaniment pieces published during the 1910s."[84] Focusing specifically on the content of Simon's music for the 1912 film *An Arabian Tragedy*, Marks observes that many of the numbers consist of fragments that are "for the most part tuneless" and that the work as a whole, which "could never be mistaken for a unified score" like Saint-Saëns's, "resembles a compilation in its unyielding discontinuity."[85] Nevertheless, Marks writes, the score "speak[s] eloquently for the film in several ways, despite halting syntax and limited vocabulary," and there is no denying that "Simon's music *is* original."[86]

Among the studios that joined Kalem in the issuance of "special music"—mostly for solo piano—were Thanhouser, Kleine-Cines, Pathé, All-Star, Famous Players, Solax, and Vitagraph. By 1914, however, the publication of "special music" to accompany specific films had all but ceased. Even though the scores were offered for reasonable prices, sales were so poor as to make publication unprofitable. Resistance had to do not with the music's artistic worth but with its impracticality. The scores may have been relatively simple, but they were nevertheless beyond the reach of most pianists who week after week had to prepare accompaniments on very short notice; for music directors who had ensembles at their disposal, allegiance to "special music" meant spending valuable time to adapt the scores for the resources at hand.

Using the film-music columns in the trade journals as their forum, accompanists did not hesitate to express their opinions about "special music." Commenting on the Verdi-based score that Pathé published in conjunction with its 1911 release of *Il Trovatore*, a pianist from Ohio complained: ". . . I can read a good deal of the popular music, yet I couldn't begin to handle this special music at all. I did not see the music till the day before I was supposed to play it and when I did see it I gave up at once. . . . If I have to be able to sight-read this kind of music for picture shows[s], I might as well quit. . . ."[87] Regarding the Kalem music in general, in 1912 a music director from Brooklyn who identified himself as E.J.L. wrote: "I have been unable to find it practical, as . . . it would mean the outlay of a great deal of money per week—and lengthy rehearsals for proper rendition."[88] Responding specifically to the Kalem piano score for *The Cheyenne Massacre*, an accompanist from Connecticut in 1913 bluntly declared: "I did not use it, as I would have had to make an orchestration."[89]

For various reasons, not the least of which was its perceived infringement on accompanists' creativity, "special music" was simply not compatible with the practice that had developed and then become codified during the nickelodeon period. Generally unsuccessful though they were, however, the "special" scores that faded from the scene ca. 1914 pointed toward one of the directions in which film music would soon move. Indeed, once the American film industry adjusted to some fundamental changes, the concept of "special music" would make a comeback that was nothing less than spectacular.

Changes in the Industry

There is no question that "vernacular" music played an important role in nickelodeon accompaniments. Along with holding up for ridicule examples of popular songs used in ways they deemed egregiously inappropriate, music columnists for the trade journals often offered tips as to how such material might be put to good effect. "Popular songs are useful," advised one expert, "especially in sentimental pictures and comedies."[90] In order to make their theatrical point, advised another, songs need not be played in their entirety; in many cases "one can use just the title of these popular songs, or the first few lines of the chorus."[91] One of the first anthologies of utilitarian film music, published in 1911, consisted of "an assortment of melodies . . . brilliantly yet simply arranged for piano."[92] That these were vintage melodies mattered little. "As long as the words fit the situation or action on the screen," wrote a film-music columnist in 1914, "use the song of those words, no matter how old the tune."[93]

Nickelodeon audiences doubtless would not have cared, but there is of course a difference between old tunes that belong to the public domain and new tunes whose lyricists and composers were likely to have registered their work for copyright.[94] Taken literally, the term "copyright" is simply the right to control the making of physical copies of protected material. At least in the early years of the nickelodeon, for music publishers the wide-spread use of copyrighted songs posed no threat whatsoever. Indeed, there was something to be gained.

Even before the nickelodeon became an established venue, American film producers maintained a close relationship with the music publishers who collectively, but quite unofficially, were known as Tin Pan Alley.[95] The involvement had less to do with music that accompanied films, however, as with films—in the form of the "illustrated song"—that accompanied music. The financial connections between Tin Pan Alley and the members of the Motion Picture Patents Company is an area that warrants exploration, but Rick Altman suggests that "until the 1913 demise of the illustrated song . . . popular music publishers saw nickel theaters as little more than loss leaders for sheet music sales."[96]

In 1914 there began a marked shift in the relationship between music publishers and the film industry, for that year saw the founding of the American Society of Composers, Authors and Publishers.

ASCAP's primary purpose was to protect its members' performance rights. Quite apart from the system of royalties that provided songwriters with a percentage of revenues generated by sales of their copyrighted works, ASCAP established tariff schedules by which songwriters would receive payment whenever their works were performed in for-profit situations. Thanks to lobbying from an ASCAP predecessor called the Music Publishers Association, in 1897 the copyright law had been adjusted so that permission from copyright holders was required for profit-oriented public performances of protected works, but it was generally assumed that this restriction applied only to formal concerts and theatrical productions. Under the new ASCAP regulations, tested in 1915 with a much-publicized lawsuit and supported in 1917 by a Supreme Court ruling,[97] fees were required for use of protected material in *any* commercial context. ASCAP was vigilant in the enforcement of its members' rights. Especially after the 1917 Supreme Court decision, entrepreneurs of all sorts—certainly including operators of motion-picture theaters—were at serious financial risk if they used ASCAP material without first paying a "music tax."

* * *

Along with restrictions on the use of music in conjunction with motion-picture exhibitions, there were other changes that profoundly affected the American film industry—and with it American film music—in the years surrounding World War I. These had to do as much with the nature of the newer films as with the venues in which these films were shown.

The magazine writers quoted at the start of this chapter marveled at the fact that in 1907 the entire country boasted some four or five thousand nickelodeons and that daily attendance numbered more than two million. By the middle of the twentieth century's second decade, writes film historian Dennis Sharp, "it [was] estimated that 25,000 picture theaters were in use and the average daily attendance was in the region of six million people."[98]

Even in medium-sized cities, the modest nickelodeons that seated at most several hundred customers gradually were replaced by more sumptuous venues that accommodated much larger audiences. Opened in 1913, the 2,460-seat Regent Theater billed itself as "the first de luxe theatre built expressly for showing movies in New York."[99] While the Regent may have been built "expressly" for films, in fact it hosted a variety of entertainments, and its multi-purpose model was quickly followed. The new "movie palaces" in New York, for example, included the 3,500-seat Strand (1914), the 1,900-seat Rialto (1916), the 2,100-seat Rivoli (1917), and the 5,300-seat Capitol (1919); Chicago had its 2,400-seat Central Park Theater by 1917, and the same year witnessed the debut of the 2,100-seat Million Dollar Theatre in Los Angeles.[100] A film shown in a theater of this size, obviously, could not have been accompanied by a mere piano. To accompany films as well as vaudeville acts, most of these venues had orchestras on their payrolls. Most of them, too, installed in their orchestra pits the elaborate and expensive new instrument called the theater organ.[101]

As the theaters grew in number and size, so the films they hosted grew in length and scope. As noted above, the MPPC members were interested almost exclusively in providing a weekly supply of one-reel films to "licensed" distributors and theater operators.[102] Following the lead of Carl Laemmle in New York and William Swanson in Chicago, independent exhibitors sought films that were not only longer than the typical MPPC release but also more obviously cast with recognizable performers. As John Belton points out, while "the [MPPC] resisted the publicization of its stars in the popular press in a deliberate attempt to prevent the creation of a costly star system," the independent producers seemed to realize that what the audience wanted was "feature-length films with sensational dramatic content and stars."[103] Thanks to the independent producers, by 1915—when the United States court system declared the MPPC illegal on the grounds that it violated the Sherman Antitrust Act—such actors as Lillian Gish, Mary Pickford, Douglas Fairbanks, Theda Bara, Charles Chaplin, and Roscoe "Fatty" Arbuckle were well on their way to being movie stars.

4

FEATURE FILMS, 1915–27

We searched for composers who would supply what we needed and we found them. They were fine musicians, but they were specialists in just one phase of music, film music, and most of them are forgotten today. Who still knows the compositions of Walter Simon, Herman Froml, Gaston Borch, Chas. Herbert, Irene Berge, Leo Kempinski, Maurice Baron, Hugo Riesenfeld? Very few, if any, will still remember them—and yet, in those days, gone only a few decades, their music was heard by more people in this country than the music of all the great masters combined.

Max Winkler, 1951[1]

Judging from the commentary in the trade journals, as early as 1910 the relationship between music and film imagery had permanently shifted. Whereas "early practice seemed more like the accompaniment of a musical concert by film projection," Rick Altman writes, "the new approach . . . enforce[d] clear subordination of the music to the moving picture."[2] Five years later, when star-studded features had all but displaced the nickelodeon's one-reel fare, music subordinated to a film's dramatic content was more in demand than ever before. With the newly created ASCAP regulations, however, there were limitations on the type of music that might serve as accompaniment.

Music by ASCAP members could indeed be used in the movie theaters, but only if exhibitors paid fees based on the size of the audience, the number of usages, and various other factors. In the case of potentially very lucrative feature films, exhibitors determined that the use of ASCAP-protected material was clearly worth the investment. Usually, however, exhibitors opted to have their cinematic attractions accompanied by music that—at least in terms of its acquisition—was much less costly.

As will be discussed later in this chapter, 1915 was a landmark year in film-music history because it witnessed—with J.C. Breil's music for *The Birth of a Nation*—the introduction into the industry of the specially composed/compiled score that could only be performed by a large, well-rehearsed orchestra. But music of this sort, far more sophisticated than the examples of "special music" issued during the twilight of the nickelodeon period, was limited both in number and influence. Although they contributed enormously to the box-office appeal of the multi-reel features with which they were associated, these lavish scores were heard only when their films played extended runs at movie palaces in the largest cities and when they toured the country as high-priced "road show" attractions. For audience members who attended the movies week after week, aurally spectacular orchestral scores were certainly not the norm.

For everyday showings of run-of-the-mill films, the most efficient solution to the problem of where to find effective yet affordable musical accompaniments involved—not surprisingly—a revamping of earlier practices. By 1915, with audiences adjusting to the comforts of the new movie palaces, an accompaniment based on nickelodeon-style improvisations of course would have seemed woefully old-fashioned. Similarly old-fashioned would have been the accompaniment that relied on those relatively few classical pieces that during the nickelodeon period were deemed sufficiently "iconographic"

Figure 4.1 Interior of the Roxy Theater, with view of orchestra pit and stage, New York City. Courtesy of Library of Congress.

for filmic purposes.[3] But film accompanists knew that there was still a rich lode to be mined from the public domain, and among them there was no disputing the communicative value of the old melodrama clichés.

More rapacious in its appetite and supposedly more sophisticated in its tastes, the movie audience ca. 1915 remained psychologically dependent upon familiar film-music tropes but would accept them only if they were presented in fresh guises and varied from week to week. While it was all but impossible to add to the number of classical compositions that for the average American might immediately "signify" a filmic situation, it was fairly easy—for musicians well-versed in the repertoire—to come up with a virtually endless supply of public-domain pieces whose emotive content was at least in some ways similar to that of the familiar musical symbols. As for the tried-and-true clichés of melodrama, it was simply a matter of distilling their expressive essences and packaging them anew.

As the humble nickelodeon gave way to the sumptuous picture palace, thoughtful film accompanists across the country might well have realized all this on their own. In case they did not, however, there was plenty of assistance to be had from aggressive players in the burgeoning film-music industry.

More Cue Sheets

Thanks in large part to his efforts at self-promotion, Max Winkler is credited in many books on film music as being the inventor of the cue sheet. According to Winkler's much-quoted autobiography, the "invention" allegedly took place in 1912. That date is easily challenged, not just because cue sheets can be traced back to 1909 issues of the *Edison Kinetogram* but also because reports on Winkler's "invention" do not start appearing in the trade journals until 1915. All that notwithstanding, it remains that Winkler had considerable impact on the nature of film music as American cinema—in the World War I period—made the transition from single-reel nickelodeon entertainments to multi-reel features.

No matter when his brainstorm actually occurred, Winkler's account of it remains of interest. Since his immigration from Romania in 1907, Winkler had been a clerk at the New York offices of publisher Carl Fischer, the firm that along with G. Schirmer dominated the American market for classical music early in the twentieth century. He had been exposed far too often, he writes, to examples of "jackass music" that turned showings of serious films into farces, and he was keenly aware that frustrated film exhibitors were often turning to Carl Fischer for advice. Suddenly, he had an idea:

> One day after I had gone home from work I could not fall asleep. The hundreds and thousands of titles, the mountains of music that we had stored and catalogued and explored, kept going through my mind. There was music, surely, to fit *any* situation in *any* picture. If we could only think of a way to let all these orchestra leaders and pianists and organists know what we had! If we could use our knowledge and experience not when it was too late but much earlier before they ever had to sit down and play, we would be able to sell them music not by the ton but by the trainload!
>
> The thought suddenly electrified me. It was not a problem of getting the music; we had the music, plenty of it, any conceivable kind, more than anybody

could ever want. It was a problem of promotion, timing and organization. I pulled back the blanket, turned on the light and went over to the little table in the corner, took a sheet of paper and began writing feverishly.

Here is what I wrote:

MUSIC CUE SHEET
for
The Magic Valley
selected and compiled by M. Winkler

Cue No.

1 Opening—play Minuet No. 2 in G by Beethoven for ninety seconds until title on screen "Follow me Dear."

2 Play—"Dramatic Andante" by Vely for two minutes and ten seconds. Note: Play soft during scene where mother enters. Play Cue No. 2 until scene "hero leaving room."

3 Play—"Love Theme" by Lorenze—for one minute and twenty seconds. Note: Play soft and slow during conversations until title on screen "There they go."

4 Play—"Stampede" by Simon for fifty-five seconds. Note: Play fast and decrease or increase speed of gallop in accordance with action on the screen.

I kept on writing for hours. *The Magic Valley* was just an imaginary picture with imaginary scenes, situations and moods, but the music was real music. It was music I knew. The endless years of close contact with it, of carrying it around, of sorting it out, of hearing it, listing it, handling it, living with it, now began to bear unexpected fruit. I went to bed exhausted, and when I woke up the next morning it took me a little time to remember how these densely covered sheets of paper had come into my room.[4]

Winkler goes on to explain that he immediately pitched his idea, via a letter, to the Universal Film Company.[5] Two days later, he says, he was called in for an interview with Universal publicity director Paul Gulick, and he was invited to apply his idea the next evening to a number of soon-to-be-released new films:

Between seven o'clock and a half-hour past midnight the next day I had been shown sixteen different subjects—slapstick comedies, newsreels, a trip through the Sahara, a Westerner. I had been provided with a little desk, a stop watch, a stack of paper, a little mountain of pencils. I looked and stopped my watch and wrote. As the pictures flashed by, the bins in the Fischer store appeared before my eyes—I not only *heard* the music that would fit perfectly to the camels slowly swaying through the sand, I *saw* the bin that stored Tchaikovsky's "Dance Arabe" and the title in print and the little card I had written out for the piece, and while the camels trotted across the screen I wrote it down on the cue sheet without a moment's hesitation.[6]

The next day, Winkler says, he was offered a four-week contract under the terms of which he would preview Universal films, "regardless of character or length," and prepare cue sheets that contained "only musical compositions published and easily available to our distributors and exhibitors."[7] Whenever it was that Winkler actually entered into his relationship with the production company, it was not until early in 1915 that the trade press, citing an announcement in *Universal Weekly*, reported that "musical suggestions will be published for important [Universal] films far in advance, to enable orchestra leaders to secure the music."[8] Within just a few months, Winkler was publicly identified as the author of Universal's pre-release cue sheets.[9]

Responding competitively to what seemed like a good idea, the Paramount Pictures Corporation announced in October 1915 that in advance of the most important films made by its various subsidiaries (Famous Players, Lasky, Morosco) the company would issue "special orchestrations" of classical works crafted by the Canadian-born, German-trained composer George W. Beynon and published by G. Schirmer. Unfortunately for the Paramount–Schirmer alliance, only the most lavish movie theaters could afford the large ensembles specified in Beynon's scores. More practical and profitable—beginning in December 1915, and for the most part involving pictures released not by Paramount but by Metro—was Schirmer's linkage of advertisements for both piano-solo and small-orchestra editions with suggestions for film accompaniment offered in *Moving Picture World* by S.M. Berg.[10]

Anthologies and Handbooks

Berg is not nearly so prominent as Winkler in film-music lore, yet his innovations were every bit as influential as those of his eventual business partner. Initially a journalist who enjoyed a "cozy" relationship with a major publisher of classical music, by September 1916 Berg—still working as a journalist—had set up his own publishing house. Oblivious to charges of conflict-of-interest, Berg in his "Music for the Picture" columns brazenly recommended works that in the very same issue of *Moving Picture World* were advertised as part of *Berg's Incidental Series*.

Significantly, most of the music that Berg published and sold—unlike the music that he recommended during his brief collaboration with Schirmer—did not belong to the public domain. To be sure, the music was derivative to the extreme, its primary models being those relatively few classical works well-enough known to have achieved symbolic status even among unsophisticated listeners, the "action music" and "heightened emotion" sequences endemic to European opera, and—most fruitful—the reliable clichés of melodrama. No matter how much its essence owed to tradition and a pre-existing literature, the specific content of the music in *Berg's Incidental Series* was original enough to qualify for copyright protection. It was not subject, however, to the ASCAP "music tax" that in the World War I years became more and more onerous to proprietors of motion-picture theaters. As a publisher, Berg dealt exclusively with composers who opted not to join the increasingly powerful performing-rights organization.

That the tax-free compositions in *Berg's Incidental Series* were created for motion-picture accompaniment is evident from their annotated titles. In an advertisement from November 11, 1916, for example, Berg offers a *Misterioso* "for burglary or mystery" and a *Pizzicato Misterioso* "for burglary and stealth," a *Hurry* "for general use" and another "for pursuit and races," and a "characteristic" *Galop* by Adolf Minot; the advertised pieces by Carl Kiefert include an *Allegro Agitato* "for general use," an *Agitato* "for angry discussion or riot," and a *Furioso* "for riot or storm scenes," and Gaston Borch is vividly represented by a *Misterioso Dramatico* "for sudden or impending danger," a *Dramatic Andante* "for suppressed emotions," and a *Gruesome Misterioso* "for infernal or witches' scenes."[11]

Along with original music by Minot, Kiefert, and Borch, *Berg's Incidental Series* (1916–17) offered works by J.E. Andino, Irénée Bergé, Charles K. Herbert, and Walter C. Simon. But these were just a few of the composers who contributed to what by the start of World War I amounted to a relatively huge repertoire of tax-free music designed specifically for the movies.

Pre-dating the ASCAP regulations, the earliest American compilation of film music seems to be Gregg A. Frelinger's 1909 *Motion Picture Piano Music: Descriptive Music To Fit the Action, Character or Scene of Moving Pictures.* Published in Lafayette, Indiana, the anthology contains fifty-one relatively easy pieces for piano. A few of them paraphrase familiar songs whose lyrics an audience would presumably find meaningful (Stephen Foster's "Old Black Joe," for example, and the drinking song "How Dry I Am"), but most of them are entirely original. They bear generic labels reflective of their tempos, emotive affects, and—in a few cases—specific character or ethnic evocations, and they are elaborately indexed according to the types of dramatic situations they might illustrate. Vis-à-vis accompaniment for film, *Motion Picture Piano Music* is a prototype, yet at the same time it reflects long-standing tradition. Marks observes that the compositions are "all headed with functional titles similar to those that appear in later, more elaborate [film-music] anthologies,"[12] while Altman, regarding Frelinger's work from a different historical perspective, compares both its content and its design with "the earlier collections published for melodrama theaters."[13]

After Frelinger's, the next anthologies of film music were the *Emerson Moving Picture Music Folio* (Cincinnati, 1910), the *Orpheum Collection of Moving Picture Music* (Chicago, 1910), and *F.B. Haviland's Moving Picture Pianist's Album* (New York, 1911). No composer is listed for the more than 125 pieces that make up the *Emerson* collection, but the music in the *Orpheum* set was apparently the handiwork of Clarence E. Sinn, who served as his own publisher before taking over the film-music column at *Moving Picture Weekly.* Whereas the *Emerson* and *Orpheum* anthologies featured original music, the *Haviland* album consisted of simple arrangements—by Eugene Platzman—of music drawn mostly from the classical repertoire.

Like Frelinger's, all of this material was scored for solo piano. And all of it, to judge from the advertisements, was pitched to the market largely on the basis of its flexibility and functionality. The Frelinger anthology of "real music that really fits the picture" consisted of "descriptive music to fit all probable scenes, actions, characters, etc., shown in moving pictures."[14] The pieces in the *Emerson* folio, a "great work" that "has taken over six months to compile," were "adapted for any style or kind of pictures that may be shown."[15] One of Sinn's ads asked accompanists if they were properly "working up" their pictures; if they were not, the copy suggests, accompanists would do well to make use of the "good melodramatic music"[16] in his *Orpheum* collection. With its "assortment of melodies adapted to every class and style of pictures," the *Haviland* album contained "the music that every pianist needs in a moving picture house."[17]

In 1912 Max Winkler's employer issued the first installment of the *Carl Fischer Moving Picture Folio, Especially Designed for Moving Picture Theatres, Vaudeville Houses, etc.* The fifty-eight pieces contained in this "up-to-date folio of melo-dramatic music"[18] were arrangements (mostly by Mayhew L. Lake) not for piano but for small orchestra. Like the *Haviland* album, the *Carl Fischer Moving Picture Folio* consisted largely of treatments of music in the public domain, but it resembled all its predecessors in that it was presented as an omnibus "covering positively every conceivable phase of human emotions."[19]

Film-music anthologies from 1913 include *Denison's Descriptive Music Book for Plays, Festivals, Pageants and Moving Pictures* (Chicago), with approximately 150 arrangements by Adam Gregory of more or less familiar classical and popular compositions; a pair of *Dramatic and Moving Picture Music* collections (Chicago) that each contained more than thirty original compositions, for piano, by John L. Bastian; the *Carl Fischer Professional Pianist's Collection for Motion Picture Theatres, Vaudeville Houses, Theatrical Programs, and Dramatic Purposes* (New York), featuring original music by George Smith; and the first two volumes of the *Sam Fox Moving Picture Music* series (Cleveland), which offered a total of forty-nine original pieces, for piano, by John Stepan Zamecnik.

Of the collections named above, those compiled by Zamecnik remain the best known; indeed, in most accounts of film-music history, the various anthologies that Zamecnik compiled for the Cleveland-based Sam Fox Company are the *only* published materials cited in the sections that deal with the period during which cinema completed its migration from the nickelodeon to the picture palace. This is due at least in part to the fact that numerous copies of the low-priced, widely distributed Fox volumes have managed to survive. But Zamecnik's enduring fame doubtless has at least something to do with the nature of his music.

Educated at the Prague Conservatory under the tutelage of Antonín Dvořák, Zamecnik (1872–1953) worked for several years as a violinist in the Pittsburgh Symphony Orchestra before taking up the post, in 1907, of music director at the Hippodrome Theater in his native Cleveland. Along with conducting the theater's orchestra, Zamecnik composed prolifically for its various vaudeville, melodrama, and filmic attractions. By 1913 Zamecnik had become well attuned to the musical needs of the evolving cinema. Graceful though they are, the piano pieces he wrote for the *Sam Fox Moving Picture Music* collections are remarkable not so much for their "artistic quality" as for their functionality.

Zamecnik's music, of course, smacks of melodramatic cliché. Whether they lived in cities large or small, movie-goers ca. 1913 would have expected—indeed, demanded—accompanimental music that embellished narrative films according to established conventions. Scenes whose dramatic content was mysterious or agitated had to be supported by music of a *misterioso* or *agitato* nature; if this were not the case, a filmic experience likely would have seemed seriously flawed. Zamecnik knew this and responded accordingly, with "Storm Music" featuring rumbling minor-key tremolos, "Burglar Music" marked by suspenseful silence and sharply accented dissonances, and "Hurry Music" propelled by rushing chromatic and scalar passages.

Itemizing film-music clichés prevalent ca. 1913, Altman notes that

> Indians were signified by eighth-note drumming of open fifths in the bass. Chinese ambience was created by high treble grace notes associated with discords and triplets. Death scenes were represented by a minor-key melody played in the left hand. War scenes could be evoked by bugle and cannon imitations. The gait of a cowboy's horse was figured by alternation between quarter and eighth notes in a 6/8 major key. A mysterious atmosphere could be

summoned by the broken, pizzicato, syncopated selections known as "burglar" or "sneaky" music, whereas hurry music employed eighth- or sixteenth-note runs of touching notes (chromatic or not) against a regular beat of quarter notes in the bass. Imminent danger could be signified by a dissonant *tremolo* in either or both hand.[20]

All this is exemplified, if not epitomized, in Zamecnik's music for the *Sam Fox Moving Picture Music* collections. And it is presented, remarkably, in a way that encourages creative input from the performer. The various pieces are closely enough related in key so that a pianist might switch easily from one to another without much of a jolt; within compositions modulations are infrequent, and the largely symmetrical phrases typically cadence with an open-ended finality that invites repetition with improvised embellishment *ad infinitum*. Unlike most of the pieces included in film-music anthologies toward the end of the nickelodeon period, Zamecnik's compositions are not just affectively on-the-mark but, in terms of possible usage, enormously flexible. Altman does not exaggerate when he writes that the Zamecnik anthologies were "precisely the kind of support that film accompanists were seeking in the early teens."[21]

Zamecnik authored his third volume of *Sam Fox Moving Picture Music*, containing twenty-one pieces, in 1914. The fourth installment in the series, with twenty-six original compositions, did not appear until 1923, but the interim saw the publication of numerous similarly structured anthologies; indeed, the flow of collections devoted to tax-free, utilitarian film music continued even after the debut of the so-called sound film.

The long list of film-music anthologies that followed Zamecnik's model includes the multi-volume *Remick Folio of Moving Picture Music* (New York: Jerome H. Remick & Co.), launched in 1914 and containing several hundred keyboard pieces arranged or composed by J. Bodewalt Lampe; the series of *Metzler's Original Cinema Music* (London: Metzler & Co.), also launched in 1914 and featuring piano/organ pieces by G.H. Clutsam, "so arranged that two or three separate numbers suitable for one particular type of picture are always to be found together in nearly-related keys";[22] the three volumes (1915, 1916, and 1918) of *Carl Fischer's Loose Leaf Motion Picture Collection for Piano Solo*, featuring a total of forty-five compositions by Mayhew L. Lake and Lester Brockton; a series of albums brought out by the New York-based Photo Play Music Company that offered pieces, mostly by Ernst Luz, "arranged for piano, organ, one man orchestral player or orchestral combinations from 2 to 35 pieces";[23] the 1916 *Carl Fischer Moving Picture Series*, with music by Emil Ascher, W.L. Becker, Fred Luscomb, and Max Winkler; the seven volumes (1916–29) of *Schirmer's Photoplay Series: A Loose Leaf Collection of Dramatic and Descriptive Musical Numbers …*, which contained music for small and large ensembles by the above-mentioned Andino, Borch, and Minot and also by Irénée Bergé, W.W. Bergunker, Arcady Dubensky, Edward Falck, William Lowitz, Otto Langey, Hugo Riesenfeld, Domenico Savino, and Walter C. Schad; *Joseph Carl Breil's Original Collection of Dramatic Music for Motion Picture Plays* (London: Chappell, 1917), consisting of twelve pieces for various instrumental combinations set up so that "it is possible to pass from one section of one number into almost any section of another";[24] *Ditson's Music for the Photoplay* (Boston: Oliver Ditson, 1918–25), a series of five loose-leave packages containing ensemble music by Nicolas Amani, Gaston Borch, Lucius Hosmer, Otto Langey, Christopher O'Hare,

T.H. Rollinson, and Berthold Tours; the two-volume *Picture Music: A Collection of Classic and Modern Compositions for the Organ Especially Adapted for Moving Pictures* (New York: H.W. Gray, 1919), featuring both public-domain music and new works by Lacey Baker; the *Guide musical à l'usage du pianiste de cinéma* (Paris: Édition A. de Smit, 1919), with twenty-five piano pieces by Charles Grelinger; *Feldman's Film Settings* (London: B. Feldman, 1925), a collection of twelve generic pieces by Hubert Bath; and eight volumes of *Ascherberg's Ideal Cinema Series* (London: Ascherberg, Hopwood & Crew, 1928–9), featuring music for both orchestra and solo piano by H. Baynton-Power, Philip Cathie, Walter R. Collins, Percy Elliot, Herman Finck, Walford Hyden, Reginald Somerville, and Arthur Wood.

Along with Zamecnik's, the film-music collections that remain best-known today are those compiled in the 1920s by Giuseppe Becce and Erno Rapee. Becce (1877–1973) was an Italian composer who already had several operas to his credit before he moved to Germany in 1913 and found a niche in the film industry; Rapee (1891–1945) was a Hungarian-born pianist-conductor who immigrated to the United States in 1912 and between 1917 and 1923 served as music director for various large motion-picture theaters in New York and Philadelphia. In terms of service to the cinema, both musicians had long paid their dues by the time they issued their anthologies and supplementary guidebooks.

The twelve volumes of Becce's *Kinobibliothek* (Berlin: Schlesinger, 1919–27) contained a total of eighty-one pieces for solo piano,[25] some of them composed by Becce but most of them drawn from the classical repertoire. Categorized along the lines of "Lyrisches Drama," "Hochdramatisches Agitatos," "Exotika," and so on, the content of the Becce anthologies is remarkable for "the manner in which established pieces of music were re-arranged to adjust them to the requirements of collective use."[26] Commenting from the perspective of 1936, pioneering film-music critic Kurt London observed that in the Becce anthologies

> even pieces which were characteristic in themselves could have their nature transformed in the melting-pot of compilation. There arose a new style, which absorbed all the earlier individuality of the single piece in favour of a new collective character. This went so far that even the rhythm, tempo, key, form, instrumentation, and actually the melody of a piece of music had to be remodeled.
>
> This arbitrary treatment made the use of renowned works of great masters, which appeared in increasingly large quantities in the repertoires of film musicians, a knotty problem indeed. On the one hand, serious music was indispensable; on the other hand, often enough it was not allowed to retain it own character. Change in its form was the least significant thing which could happen to it.[27]

Becce's *Kinobibliothek* volumes, also known as *Kinothek: Neue Filmmusik* or simply *Kinothek*, were originally issued in Germany, but in short order their content was licensed in the United States by Belwin, a New York company that had been founded in 1918 by Berg, Winkler, and Sol Levy. Even before it picked up the *Kinothek* series, however, Belwin had established market dominance with its 1924 publication of Rapee's *Motion Picture Moods for Pianists and Organists: A Rapid Reference Collection of Selected Pieces, Adapted to 52 Moods and Situations.*[28]

This thick volume contained almost three hundred pieces. While a sizeable number of them were simplified and abridged arrangements of classical pieces, the vast majority were original compositions by film-music "specialists" of the sort Winkler describes in the epigraph at the start of this chapter. That *Motion Picture Moods* was truly intended to be a "rapid" reference is evidenced by the fact that the music's categories are listed alphabetically, along with their locations, in the outer margins of each and every pair of pages.

The "moods and situations" in Rapee's book for the most part match the affective typology of the Zamecnik collection. Lest a mere fifty-two dramatic pigeonholes seem too limiting, however, Rapee in 1925 authored an *Encyclopedia of Music for Pictures* that itemizes tax-free music for tenfold more categories.[29] Whereas earlier anthologies might have been content with a simple "exotic" category, Rapee's *Encyclopedia* lists compositions that qualify "distinctly" as "Abyssinian, Arabian, Argentine, Armenian, etc.," and it sorts pieces of an "agitato" nature that previously might have been lumped together into "light, medium and heavy" groups.[30] Apparently thinking along the same lines, in 1927 Becce—in collaboration with Hans Erdmann—issued a two-volume *Allgemeines Handbuch der Filmmusik* that applies a tempo/affect categorization to no less than 3,050 readily available compositions.

Whereas Rapee's *Motion Picture Moods* and Becce's *Kinobibliothek* were clearly anthologies of keyboard music suitable for films, these same writers' *Encyclopedia of Music for Pictures* and *Allgemeines Handbuch der Filmmusik* were combinations of extensive indexes of film-music titles and instructional manuals aimed at musicians who found themselves in charge of motion-picture accompaniments. As was noted in the previous chapter, the tradition of such manuals seems to have begun in 1913, shortly after the advent of music-related columns in the trade journals, with Eugene Ahern's *What and How to Play for Pictures*, and it continued throughout the period of the so-called silent film. Among the other guidebooks were Lyle B. True's *How and What to Play for Moving Pictures* (San Francisco: Music Supply, 1914), Edith Lang and George West's *Musical Accompaniment of Moving Pictures* (Boston: Boston Music, 1920), George W. Beynon's *Musical Presentation of Motion Pictures* (New York: G. Schirmer, 1921), P. Kevin Buckley's *The Orchestral and Cinema Organist* (London: Hawkes and Son, 1923), and George Tootell's *How to Play the Cinema Organ* (London: W. Paxton, 1927).

The handbooks published between 1915 and 1920 tended to formalize the advice that film-music columnists had been offering in the first half of the decade. Like their predecessors, the authors recognized that gimmickry quickly wears thin and therefore admonished against the over-use of tunes whose associated lyrics somehow related to the plot and any sort of music synchronized with specific filmic action. Often referring to material available in the anthologies, the writers of the handbooks advocated the selection of music whose mood was suitable to the entirety of a scene, and they recommended changing music within a scene only when such a change was truly warranted by a shift in the narrative. That the authors felt the need to make these points suggests they were aware that at least some of their contemporaries were still applying to film the old-fashioned gimmicks of the nickelodeon and the vaudeville house. Altman observes that "not until the teens would musicians regularly adopt an aesthetic of continuous music matched not to transient images or actions but to each scene's overall atmosphere."[31] To judge from the tenor of the suggestions in the later handbooks, the adoption of this aesthetic by 1920 was a *fait accompli*.

Breil and *The Birth of a Nation*

The film-music anthologies listed above include a 1917 publication titled *Joseph Carl Breil's Original Collection of Dramatic Music for Motion Picture Plays*. A native of Pittsburgh, Breil (1870–1926) is an important figure in the history of American film music. Not only was the orchestral accompaniment he prepared in 1915 for D.W. Griffith's twelve-reel *The Birth of a Nation* the longest and most elaborate example of "special music" that audiences anywhere had ever heard; with its numerous themes and mid-cue synchronization points, Breil's music for *The Birth of a Nation* might well be considered the first "modern" film score.

As was shown in the previous chapter, orchestral scores occasionally accompanied screenings during the transition from the nickelodeon period to the era of the feature film. "Special music" was associated in particular with pictures imported from Italy, whose government-supported film industry hit upon the idea of the multi-reel "epic" several years before the independent American producers did. Of the half-dozen or so Italian imports that entertained American audiences on the eve of World War I, however, only *Dante's Inferno* (1911) and *Cabiria* (1914) crossed the ocean in the company of "special music" that had been prepared in Italy.[32] The others—*Homer's Odyssey* (1912), *Quo Vadis?* (1913), *The Last Days of Pompeii* (1913), *Antony and Cleopatra* (1914), and *Spartacus* (1914)—were all presented in the United States with music by American composers,[33] and even the original orchestral-choral score for the twelve-reel *Cabiria* was eventually replaced before the film went on its nation-wide tour.

The composer who re-scored *Cabiria* was Breil, although "the full extent of his role," as Marks points out, is "difficult to determine."[34] Various reviews of the *Cabiria* production that traveled from city to city cite Breil as the conductor, but these same reviews typically refer to the music as being of Italian origin. On the other hand, Breil in a trade-journal essay from 1916 claimed that when the film was still in the making "the American managers called upon me to provide it with a musical setting."[35] He claimed, too (in a 1914 letter), that at least two of the choruses were entirely his own compositions.[36] However much of the *Cabiria* music he wrote himself, it remains that Breil's experience with an accompaniment of this length served him well when it came time to work with Griffith.

Breil, who had to his credit not only the *Cabiria* score but also music for three French films from 1912[37] and at least three films from the Hollywood-based Famous Players studio in 1913,[38] was Griffith's first choice as composer for *The Birth of a Nation*. He was not engaged in time, however, to provide music for the film's premiere (under the title *The Clansman*) at Clune's Auditorium in Los Angeles on February 8, 1915. On that occasion the accompanying score—performed by a forty-piece orchestra and a twelve-voice chorus that included six vocal soloists—was the handiwork of the Romanian-born composer Carli D. Elinor. Noted in advertisements as the result of "a diligent search of the music libraries of Los Angeles, San Francisco and New York,"[39] Elinor's score was clearly a compilation of music not subject to the ASCAP tax; along with a few items credited to J.E. Nurnberger, K. Bela, A.V. Flelitz, T.W. Thurban, L. Brown, and Elinor himself, the music consisted entirely of fairly well-known, mostly operatic, works by Beethoven, Bizet, Massenet, Meyerbeer, Mozart, Offenbach, Rossini, Schubert, von Suppé, Verdi, and Wagner.

Griffith apparently considered the Los Angeles run to be little more than a preview. He had signed a contract with Breil as early as November 1914, and even before the film's Los Angeles opening he was publicly singing the praises of a score that, Griffith said, would feature not only Breil's music but also a few pieces of his own. According to a report that appeared in the *Los Angeles Times* on the day of the premiere:

> Mr. Griffith has decided notions on the arranging of music for pictures.
>
> "Too long," he said, "we've been fitting the pictures to music, rather than the music to pictures. If there's a lady to die, and the orchestra leader happens to want to play *A Hot Time in the Old Town*, the poor lady has to die in two hops, so as to keep time to the music; or if there's a battle on and the orchestra wants to play *Hearts and Flowers*, that battle scene looks like a calisthenic exercise in the Old Ladies' Home."
>
> The Russian Symphony Orchestra in New York is to play the music for *The Clansman*. Carl [Breil] ... is composing music and adapting certain compositions. Mr. Griffith has also written two compositions to be used in displaying the pictures.
>
> A tremendous idea that of Mr. Griffith, no less than the adapting of grand-opera methods to motion pictures! Each character playing has a distinct type of music, a distinct theme as in opera. A more difficult matter in pictures than opera, however, inasmuch as any one character seldom holds the screen long at a time. In cases where there are many characters, the music is adapted to the dominant note or character in the scene.[40]

Under its more enduring title, the 187-minute film opened—not without controversy triggered by narrative themes that many in the audience considered to be blatantly racist—at New York's Liberty Theatre on March 8, 1915.[41]

Like Elinor's score for the *The Clansman*, Breil's score for *The Birth of a Nation* included classical music drawn from the public domain. Along with excepts from the overtures to Bellini's *Norma*, Hérold's *Zampa*, Weber's *Der Freischütz*, and Wagner's *Rienzi*, it referenced the fourth movement of Beethoven's *Symphony No. 6*, von Suppé's *"Light Cavalry" Overture*, "In the Hall of the Mountain King" from Grieg's incidental music for *Peer Gynt*, Tchaikovsky's *"1812" Overture*, the "Gloria" movement from Mozart's *Mass in G Major*, and—in what is arguably the film's climactic scene—the "Ride of the Valkyries" segment from Wagner's *Die Walküre*. Apparently recognizing the Wagner material but misidentifying it in part and erroneously characterizing it not as a quotation but as a paraphrase by Breil, a reviewer nonetheless captured the impact of its use as underscore, early in the final reel, for a scene depicting a vengeful rescue mission:

> One leaves the play with the strange, weird, melodic calls of Wagner's "Ride of the Valkyries" and "Flying Dutchman" ringing in the ears. This is because the call sounded in reeds and trumpets in the rush of the Ku Klux Klan are modifications of those themes. The call is sounded most impressively, and more than any stage mechanism brings right to mind the rush of legions of men. It brings convincingly the idea that these men of the play had an absolute consecration to a cause that they believed to be a holy one.[42]

Quite unlike Elinor's score, Breil's quoted from more than two dozen public-domain songs (for example, "Auld Lang Syne," "Camptown Races," "Comin' Through the Rye," "Dixie," "Home! Sweet Home!" "Listen to the Mockingbird," "My Old Kentucky Home," "Tramp, Tramp, Tramp," and "We Are Coming, Father Abraham"), whose familiar lyrics the audience doubtless would have found meaningful in the context of the filmic narrative.

Long as the lists of quoted material from classical works and familiar songs might seem, it remains that the bulk of the music for *The Birth of a Nation* consists of original material. Breil's original music is almost always linked with one or another of the narrative's distinctive entities, and at least fifteen of his themes are heard on more than one occasion.[43] Most of Breil's themes, in other words, circulate through the score as leitmotifs.[44] In their simplest forms, they signal the mere presence of whatever character, object, action, or emotion with which they are associated; more complexly (as when the originally *allegretto jocoso* D-major "Elsie Stoneman" motif is recapitulated, *molto lento*, in E minor), they indicate serious changes in affect or situation. Dramatically motivated manipulation of leitmotifs was endemic to nineteenth-century European opera, and after the mid-1930s it would be endemic, too, to scores for classical-style Hollywood films. Before *The Birth of a Nation*, however, purposeful transformation of basic thematic material was virtually unheard of in film accompaniment.

Also remarkable in Breil's score for *The Birth of a Nation* is the relatively large number of indications for synchronization between music and image. Notwithstanding Saint-Saëns's anomalous 1908 score for *L'Assassinat du Duc de Guise*, affective shifts in earlier film accompaniments tended to coincide with marked shifts in the narrative. Documented in "special music" and cue sheets, and theorized aplenty in film-music columns, these changes typically were cued not by filmic action but by the appearance of intertitles whose content made obvious whatever subtleties might have been conveyed by the ensuing music.

Many of the 214 musical segments of Breil's score are similarly triggered by intertitles, but within the segments there is an impressive amount of verbal information that fairly demands that particular musical phrases be synchronized with specific on-screen events. For example, the segment in the first reel that introduces Lydia Brown, housekeeper for the villainous Austin Stoneman, consists (including the two repeated sections) of 130 measures; within this span, one finds such cues as "Mulatto aroused" and "Sumner orders hat" (at the two cadences of the first repeated section), "Lydia picks up hat" (two measures before a caesura that precedes an accelerating *energico* passage), "Lydia spits out of door" (at the start of a modulatory passage that leads from F minor to G minor), "Lydia on floor" (at the start of an *allegro* passage filled with diminished seventh chords), "Lydia sits up" (at the start of a chorale-like passage that cadences on F major), "Lydia puts hand to mouth" (at the start of a recapitulation of the opening F-minor passage), and "Leader's weakness" (at the first cadence of the repeated section).[45]

Referring to a scene in the seventh reel of *The Birth of a Nation* during which the heroic character Colonel Ben Cameron deals with another villain, Manvell and Huntley observe that music filling only two pages in the piano score contains cues for

> Lynch's second time with Colonel.
>   As Lynch's arm crosses chest.
>   Offers hand second time.

Lynch exits.
Title "Lynch the traitor."
Lynch swearing.
 The Union League Rally.
Eye in door.
Wait for door close.
Lynch at speaker's table second time.
First time: If I don't.
Picture.[46]

Granting that such words seem vague when read out-of-context, the authors note that "the film composer of today will have no difficulty in recognizing the technique of the single 'prompting' phrases which suggest the care that lay behind the preparation of the score."[47] Written in the late 1950s, their comment is still on the mark today.

Considered as a composition with a duration of more than three hours, Breil's contribution to *The Birth of a Nation* is indeed a "sprawling, kaleidoscopic pastiche . . . [whose] pieces do not always fit together in a manner pleasing to the musician's or music-lover's ear,"[48] an evening-length work that, "musically speaking, merits little attention today."[49] But to consider Breil's effort as a composition unto itself would be to seriously miss the point. Breil's music for *The Birth of a Nation* was not a wordless opera or a tone-poem or an extended symphony; it was simply a film score, governed in virtually all its aspects by its creator's response to the film's narrative needs as modified by the opinions—in this case, very strong—of the film's director.[50]

The last point ought not be underestimated. Apparently the "selection of theme music" was something that "obsessed Griffith,"[51] and "the two men [Griffith and Breil] had many disagreements over the scoring of the film."[52] In disagreements, of course, Griffith invariably prevailed, and thus Breil, along with generating "one of the first deliberate attempts to create a score specifically for a single picture,"[53] seems to have been "among the first to have his painstakingly musical solutions cut to conform to the demands of the director."[54] In its underlying process as well as in the product itself, then, Breil's score for *The Birth of a Nation* stands as "one of the first great exemplars of the film composer's craft."[55]

Other "Roadshow" Pictures

There is no denying that *The Birth of a Nation* marked a turning point in American cinema. Its impact had to do in part with its subject matter: the events portrayed in the final reels (the Civil War, the assassination of Lincoln, the explosions of racial tension during the Reconstruction period) remained fresh in the memories of at least a few of its viewers, and although in some quarters the film was loudly decried as racist, at the same time it was widely celebrated as being supportive—in a general way—of American values. More significant, *The Birth of a Nation* in purely cinematic terms differed enormously from anything that had preceded it to the screen. Every bit as spectacular as the earlier Italian epics, Griffith's film reveled in state-of-the-art photography and editing techniques, and its more intimate scenes were conveyed by an acting style unprecedented in its realism. In terms of dramatic content

[*The Birth of a Nation*] is both strikingly complex and tightly whole. It is a film of brilliant parts carefully tied together by the driving line of the film's narrative. Its hugeness of conception, its acting, its sets, its cinematic devices had not been equaled by any film before it and would not be surpassed by many that followed it. Yet surprisingly, for such an obviously big picture, it is also a highly personal and intimate one. Its small moments are as impressive as its big ones. Though Griffith summarizes an entire historical era in the evolution of the nation in general and the South in particular, his summary adopts a human focus. . . .[56]

As for the meticulously crafted music that accompanied public showings of *The Birth of a Nation*, it is interesting that Breil's score was loudly trumpeted in advertising materials and newspaper 'blurbs' yet rarely commented upon in reviews. It may well be that, in Europe, "*The Birth of a Nation* led many leading film makers to see music . . . as something integrally linked to the experience of cinema."[57] In the United States, however, Breil's contribution seems to have been taken almost for granted. American film critics of course mentioned Breil's score, but almost always in a manner that is merely reportorial; their prime concern, clearly, was with the film's considerable dramatic impact, and perhaps it is testimony to the music's craftsmanship that its effect was felt but not noticed.

In his dissertation on accompaniments for silent film, Charles Berg argues that Breil's score for *The Birth of a Nation* "established the symphony orchestra as a permanent feature of the picture palace."[58] In fact, accompanying ensembles in smaller picture palaces were hardly of symphonic proportion, and in many theaters films were regularly accompanied not by orchestra but by organ. Quite aside from its forward-looking relationship with filmic imagery and the medium by which it could be delivered, perhaps the most significant precedent established by Breil's score for *The Birth of a Nation* had to do with its marketplace linkage with an expensive and hugely touted commodity.

As noted above, the Italian epics were presented not as everyday fare at neighborhood movie theaters but as special attractions at venues that catered to relatively affluent audiences. From the start, *The Birth of a Nation* was similarly marketed as an up-scale film. Upon its initial release it played for extended runs only in select theaters in the largest cities, and long before it entered general circulation (concomitant with publication of the score in piano reduction) the film toured the country accompanied not by local ensembles but by orchestras that were part of the production's entourage. Masterminded by entrepreneur J.J. McCarthy, the tours of *The Birth of a Nation* easily eclipsed those of previous filmic "road shows."[59] Looking back from the perspective of 1926, a commentator for *Variety* concluded that, despite earlier efforts, "all honors were still carried off by *The Birth*, in reality the first screen production playing in . . . legitimate theatre[s] for which an admission charge of $2 was made."[60]

By the time the era of the so-called silent film neared its end, "$2 picture" had evolved into an almost legendary term of praise. With millions of dollars in profits looming as their potential reward, studios of course tried to duplicate the fiscal success of *The Birth of a Nation*. Among the attempts were Griffith's own *Intolerance* (1916, with music by Breil), *Hearts of the World* (1918, Joseph E. Nurnberger), *Broken Blossoms* (1919, Louis F. Gottschalk), and *Dream Street* (1921, Louis Silvers); Fox's *A Daughter of the Gods* (1916, Robert Hood Bowers), *Over the Hill* (1920, Erno Rapee), *A Connecticut Yankee at King Arthur's Court* (1920, Rapee), *The Queen of Sheba* (1921, Rapee), *Nero*

(1922, Rapee), *If Winter Comes* (1923, Rapee), *The Iron Horse* (1924, Rapee), and *What Price Glory* (1926, Rapee and R.H. Bassett); Metro's *The Four Horsemen of the Apocalypse* (1921, Gottschalk) and *The White Sister* (1923, Breil); Metro-Goldwyn's *Romola* (1924, Gottschalk); Paramount's *Humoresque* (1920, Hugo Riesenfeld); and Cosmopolitan's *When Knighthood Was in Flower* (1922, William Frederick Peters).[61]

But although many were called, few of the "road show" pictures were chosen for financial success. Each of the above-named films indeed traveled, at no little cost to their producers, in the company of well-rehearsed orchestras that played a commissioned score at least in some ways emulative of Breil's music for *The Birth of a Nation*. Less than a quarter of them, however, managed even to break even. According to a *Variety* report from 1928, only a half-dozen "road show" pictures actually "profited by special showings at special prices"[62]—along with *The Birth of a Nation*, the pantheon included Griffith's 1920 *Way Down East* (with music by Silvers and Peters), Paramount's 1920 *The Covered Wagon* (Riesenfeld and Zamecnik) and *The Ten Commandments* (Riesenfeld, with Milan Roder, L. Saminsky, Carl Gutman, and Edward Falck), and MGM's 1925 *The Big Parade* and *Ben-Hur* (both with scores by William Axt, orchestrated by Maurice Baron).

Before the advent of the so-called sound film, many composers besides those just mentioned graced picture presentations with original orchestral scores. A perusal of Clifford McCarty's encyclopedic *Film Composers in America: A Filmography, 1911–70* turns up such additional names as James C. Bradford, Charles Wakefield Cadman, Cecil Copping, Henry Purmont Eames, Vern Elliott, Michael Hoffman, Leo Kempinski, Noble Kreider, Sol Levy, Ernst Luz, Ulderico Marcelli, William J. McKenna, David Mendoza, Wedgewood Nowell, Nicholas Orlando, Albert Pesce, Edward Rechlin, Herman Rosen, Domenico Savino, Elliot Schenk, Victor L. Schertzinger, Adolph Schmidt, Gino Severi, Hermann Spielter, Frederick Stahlberg, William Stickles, and Mortimer Wilson.

With few exceptions, however, the film-specific scores of these composers were heard only in the theaters at which the composers were employed. The vast majority of film accompaniments during the heyday of the silent-film feature were strictly localized phenomena. Musical directors at the more sumptuous movie theaters around the country of course had to step aside whenever their places of employment were temporarily taken over by "road show" films. But touring films equipped with "special" scores, historically significant though these scores might be, were few and far between. Like accompanists who week after week labored at less prestigious venues, their counterparts even at the larger theaters were—most of the time—left to their own resources.

Common Practice

Two-staff reductions of complete scores for big-budget films circulated, but only after the music had made the rounds in its original orchestral format. Re-orchestrating such material to suit a provincial ensemble would have proved time-consuming, and so in all likelihood these reduced scores were realized only by organists or—in the rare instances of small theaters gaining access to especially ambitious films—by pianists. The studio-issued score indeed paved the way for the built-in accompaniments of the so-called sound film. So long as the musical support for silent films was left to the discretion of individuals, however, the studio-issued score for the most part served as just one example of how a particular film *might* be accompanied.

Examples came as well in the form of suggestions from trade-journal columnists, although by the early 1920s such writers tended to focus less on prescriptions for particular films than on general principals of accompaniment. At least for a while, examples of a more influential sort came directly from the film companies in the form of cue sheets that grew more and more specific as the era of the silent film rolled on.

It soon enough became obvious that cue sheets issued by certain film studios involved only the products of certain music publishers. A columnist in 1918 euphemistically suggested that compilers of such cue sheets were somehow "subsidized,"[63] and a year later one of his colleagues opined that cue sheets tended to promote the wares of "corporations not wholly connected with art."[64] Moralizing aside, it remains that after World War I tight relationships between studios and music publishers were fundamental to the burgeoning film industry. Whereas S.M. Berg's 1915 columns in *Moving Picture World* catered almost exclusively to films produced by Metro, his columns in 1916— when he was running his own publishing company—paid attention to films issued by Metro, Selznick, Triangle, Vitagraph, and World. By this point, Winkler had broadened the scope of cue sheets featuring Carl Fischer publications to include not just Universal films but also films issued by Bluebird, Fox, Paramount, and World. In July 1918

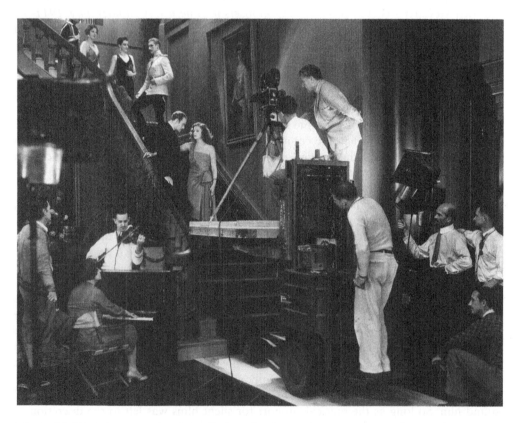

Figure 4.2 Musicians accompany the filming of MGM's *The Mysterious Lady* in 1928.
© The Kobal Collection.

Winkler left Fischer to form, with partner Sol Levy, a publishing-distribution business called Cinema Music. Shortly after that Cinema Music merged with Berg's company to form Belwin, Inc. "Soon we went places," Winkler writes, "Berg and I had, in the past, been the real stars in the cue sheet world and now that we had become united, we established a virtual monopoly. We supplied the musical cue sheets for Universal, Triangle Films, Douglas Fairbanks, . . . William S. Hart, Fox Films, Vitagraph, and Goldwyn."[65]

Altman notes that while cue sheets for feature films at first were "bankrolled entirely by film studios and music publishers," by the early 1920s they evolved into "an independent entrepreneurial product."[66] Important new participants in the independent cue-sheet industry were the Cameo Music Service Corporation, a New York firm that under the editorship of M.J. Mintz issued "Thematic Music Cue Sheets" for films made by numerous studios, and the Synchronized Scenario Music Company, a Chicago operation that successfully published not cue sheets but complete scores—in orchestral as well as keyboard format—compiled by the likes of Bradford, Breil, Riesenfeld, and Rapee.[67] But the major player, clearly, was Winkler's and Berg's Belwin, Inc., which not only continued to promote its products in the form of published cue sheets but also "had arrangements with some seventy theaters all over the country to view the pictures they booked and to make special musical cue sheets for their orchestras."[68]

Cue sheets based on specific films were important to silent-film features, but Altman perhaps exaggerates with his claim that they were "at the heart" of 1920s film-music practice.[69] As a prescription, the cue sheet was obviously useful to the musical director who lacked time, ability, and/or inclination to devise an accompaniment of his own for a particular film. The cue sheet would be practical, however, only if the theater's library already contained or could quickly acquire whatever pieces the cue sheet specified; assuming the theater employed an orchestra, it would likewise be practical only if the prescribed music existed in arrangements that suited the instrumentation and the performance ability of the accompanying ensemble. Likening the independent cue sheet industry to "a national scoring service," Charles Berg suggests that the most formidable obstacle facing such a service was "the variety in instrumentation and musicianship in the film orchestras across the country," but he also notes—tellingly—that "many music directors felt their own musical tastes superior to the [cue sheet] arranger's and therefore chose to compile their own scores."[70]

Notwithstanding the bounty of documentary evidence offered by published cue sheets and the performance histories of complete scores that traveled with would-be blockbuster films, it seems that film-music practice throughout the age of the silent feature depended most of all on the creativity of individual accompanists. Doubtless it was true, as Samuel "Roxy" Rothapfel told an interviewer in 1914, that because of the required preparation time "first-run pictures are the bane of a picture man's existence,"[71] yet Rothapfel was just one of the managers of "deluxe" theaters who early in the silent-feature period generally rejected ready-made cue sheets in favor of scores personally compiled by him or by a trusted colleague.

For a multi-reel feature film, the effort of compiling and rehearsing a theater-specific orchestral score at relatively short notice was considerable. Referring to comments from film accompanist Hyman Spitalny that had been reported in the *Cleveland Plain Dealer*, a magazine article from 1918 described the process:

When a new film is booked for an engagement the print to be used is sent on a week ahead for a private screening. This may occur in a private projection room, in the theater proper before the performance time, or in the studio of some film exchange. In any instance, it is at the private screening [that] the work of the musical director begins. It is there he lays the foundation for his next week's score. The picture is projected at the same speed at which it will be shown to the public. As the scenes flash across the screen, the director jots down his notes as to varying incidents and characters. Three or four of the leading characters are selected as vital to the action. Varying themes may be given them, . . . or the basic principle of the play may be themed. . . .

Elaborate notes are made as to the varying scenes, with memoranda whether the action is fast or deliberate, long or short, and what character participates in them. This is the working model, as it were, the skeleton upon which the director fastens his themes and builds up a musical composition to fit the performance.

Then comes the real task—the arranging of the score.

The average feature of the program presented today runs from five to ten reels, with an average of 1,000 feet of film to a reel. The six- and seven-reel feature is employed as frequently as any. The total of musical numbers selected in making up the score for such an offering may number from eighty to one hundred different compositions, irrespective of repetitions; the number is never less than from forty to fifty.

When these arrangements are completed, the music selected, the themes worked out, the cuttings indicated, and the rough version of the setting is ready, then comes the second showing of the film, which is reviewed by the director and the pianist. Then . . . the music is made to fit. Some bits may be found to be too long; some may run too briefly; all this is noted, tried, rearranged, and, finally, when the session is ended, the score has been synchronized to a nicety. The musical arrangement is reviewed. The part for each of the various instruments is made to correspond with the master score. Then, when this is done, all is ready for the dress rehearsal, at which not only orchestra and operators, but stage-hands, electricians, and others may be present.[72]

Time-pressed though this procedure must have been, apparently more than a few theater managers deemed it worth the effort. Responding to the needs of orchestra leaders who chose to concoct their own accompaniments, American music publishers found that by 1920 their most lucrative product was the "constantly growing library of music . . . written and published for no other public than that made up of professional [film] musicians."[73] Indeed, demand for repertoire was so great that the industry struggled to keep pace. Max Winkler colorfully described Belwin's happy predicament:

Every scene, every situation, character, action, emotion, every nationality, emergency, wind storm, rain storm and brain storm, every dancer, vamp, cowboy, thief, and gigolo, eskimos and zulus, emperors and streetwalkers, colibris and elephants—all this plus every printed title that flickered in the faces of the five-cent to twenty-five-cent audience had to be expressed in music, and soon we realized that Belwin's catalogue of so-called Dramatic and Incidental Music was quite insufficient to furnish the simply colossal amounts of music needed by an ever-expanding audience.[74]

Although composers under contract with Belwin "were writing film music by the mile," in order to meet its customers' needs the firm "began to import music from Europe, where a whole battery of writers were busy turning their talents towards picture music."[75] But demand still exceeded supply, and so "in desperation [Belwin] turned to crime. We began to dismember the great masters. We began to murder ruthlessly the works of Beethoven, Mozart, Grieg, J.S. Bach, Verdi, Bizet, Tschaikovsky and Wagner—everything that wasn't protected from our pilfering by copyright."[76]

Writing from the perspective of a score compiler who worked for a number of New York picture palaces, Hugo Riesenfeld in 1926 observed that

> The chief difficulty in score writing or arranging is keeping the music subordinate to the action on the screen. It must never obtrude itself. The audience must never be conscious of hearing a familiar tune.
>
> To achieve this, the musical director who is obliged to prepare a new score every week must have at his disposal a limitless supply of music. For this purpose the metropolitan theaters maintain enormous libraries, some of them containing 25,000 pieces of music. These are all catalogued, not only by titles and authors, but also by the type of emotion or kind of action which they suggest. When the score writer wishes a piece of music giving the atmosphere of the opening scene of *MacBeth*, he refers to the sections marked "Witch Dances" or "Ominous Music." In the same way he may instantly put his hands on music which suggests the sound of an aeroplane, anger, a runaway horse, a canoe drifting down a quiet stream.
>
> A staff of trained librarians is required to keep this stock of music constantly replenished with fresh works. The larger music publishing houses have a standing order to send everything that comes off their presses. Material is sought in France, Germany, England, Italy and even the Orient.
>
> The musical scores of every country are assiduously combed for melodies that will create just the right illusion. . . . The compiler or arranger of scores searches down every possible alley, in every corner for something that will give just the right effect.[77]

Riesenfeld goes on to describe the intellectual process by which a theater's musical director typically compiles a score, and he emphasizes that "very often, if the arranger cannot find satisfactory music for a certain bit of action, he is obliged to compose some himself."[78] He grants that compositional talent might not be so abundant in the provinces as in the larger cities, thus necessitating a certain reliance on published cue sheets and "syndicated" scores. But his implication is clear. For Riesenfeld, the most effective film accompaniments were not mere realizations of prescriptions but, rather, original compilations that sprang from the minds of musicians who responded—creatively and artfully—to the needs of their individual audiences.

* * *

Penned for a learned journal whose special issue concentrated on "The Motion Picture in Its Economic and Social Aspects," Riesenfeld's 1926 article in its final pages looks curiously in two different directions. On the one hand, Riesenfeld waxes optimistically on the financial prospects of "the army" of musicians "necessary to man the orchestras in our 18,000 film theaters."[79] On the other hand, he sings the praises of the Vitaphone, a newly invented device that allowed recorded sounds—including those of orchestral music—to be synchronized with a projected film.

Altruistically, Riesenfeld observed that the Vitaphone makes it possible "for certain films requiring the finest musical accompaniment to be shown in places where there is no orchestra available."[80] Naively, Riesenfeld also expressed the opinion that "it is not probable that the Vitaphone will ever entirely replace the [live] orchestra."[81] In terms of how technology would impact the burgeoning art of film music, little did he know what was just around the corner.

Part 2

MUSIC AND
THE EARLY SOUND FILM
(1894–1933)

Chapter 5

THE LONG ADVENT OF SOUND,
1894–1926

The future of the motion picture in the amusement line will be in the form of a combination between it and the phonograph, although of course to make the illusion perfect the phonograph will have to be improved with a view of securing a much louder reproduction. Stereoscopic photography will probably also be applied to motion pictures, so that they will stand out in bold, sharp relief. Finally, color photography will be employed, presenting scenes in natural colors and tints. Thus the motion picture of the future will show apparently solid objects projected in natural colors and accompanied in natural reproduction by all the concomitant sounds.

Thomas Edison, 1910[1]

Edison's predictions, as they often did, overshot the mark only slightly. "Stereoscopic photography" in the form of what eventually came to be known as 3-D cinema was indeed applied to motion pictures, but not until the 1950s, and primarily as a short-lived gimmick designed by film producers to attract audiences they feared were being lost to the burgeoning medium of television. Color cinematography, on the other hand, had been in existence since 1908, when Charles Urban, an American working in England, patented a process called Kinemacolor, and it would become widespread after the 1917 founding, in the United States, of the Technicolor Corporation.

The quotation comes from an interview with Edison that appeared, in an unsigned column titled "Who's Who in the Film Game," in the fourth volume of *The Nickelodeon*. That by 1910 a trade journal aimed at manufacturers and exhibitors of motion pictures was already in its fourth year of publication suggests that cinema, as a cultural institution, had come a long way since its wild and wooly origins in the mid 1890s. Likewise, the headline's casual reference to a film "game" suggests that cinema by this time was well on its way to becoming an industry. Indeed, the establishment of the enormously influential Hollywood studios—and with them the creation of "movie stars" and the solidification of standard plot genres—was just a half-decade in the future.

Anticipating technology that would not be developed until the late 1920s, Edison forecasts that the synchronization of recorded imagery with recorded sound will "revolutionize the stage." Edison, ever the champion of the economically deprived, enthuses: "What a boon it will be to the middle and poorer classes! ... The world's greatest musicians, singers and actors can then be heard in the most insignificant hamlet

71

at a nominal price, where they can now be heard only in the large cities and at prices which only the wealthy can afford."[2] Then he expounds on the sound film's educational value, especially in the areas of geography, history, literature, botany, surgery, and chemistry.

Nowhere in his prognostications does Edison mention filmic narratives in combination with accompanying music. The inventor, of course, was well aware of the commercial potential of this multi-media blend; it was because of inducements from the marketplace, after all, that Edison's own company presaged modern film-scoring practice by publishing the first "cue sheets."[3] But apparently Edison reaped more than just monetary rewards from music-supported "silent" film. "One of his favorite diversions," writes the anonymous columnist, "is to slip away by himself and make his way unostentatiously into some nickelodeon in Orange [New Jersey], paying his five-cent admission like any other plain, every-day citizen, and spend an hour or two watching the pictures."[4]

Thanks at least in part to the suggestions for musical accompaniments regularly offered in the *Edison Kinetogram*, exhibition practice in nickelodeon theaters by this time was well on its way to being standardized. The music that Edison heard as he sat "watching the pictures" was likely similar, in content as well as usage, to the music heard by members of cinema audiences in countless other cities. Of all the musical bits and pieces that Edison experienced during his secret outings to the nickelodeon theaters, surely some of them struck him as "working" better than others; quite apart from whatever aesthetic sensibilities he might or might not have owned, Edison as a profit-minded industrialist surely would have noticed that some accompaniments at least seemed to be more successful than others in convincing members of the paying audience that they were, indeed, getting their money's worth. There is no evidence, however, that at this stage of "the film game" Edison gave even the slightest thought to the mechanical reproduction of apparently successful film accompaniments.

Despite the fortunes that he earned through entertainment-oriented applications of his inventions, Edison's personal interest in recording devices of any sort seems always to have been focused on the devices' potential as documentary tools. Although in 1910 Edison waxed enthusiastic about preserving both aurally and visually speeches by civic leaders and performances by renowned artists, it seems never to have occurred to him that the recorded sonic elements of the future cinema would include—along with dialogue and more or less realistic sound effects—music of the sort that today is known as underscore.

Early Sound Film Technologies

The earliest surviving motion picture with synchronized recorded sound, in fact, is an Edison product. It dates from sometime between September 1894 and April 1895, more than six months, at least, before the Lumière brothers in Paris exhibited the first projected motion pictures. Lasting a mere twenty-three seconds and bearing the ungracious title "Dickson Experimental Sound Film," it features Edison engineer William Kennedy Laurie Dickson standing with a violin at the mouth of an enormous acoustical horn and fiddling a humble waltz as a pair of unidentified men awkwardly dance.[5] The original content of the "Dickson Experimental Sound Film" is preserved on both a 35-mm filmstrip and a wax cylinder audio recording; had it been intended for public consumption, its means of transmission would have been the showing of the filmstrip (seen through the peephole of a Kinetoscope) simultaneous with the playback of the sound recording (heard through a megaphone or, more likely, a pair of stethoscope-like earphones[6]). But attempts to combine recorded sound with a motion picture predate even this 1894–5 experiment. According to Dickson's published memoir, Edison upon his return from a visit to the 1889 Paris Exposition was greeted with a sound film that had Dickson saying: "Good morning, Mr. Edison, glad to see you back. I hope you are satisfied with the kineto-phonograph."[7]

Edison, alas, was not satisfied,[8] and a practicable "kineto-phonograph"—a single device that could record both moving image and sound—would not be developed until almost four decades later. Yet it is significant that Edison was thinking about and investing in such a device as early as 1889, when the motion picture was barely past its embryonic stage. Indeed, the idea of the sound film—at least in the abstract—predates even Edison's earliest experiments.[9] In what film historian Tom Gunning describes as "a *locus classicus* for discussions of cinema's origin," a passage in the 1886 *L'Eve future* by French novelist Villiers de L'Isle-Adam describes a scene "in which a fictional Edison reveals a six-minute motion picture of a Spanish dancer accompanying herself with shouted *olés*."[10] Whether the evidence is drawn from fiction or historical fact, it seems that right from the start of what Walter Benjamin famously labeled the Age of Mechanical Reproduction[11] it was a foregone conclusion, among futurists, that audio and video recording would eventually be linked.

In 1891, with the Lumière projections a few years in the future, Edison waxed enthusiastic about his kineto-phonograph. "Should [soprano Adelina] Patti be singing somewhere," he declared, "this invention will put her full-length picture upon the canvas so perfectly as to enable one to distinguish every expression and feature on her face, and all her actions, and listen to the entrancing melody of her peerless voice." The work-in-progress was not yet ready to record the refined performances of an international opera star, but apparently Edison felt it was good enough for the rough content of a boxing match. "I have already perfected the invention so far as to be able to picture a prize fight—the two men, the ring, the intensely interested faces of those surrounding it—and you can hear the sounds of the blows."[12]

That Edison invested in the audio-video recording of a pugilistic contest—as opposed to, say, a foot race or a rodeo—says a great deal about his intentions. Whereas most athletic events would yield only noises of a general nature (the proverbial "roar of the crowd," rising and falling), a boxing match is characterized by percussive thumps that, in the context of a sound film, would impress an audience only if they were precisely synchronized with the sight of fast punches. Indeed, precise synchronization of the recorded materials, realizable in playback by means of a single belt drive that regulated the speed of both the audio and the video mechanisms, was clearly the goal of Edison's experiments in the early 1890s. But the research proved costly, and the anticipated financial rewards were not enough to make it seem worthwhile. Like the boxing-match film with its allegedly synchronized audio concomitant, the "Dickson Experimental Sound Film" was never circulated. The best that Edison could offer to the public, in 1895, was a set of short films accompanied by music arguably related in affect to, but not synchronized with, the film's content. These pairings of film and music came by way of a contraption that Edison called the Kinetophone, which was simply a Kinetoscope whose playback mechanism was connected to a phonograph. Domestic sales were unimpressive; whereas Edison was able to sell more than a thousand Kinetoscopes, he sold only forty-five Kinetophones.[13] Edison hoped to market the Kinetophone abroad, but he was stymied by a legal action. On June 30, 1895, the *New York Times* reported:

> [The magistrate] to-day reserved decision in the case of the North American Phonograph Company against Thomas A. Edison and the Edison Phonograph Company, on an application for an injunction to restrain the defendants from selling Kinetophones in foreign countries. The complaining company holds an assignment from Edison of all foreign rights for the sale and use of the phonograph, with the exception when it is used in connection with toys, dolls, &c. They allege that Edison has infringed on the right by combining the phonograph and kinetoscope under the name of kinetophone, and placing it in the foreign market. The defense holds that the kinetophone is a toy.[14]

To speak dismissively, for the sake of a courtroom skirmish, of his Kinetophone must have chagrined Edison to no end. But by this time the inventor was already disappointed. During the legal proceedings, "one of the new instruments was in court and [the magistrate] took a peep into it, beheld Loie Fuller doing her famous serpentine dance, and heard the music accompanying it."[15] Doubtless Edison would have much preferred that the magistrate beheld something other than a popular dancer[16] and heard not just "music accompanying" but genuinely synchronized sound. The presumably wiggly music that was paired with Fuller's dance surely counts as one of the very first examples of recorded film "underscore." For Edison, however, it was not a claim to fame but a mark of failure.

The 1895 marketplace flop of the Kinetophone prompted Edison to busy himself with other projects. But fifteen years later—perhaps trying to prove that the Kinetophone was not, as he had claimed in court, just "a toy"—he would return to both the device's name and the idea behind it. In the meantime, numerous other inventors tried their hands at what would soon be known as "talking pictures."

* * *

After Edison's efforts ca. 1889–95, the next major attempt to coordinate moving pictures with recorded sound came from French inventor and filmmaker Léon Gaumont, who at the 1900 Paris Exposition demonstrated something called the Chronophone.[17] Like the Kinetophone, Gaumont's Chronophone consisted in essence of a simple pairing—first mechanical, then electrical—of independent playback devices for film and sound. But one important difference had to do with the fact that Gaumont's films would have been projected, not viewed through peepholes, and beginning in 1906 their audio concomitants—preserved not on fragile wax cylinders but on relatively durable shellac discs—would have been literally "aired" by means of pneumatic pumps that blew the sound toward the audience through the acoustical horns of multiple phonographs.[18] Another important difference had to do with the films' content. Whereas Edison's commercial Kinetophone offered action merely accompanied by music, the Chronophone offered action and sound that—as the device's name suggests—were precisely synchronized.

74

Following the same inclination that led Edison in 1891 to imagine an audio-video recording of Adelina Patti, Gaumont for his Chronophone material looked to popular performers in whose acts sound was a crucial element. Gaumont's first commercial products, exhibited in Paris ca. 1905–6, featured French comedians, cabaret and opera singers, and—occasionally—actors from the "legitimate" theater.[19] His move into the London market, in 1907, was strategically based on recordings of Scottish vaudevillian Harry Lauder and English music-hall singer Victoria Monks; for his trans-Atlantic foray, beginning in May 1908, Gaumont presented not just international attractions derived from opera but also "an 'All-American' programme . . . with standard ballads and new popular successes."[20]

With such a diverse Chronophone catalogue, Gaumont "performed an audacious balancing act between high-flown bombast and naughty remarks"[21] that one supposes was perfectly suited to the period's eclectic tastes. But the Chronophone was hardly without its problems. Whereas for Edison's 1895 Kinetophone the physical distance between video and audio playback mechanisms was a matter of inches, for Gaumont's Chronophone the film projector at the rear of the exhibition space and the phonographs at the front of the space were separated by a hundred or more feet. The projector and phonographs were connected by a system of cables, and synchronization was managed by means of a rheostat mechanism that allowed a person in the projection booth to adjust their speeds; not surprisingly, breakdowns in communication between the various devices were fairly common. More significant, Gaumont's audio recordings could only service films whose maximum length was 1,500 feet; by 1908 the American film industry, affiliation with which was crucial to Gaumont's business plan, was seeking products considerably longer than that, and thus development of the Chronophone was abruptly halted.[22]

After the Chronophone came the Cameraphone, developed in 1907 by American entrepreneur Carl Herbert and inventor E.E. Norton, a former mechanical engineer at the American Graphophone Company. The Cameraphone's playback mechanism was similar to that of the Chronophone, but the preparation of the material was markedly different. Like Edison's noncommercial Kinetophone experiments, Gaumont's Chronophone products were all recordings of "live" performances; in the case of Cameraphone products, the audio recordings were invariably made first, and the motion pictures were in effect images of the performers "lip syncing."[23]

At first glance, the Cameraphone method seemed to offer several advantages. Not having to concern themselves with anything but their voices or musical instruments, performers during audio recording could be ideally positioned before the acoustic horns; conversely, during filming the performers—in no way constrained by the demands of sound equipment—could move without inhibition and could benefit from theatrical lighting, special stage effects, and so on. But getting performers, most of whom Herbert and Norton recruited from vaudeville, to mime convincingly to their pre-recorded sounds was no easy task. And the pre-recorded sounds, according to Herbert's own testimony, were by the standards of the day not very good. "Most prominent vaudeville actors and actresses make poor records," Herbert eventually admitted to the trade press. "So true is this that of a score of high salaried 'headlines' so employed, barely two or three have proved more than provoking disappointments."[24]

Like most show-business novelties, the Cameraphone at first enjoyed a fair amount of success. By 1908 the Cameraphone Company was marketing "shorts" featuring such famous vaudevillians as George M. Cohan and Eva Tanguay; at the same time, it was offering multi-reel productions (the moving pictures accompanied, of course, by multiple phonograph discs) of *The Mikado, H.M.S. Pinafore*, and other musical theater favorites.[25] But the purchase price of Cameraphone sound films was unusually high,[26] and likewise expensive was the equipment necessary to present Cameraphone material in nickelodeon-era venues. In January 1909 the *New York Times* used a photograph captioned "Rehearsing before the Cameraphone" to help illustrate, doubtless enthusiastically, a full-page article about the popularity of moving pictures;[27] seven months later the same newspaper ran a tiny item announcing that the Cameraphone Company had gone bankrupt.[28]

In February 1910 the *New York Times* reported that there had just been "a private exhibition of the American Cinephone, a new apparatus for combining motion pictures with talking machine records":

> The novelty of the machine was the simple method of synchronizing the speed of the picture film and the sound reproducing disc.
>
> By means of two slowly moving illuminated pointers, one appearing in the picture and the other attached to the side of the talking machine mechanism, the picture operator is able to control the movement of the film so that the gestures of a singer and actor appear at practically the same instant as the sound of the voice.[29]

The Cinephone had been imported the year before from England, where its developers—filmmakers William Jeapes and Will Barker—had already installed their system in more than a thousand venues. Along with being less expensive and more mechanically reliable than the Cameraphone, the Cinephone had the advantage of a relationship with the Victor Talking Machine Company. Not only did Victor provide Cinephone exhibitors with state-of-the-art sound-reproducing equipment; it serviced the Cinephone Company with audio recordings made in its own studios by its prestigious stable of British music-hall artists.[30] By the summer of 1910 the company was making sound films geared specifically for the American market. Within a year the Cinephone joined the Chronophone and the Cameraphone in the group of sound-film technologies that in the years before World War I quickly won the attention of journalists and investors and then, almost as quickly, went out of business.

This meteor shower of sound-film devices included not only those described above but also such colorfully named inventions as the Animatophone; the Biographon, Biophon, and Biophonograph; the Chronophotographoscope; the Cinemacrophonograph, Cinematophone, and Cineograph; the Graphophonoscope; the Kinematophone and Kosmograph; the Phoneidograph, Phono-Cinéma-Théâtre, and Phonoscope; the Photophone, Foto-Fone, and Photokinema; the Picturephone; the Synchrophone and Synchroscope; the Talkaphone; and the Vivaphone.[31] But foremost among them, at least in terms of initial reception, was Edison's new and improved Kinetophone.

* * *

The second round of Kinetophone films was not exhibited in theaters until 1913. But as early as 1910 the American press, having been invited to a preview, was raving about the films' superiority over all others in an obviously crowded field.[32] Apparently forgetting what Edison had done fifteen years before, and perhaps choosing simply to ignore the hardly invisible competition, the *New York Times* gave its report a multi-deck headline that declared: "Motion Pictures Are Made to Talk/Edison Invents a Machine that Combines the Kinetoscope and Phonograph/Records Taken Together/When the Pictured Man Acts the Voice in the Box Speaks, and Illusion Is Perfect."[33] Similarly, the *Los Angeles Times* announced: "Edison's Latest Invention/He Demonstrates Success in Machine for Making Moving Pictures Talk, Calls It Kinetophone."[34] The New York and Los Angeles newspapers described what transpired during the demonstration at Edison's New Jersey facilities, but the most detailed account came from the *Chicago Daily Tribune*:

> The demonstration opened with an exhibition of moving pictures, but it has to be remarked that the pictures moved with a peculiarly even flow. There was less vibration than is usually to be seen. It might be said that the series depicted the efforts of a thirsty man to obtain a drink, but the series had a moral.
>
> However, after this series came the real test of the evening. A big man walked forward on the screen, bowed to the audience, and began to speak. As soon as he opened his mouth the sounds came as naturally as they would from an actor on the stage, or to be more precise, it might be said they came like the sound of the voice of a manager who comes before the curtain on the stage and makes such announcement as the stage manager may desire to put before his patrons.
>
> He took a ball from the table and the rebound coincided with the enunciation of the words, not only the sight of the ball, but the sound of its impact on the platform. He then said:
>
> "I will now show you more distinctly by taking a plate which you see from the table and smashing it on the floor."
>
> Exactly as he did so the plate went to the floor, as the audience could see, and smashed into smithereens, the sound of the smash and the rebound of the splinters coinciding with the motion and the words of the picture man.[35]

A sound-film of a man smashing a plate was part of the program when the new Kinetophone was publicly exhibited at vaudeville theaters in numerous cities in February and March 1913. But the bill also featured a piano–violin–soprano rendition of "The Last Rose of Summer," some comic tooting from a bugler, a scene involving barking dogs, and—after a brief intermission—a minstrel-show number complete with "orchestra, soloists, end men, and interlocutor, large as life and quite as noisy."[36] Entertainment critics were impressed, especially with the high quality—relatively speaking—of the recorded sound. But the synchronization of sound and moving image, announced in advance as now perfected, sometimes proved problematic. According to the reporter for the *New York Times*,

> The real sensation of the day was scored quite unintentionally by the operator of the machine at the Union Square Theatre.... He inadvertently set his pictures some ten or twelve seconds ahead of his sounds, and the result was amazing. The [minstrel show] interlocutor, who, by a coincidence, wore a peculiarly defiant and offended expression, would rise pompously, his lips

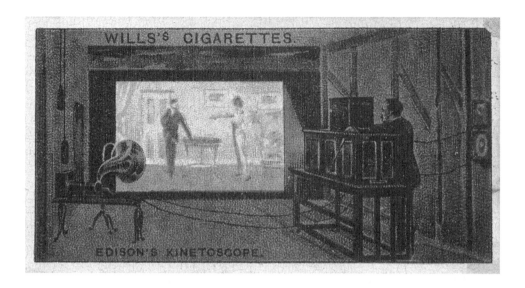

Figure 5.1 Thomas Alva Edison's kinetographic theater, ca. 1892. From a cigarette card published 1915. © Oxford Science Archive/Heritage-Images/The Image Works.

would move, he would bow and sit down. Then his speech would float out over the audience. It would be an announcement of the next song, and before it was all spoken the singer would be on his feet with his mouth expanded in fervent but soundless song.

This diverted the audience vastly, but the outbursts of laughter would come when the singer would close his lips, smile in a contended manner, bow, and retire while his highest and best notes were still ringing clear.[37]

A similar malfunction, not so disastrous, occurred at the Orpheum Theater in Los Angeles, where the reporter politely noted that "sound and movement do not quite 'hitch.'" Suggesting an explanation that was scientifically erroneous but psycho-perceptually on the mark, he wrote:

The musical part goes better than the talking—it may be because here [that is, in the music] we do not notice so plainly that light travels faster than sound, and that therefore the lips move a perceptible time before any sound is heard.[38]

News items in advance of the 1913 public exhibition of Edison's new Kinetophone typically emphasized not only the device's improved technology but also its "great educational value"[39] and its inventor's stated hope that the device would "put the finest operas and the best dramas within the reach of the poorest man," that it would "be a big agency for the uplift of the poor."[40] But one Chicago columnist, apparently bedazzled not at all by the altruistic statements emanating from Edison and his corporate publicists, did some quick calculations and wryly observed: "By way of emphasizing what a wonderful thing the kinetophone is, the exchequer of the Edison interests will be improved by $50,000 weekly—the amount of the toll to be paid by the vaudeville theaters which employ this wonderful apparatus."[41] The same columnist, reporting on a public exhibition during which synchronization apparently was *not* a problem, summarized the program as just one "stunt" after another; he identified the Kinetophone as "this new Edison toy" that for the moment is just "an inspiring fillip—not as impressive as looking at the stars, but a punch showing us how wonderful are some of the others of us."[42]

Edison's "wonderful apparatus" had at least three purely technological advantages over its competitors. One of these was a synchronization system that had the electrically powered phonograph (which played cylinders, not discs) and projector driven by identical sets of gears and connected by a long belt in such a way that the speed of the projector was governed, at least in theory, by the speed of the phonograph.[43] The mechanism was hardly foolproof, but when it functioned properly it offered better linkage of sound and image than earlier systems that aspired to the same goal.

Another advantage, significant for a device marketed not to small nickelodeon theaters but to large vaudeville houses, was the sheer amount of sound that the new Kinetophone could produce. As Gaumont had been doing since 1906, Edison in 1913 pumped air through his phonograph horns to increase both their decibel levels and the extent of their range. Whereas Gaumont in his Chronophone installations used pairs of conventional phonographs positioned at either side of image-receptive surfaces that likely were white-painted solid walls, Edison in each of his Kinetophone installations used just a single phonograph located, invisibly, behind a porous canvas or muslin screen; the considerable difference in audio output between the Chronophone and Kinetophone had to do with the simple facts that the latter's phonographs had horns that were quite huge—more than six feet in length—and were fitted with compressed-air pumps that, compared with Gaumont's, were extremely powerful.

A third advantage that the "new Edison toy" had over other systems involved the means by which the audio content of its sound-films was recorded. The public exhibitions of the new Kinetophone took place more than a decade before the advent of electrical recording, so called because the styluses that etched analogues of sound waves into receptive surfaces were activated not by acoustic vibrations but by electrical signals that, before reaching the styluses, could be electronically amplified. But as early as 1910 Edison had devised an entirely acoustic method of pre-amplification that allowed, as did the later electrical technology, for relatively sensitive recording. This meant that performers whose vocal or instrumental iterations went into Kinetophone productions were not obligated, as were artists who did "live" recording for other sound-film systems, to locate themselves in close proximity of the recording horn. It is not true, as one film historian has suggested, that "any early films that used synchronously recorded sound would have had to include [a recording] horn in the frame";[44] many of Gaumont's Chronophone films, for example, showed performers in medium-close shots, with the recording horn nowhere in sight but positioned, presumably, just behind the camera or above the performers' heads. Nor is it true, as Douglas Gomery writes in his otherwise reliable book on early sound-film technology, that the new Kinetophone "employed a microphone sensitive enough to pick up sounds from 300 [!] feet away";[45] in reality, the Kinetophone was credibly responsive only to sounds whose sources were located within forty or so feet from the microphone-horn combination.[46] Compared to the limits that constrained earlier sound-film experimenters, the Kinetophone's forty-foot range was nevertheless enormous. Such audiophonic sensitivity meant that Kinetophone artists whose routines in some way involved physical movement had all the freedom they needed. Just as significant, the Kinetophone's state-of-the-art audio sensitivity meant that sounds of a subtle nature—the delicate nuances of a dramatic recitation, for example—could not only be recorded but also played back with an unprecedented degree of sonic fidelity.

The Kinetophone's sound quality was indeed much better than what had previously been offered by talking-picture devices. This is not to say, however, that the sound was anywhere near what would be considered good, or even acceptable, by modern standards. To be sure, the Kinetophone's ingenious pre-amplifier increased the sensitivity of the mechanism's "ear," but at the same time it also increased the cylinder recordings' surface noise. After listening to all the Kinetophone recordings preserved at the Library of Congress, a film historian recently wrote:

> The sound is that of a static-filled radio broadcast—the performers are intelli-gible, but you have to concentrate. What finally makes the invention insupportable is the fact that they're all virtually screaming their lines. Initially funny, it's wearing after five minutes; an entire program of it would be maddening.[47]

But even when the Kinetophone was new, at least a few critics observed that the recorded sound was, as they say, not quite right. Obviously aware of and perhaps even sympathetic with Edison's conviction that the Kinetophone would soon enable "the poor man" to experience masterworks of opera and theater, but perhaps skeptical, a writer for the *New York Dramatic Mirror* observed:

> The metallic sound from the phonograph has been greatly diminished, but not overcome, neither is the volume of sound at all times sufficient for a large theater. The spectator feels that the words spoken were uttered by the figure on the screen, but it is difficult to forget that they are being transmitted through a phonograph.[48]

In essence, the Kinetophone was not much different from its many and sundry sound-film predecessors. Advanced though surely it was, the synchronization technology failed far too often to convince exhibitors of its long-term viability. Despite Edison's ambitious dreams, the limited capaciousness of his audio cylinders meant that the running time of a typical Kinetophone product—like the running times of the disc-accompanied films—could be no more than six minutes.[49] Although with its oversized horn the Kinetophone easily surpassed the sonic output of all its predecessors, it was nevertheless hardly loud enough to fill the space of the new "movie palaces" that were starting to be built right around the time the Kinetophone made its debut.

In terms of acoustics, the Kinetophone's only viable venue was the mid-sized vaudeville house that seated approximately 500. Not surprisingly, its repertoire favored material of the sort that played well with vaudeville audiences. Ever dreaming that his device would have a cultural impact, Edison invited writers to submit scripts for serious dramas, specifying only that "each play should be figured to run six minutes," that "the characters should be few and the action laid in one act," and that, along with being unrestricted by copyright, their contents be "clean and free from offense."[50] But most of what came out under the Kinetophone label amounted to mere comedy routines or song-and-dance numbers.

Since in content most of its material was so similar to what vaudeville audiences were getting on a regular basis from live performers, Edison's Kinetophone—once its initial novelty had faded—proved to be a very tough sell. Contrary to the financial predictions of the above-quoted Chicago columnist, managers of vaudeville houses did *not* hand over fortunes for the weekly privilege of renting Kinetophone sound-films and the elaborate equipment necessary for their exhibition. With a glaring headline, *Variety* in March 1914 described the Kinetophone as "The Sensation That Failed."[51] Undaunted, Edison stepped up his effort to market the Kinetophone in Europe, but his hopes were dashed on June 28, 1914, when the assassination in Sarajevo of Austria's Archduke Ferdinand triggered the outbreak of World War I.

In December 1914 a fire all but destroyed the Edison plant in West Orange, New Jersey. Edison was able to rebuild, but his restoration project—significantly—did not include the elaborate research and production facilities that for the previous four or five years had been devoted to development of the sound film. "The West Orange fire," writes film historian Douglas Gomery, "not only marked the end of the Kinetophone but signaled the demise of all serious efforts to unite mechanically the phonograph with motion pictures."[52] Like all the early experiments in sound film, Edison's "wonderful apparatus" proved to be just another flash in the pan.

A Turning Point in Cinema

Hailed as a technological triumph but then ridiculed as a failure, Edison's revitalized Kinetophone made its foray into the marketplace at an important turning point in the history of both film and film music. The Kinetophone would have succeeded only if its recording and synchronization technology had improved significantly while the film culture all around it remained absolutely frozen. Film culture at this time, of course, was hardly frozen; in terms of production and exhibition practice, and thus in audience expectations, the years 1913–15 form one of cinema's most dynamic periods of transition.

At first glance, it seems a wonder that the so-called Wizard of Menlo Park failed to recognize that the changes put the Kinetophone, even at its inception, sorely behind the times. It should be remembered, though, that Edison at this time was heavily invested in an old-fashioned type of cinema. The Motion Picture Patents Company that Edison helped found in 1908 was committed to the quick production of vast quantities of low-budget short films that, according to the cartel's marketing scheme, precisely suited the needs of nickelodeon-style theaters. Thanks to the persistence of filmmakers and exhibitors who resisted pressures from the MPPC, simultaneous with the debut of the new Kinetophone it was becoming clear in cities all across America that audiences seemed to prefer not inexpensively made short films but, rather, longer films whose "production values" entailed considerable financial investment.

In March 1913, when the new Kinetophone was first publicly exhibited, the MPPC was still very much in business. Less than a year before, however, the federal government had filed a civil suit against the MPPC, charging that "unreasonable and oppressive restraints and conditions have been arbitrarily imposed on the manufacture and leasing of films and machines" and noting that the cartel's primary function seemed to be "to harass and oppress all persons engaged in the motion picture business who have not obeyed its mandates."[53] Naturally, the MPPC resisted, and final arguments in the case were not made until December 1914; the decision of the Philadelphia-based United States District Court came ten months later, and it declared "that the defendants went far beyond what was necessary to protect patent rights and that their acts constituted a violation of the anti-trust laws."[54]

The October 1, 1915, court order that "the moving picture trust" be dissolved forthwith perhaps marks the "official" end of the nickelodeon period. But already for several years before this the nickelodeon-style film, and the small venues that neatly accommodated it, had been on the way out.

The American filmmakers affiliated with the MPPC were all based on the East Coast; since 1909 independent filmmakers had been making their way to Southern California— in part to take advantage of the region's abundant space and consistently sunny climate, but also to escape harassment from MPPC lawyers and thugs—and within just a few years there was a sizeable concentration of film studios in the Los Angeles suburb of Hollywood.[55] Some of the early Hollywood studios made only single-reel films that they attempted to market, without much success, to MPPC-affiliated exhibitors; others of them, more attuned to shifting audience tastes, focused on the production of multi-reel films of the sort that as early as 1911 were being imported from Italy and, despite obstacles imposed by the MPPC, profitably shown. Like some of the Hollywood producers, at least a few entrepreneurs seem to have been gifted with foresight. America's first "movie palace," New York's 2,460-seat Regent Theater, opened for business in February 1913; this was a full month before Edison's Kinetophone, with its pneumatically enhanced sound-reproducing mechanism, in vaudeville houses in the same city struggled to reach the ears of a mere five hundred or so listeners.

As had been the case for more than a decade, in 1913–15 the synchronization of any type of recorded sound with motion pictures surely seemed a technological marvel. But only someone close to being deaf—as Edison at this time apparently was—would have suggested that in terms of audio quality the music in a Kinetophone-style "talking picture" compared favorably to the sound of a theater organ or well-rehearsed orchestra accompanying a "silent" movie. And only the most obtuse observers of the entertainment scene would have thought, even for an instant, that the musical goals of these two forms of sound/film combinations were in any way similar.

At least since 1905, music had regularly accompanied exhibitions of narrative "silent" film in ways that, for better or worse, supported the films' content. Not since Edison's first Kinetophone, in 1895, had the sound film featured musical accompaniment, but that early effort had been a fluke, resulting not from intention but from the inability of Edison and his engineers to synchronize the device's separate audio and video playback mechanisms. With improved synchronization between phonograph and projector, all the subsequent "talking picture" devices up until the time of World War I attempted to intrigue audiences only with sounds that at least seemed to emanate directly from whoever, or whatever, was being portrayed in the film. Although their content included opera arias, popular songs, instrumental numbers, and music-supported scenes from melodrama, the sound films made between 1900 and 1915 for the most part were documentary recordings of in-studio performances; the exceptions were those products that involved music recorded in advance of filming, but even with these the entrepreneurial aim was to provide audiences with mechanical reproductions of material they might otherwise have experienced in a "live" theatrical setting.

In 1913–15 the American cinema was fairly exploding with newfound sophistication. Pictures coming from the independent West Coast studios were considerably longer than those the East Coast MPPC members persisted in making, and along with enormous sets and casts of thousands they featured genuine movie "stars." To accommodate offerings that were growing expansive metaphorically as well as literally, relatively large venues designed specifically for film sprang up in all the major American cities. And after a decade of trial and error, musical accompaniment for narrative film was starting to settle into a common practice whose success depended in large part on meeting the expectations of veteran moviegoers.

In this context, even the most advanced of the "talking picture" devices must have seemed like throw-backs to the time when cinema itself was a novelty. As audiences adjusted to narrative films two or three hours in length, documentary sound-films— because of the limited capacity of the discs or cylinders that held their sonic material —could run just five or six minutes. As audiences were learning to appreciate the visual splendor and physical comforts of new "movie palaces" that seated thousands, the sound-film was confined to vaudeville houses where pneumatically enhanced phono- graphs struggled to reach the ears of just a few hundred listeners. And as audiences in 1913–15 came to accept the musically accompanied "feature" film as a form of entertainment thoroughly of their own time, the contemporaneous sound film seemed modern only by virtue of its technology.

Sound film and "silent" film ca. 1913–15 both involved cinematic projections, but that is just about all they had in common. "As this writer sees the talking picture situation," opined Robert Grau in a 1914 monograph, "the outlook for its survival as a tremendous factor in public entertaining is better than it has ever been." One suspects that Grau, obviously a technophile, was attempting to see the future through rose-colored glasses. But his vision seems to have been undistorted when he noted, in an aside, that the sound film "should never be regarded as a competitor of the moving pictures."[56]

Sound Film Technology's Second Wave

Only when the moving picture in and of itself counted as a novelty was the sound film a serious rival for the public's attention. On the eve of World War I, after the "silent" film had begun to develop relatively sophisticated conventions for story-telling, the "talking picture" remained little more than a sonically enhanced example of the "cinema of attractions."

Not for lack of good reason, the "talking picture" at around this time vanished from the scene, but over the course of the next decade the "silent" film only gained in sophistication. As "silent" film's modes of exhibition became ever more standardized, so its system of manufacture and distribution became ever more institutionalized; as the loyalties of its audience solidified, so the profits reaped by its moguls grew. The American film industry as early as 1912 was estimated to be worth $100,000,000;[57] by the middle of the so-called Roaring Twenties, amidst a booming post-war economy and a culture that emphasized fun on all social strata, the industry's value had increased astronomically. The fabulous success of the American-style "silent" film was based at least in part on the fact that its offerings were indeed "silent"; the films of course featured non-stop musical accompaniments, but their actors—who by the mid 1920s were communicating with audiences far beyond the borders of the United States—remained glamorously mute. Vis-à-vis the cliché that cautions "if it ain't broke, don't fix it," the "silent" film ca. 1925, in terms of its sonic component, was not at all in need of repair.

The urge to link recorded sound with moving pictures nevertheless endured. But whereas in the twentieth century's first decade the idea for sound film was cultivated by and large by impresarios, during the heyday of "silent" film ambitions to develop a viable sound-film technology were harbored almost exclusively by scientists. Presciently, a physicist in 1921 wrote: "The talking picture . . . is gathering strength in the laboratory. When the proper time comes, it will soon live down its unfortunate past."[58]

Sound film's "unfortunate past" had to do in part with the limited volume levels of the phonographic equipment. But volume-related criticism applies only to the Kinetophone and other devices that attempted, ca. 1914, to satisfy audiences in relatively large venues. Before this, when sound films were exhibited in nickelodeon-style theaters, the output of purely acoustic phonographs would have been quite adequate.

Most of sound film's "unfortunate past" resulted from the persistent failure of inventors to manage synchronization between a pair of mechanical devices whose movement styles were decidedly different. There was never—nor could there ever be—a photographic picture that actually moved; a so-called moving picture offers only an illusion of movement that results from the attempts of the spectator's eyes to comprehend a rapid succession of pictures that, in fact, do not move at all. In marked contrast to the start-stop/start-stop activity of the film projector was the necessarily uninterrupted rotation of the phonograph cylinder or disc. No matter how ingenious were the connecting systems of gears and belts and pulleys, the precise co-ordination of a machine that moved intermittently with one that moved continuously was near impossible. Advertisements for each new device declared that the synchronization problem had finally been solved, but reviews testify that this was not the case.

The two problems—one having to do with volume level, the other with synchronization—might seem not much related. But the solutions to both problems, as would be discovered, involved the management of electricity.

*　　*　　*

Edison's 1877 phonograph was based on the idea that a series of intangible sound waves could be converted into impressions etched into a solid surface. Working in England, in 1904 Eugene Augustin Lauste, an engineer who had been employed by Edison from 1886 to 1892, began to develop a device that converted sound waves into physical movement that could be photographed.[59] Edison's and Lauste's methods both featured a sensitive diaphragm that vibrated—like a human eardrum—in response to sound. In Edison's case, the diaphragm was connected to a stylus that etched into a receptive surface a single long groove whose "hills" and "valleys" were analogous to the undulations of sound waves. In Lauste's case, the diaphragm was connected to a thin strip of metal set over a slit through which shone a beam of light; against the light, Lauste's sound-activated metal strip made a wiggling silhouette whose movement could easily be captured with a motion-picture camera. As with Edison's phonograph, playback for Lauste involved a reverse procedure. The "moving picture" of the sound waves was projected not onto a screen but simply onto the surface of a selenium cell; the photosensitive cell vibrated in sympathy with the stimulus, and these vibrations—like the vibrations of the needle that followed the groove of an Edison recording—were transmitted to a diaphragm whose movement made the sound once again audible.

The sound was audible, but just barely. With no electrical or electronic amplification, the audio component of Lauste's sound films was perceivable only by persons who listened—as did patrons of the 1895 version of Edison's Kinetophone—through earphones. By 1907, when Lauste first exhibited his Photocinematophone in London, the audience for sound-film novelties was already accustomed to hearing music or spoken words pour out from phonograph horns. In terms of public appeal, right from the start the Photocinematophone was hopelessly out-of-date. In terms of its underlying technology, however, it was very much ahead of its time.

Lauste's device is remarkable because it convincingly demonstrated that sound waves, up to this time thought to be transcribable only in a physical way by means of the continuous movement of an etching stylus, could in fact be recorded photographically by means of the intermittent movement of a motion-picture camera.

To make his early Photocinematophone sound films Lauste used a pair of cameras— one for image, one for sound—whose recorded materials were then played back via a pair of mechanically linked projectors. The logical next step was the development of a device that could record, entirely by photographic means, image and sound simultan- eously. Once this step was successfully taken, the problem of sound/image alignment would indeed be solved once and for all; recorded on a single strip of film by one intermittently moving device equipped with an "ear" as well as an "eye," the material upon playback via a single sound/image projector could not possibly be out of sync. Thanks to Lauste's experiments, scientists all over the United States and Europe by 1910 were aware of the possibilities of what eventually would be known as sound-on-film recording.

By that time, too, they were at least starting to become aware of the possibilities of the so-called audion tube that American engineer Lee de Forest invented in 1906 and patented in 1907. Born in Iowa and educated at Yale, de Forest had worked in both the radio and telephone industries, and hence his name for the invention. The audion was a "thermenionic triode valve," a gas-filled tube with three filaments whose electron activity was controllable by independent electrodes, and it allowed an electrical signal— for the first time ever—to be slightly amplified.

The audion tube naturally captured the attention of Western Electric, the manufac- turing division of American Telephone and Telegraph (AT&T), which in the years before World War I was anxiously seeking ways to make telephonic signals strong enough to travel more than just a few thousand miles. It also caught the notice of General Electric, which along with light bulbs produced radio equipment and thus was interested in boosting the power of broadcast signals. In 1913 Western Electric bought the patents for de Forest's audion; shortly thereafter one of its scientists discovered that simply by removing the gas from the tube—in other words, by housing the filaments in an almost total vacuum—the strength of the amplification could be increased more than a hundredfold. During the war, thanks to heavy subsidy by the United States govern- ment, both patent-holder Western Electric and licensee General Electric worked hard on improvements to and applications of the vacuum tube. At the war's end, that is, "on the eve of the introduction of commercial sound film,"[60] these two American companies held a virtual monopoly on vacuum-tube technology.

Civilian use of radio had been prohibited during the later years of World War I; while broadcast facilities were certainly ready for the new technology, commercial radio receivers were not, and thus the first public demonstration of amplified sound came by way of a public-address system during a "Victory Day" parade in New York City in September 1919. Electrically powered loudspeakers were put to good use at both the Republican and Democratic national conventions the next summer and again in March 1921 when the newly elected president, Warren G. Harding, made his inaugural address; within a few months the concept of the loudspeaker had been successfully adapted to the needs of long-distance telephone lines, and Harding's speech upon the dedication of the Tomb of the Unknown Soldier, in November 1921, was broadcast live to large crowds gathered in auditoriums in New York and San Francisco. Seeing commercial potential in all this, soon afterward theater manager Samuel "Roxy" Rothapfel arranged with Western Electric for installation of an amplification system in his 5,300-seat Capitol Theater in New York.[61]

Rothapfel's interest in Western Electric's amplification system, it is important to note, had to do with live sound broadcast directly, in closed-circuit fashion, from special events, not with recorded sound offered in conjunction with motion pictures. As noted, public interest in the sound film by and large died with the failure of Edison's Kinetophone; by 1921 audiences in America and most other countries had come to equate the movie-going experience with star-studded evening-length "silent" films whose accompaniments, more or less sophisticated, were invariably provided by live musicians. But also as noted, even during this dawn of the "silent" film's heyday the "talking picture" was "gathering strength in the laboratory."

* * *

One laboratory in which the "talking picture" gathered strength was Western Electric's, where entire teams of engineers were assigned not just to both sound-on-disc and sound-on-film technology but also—and significantly—to amplification systems and methods of electrical recording. Another was at the University of Illinois, where Joseph Tykocinski-Tykociner, a researcher in electrical engineering, in 1921–22 developed a sound-on-film system that involved a fast camera speed and thus delivered audio results of relatively high fidelity. Still another was the New Jersey laboratory of Lee de Forest, who after his lucrative work on the audion tube busied himself with combining Lauste's pioneering photographic sound-recording techniques with amplified sound. As early as 1913 de Forest was experimenting with both a recording device that captured sound and image simultaneously and a playback mechanism that delivered amplifiable sound perfectly synchronized with the moving picture; in 1919 he patented a sound-on-film process he called DeForest Phonofilm, and by 1922 he was marketing short features called Phonofilms in the United States, Australia, and Europe. In the same year that de Forest patented his Phonofilm process, a trio of German inventors—Josef Engl, Joseph Massolle, and Hans Vogt—patented a similar process they called, because it was the work of three men, Tri-Ergon. De Forest recalled that in June 1921 he was approached "by two German engineers" with an offer to collaborate; he does not name the Germans, but it is possible there was a connection with the Tri-Ergon developers.[62] In any case, in

October 1921 de Forest moved to Berlin, where the Tri-Ergon laboratories were located, and he remained there until September of the following year.

Tykocinski-Tykociner's sound films were academic experiments, and in terms of both content and audio quality de Forest's commercial products were not much different from the vaudeville-based sound films that attempted to entertain audiences before the war. Although they tried, neither Tykocinski-Tykociner nor de Forest could interest major players in the international film industry—which by the early 1920s was clearly centered in Hollywood—in supporting their work, and the Tri-Ergon group was similarly unsuccessful in their attempts to win the attention of European filmmakers. Being as it was a subsidiary of what at the time was the second-largest privately owned corporation in the entire world, AT&T's Western Electric felt no compulsion to leap into the marketplace with products that were not yet perfected; it remains, though, that by 1924 Western Electric had fully developed not just a sound-on-disc playback device in which both projector and phonograph were driven by a single motor but also electrical recording and a credible sound-on-film system.[63]

All things considered, during the early 1920s the "talking picture" gathered strength, indeed. But by this time motion-picture culture had grown to a mature and stable level; audiences worldwide had a well-defined appetite, and filmmakers worldwide, by and large following the example set by Hollywood, knew more or less precisely how to deliver what their audience expected. In the context of an enormously profitable scheme built on a steady flow of products that were both attractive and reliable, there was simply no place for experimental sound films. As much aware of the marketplace as of laboratory developments, film stock manufacturer George Eastman was on the mark when, apropos of sound-film technology ca. 1922–23, he commented: "I wouldn't give a dime for that invention. The public will never accept it."[64]

Chapter 6

VITAPHONE AND MOVIETONE, 1926–8

No producer in five years will think of making anything but talking pictures. It will take five years to permit us to perfect the sound and screen devices, to achieve the required results in recording the sound, without any flaws. We want this time just as we took time to get where we are today.

William Fox, 1927[1]

In 1926–7 the public *did* accept sound film, and the film industry responded—both to the invention and to the public's obvious taste for its results—with astonishing speed.

How is it, one must wonder, that an audience apparently very comfortable with the sophisticated Hollywood-style "silent" film could, almost overnight, shift the focus of its attention? How could it be that an entire industry, including participants whose involvement with filmmaking was more artistic than commercial, in a flash embraced an idea that for years it had scornfully dismissed? For quite a long time the sound film had been unsuccessfully clamoring for the public's attention; why did it so suddenly not just enter into but take over the industry's mainstream? The answers to all these questions can be distilled down to a single word: timing.

In this momentous case, the fortunate timing had little to do with film aesthetics or ideology. Rather, it involved the coincidence of disparate and relatively mundane forces that all pertained—specifically, albeit in various ways—to the situation of the United States in the wake of World War I. As film historian Leo Enticknap notes, "during a period spanning some four decades (1885–1925, approximately), moving image and audio recording technologies evolved through distinct sets of business practices and cultural models—ones that were essentially incompatible until a number of factors combined to enable their successful and widespread integration in the late 1920s."[2]

Once the Lumière brothers figured out, in 1895, how to project moving pictures onto screens, film exhibition worldwide followed the long-established cultural model of the staged performance presented to a relatively large audience. Before the advent of the electrically powered amplifier, audio recordings—because of the limited output of their purely acoustic playback devices—followed the cultural model of domestic music making. Quite aside from their persistent difficulties in synchronizing one playback mechanism with another, all the early sound films failed at least in part because they tried to place an essentially private aural medium into an essentially public venue.

Another incompatibility of cultural models had to do with disparity of content offered by early "silent" films and early sound films. Over the course of the nickelodeon period (roughly 1905 to 1915), audiences worldwide grew accustomed to films much longer than contemporaneous audio recordings could be; reels of celluloid film could easily last twelve minutes or more, but audio recordings on cylinder or disc had durations of just three or four minutes. Makers of "silent" films were thus able to present relatively complex narratives, but makers of early sound films, because of the temporal restrictions of the films' audio concomitants, were limited to necessarily brief attractions; whereas most early "silent" films told stories, most early sound films presented isolated "numbers." Generally speaking, both types of entertainment—for those who could afford the price of admission—were available elsewhere: as had been the case for centuries, enacted stories formed the essence of theatrical productions, and "numbers" abounded in post-Victorian vaudeville houses and music halls. As late as 1914, the year in which Edison finally abandoned his second Kinetophone project, sound films merely replicated, or documented, what at the time was being offered in "live" venues; as early as 1903, "silent" films (e.g., Edison's *The Great Train Robbery*) were spicing their stories with narrative/visual effects that could not possibly be realized in "real time" on a theatrical stage. The makers of "silent" films were free to experiment with such things as close-ups, pans, quick cuts, dissolves, cross-fades, flash-backs, and montages, all of which arguably had roots in traditional theater and literature but which, in their realization, were unique to the newly evolving medium of cinema; in marked contrast, the makers of early sound films could do little more than roll the recording machines and entice popular entertainers to "do their thing."

The basic business practices of audio recording and film were not incompatible but simply different. Almost from the start, audio recordings as well as their playback devices were sold to individual customers; films, on the other hand, were by and large not sold but rented to exhibitors. Once purchased, an audio recording could theoretically be experienced whenever or wherever its owner wished; in contrast, a film could be experienced only at times and in places determined by an exhibitor. In each field there was at the outset intense technological competition, which meant that a company's "software" typically was playable only on a certain type of "hardware." Record companies as well as filmmakers realized that "format wars" were not to their advantage, however, and soon enough industry-wide standards were instituted. After having invested in just one phonograph, customers could buy and listen to recordings from a variety of companies; likewise, proprietors of movie theaters—having invested in a single projector—could rent and exhibit products from a variety of filmmakers. And all was well, so long as each medium held to its own cultural model.

But severe incompatibility resulted when the two media were mixed. Except for the efforts of Edison, all the pre-1926 experiments in sound film were conducted not by major players in either industry but by independent inventors who in most cases also served as their own promoters and marketers. The chief selling point of every one of the early sound-film products, of course, was novelty. Allegedly the novelty pertained to the sound films' content; certainly the word "novelty" described the sound films' necessary machinery. Whereas not just the equipment but also the manpower required for the presentation of "silent" films was more or less standardized, the equipment and manpower needed for any type of early sound film was inevitably unique; before a sound film could be exhibited, special equipment first needed to be installed, and then that equipment needed to be operated, and maintained, by specially trained personnel. Innovative though the early sound films might have been, as commodities they were all doomed to failure; in the context of an industry that almost from the start gravitated toward a business practice that depended vitally on the widespread distribution and smooth delivery of more or less standardized products, the idea of parochial sound-film novelties—quite apart from their many technical glitches—was almost ridiculously out of place.

But what if sound films, with their requisite playback equipment, *were* standardized? What if the perennial problems of synchronization and volume level—thanks to new technologies developed not by maverick inventors but by the concerted research forces of a major corporation—were finally solved? What if both production and distribution of sound films were controlled not by independent entrepreneurs but by an established studio? What if the exhibition of such films, on a regular basis, took place in theaters where installation and operation of the necessary equipment were closely monitored by the heavily invested filmmaker? What if the sound films were appealing enough in both quality and content so they could replace the vaudeville-style acts that audiences, in the better movie palaces, were accustomed to experiencing in advance of the feature-length screen attractions?

Before the mid-1920s such questions would have been mere speculation; by the summer of 1926, all the conditions had been met. And while the incompatible business practices and cultural models that previously stymied the sound film were quite international, the crucial factors that turned the tide were clearly American.

Vitaphone

When AT&T's Western Electric began to market its electrical recording technology early in 1924, it immediately found clients in the record business, notably the Columbia and Victor labels, but not in the film industry. Not until May 1925 would there be interest from a film studio; this was Warner Bros., a relatively small yet nonetheless successful Hollywood company that just a month earlier—for the sake of improving international distribution of its products—had acquired the fifty or so theatrical venues owned by the almost bankrupt Vitagraph studio. In the course of its rapid expansion, richly financed by a Wall Street firm (Goldman, Sachs), Warner Bros. also purchased a radio station in Los Angeles. This brought one of the Warner brothers, Sam, into contact with a Western Electric salesman who, naturally, sang the praises of the new recording technology and its potential relationship with motion pictures. Intrigued, Sam Warner convinced his brother Harry to travel to New York to attend a demonstration. As Douglas Gomery tells the story:

> Harry almost did not go for, as he later recalled, "if [they] had said talking pictures, I never would have gone, because [talking pictures] had been made up to that time several times, and each was a failure."
>
> A recording of a five-piece jazz band sparked Harry's interest, and within a week he had conceived of a plan to use this new invention. He explained to [Sachs, Goldman investment director Waddill] Catchings, "If it can talk, it can sing."[3]

Told another way, the story has it that Harry Warner

> was instantly impressed and feigned indifference to the [Western Electric] executives, but at home it was a different story. "I could not believe my own ears. I walked back of the screen to see if they did not have an orchestra there synchronizing with the picture," he later recalled. "I myself would not go across the street to see or hear a talking picture. But music! That's another story."[4]

Warner Bros. contracted, in June 1925, for at least a year's worth of experimentation with Western Electric's sound-on-disc system. At the same time, Warner Bros. launched a subsidiary it called Vitaphone, the production facilities of which were housed at first in the old Vitagraph studios in Brooklyn but later relocated to the acoustically more favorable Manhattan Opera House on 34th Street in New York City. Fourteen months after Warner Bros. signed on with Western Electric, its Vitaphone was ready for public display. The premiere took place on August 6, 1926, at the New York movie palace formerly known as the Piccadilly but after acquisition by the Hollywood studio called simply Warners' Theatre.

Especially as it relates to the history of film music in the accompanimental sense, the program of this first-ever Vitaphone exhibition is worth noting in detail.

It opened not with anything at all musical but with a congratulatory speech by Will Hays, president of the self-policing Hollywood organization known as the Motion Picture Producers and Distributors of America. After this came eight short sound-film attractions, each of them rich with musical content. These were the overture to Wagner's *Tannhäuser* performed by the New York Philharmonic under the direction of Henry Hadley, Dvořák's *Humoresque* performed by violinist Mischa Elman and pianist Josef Bonimo, the "Caro nome" aria from Verdi's *Rigoletto* sung by soprano Marion Talley, a song-and-dance number called "An Evening on the Don" delivered by a troupe of supposedly Russian performers, a vaudeville-based routine featuring the "seductive twanging of a guitar manipulated by Roy Smeck,"[5] a set of variations on a theme from Beethoven's "Kreutzer Sonata" by violinist Efrem Zimbalist and pianist Harold Bauer, the "Vesti la giubba" aria from Leoncavallo's *Pagliacci* performed by tenor Giovanni Martinelli with full orchestral accompaniment, and—finally—a "pleasing and extraordinarily effective" number by popular singer Anna Case "supported by a dance divertissement of the Cansinos" and "accompanied by the Metropolitan Opera chorus and Herman Heller's orchestra."[6]

Only after this lengthy and variegated prelude did Warner Bros. show its main attraction, a 111-minute swashbuckler titled *Don Juan*. Remarkably, considering the press's eager identification of the new Vitaphone products as the latest incarnations of the "talking movie," the sixteen-inch phonograph discs that accompanied each reel of *Don Juan* featured not one spoken word. A big-budget feature starring John Barrymore and Mary Astor, *Don Juan* had been completed earlier in 1926 and was originally intended for release as yet another "silent" film. Along with occasional pre-recorded sound effects, all that differentiated it from its 1926 box-office competitors was the fact that its score—composed mostly by William Axt, with contributions from David Mendoza[7]—was not performed "live" by a theater orchestra but delivered via phonograph. That the film's musical concomitant seemed in no way unusual is evidenced by the *New York Times*'s rather detailed account of the Vitaphone debut. Veteran film

91

critic Mordaunt Hall waxes eloquently over the fidelity of mechanically reproduced sound, and its synchronization with moving imagery, in the program's introductory bits; regarding *Don Juan*, he writes extensively on the narrative, the mise-en-scène, and the acting, but on the accompanying music—presumably taking it for granted—he comments not at all.[8]

Ordinary though the music for *Don Juan* may have been, it was not without its problems. According to J.C. Rosenthal, general manager of the American Society of Composers, Authors, and Publishers, Axt's score included two segments of generic yet published film music ("The Fire Agitato" and "In Gloomy Forests") whose copyrights were held by ASCAP member Robbins-Engel, Inc. According to a newspaper report that followed the Vitaphone premiere by less than three weeks, "six pieces by French composers, whose copyrights are owned by French publishers, also were used in the production," and Rosenthal promised that ASCAP "would act to protect these also because of a cooperative arrangement it has with the French publishers' organization."[9] ASCAP was preparing to sue for royalty payments, but the next day it "was indicated . . . by representatives of the publishers' association and the motion picture concern" that the matter "very likely will be settled by mutual agreement without recourse to legal action."[10]

Warner Bros. had good reason to want to settle quickly, for the relatively minor legal tiff with ASCAP transpired amidst staggering news from Wall Street. Just a day after the announcement of the imminent settlement, the *Los Angeles Times* reported: "In Warner Bros. Pictures, the New York stock market has another sensation supplied from the Pacific Coast, or more particularly, from Hollywood. Warner Bros. 'A' stock is perhaps the most popular of the so-called specialty group, having performed the remarkable feat of rising from 15, the price at which the stock was sold to the public in February, to a high yesterday of 50. Only a few weeks ago the stock was selling at 18."[11]

Clearly a hit, the original Vitaphone program within a month of its premiere was being presented at venues in Atlantic City, Chicago, and Los Angeles. With the *Don Juan* program still playing at Warners' Theatre on Broadway, on October 7, 1926, Warner Bros. launched a second Vitaphone program at New York's Colony Theater. In this case the feature-length film was *The Better 'Ole*, a wartime comedy starring Syd Chaplin (half-brother of Charles Chaplin). As with *Don Juan*, the disc recording that accompanied *The Better 'Ole* involved sound effects and a musical score;[12] voiced words (in the form of "Tipperary" and other marching songs) figured into the score, but the film featured no dramatic speaking.

There was indeed speaking, however, in some of the short films that preceded the intermission, and it was audience reaction to this sometimes casual banter that in part determined the sound film's immediate future. Along with performances by comedy duo Willie and Eugene Howard, vaudeville vocalist Elsie Janis, "old time" ballad singer Reinald Werrenrath, and the vocal group known as The Four Aristocrats, the first half of the second Vitaphone program showcased numbers by Broadway stars Al Jolson ("Red, Red Robin," "April Showers," and "Rockabye Baby with a Dixie Melody") and George Jessel ("At Peace with the World and You").

For more than a year Jessel had been appearing in the Broadway production of Samson Raphaelson's *The Jazz Singer*. Even before the second Vitaphone program debuted, it was generally known that Warner Bros. intended to turn *The Jazz Singer* into a "talking picture." Soon, Harry Warner explained, the Vitaphone will not only be used as a prologue and to synchronize the musical accompaniment to the picture, but will also be employed to transmit the voice of the players synchronized with their actions through the story.

This makes possible bringing to the screen musical stage successes without sacrificing any of the music. It also indicates that the artists will be engaged for their voice and singing ability as well as their pantomime.

On the legitimate stage at the present time there are numerous players who have gained fame by their versatility in singing and other musical accomplishments, added to their histrionic ability, which will to the screen be a greater asset than appearance or pantomime.

A good example of both of these cases is "The Jazz Singer," the New York stage success, which we will produce in the early spring, featuring George Jessel. . . .[13]

At the end of April 1927 it was generally believed that Jessel was "soon to leave for Hollywood to star in the film version of his stage success, 'The Jazz Singer,' which will be the first into which the Vitaphone has been introduced for dramatic effect."[14] But a month later it was announced that the first Hollywood-based Vitaphone production would feature not Jessel but Jolson. The *Los Angeles Times* reported that Jessel was still under contract with Warner Bros., but "it is rumored that when [he] heard that Vitaphone was to be used in connection with 'The Jazz Singer,' he requested an addition to his salary, which gave rise to some argument, and resulted in the Warners looking about for another famous comedian to play the role."[15]

Starring Jolson, *The Jazz Singer* opened at the Warners' Theatre in New York on October 6, 1927.[16] By this time, more than a hundred and thirty American movie theaters had already installed Western Electric's projection and amplification devices, and hundreds more—not just in the United States but in England, Canada, and Australia—were waiting to be equipped. When they finally experienced it, audiences worldwide got from *The Jazz Singer* not only their money's worth of entertainment but also a paradigm shift in cinematic possibility.

The Jazz Singer lasts eighty-nine minutes. A large portion of it is, like *Don Juan* and *The Better 'Ole*, a "silent" film accompanied by a recorded orchestral score.[17] But small portions of it are devoted to musical "numbers" in which recorded sound is synchronized with on-screen action, and three of these include not just singing but also spoken words.[18] In two of these cases, the spoken words amount to asides likely improvised by Jolson in the course of his delivery of songs. In one case, however, a single word—"stop," voiced angrily by the father of the title character—is obviously scripted.

In terms of sonic content, these nine "numbers" are perhaps not much different from what Warner Bros. had lately been offering in its pre-intermission Vitaphone programs. In terms of dramatic content, however, they are hugely different, for in all cases they are presented not as documentations but as enactments. Whereas in the prelude to *The Better 'Ole* audiences saw and heard Jolson himself delivering "April Showers" and other of his trademark songs, in *The Jazz Singer* they witnessed such songs as "Dirty Hands, Dirty Face," "Toot Toot Tootsie," "Blue Skies," and—most famously, in the final scene—"My Mammy" rendered not so much by Jolson as by the character he portrayed.[19] The aural component of *The Jazz Singer* combined what at the time was standard practice for "silent" film musical accompaniment with sound-film "novelty" numbers of the sort that had intrigued entrepreneurs since the turn of the century. But, *pace* a conclusion drawn by film scholar Alan Williams, it was more than "this co-presence of two kinds of [sound-film] discourse within a single work" that represents "the crucial difference between *The Jazz Singer* and all previous attempts to market recorded [film] sound."[20] Rather, the crucial difference between *The Jazz Singer* and every single one of its sound-film predecessors had to do with the idea that its quasi-realistic sonic elements communicated not fact but fiction.

In real life Jolson was a singer, but in this landmark 1927 film he was an actor *portraying* a singer. It may be that Harry Warner entered into the Vitaphone project believing that audiences would be interested only in "musical" pictures. The phenomenal success of *The Jazz Singer*, however, convinced many in the film industry that the time for "talking" pictures had indeed arrived.

*   *   *

After *The Jazz Singer* opened in Los Angeles at the Criterion Theater shortly after Christmas 1927, Frances Goldwyn, wife of MGM executive Samuel Goldwyn, supposedly remarked that the West Coast premiere was "the most important event in cultural history since Martin Luther nailed his theses on the church door."[21]

All things considered, that seems an exaggeration. But it is fact that within just a few months after *The Jazz Singer*'s arrival MGM and several other Hollywood studios were investing hugely in the building of facilities that would allow them to compete with Warner Bros. In an August 1928 article illustrated by an architectural drawing and four wide-angle photographs of construction projects, the *Los Angeles Times* reported:

> Several million dollars has or shortly will be expended by six leading motion-picture producers in the novel construction of sound stages, recording buildings and other paraphernalia incidental to the proper rearing of Hollywood's favorite daughter—the film industry.
>
> Executives and technicians are in accord: the daughter must have voice culture. And it's like the rearing of any child, this new development of talking. Just as an infant progresses from crawling to walking and then talking, the motion-picture industry is in the throes of another transition as important as the evolution of silent drama from the prototype, the nickelodeon. Silent drama is about to be silenced forever, if one will note the activity of Fox, Metro-Goldwyn-Mayer, Warner Brothers, United Artists, Christie and Sennett.[22]

After describing in detail the considerable acoustic and technological needs of sound stages—that is, buildings designed to accommodate not just the filming of theatrical action but also the recording of that action's audio components—the reporter noted that to date only five hundred of the United States' fourteen thousand motion-picture theaters had been properly wired for amplified sound. Estimating that even a "rushing of work will not permit more than two picture houses per day to be equipped for talking pictures," the writer calculated that "a year from now less than 1,300 [American] houses will have been placed in the market for talking pictures."[23] Studio executives were perhaps frustrated by that slow installation pace, but they were hardly daunted; as far as the reporter could tell, the path to the future seemed clearly enough marked.

The rapidity with which cinema converted—or attempted to convert—to the new sound-film technology has been mythologized, very entertainingly in the screenplay of MGM's 1952 musical comedy *Singin' in the Rain* but also quite dryly in a great many academic treatments of film history. "The standard textbook account," writes Alan Williams, "is of massive disruption: producers panicked; careers were ruined; no one knew how to use the new technology, and so sound recordists became *de facto* directors; the art of film took a giant, if temporary, step backwards, particularly in editing and camera movement."[24] As with all myths, there is a certain amount of truth in this. Still, as Williams cautions, "some specific points in this account are clearly in need of revision."[25]

Figure 6.1 "The Talkie," featured on the cover of *Life* magazine, November 30, 1928. Courtesy of Library of Congress.

Resistance to the "Talkies"

One point in need of revision has to do with the sound film's reception, which in most cases was warm—indeed, feverish—but which in some instances was decidedly cool.

It is true, as the myth has it, that Hollywood as a whole moved quickly to adopt the new technology and that film industries elsewhere soon enough followed suit. But not all filmmakers equated the coming of the sound film with the end of silent film. Even as his MGM studio was in the process of constructing elaborate sound stages on its Culver City property, Samuel Goldwyn emphasized what he saw as essential differences between the well-established medium of the silent film and the just-arrived "talkie," and he sincerely believed that the silent film—precisely because of those differences—would endure. "I am by no means opposed to sound film," he told an interviewer,

> but I do think that the hysteria that reigns here at present may mean that so many inadequate talking subjects will be issued that people will eventually long for the peace and quiet to which they have been accustomed with the silent features. . . .
>
> The producers [of silent films] had in their hands a medium that was international, one in which screen performers while silent were able to talk to any country in the world. It is to be hoped that this [new] combination of shadow and sound will not destroy all interest in the silent picture, for after all is said and done there is something gentle and poetic in the idea of being able to tell a story by animated shadows that flit across a screen.[26]

Audiences in England did not experience *The Jazz Singer* until almost a year after the film had opened in New York. At least among British critics and members of the British film industry, however, the Vitaphone package was the talk of the long town before it arrived at London's new Piccadilly Theatre. A consensus had it that the sound film—while not without merit—was not likely to replace the silent film. A special report to the *New York Times* summarized British opinion:

> The British cinema world is . . . quite prepared to believe what Mr. [Jesse] Lasky [an executive at Hollywood's Paramount studio] calls "the new art form" has a place in the scheme of things. They are convinced that it will abolish cinema orchestras, that it will be a boon to the makers of "news reels," that it will provide "atmosphere" instead of disconnected "incidental noises" for such films as "Chang" and "Wings," that it may popularize a musical comedy type of picture on the lines of "Show Boat" or "The Jazz Singer." But they do not think it will oust the silent film. They base their belief chiefly on the fact that the silent film is a distinct art form, while the talking picture would, in the last analysis, be a more or less imperfect imitation of the stage.[27]

That belief, like Goldwyn's, is in keeping with attitudes voiced by conservative film-lovers and filmmakers both in and outside the United States. More remarkable is the British filmmakers' conviction that the sound film would have a positive effect on film production in their own country. England's film industry, like indigenous film industries worldwide, had for more than a decade and a half been outshone by Hollywood's wide-reaching glow. Its films, cultural loyalists might have argued, were more artistically refined, and certainly more attuned to the needs of an insular audience, than were the mass-market commodities that since the days of World War I had flowed steadily out of Southern California. But British films were limited, not just in number but in budget, and this meant that they were also limited in spectacle, star-content, and most of the other elements that together added up to a rather colossal amount of appeal for an international audience. That being the case,

> What few in the British film industry would have expected is that Hollywood should ever sponsor the talking picture. For Hollywood, at least, silence should be golden on the silver screen. How, otherwise, is it to maintain its practical world monopoly? A picture made in Los Angeles can be comprehended in Tibet. But how about a picture which depends for its exposition not entirely on pantomime but on dialogue expressed in 100 per cent American?[28]

In summary, the June 1928 report from London noted that British filmmakers regarded the sound film "with great equanimity." And perhaps their equanimity disguised some optimism. "If [the sound film] is to be a permanent development then, so runs the argument here, it means the end of American film dominance."[29]

*   *   *

The Jazz Singer opened in London in late September 1928. In the same month it was presented in Berlin, albeit as a silent film; not until January of 1929 did German audiences, and audiences in Paris, experience the full Vitaphone package. But members of the film industries in France and Germany, like filmmakers in England, were well aware of the film's content and its likely impact on their audiences. They were aware, too, of the technological superiority of the securely patented Vitaphone system—which involved not just disc recordings synchronized with the moving picture but also, importantly, effective amplification—over their own efforts toward sound film.

Although film aesthetics certainly entered into their discussion, it was largely for the purpose of protecting their technological and physical "turf" that various German patent holders, producers, and exhibitors convened at Berlin's Kaiserhof in July of 1928. Summarizing the conference that resulted in the forming of Germany's hopeful but short-lived Tobis syndicate, *Film-Kurier* commented:

> Can we resist the onslaught from abroad? The very strong and fruitful development of German sound film compels us to say yes. But sound film should not be or become a competitor of silent film—on the contrary, but neither should it be an aggregate.[30]

In the Soviet Union there was not much worry that a capitalist "onslaught from abroad" would upset the government-supported homegrown film culture. Indeed, at least some Soviet filmmakers seemed to welcome the news of technological breakthroughs in the West. This is not to say, however, that they were eager to imitate Western productions of the sort that in the summer of 1928 they had yet to experience firsthand. Rather, they imagined a uniquely Soviet form of sound film. Just a month after representatives of the German film industry collectively girded their loins for a commercial skirmish, a trio of Soviet filmmakers issued a purely artistic "Statement" that began:

> The dream of a sound film has come true. With the invention of a practical sound film, the Americans have placed it on the first step of substantial and rapid realization. Germany is working intensively in the same direction. The whole world is talking about the silent thing that has learned to talk.
>
> We who work in the U.S.S.R. are aware that with our technical potential we shall not move ahead to a practical realization of the sound film in the near future. At the same time we consider it opportune to state a number of principal premises of a theoretical nature, for in the accounts of the invention it appears that this advance in films is being employed in an incorrect direction. Meanwhile, a misconception of the potentialities within this new technical discovery may not only hinder the development and perfection of the cinema as an art but also threaten to destroy all its present formal achievements.[31]

The authors—Sergei Eisenstein, Vsvolod Pudovkin, and Gregori Alexandrov—argue that to date the "success of Soviet films on the world's screens [has been] due, to a significant degree," to the effective use of montage, that is, the collective impression that results from the presentation in quick succession of images that on first glance might not seem to be logically connected. Indeed, they argue that Soviet-style montage "has become the indisputable axiom on which the worldwide culture of the cinema has been built." That being the case, they suggest, the cultivation of montage should continue, and the idea of montage should simply be expanded to include elements of sound.

Collectively, the writers grant that "it is most probable that [sound's] use will proceed along the line of least resistance, i.e., along the line of satisfying simple curiosity." They predict that the first wave of sound film will involve "naturalistic" films that feature "a certain 'illusion' of talking people, of audible objects, etc."; in the second wave, they predict, the sound film will be used "for 'highly cultured dramas' and other photographed performances of a theatrical sort." And this, they say, "will destroy the culture of montage, for every *adhesion* of sound to a visual montage piece increases its inertia as a montage piece." "*Only a contrapuntal use* of sound in relation to the visual montage piece," they declare, "will afford a new potentiality of montage development and perfection." Therefore, "*the first experimental work with sound must be directed along the lines of its distinct nonsynchronization with the visual images*. And only such an attack will give the necessary palpability which will later lead to the creation of an *orchestral counterpoint* of visual and aural images." They conclude:

> The *contrapuntal method* of constructing the sound film will not only not weaken the *international cinema* but will bring its significance to unprecedented power and cultural height. Such a method for constructing the sound film will not confine it to a national market, as must happen with the photographing of plays, but will give a greater possibility than ever before for the circulation throughout the world of a filmically expressed idea.[32]

This was an archly didactic view, and it did not have much immediate effect.[33] In retrospect, perhaps one of the most interesting things about the "Statement" is the accuracy with which its authors forecast the immediate future of the sound film; in the Soviet Union, where sound-film technology in fact was slow to develop, there was no quick cycling through "illusions" of "talking people [and] audible objects" to "photographed performances of a theatrical sort," but that description certainly applies to what transpired in the market-driven West. Certainly another interesting thing about the "Statement" is its essentially positive attitude toward sound film; instead of waxing nostalgic over a familiar but soon-to-be-*passé* medium, the authors of the "Statement" eagerly look forward to new possibilities.

Also looking forward to new sound-film possibilities around this time was the American film critic Harry Alan Potamkin. Because of his active involvement in New York's Communist circles, Potamkin was likely aware of developing Soviet film theory long before that theory was ever realized.[34] But he did not refer to Eisenstein et al. in the article he published in April 1929 in the prestigious *Musical Quarterly*. For the most part, his article is a nostalgic paean to "good" accompaniments for silent films and a rant against "poor" accompaniments of the sort that had gone out of fashion more than a decade earlier. Like the Soviet writers, however, Potamkin recognized the reality of the sound film, and regarding the new genre's use of music he offered potent advice:

> Since music is inevitable, we can make the best use of silence by selecting the intervals carefully at which the music will be hushed. At all other times the music is to be subdued—I might even say, made bashful. Long periods of silence separated by music will emphasize not the silence but the sound. And only by emphasizing silence can we stress the silent image. Though in the emphasis of silence in sound, there is still an emphasis of the sound arrangement. To this I answer: subdue the silence in sound, use it sparingly. But see that the music neither distracts nor deceives the sight. Hide the orchestra.[35]

Expressions of optimism, and suggestions for future developments, can be found as well in a document produced in May 1929 by the French journalist-turned-filmmaker René Clair. To detect hopefulness, however, one has to read between the lines. On first glance, Clair's letter from London (published decades later, in essay form, as "The Art of Sound") comes across only as a bitter screed against the new "talking" film:

> The talking film exists, and those skeptics who prophesy a short reign for it will die themselves long before it's over. It is too late for those who love the art of moving pictures to deplore the effects of this barbaric invasion. All they can do is try to cut their losses.[36]

Whereas the "onslaught from abroad" mentioned almost a year earlier by the German industrialists had to do mostly with the technology marketplace, the "barbaric invasion" for Clair had entirely to do with aesthetics. To his credit, Clair seemed to be not entirely immune to the entertainment value that came with certain of the "barbaric" products. Late in his letter, he sang the praises of *The Broadway Melody*, an MGM production advertised upon its release in February 1929 as the first-ever "all-talking, all-singing, all-dancing" film. "Of all the films now showing in London," Clair wrote,

> *Broadway Melody* is having the greatest success. This new American film represents the sum total of all the progress achieved in sound films since the

appearance of *The Jazz Singer* two years ago. For anyone who has some knowledge of the complicated technique of sound recording, this film is a marvel. . . . In *Broadway Melody*, the talking film has for the first time found an appropriate form: it is neither theater nor cinema, but something altogether new. The immobility of planes, that curse of talking films, is gone. The camera is as mobile, the angles are as varied as in a good silent film. The acting is first-rate. . . . The sound effects are used with great intelligence, and if some of them still seem superfluous, others deserve to be cited as examples.[37]

Clair indeed cites examples of sound effects in *The Broadway Melody* that he deems praise-worthy. In conclusion, though, he mourns the passing of the silent film, the art form that just a year before had been described as so "gentle and poetic" by Hollywood mogul Samuel Goldwyn. "At its best," Clair writes,

the talkie is no longer photographed theater. It is itself. Indeed, by its variety of sounds, its orchestra of human voices, it does give an impression of greater richness than the silent cinema. But are such riches not in fact quite ruinous to it? Through such "progressive" means the screen has lost more than it has gained. It has conquered the world of voices, but it has lost the world of dreams. I have observed people leaving the cinema after seeing a talking film. They might have been leaving a music hall, for they showed no sign of the delightful numbness which used to overcome us after a passage through the silent land of pure images. They talked and laughed, and hummed the tunes they had just heard. They had not lost their sense of reality.[38]

Clair's dismay was triggered for the most part by films that prominently featured spoken dialogue. But "the talking film is not everything," he noted. "There is also the sound film."[39] Whereas this book—following the trend of most recent writing on cinema—uses the term "sound film" to denote a film that in one way or another includes a recorded sonic component, Clair reserved the term "sound film" (in the original French, "*film sonore*") for a film whose recorded sonic elements were of a certain type. Contrasting the "sound film" with the mere "talkie" (the "*film parlant*"), Clair suggested that whereas the latter depended vitally on its dialogue, the former kept words to a minimum and instead made creative use of what nowadays would be called sound effects. For Clair, the "sound film" was a genre "on which the last hopes of the advocates of the silent film are pinned," but he worried that "this solution will only half-satisfy the public." And while he over-generalized when he stated that at the time there was "almost universal agreement about the advantages of a mechanical musical accompaniment" over live accompaniments performed by theater orchestras, he was on the mark when he admitted:

[O]pinions vary as far as noises accompanying the action are concerned. The usefulness of such noises is often questionable. If at first hearing they are surprising and amusing, very soon they become tiresome. After we have heard a certain number of sound films, and the first element of surprise has worn off, we are led to the unexpected discovery that the world of noises seems far more limited than we had thought.[40]

100

Written in response to the filmic attractions that were all the rage in London early in 1929, Clair's letter points to the directions in which he would attempt to move with his own work. Clearly opposed to the fast-paced and word-filled "talkie," Clair produced "sound films" in which he attempted to balance a requisite amount of spoken language with judiciously chosen sound effects, purposeful musical accompaniments, and—most significant—long moments of actual silence. At a time when Hollywood, and most of its international imitators, sought to attract the largest possible crowds with entertainment commodities, Clair appealed to an arguably more select audience with films that possibly might qualify as works of art. And in this effort, a struggle wholly in keeping with the spirit of the times, Clair as a filmmaker was hardly alone.

*   *   *

"Throughout the 1920s and early 1930s," film historian Des O'Rawe reminds us, "the relationship between commercial filmmakers and avant-garde artists and theoreticians (particularly in Germany and France) was more intimate than ever before (or since)." Alas, as O'Rawe also reminds us, "the modernist dream of a cinema shaped by a productive symbiosis between film and the other arts (painting, music, architecture, theatre, poetry, and so on)" soon enough became "a casualty of the 'sound era' and its fetishization of sound-image synchronicity."[41]

The "modernist dream," in any case, resulted in a handful of films that made use of the new sound technology but nevertheless remained aligned with certain of the practices and aesthetics of older cinema. In keeping with the montage idea championed by Eisenstein et al., the makers of these films experimented with sound that was deliberately not synchronized with images. Eschewing chatter and clatter, they kept both dialogue and sound effects to a minimum; for the sake of dramatic effect, they used naturalistic sounds that were sometimes exaggerated in volume level or in other ways distorted. They devised fantastic scenes that, à la the silent film, were in essence pantomimes supported by music either diegetic or extra-diegetic; more daringly, recognizing that "silence exists as one aspect of a pluralistic sound universe,"[42] they created stunningly realistic scenes that for all intents and purposes were devoid of sound altogether.

Sometimes called "silent sound films,"[43] these deliberately modernist efforts include such works as Alfred Hitchcock's *Blackmail* (1929); Walter Ruttmann's *Melodie der Welt* (1929); Josef von Sternberg's *Der Blaue Engel* (1930); Dziga Vertov's *Entuziazm* (1930); Lewis Milestone's *All Quiet on the Western Front* (1930);[44] René Clair's *Sous les toits de Paris* (1930), *Le Million* (1931), and *À nous la liberté!* (1931); Georg Wilhelm Pabst's *Kameradschaft* (1931); Fritz Lang's *M* (1931) and *Das Testament der Dr. Mabuse* (1932); and Carl Theodor Dreyer's *Vampyr* (1932). These films' subtle mix of actual silence with accompanying music and more or less realistic sound effects has drawn—and doubtless will continue to draw—serious analytical attention from film scholars.[45] And even in their own time they drew due attention aplenty from critics of avant-garde persuasion.[46]

The mere fact that these films differed from the sonic norm attracted the notice, if not always the praise, of movie reviewers for the popular press. Writing from London, a special correspondent for the *New York Times* observed that Hitchcock's *Blackmail* "goes some way to showing how the cinematograph and the microphone can be mated without their union being forced upon the attention of a punctilious world as mésalliance. The talk is not allowed to be the shrew of the combination, nagging the poor silent screen into pathetic subjection."[47] A few days later the *Times* published an editorial in which an anonymous writer, boldly and perhaps cynically pointing to "a road which artists in the talkies, if such there be, should wish to follow," didactically declared:

> The technique of the novel and of the stage must be completely forsaken. Sound and words must be used not to tell the story, not to get the action forward, but to supplement and enrich the story and mood as they are already presented on the film. An example of the correct use of sound is to be found in "Blackmail."[48]

But when Hitchcock's film finally crossed the Atlantic a *Times* reviewer, although noting a scene in which "three words are uttered and [followed by] a curious and artificial silence," for the most part carped about what he perceived to be the slowness of plot.[49] A year later, the same newspaper's regular film critic described Clair's *Sous les toits de Paris* as "a curious combination of clever cinematic work, silent episodes with music, others with dialogue and some with singing."[50]

Vis-à-vis their use of music and sound effects, films such as *Blackmail* and *Sous les toits de Paris* were indeed recognized, and sometimes lauded, for their inventiveness. But they were also identified, precisely because of their "curious" sonic novelty, as being far removed from what at the time was the sound-film mainstream. Estimable though these sonically adventurous films may seem today, in their time—like the theories that buttressed them—they had very little influence.

* * *

Remembering cinema's not-so-long-ago "good old days," René Clair was chagrined when in 1929 he witnessed London filmgoers emerging from theaters not in a state of "delightful numbness" but, rather, in a state of arousal that presumably had something to do with the lively musical content of their just-experienced films. With this, although doubtless without knowing it, Clair was rather precisely identifying what Hollywood producers of the time perceived to be the tastes of their audiences. As the Soviet theorists predicted would be the case, once fascination with "illusions . . . of talking people" had passed, Hollywood moved quickly to "photographed performances of a theatrical sort," and in terms of content the first round of these "photographed performances" had much in common with attractions associated with the music hall.

Potamkin's advice to "hide the orchestra" would indeed be heeded, but not until ca. 1932–3, when Hollywood began to move toward a consistent mode of production that would eventually come to be known as the "classical" style. As will be explained later in this chapter, midway along the path that led to the long-lived classical-style "the orchestra" was not so much hidden as eliminated altogether. Before that transitional stage, however, the sound film's "orchestra" was as much in the foreground as were the movements and vocalizations of its featured performers.

Whether in England, Germany, France, the United States, or anywhere else in the world, film audiences in general ca. 1929–30 were not much interested in "artistic" treatments of sound and music. Especially as the realities of a worldwide economic depression began to set in, what audiences cared most about—what they were willing to pay for, repeatedly—was escapist entertainment. At least during the sound film's first few years, that entertainment was richly musical.

The Spread of Sound

Another point in the sound-film myth that warrants revision concerns the actual speed with which cinema culture in general—not just Hollywood but film industries worldwide, and not just production facilities but exhibition venues—managed the change.

Relatively speaking, the adaptation to sound film was indeed swift, at least in part because of the timing of the development of sound-film technology vis-à-vis the economic climate of the late 1920s. On the coincidence of scientific achievement with a prosperous economy, film historian Kenneth MacGowan has astutely observed:

> It was doubly fortunate for the Hollywood studios that they had largely taken to sound before the depression began in the fall of 1929. The Wall Street boom and the quick success of the talkies enabled exhibitors to borrow and to pay off the money needed for new sound equipment; the cost per theater ran from $8,500 to $20,000. If the producers had waited till October 26, 1929—as they

Figure 6.2 Billboard advertising Al Jolson in Warner Bros.' *The Jazz Singer*, 1927.
© ArenaPal/Topham/The Image Works.

might well have done except for Warner Brothers and Fox—sound would have been impossible for ten more years; and receiverships would have come to Hollywood quite a time before 1932.[51]

Sound film came fast, but the transition did not happen overnight. Even if, hypothetically speaking, it had been the case that every single person on the face of the globe had in an instant been turned into a true believer in the sound film, it remained that individual filmmakers had to acquire the necessary physical equipment and then produce—after first pondering how such things might be conceived—marketable sound-film properties. For hopeful exhibitors, excluding those lucky few whose big-city venues had been designated as showcases, it remained that embracing the new sound film meant filling out an application and then waiting until they could be paid a visit by properly licensed technicians. Obviously, all of this—the making of sound films and the preparation of exhibition spaces that could accommodate sound films—took some time.

As early as February 1927, five Hollywood studios (MGM, Paramount, Universal, First National, and Producers Distributing Corporation) signed an agreement to the effect that they would *en masse* decide upon a single method of sound-film production as soon as the dust had settled on the competition between Warner Bros.' sound-on-disc Vitaphone system and a new sound-on-film system, promoted by Fox, called Movietone.

Developed in conjunction with RCA and announced to the public in November 1926, just three months after the debut of Warner Bros.' *Don Juan*, the Movietone system was first demonstrated in January 1927 to an invited audience at Fox's New York studios; the film topics were a crying baby, a chirping canary, and songs performed by Frieda Hempel and Raquel Meller, but more significant than the films themselves was the announcement, made during the demonstration, that Fox had recently "granted the Vitaphone Corporation licenses under its patent and patent applications and the right to use its device."[52] The first public showing of a Movietone product took place at New York's Roxy Theater in May 1927; it was notable for its precise synchronization of sound and image, but it "did not by any means stop the show or cause audible comment," for the brief newsreel-like film featured nothing more than a drill team at the West Point military academy, and its sonic component involved only "trumpet signals, orders by the drill master, and a speech by an army official."[53] Much more impressive was the Movietone program that Fox offered on September 25, 1928, at the Carthay Circle Theater in Los Angeles; along with a newsreel featuring United States president Herbert Hoover and yachtsman Thomas Lipton, the bill of fare included an address by playwright George Bernard Shaw, a vaudeville comedy routine, and a full-length film— a music-related romance—titled *Mother Knows Best*.[54]

Also impressive, two months later, was an entertainment that used a sound-on-film system that was similar to Movietone but which actually was a variation on the Phonofilm technology developed early in the decade by Lee de Forest. This was *Steamboat Willie*, the third of Walt Disney's animated cartoons to feature the character Mickey Mouse but the first to use a tightly synchronized soundtrack.[55] "It is an ingenious piece of work with a good deal of fun," wrote a reviewer for the *New York Times* after the November 18, 1928, premiere; "it growls, whines, squeaks and makes various other sounds that add to its mirthful quality."[56]

Although Vitaphone and Movietone would be in competition for a few more years, there was little debate as to how sound recorded by one system or the other would be shared with members of a theater audience. Vitaphone used sound recorded on discs; Movietone used sound recorded, photographically, on the edge of standard filmstrips. But both systems used electric microphones, and—significantly—for playback they both used the amplifiers and loudspeakers developed by Western Electric.

With consolidation of sound-film playback technology fast becoming the norm, the more or less official transformation of the American film industry, and with it the international film industry, occurred on May 15, 1928. It was on that date that MGM, Paramount, and United Artists simultaneously contracted with Electrical Research Products, Inc. (ERPI)—the Western Electric subsidiary established to handle the licenses for AT&T's sound-film patents—for the same equipment that was already being used with considerable commercial success by Warner Bros. and Fox.[57] The contract involved not only the acquisition of cameras and sound-recording devices for use on the studio lots; it also involved the installation of amplification systems in all the theatrical venues owned by these studios.

*   *   *

For the musicians who constituted these theaters' orchestras, this was not good news. Naturally, they resisted. Less than a month after the above-mentioned studios signed their contract with ERPI, the American Federation of Musicians (AFM) at their convention in Louisville, Kentucky, prepared for serious battle. On June 29, 1928, union president Joseph N. Weber issued a statement that informed Hollywood that the AFM "had established a war chest of $1,500,000 to prevent the introduction of recorded music into movie theaters." The AFM had no quarrel with the sound film *per se*, Weber said, but only with the use of amplification equipment "as a substitute for vocal and orchestral music."[58]

Just as *The Jazz Singer* was opening in Los Angeles—at Christmastime, 1927—a writer for that city's leading newspaper reported: "At the present time, there are 250 [American] theaters with Vitaphone in operation, and 100 more awaiting installation— a great percentage of them on the Pacific Coast."[59] As the musicians' union saw it, this was an understatement. In an effort to enlist the Chicago local as an opposition force, the AFM's Weber in July 1928 declared that while to date only 200 American movie theaters had been wired for sound "*1,000* more were planning to install sound equipment."[60]

In the face of this, public expressions of protest by AFM members were mounted not just in Chicago but also in such cities as St. Louis, Milwaukee, Detroit, New Orleans, Philadelphia, Pittsburgh, and Baltimore, and occasionally the demonstrations involved members of the actors' union (the Actors' Equity Association). On September 3, 1928, the Chicago local—led by James Petrillo, soon to be AFM president—instigated a strike against more than 250 Chicago theaters; a few days later the exhibitors and the AFM reached a settlement according to which the city's forty-five or so largest theaters, regardless of their actual needs, would for the next few years each maintain a staff of at least four musicians. Petrillo's claims of triumph, writes film historian Preston J. Hubbard, were based simply "on the AFM's not being completely annihilated from the battlefield. It was a Pyrrhic victory of the most dismal sort."[61]

Just a month before the September 1928 strike in Chicago, the entertainment newspaper *Variety* estimated that of the 75,000 or so musicians then employed in American

105

movie theaters, two thirds of them were likely to be displaced by "canned music."[62] Any optimism that might be read into that prediction is likely due to *Variety*'s belief that theaters, at least in the larger cities, would continue the exhibition practice established during the heyday of silent film and preface their on-screen feature presentations with vaudeville-style "live" entertainment. While that conviction perhaps seems logical in the context of the still-booming economy of August 1928, it seems quite absurd if projected forward to the situation that followed the stock-market crash of October 1929.

Whereas in the summer of 1928 the AFM nervously predicted that some 1,200 American theaters would soon be wired for sound, by December 1929 the number of American venues that had invested in the conversion in fact was close to 9,000.[63] At the end of 1929, nevertheless, 10,000 American theaters—more than half the total—did not have sound equipment, and a year later "almost one-fourth of all theaters in the United States still could present only silent films."[64] Almost all of these, it should be stressed, were small theaters in small towns, and the reason for their not installing sound equipment had nothing to do with aesthetics but simply with the fact that in the depressed economic climate they could not afford the cost of conversion. Even in 1933 a small percentage of American theaters exhibited only silent films; it was not until 1935 that the last of these went out of business.[65]

Knowing that a large number of American theaters had still not converted to sound, Hollywood in 1929 released 175 feature-length silent films. But all of these were "silent" versions of films that were being released in conjunction with some sort of sonic component. Hollywood's sound films from 1929 included seventy-five that followed the model of *Don Juan* and featured recorded musical scores but no recorded dialogue; the 1929 output also included ninety-five sound films that followed the model of *The Jazz Singer* and featured recorded scores interrupted only occasionally by dialogue or diegetic musical performance. But these numbers (which added together almost equal the number of purely "silent" releases) pale in comparison with those for feature-length films in which every bit of dialogue was recorded. In 1929 Hollywood released 175 films that in one way or another maintained a relationship with silent-film practice; in sharp contrast, during the same year it released 355 films that clearly fall into the category of "talkies."[66]

A mere four months after the start of the so-called Great Depression, an editorial in the *New York Times* noted, regrettably, that "nearly all of those [musicians] who formerly found employment in [movie] theaters are now out of work."[67] The layoff of musicians was not limited to the United States. In September 1930—by which time the film industry's conversion to sound was virtually a *fait accompli*[68]—the relatively low number of "unemployed men and women in all of France" was suddenly increased when "500 French musicians were thrown out of work as a result of installation of talking-picture apparatus in the cinemas where they were employed."[69] While there are scarce available data on the sound film's effect on the employment of cinema musicians worldwide, it seems likely that what occurred worldwide was similar to the documented displacement in France and the United States.

* * *

Theater musicians' resistance to the sound film, however much it amounted to, was by and large of no avail. Having heard about the sound film, audiences almost everywhere wanted to experience it for themselves, and the companies that controlled the technology were happy to oblige. In June–July 1930 a conference in Paris brought together representatives of Western Electric (which developed, and thus controlled, the requisite equipment), the Radio Corporation of America (which manufactured the equipment), most of the major Hollywood studios (who by this time had become quite expert at using the equipment), and Germany's Tobis-Klangfilm company (which still held certain patent rights to the sound-on-film technology). After a month of secretive discussion, the three hardware groups—with considerable input from the prolific American filmmakers —in effect established an international cartel whose rules specified not just the sharing of any new technical developments but also the charging of a handsome royalty fee for every single film made using the licensed sound-film technology.

Legal wrangling, instigated for the most part by the Hollywood studios, in fact continued until 1932, but this proved a relatively minor wrinkle. For all intents and purposes, by the middle of 1930 "the economic struggle [was] over," as film historian Douglas Gomery writes, and at least theoretically the worldwide "diffusion of sound seemed to be complete."[70] Anticipating that this would be the case, over the course of 1929–30 ERPI recruited, trained, and then sent far and wide virtually an army of eager salesmen. Thus "the expanding wave [of sound-film technology] migrated far beyond its country of origin, and the expansion did not stop until a global empire of sound was constructed. From Fiji to Spain, rural New Zealand to the streets of Tokyo and Calcutta, the arrival of talkie technology was heralded with banners, signs, and parades."[71]

Released in June 1929, Hitchcock's *Blackmail* (produced by British International Pictures) is often cited as England's first sound film. In fact, *Blackmail* had been preceded in March 1929 by *The Crimson Circle* (a British Sound Film Productions re-issue, fitted with English dialogue, of the 1928 German-made silent feature *Der Rote Kreis*) and *The Clue of the New Pin* (a British Lion production utilizing the sound-on-disc Photophone system) and in May 1929 by *Black Waters* (an all-talkie film shot entirely in Hollywood but produced by the British and Dominion Film Corporation).[72]

Germany's first sound film, and likely the first sound film made anywhere in Europe, was *Ich küsse ihre Hand, Madame*, a sound-on-film effort (made with the Dutch-German Tobis system based on the Tri-Ergon patent) that featured no dialogue but, rather, a continuous score and a few minutes of operetta-style singing by tenor Richard Tauber. *Ich küsse ihre Hand, Madame* was released in January 1929; it was followed in September by *Das Land ohne Frauen* (a Tobis-Klangfilm production with dialogue in about a quarter of its duration), in October by *Atlantik* (an "all-talkie" film co-produced with British International Pictures and, in fact, shot at the Elstree studio in England), and in November by *Dich hab ich geliebt* (an "all-talkie" made entirely in Germany by Aafa-Film).[73] Austria's entry into the sound-film market seems to have been made with a "talkie" (released in August 1929 by Eagle Film-Ottoton Film) titled *G'schickten aus der Steiermark*.[74]

In France, the first sound film—released early in October 1929—was the Epinay studio's *Le Collier de la reine*, originally made as a silent film but then retrofitted (by means of the sound-on-film Tobis system) with a continuous score and just a bit of dialogue. Later in October 1929 French audiences experienced *Les Trois masques*, a "talkie" produced by the Pathé-Natan studio but shot (as had been the case with Germany's *Atlantik*) at England's Elstree facilities. And a month later they had *La Route est belle*, a "talkie" produced by Braunberger-Richebé but also shot at Elstree.[75]

It is tempting here to offer just a summary statement, to note simply that elsewhere in the world filmmakers, and their audiences, were as interested in the possibilities of the sound film as were their counterparts in the United States and western Europe.[76] Such a synopsis would not be inaccurate, but it would hardly convey the impact of the new sound-film technology. At least a few more details, presumably, will demonstrate the sound film's seismic force.

As early as October 1929 Sweden had a "talkie" titled *Konstgjorda Svensson*. Using a sound-on-disc system, Poland had the music-accompanied *Moralność pani Dulskiej* in March 1930 and seven months later a "talkie" titled *Niebezpieczny romans*.[77] At around the same time, in October 1930, audiences in Italy were treated to a music-laced "talkie" called *La Canzone dell'amore*. In 1930 sound films, most of them to a large extent "talkies," were produced in Czechoslovakia, Denmark, Greece, Romania, Belgium, Canada, Brazil, Cuba, the Philippines, and Australia.[78] The Soviet Union's first sound films were *Entuziazm*, an "experimental" film without dialogue released in the spring of 1931, and *Zemlya zhazhdet*, a re-issue, with added music and sound effects, of a silent film from the year before.[79] In 1931 sound films were also being made in Hungary, Norway, Finland, Portugal, Turkey, Argentina, Mexico, and (with dialogue in Afrikaans) South Africa. Audiences in 1932 experienced the first sound films produced in Spain, Egypt, and (with dialogue in English) Ireland; in 1933 the Netherlands jumped onto the sound-film bandwagon, and a year later it was joined by Bulgaria, Chile, and (with dialogue in French) Morocco.

Although throughout the 1930s Japan sustained the tradition, borrowed from the *bunraku* puppet theater, of exhibiting films with live narrations,[80] the country nevertheless had sound-on-disc "talkies" (*Taii no musume* and *Furusato*) as early as 1929.[81] The first Chinese sound film—produced in Shanghai, with dialogue in Mandarin—was the 1930 feature-length "talkie" *Gēnǚ hóng mǔdān*; the first sound films from Hong Kong, with dialogue in Cantonese, were 1933's *Sha zai dongfang* and *Liang xing*,[82] and in 1935 Korea entered the sound-film market with *Chunhyangjeon*. India's first sound film, released in September 1930, was a mere "short" involving the addition of a sung performance to a clip from the 1928 silent feature *Madhuri*. Catering to a huge and linguistically diversified audience, the Indian film industry followed up in 1931 with such music-filled "talkies" as *Alam Ara* (in Hindi-Urdu), *Kalidas* (mostly in Tamil, with some parts in Telugu), *Jamai Sasthi* (in Bengali), and *Bhakta Prahlada* (all in Telugu); in 1932 with *Ayodhyecha Raja* and *Sant Tukaram* (both in Marathi), *Narsimha Mehta* (in Gujarati), and *Kalava* (entirely in Tamil); in 1933 with *Dukhtar-e-loor* (in Persian); in 1934 with *Sathi Sulochana* and *Bhakta Dhruva* (in Kannada); in 1935 with *Joymati* (in Assamese) and *Pind di Kuri* (in Punjabi); and in 1936 with *Sita Bibaha* (in Oriya).[83]

Each of these countries that in the early 1930s gravitated toward the sound film of course had a unique culture, and these many unique cultures were manifest—in one way or another—in the approaches taken by the native filmmakers not just to sound film but to narrative cinema as a whole. In the early 1930s, too, each country that fancied the sound film was in a unique situation vis-à-vis a depressed global economy and, especially in Europe and East Asia, political-military posturing that would lead within just a few years to the outbreak of a second world war. Almost every film historian who has seriously addressed the fast international spread of the sound film has noted that, for various and complex reasons, the new medium developed here and there in markedly different ways. To generalize is foolish, the historians say, and the admonition is especially forceful when it comes from those whose careers have been invested in detailing the film culture of one particular nation.

Almost always, though, the film historians *do* generalize. And almost always their generalizations convey the story that film culture worldwide, no matter how strongly established indigenous traditions might have been, in the early 1930s rather quickly adjusted to the norms being set by Hollywood. Sensitively aware of the enormous variety in film style worldwide, Charles O'Brien in a recent book on the spread of sound-film technology at first seems to dismiss a vintage conclusion (drawn by Arthur Knight) to the effect that with the coming of sound "the stylistic differences that distinguished a French or Russian film from a Hollywood film during the silent era virtually disappeared."[84] But then O'Brien grants: "Although film-historical scholarship has evolved considerably in the half-century since Knight wrote his survey, few film historians today would dispute his claim regarding world cinema's post-conversion sameness."[85]

Chapter 7

HOLLYWOOD'S EARLY SOUND
FILMS, 1928–33

Eventually a man will come along who can combine the screen, the
drama and music into one harmonious whole. Today, nine-tenths of
our directors—and I don't care how expert they may be at camera
angles or dialogue—are "tone deaf."

William Axt, 1931[1]

The "sameness" of international films after the conversion to sound resulted at least in
part from the simple fact that both during and after the transition-to-sound period, as
had been the case throughout the 1920s, Hollywood collectively issued far more films
than did the film industry of any other country.

Audiences around the world, generally speaking, were happy to patronize films made
by their compatriots, and in many countries the governments not just supported but
subsidized the making of such films. But not even the largest European industries—those
in England, France, and Germany—could generate enough films to supply a large
domestic audience with a variety of new attractions week after week. And so the theater
managers relied heavily on foreign-made products; during the heyday of the silent film,
at least ninety percent of the films shown anywhere in Europe were imports, and by far
the largest number of these imports came from the United States.[2] When British
filmmakers, as quoted in the previous chapter, opined in 1928 that the "talkies" might
mean "the end of American film dominance," their hope was rooted in the bitter
knowledge that for at least a decade their own efforts had been not necessarily outshone
but certainly outnumbered by the products of Hollywood.

Having as it did a firm grip on the international market for silent film, and depending
as it did, in 1929, on overseas distribution for as much as forty percent of its profits,[3]
Hollywood was well aware of the challenges it took on with the quick switch to sound
films. Adapting a silent film for distribution in a country where the language was
somehow "foreign" involved the simple substitution, easily done in an editing room, of
one set of intertitles for another. Adapting a sound film whose main attraction was
spoken or sung words was enormously more problematic.

For a while not just Hollywood but also the major studios in France and Germany
experimented with the making of sound films in linguistic variants. Indeed, early in 1930
Paramount established a facility in Joinville, France—six miles outside of Paris—for the
sole purpose of completely remaking its sound-film products with European casts, and
by the summer of that year a number of other Hollywood studios were using the Joinville

110

facility "on a 24-hour-a-day schedule" to create "talkies" in as many as twelve different languages.[4]

The impracticalities of reproducing, again and again, with casts of various linguistic orientations, foreign language versions of what in essence were singular filmic properties quickly proved obvious.[5] And so Hollywood and the leading European film industries also engaged in the practice of "dubbing," by which a picture would be filmed with just a single cast of actors but before release in one foreign country or another would have its dialogue segments replaced by spoken translations in the appropriate language. Before the development, ca. 1932–3, of audio mixing technology that allowed for the recording of separate tracks for dialogue, sound effects, and music, "dubbing" meant wreaking havoc on whatever sonic integrity might have been achieved in the initial recording. It also meant the complete jettisoning of all the arguably significant non-linguistic vocal noises—gasps, laughs, moans, and so on—that might have been generated by the original cast's possibly star-quality thespians. Still, "dubbing" a film with the voices of heard-but-not-seen actors was far less expensive than restaging an entire film with a fully costumed photogenic cast.

In some cases, "dubbing" was a governmental mandate. Upon his rise to dictatorial power in 1929, for example, Benito Mussolini declared that the *only* language acceptable in his country's movie theaters would be Italian, and so imported films were either dubbed or retrofitted with intertitles and presented as old-fashioned silent films. Attempting to squelch separatist movements whose languages included Basque, Catalonian, and Galican, Francisco Franco issued a similar declaration in Spain, but not until his revolutionary forces seized control in 1936. At least in part for political reasons, the "dubbing" of foreign-language films was also favored in France and—especially—in Germany.[6] Regardless of the motivation, the practice of "dubbing" foreign films was most widespread in the countries where the common language was French, Italian, German, or Spanish. Elsewhere, distributors of imported films—and doubtless encouraged by the makers of those films—opted for a method of translation that was far less expensive than either "foreign language versions" or "dubbing."

Although during the early years of the sound film the press tended to refer to this method generally as "subtitling,"[7] in fact the printed translations appeared in a variety of formats relative to the screen image. The most common format, between 1929 and 1931, was similar to what had been standard for silent films; verbal material in the appropriate language appeared not below the screen but at its center, in the form of intertitles shown in advance of the scenes whose dialogue they translated or, more often, merely summarized. More theatrically effective, but more cumbersome and thus less common, was the format in which translations were displayed—by means of a second projector running simultaneous with the one that conveyed the sound film—either alongside the main screen or, literally as *sub*titles, at the screen's bottom edge. Aside from a few early experiments, the practice by which translations were actually printed on the filmstrips was not generally adopted until the late 1930s.[8]

Having the most to gain from international distribution of sound films, Hollywood, with its many competing studios, attempted other creative solutions to the language problem. Some films were altered not at all but upon their foreign release were supplemented, following a model that had been established for decades in opera houses that presented works only in their original languages, by booklets in which printed versions of the spoken dialogue appeared alongside translations. Other films were shot again and again, always using their original casts but each time with the dialogue spoken—after hasty phonetic memorization—in a different presumably marketable language. Still others were simply subjected to drastic editing, along the lines of a ca. 1929 Paramount interoffice memo that mandated: "We take out the dialogue, retain the dance numbers, and then synchronize the entire picture to a musical score."[9]

* * *

In the end, "subtitling" won out, and not just because studio accountants celebrated its cost-effectiveness or because sophisticated film critics felt that this method alone respected the directors' original concepts. Thinking along the same lines as did the early champions of the "sound film" (as opposed to the mere "talkie"), the Hungarian film theorist Béla Balázs surely had high aesthetics in mind when he wrote, in 1948, that "in the present-day sound film we understand the words" yet realize that "their meaning is unimportant;" far more important "is the tone in which [the words] are said: the cadence, the emphasis, the timbre, the husky resonance, which are not intentional, not conscious."[10] But movie audiences worldwide were coming to the same conclusion, for reasons not intellectual but simply visceral.

After scrambling frantically to find ways by which to communicate the verbal content of its new sound films to international audiences, Hollywood reminded itself that the enormous and arguably universal appeal of its products all along had to do not so much with the literary quality of screenplays as with the performances of individual actors and actresses who brought those screenplays to life. Whereas the movie stars of silent film earned their status by means of what they accomplished with their bodies and faces alone, the emerging stars of the sound film scored their successes not just with what they did physically but also with what they did vocally. As was evidenced again and again by box-office receipts within the United States, there was obviously something "special" about the way Al Jolson sang, about the way Greta Garbo sighed, about the way James Cagney and Joan Crawford spoke. The movie stars' voices, as much as their visages, were inimitable; to "overdub" them merely for the sake of translating whatever words issued from the performers' mouths, Hollywood quickly realized, would be a foolish compromise.

Contrary to what British filmmakers hopefully anticipated as they carped about objectionable accents in the voices of certain screen performers, the new sound film did not result in the end of "American dominance" of the international film industry. The new sound film resulted, rather, in a quick ascendance of Hollywood products to heights much greater than had been experienced during the silent-film era. Quite aside from the simple fact that its sound films vastly outnumbered and were more efficiently distributed than sound films produced in any other country, Hollywood—by virtue of its critical mass of technical talent and its close interaction with the developers and manufacturers of sound-film equipment—had a clear technological advantage over any and all of its international competitors.

In the early years of the sound film, audiences worldwide experienced far more products from Hollywood than from anywhere else, and thus those audiences soon grew accustomed to Hollywood's collective and commercially driven norms. Filmmakers worldwide may have preferred to cultivate nationalistic styles, but even on their home ground they remained in a small minority, and even the most defiantly non-commercial of them, although they were prone to reject Hollywood aesthetics, nonetheless were eager to adopt Hollywood technique. And this meant that the international film industry —by and large, and more or less quickly—imitated whatever Hollywood did vis-à-vis film music.

Hollywood Musical Practice

For theater musicians and for Americans in many other walks of life, the economic situation that persisted throughout the 1930s was grim. But the Great Depression is coincident with the American film industry's years of greatest prosperity (any irony seen in this will likely be amplified when one considers the difficult straits—to be detailed in Chapter Nine—in which Hollywood found itself during America's booming economy of the 1950s).

In January 1930, when the nation as a whole was still dazed by the crash of the stock market, the *Los Angeles Times* reported on how wonderful things seemed to be in Hollywood:

> Approximately 30,000 persons are now regularly employed in the studios of Hollywood. This figure has never been equaled before, even in the days when there were twice the studios there are now and almost twice as many pictures being made.
>
> These studio employees have been paid, within the past year, approximately $82,000,000, with the assurance that figure will be materially increased this year.
>
> The production budget for the industry as a whole during the 1929–30 season will exceed $165,000,000—another record-breaker in motion-picture statistics.[11]

Reflecting on the position of the film industry relative to the economy in general, the reporter noted that

> since the advent of talking pictures capital investment [in Hollywood] has been increased by $500,000,000. During the reign of the silent film the peak of investment approximated $200,000,000, which means that the total invest-ment has jumped almost 25 per cent in little more than a year. Such a rise is phenomenal. From the ninth industry of the nation motion pictures take their place now as the fourth, with the possibility of their ranking third in importance and extent, when the field of sound has run its course.[12]

"At the present time," the reporter observed, "there are approximately twenty-six operating studios in Hollywood," most of which "are utilizing sound and dialogue in many if not in all of their productions." Significantly, the reporter also observed: "Every studio now employs a large orchestra."[13]

*   *   *

What was the function, in the early 1930s, of the "large orchestra" on the payroll of every one of Hollywood's several dozen studios?

A simple answer would be that the orchestras served the studios in much the same way that other teams of employees did. Like teams of carpenters, painters, and other skilled craftsmen, the orchestras—with their associated arrangers, composers, and conductors—did whatever was asked of them by the executives assigned to particular films for the sole purpose of making those films palatable to as large an audience as possible. The studio orchestra was surely an expensive new element in the complex Hollywood studio "system" that had been steadily and profitably evolving since the years following World War I. But it did not, in essence, change the nature of what Hollywood produced and marketed. Citing David Bordwell's 1985 account as the first to make a point that is perhaps obvious to today's student of film history, Donald Crafton reminds us that both the dialogic and musical aspects of the early sound film, "far from disrupting traditional practice," made the traditional practice "even more entrenched."[14] Cast in purely economic terms, the obviously successful traditional practice had to do with the quick production and efficient distribution of filmic commodities that were entertaining enough to satisfy the immediate expectations of any given audience and at the same time compelling enough to entice a more generalized audience to return—again and again—to the movie houses. To that end, the orchestras simply—in a word—contributed.

A more complicated but more accurate answer to the question entails the markedly different ways in which the studio orchestras, over a span of just a few years, contributed to their employers' products. The shifts in approach, initiated by one studio or another but always quickly taken up by the industry as a whole, were in fact quite drastic. Indeed, it seems safe to say that between 1929 and 1933—that is, during the "transition" period whose boundaries might be defined, on one end, by Hollywood's general acceptance of the previously experimental sound film and, on the other end, by the dawn of Hollywood's so-called classical-style—the nature of film music changed more frequently, and more radically, than at any other time in the art form's history.

1929–30

Triggered by audience response to the recorded song performances by Al Jolson in *The Jazz Singer*, the first wave of sound films featured as many musical "numbers" as could be squeezed into the ca. ninety-minute time-span of a feature film.

The musical "numbers," obviously, did not come free of charge. For pre-existing songs that it wanted to include in films, Hollywood had to pay handsomely both to ASCAP (the American Society of Composers, Authors, and Publishers) and, for "mechanical reproduction" rights, to the songs' various publishers. It did not require rocket scientists to figure out that considerable savings could be had—and large profits might be made—if the studios themselves owned the copyrights. With those dual ends in mind, Warner Bros. in January 1929 strategically purchased the large New York-based music publisher M. Witmark and Sons and within the next several months acquired more than a half-dozen other imprints.[15] Before long, Warner Bros.' new Music Publishers Holding Company controlled virtually *all* the older but still viable songs that Hollywood in general might wish to include in its films.

Familiar songs of course appealed to the movie-going audience, and thus the other Hollywood studios willingly—albeit perhaps begrudgingly—paid Warner Bros. for the use of this material. But just as appealing to the audience, Hollywood realized almost in

Figure 7.1 Film images with their accompanying "push-pull" soundtrack, ca. 1934.
© NMeM/Kodak Collection/The Image Works.

an instant, were fresh songs. Whereas artistic-minded filmmakers in France, Germany, and elsewhere might have regarded the sound film as a medium for aesthetic experimentation, the more commercially minded Hollywood studios regarded the sound film in large part as a means for promoting brand new musical commodities—often presented in the form of a filmic "theme song"—whose potentially lucrative publication rights were controlled by the studios that commissioned them as "works for hire."

As early as December 1928, more than a month before Warner Bros. inked its deal with Witmark, the *Los Angeles Times* ran an article that described a veritable invasion of Hollywood by Tin Pan Alley songwriters. Among the tunesmiths already servicing the "talking and singing pictures," the reporter writes, are Irving Berlin, Billy Rose, Nacio Herb Brown, Jules Buffano, Arthur Freed, Fred Fisher, David Mendoza, William Axt, Archie Gottler, Sidney Mitchell, Con Conrad, William Kernell, Dave Stamper, Walter Donaldson, Wolfe Gilbert, Richard E. Whiting, Leo Robin, Louis Silvers, and Sterling Sherwin. "One way or another," she says, these songwriters "have gone to work for the movies." She explains:

> Every talkie that goes out must have its theme song synchronized with the film. Where before a theme song could be enjoyed only in the larger cities where good orchestral accompaniment was available, now it belongs to the picture and can be heard in any theater where there is sound-reproducing equipment. . . .
>
> Hit songs used to come out of the big musical shows in New York. As the shows went on the road, the songs traveled with them and their popularity spread.
>
> Hit songs now are coming from the movies and where thousands heard them before, millions of people are hearing and humming the new melodies within the space of a very few months.[16]

In some cases (for example, in MGM's *The Hollywood Revue*, released in November 1929), the "new melodies," along with old ones, were simply presented one after another as if they were items on a traditional vaudeville program. In other cases (perhaps most notably the same studio's *The Broadway Melody*, released in February 1929 and advertised as the first-ever "all-talking, all-singing, all-dancing" film), the bounty of musical "numbers" was cleverly worked into a narrative plot.

The Broadway Melody was a huge success, winning not just an Academy Award in the "best film" category but also a net profit of $1.6 million.[17] The film's title song, still familiar today, certainly functioned as a theme song, but its usage veered significantly from the norm. Whereas the typical theme song ca. 1928–9 was introduced in extra-diegetic fashion during the opening credits and then liberally sprinkled throughout the sound track in diegetic as well as extra-diegetic variants, "The Broadway Melody" likely owes its success to the fact that its relatively few post-credits reprises were always diegetic and always related to the plot's peak moments.

Interviewed shortly after the film's premiere, Nacio Herb Brown, who composed all of the music for *The Broadway Melody*, stated that director Harry Beaumont "did not want us [Brown and lyricist Arthur Freed] to write theme numbers. He wanted songs that carried the story and action beyond the power of the spoken word. He did not simply fit songs into his picture for the sake of having music."[18] Brown was convinced

Figure 7.2 June 8, 1929: Songwriting partners, composer Nacio Herb Brown (1896–1964) (left) and lyricist Arthur Freed (1894–1973). They worked together on *The Broadway Melody*, the first "all-talking, all-singing, all-dancing" film. (Photo by John Kobal Foundation/Getty Images.)

that with its apparently unprecedented concentration on dramatically relevant diegetic music, *The Broadway Melody* "left all other sound productions with so-called theme songs far behind." According to the article's anonymous author, Brown strongly expressed the opinion that "musical accompaniments and theme songs that serve only as an interpolation or background in sound pictures of today are as passé as the thrilling chase sequences that chilled audiences in the earliest efforts of the silent films."[19]

These bold statements, as it turned out, were premature.

* * *

On the same day that it carried the interview with Brown, the *Los Angeles Times* ran a brief item describing the vast quantities of hand-written music regularly required by the fifty-piece orchestra that Hugo Riesenfeld led at Paramount; citing Riesenfeld, who perhaps exaggerated, the reporter noted that "the average talkie in feature length, which is from six to eight reels, requires some 200 musical numbers."[20] David Mendoza gave a slightly smaller estimate, writing that "the average motion picture that is synchronized requires the blending together of between a hundred and a hundred and fifty different musical numbers."[21] While some of these "numbers" were generic pieces that, following the model of the silent film, set moods or accompanied action, many of them were original compositions that identified particular characters and were played, often in the background, "whenever he or she appears upon the screen."[22]

In July 1929 a writer for the *Times* observed that the phrase "music in the movies" had lately taken on "an entirely new significance" and might mean "anything from a mere orchestral accompaniment of a picture, the repeated singing of a theme song, to the interpolation of something akin to an excellent concert hall program."[23] But a month later another writer for the same paper cynically noted that while there was indeed talk in Hollywood of using "high-quality" music in films, "for the most part the movie makers, with customary matter-of-factness, are concentrating their efforts on the vo-de-o-dough."[24] Significantly, though, he cited J.J. Robbins, head of the publishing firm that handled the songs for MGM's *The Broadway Melody*, as saying that "the theme-song for its own sake is a thing of the past":

It is generally agreed in the trade that the interpretive ballad stands the biggest chance of success—one closely allied with the nature and plot of the picture, and not dragged in by the heels, mixed-metaphorically speaking, and crammed down the public's throat.

The most essential item in popularizing a number is "spotting" it properly. This means that it must be played or sung at the [right] psychological moment in a film.[25]

The writer granted that, for the moment, the theme song still reigned supreme. He ended his report, nevertheless, on a note of optimism:

Ultimately, when the hubbub has died down, a corps of music specialists with a knowledge of dramaturgy and the exact requirements of the sound film, will be developed; and the motion picture, which has in music a sister art, will reach its full florescence.[26]

Furthering the idea that "music specialists" might be coming to the fore, still another writer for the *Los Angeles Times* in December 1929 submitted an article that suggested the creation not just of marketable theme songs but also of extra-diegetic accompaniments was fast approaching production-line efficiency:

Proving that type is still everything in the movies, regardless of the changes wrought by sound, film music is fast becoming a game of specialization.

Composers in the future will be cast according to their suitability of creating a certain kind of tune to fit a certain kind of scene, and for other peculiarly individual qualifications.

On this basis it will be possible to have compositions for the screen that are not the product of one man's talent and ability, but the combining of various talents and abilities under the one supervising spirit.[27]

The article quotes Nathaniel Finston, head of the music department at Paramount:

118

[T]here are many composers who are individualists. . . . They feel that they must create the whole work and doubtless there are many who can accomplish this in the suitable medium.

But there is a great difference in screen work. It is a difference oftentimes better understood by the industrialist than the artist. He knows that in a factory each man can specialize in doing something exceedingly well and will confine his efforts chiefly to that thing. . . .

[W]e are faced with an industrial equation in pictures and a need for skilled accomplishments in some special line. In other words, we must be able to hold the public's attention every minute that a film is going on. Each number must be a peak of effort, and each must fit a certain mood. We could secure war-like music from one man, who was expert in writing such music, and romantic music from another who was skilled in the penning of such music. By using the director as the co-ordinator of their efforts we can achieve a unified whole.[28]

In the first half of 1929, as is evidenced by the above-cited news item on Hugo Riesenfeld, Paramount and at least a few others of the Hollywood studios remained convinced that extra-diegetic music was wholly appropriate to the sound film. By the end of 1929, however, most of the studios—including Paramount—were using extra-diegetic music only in a film's title credits and in the minute or so that preceded the emphatic on-screen words "The End." But clearly at least some directors and producers, doubtless remembering the significant role that music had played in the silent film, were thinking about the possibilities of music that did not "belong" to the on-screen action but simply accompanied it. Indeed, the same article that features Finston's comments also notes that Ludwig Berger, director of Paramount's forthcoming *The Vagabond King*, "believes that the future lies in what he terms the 'music of character.'"[29]

A few months later, shortly after the February 1930 release of *The Vagabond King*,[30] the apparently prescient Berger was quoted again on the "original score of [the] future":

It is essential that we know the tools [i.e., the microphones and recording machines] with which we work before we proceed.

But more important artistically is the necessity of not overloading our scenes. Each individual "frame" on a spool of film contains a picture. This picture must be orchestrated as carefully as each moment in an opera, but in exactly the right proportion. To play the full complicated score of a Wagner opera would be unsound, both literally and figuratively, for it would give us one of two impressions: either that the screen was too small, or that the music was too "large."

To avoid such an impression, it became imperative to reduce the orchestral arrangement originally made by Rudolf Friml for "The Vagabond King." The melodies, of course, were unimpaired, and we were not permitted to rescore in any real measure; but we did learn what may be done with music in pictures. When we start building our own original scores, you will be amazed.

Strings, for example—the pure tone of strings—will lift love scenes to undreamed-of heights in the symphonic film of the future. The pensive sadness of the woodwinds will reach into our hearts. The full strength of the brasses—unaided by either strings or woodwinds—will exalt us with the fire and fury of life.[31]

119

Such extra-diegetic musical effects would indeed be attempted and accomplished, but not for another few years. Taking its cue from MGM's spectacular success with *The Broadway Melody* early in 1929, Hollywood in general over the next two seasons fairly reveled in the production of revues and musicals. Of the 562 feature-length films produced in Hollywood in 1929, seventy-five featured Broadway-style scores; of the 509 productions from 1930, more than a hundred fall clearly into the "musical" genre.[32]

Surveying the rosy scene in May 1930, Robert Crawford, executive in charge of music at both Warner Bros. and First International Pictures, boasted that

> more than 90 percent of the creative music of America is now being written in Hollywood. The home offices of the [publishing] companies are still in New York for business purposes, but all of the finest American music is now being written in connection with the screen.
>
> We have gathered here . . . the men who have been responsible for many of the operetta and musical-comedy hits of the past ten years—Sigmund Romberg, Oscar Hammerstein II, Jerome Kern and Otto Harbach, Oscar Strauss, Herbert Fields, Richard Rogers and Lorenz Hart, and a dozen song-writing teams.
>
> Hollywood's studios today encompass all the big names of contemporary music—Irving Berlin, George Gershwin, [Buddy] DeSylva and [Ray] Henderson, Nacio Herb Brown and many others.
>
> We are moving forward with tremendous strides, daily, weekly, monthly. There is no telling how far we will go, or how much music, as spread by talking pictures, will influence the lives of people throughout the world.[33]

On the ubiquitous "theme song" that had been disparaged as being seemingly "crammed down the public's throat," Crawford stated:

> There is no such thing as a theme song any more. Music is an integral part of a story. Pictures are [now] written with complete scores, and the music is of the highest operetta type. It is my own belief that it will not be long before we are producing music far greater in its sweep than grand opera, which has always been limited by the traditions of the stage.[34]

For the moment, however, this was just wishful thinking.

Up until the middle of 1930, the use of songs in films had proved to be attractive to audiences and thus lucrative to their publishers. But toward the end of the year a downturn in box-office revenue suggested that perhaps the public had finally had its fill of films packed to overflowing with songs. Attributing the idea to songwriters DeSylva, Henderson, and Brown, then on the staff at Fox, a reporter announced that "the future of music in pictures is certain, despite the gloomy predictions of producers who have nothing but failure to show for their efforts to combine melody and movies."[35] As it turned out, the future of music in pictures was decidedly uncertain.

1931

As noted, Hollywood produced more than a thousand feature-length films in 1929 and 1930, and almost two hundred of these could be described as "musical." In sharp contrast, of the 990 feature films produced in 1931 and 1932, "musical" films numbered only twenty-one.[36] Almost overnight, it seems, Hollywood's music boom went all but bust.

In May 1931 a feature writer for the *Los Angeles Times*, in a richly illustrated article headlined "Tin Pan Alley Says Good Bye," offered a light-hearted explanation for the abrupt shift in the public's taste and the film industry's response:

> Why did Tin Pan Alley, that blazed with sudden, brilliant mazdas, darken into a shadowy side-lane?
>
> Trail along, Ivy, and maybe we'll find out what put out the incandescents— why the song writers went back home to New York. Why the air that was stirred by frantic cries of "girl-curl . . . boy-coy-joy . . . love-dove" is becalmed.
>
> When the talkies first came [the songwriters] boomed, "It's Bonanza Time in Hollywood!" But their theme song became truly a "blues." It was repeated, with lugubrious emotion, by countless disappointed song-writers returning east, and was tacitly titled "Hello, Albuquerque! We Meet Again—So Soon!"[37]

After citing a dozen or so top-selling songs that had been created especially for films, the author—apparently having done some research—states with confidence that since the dawn of the sound film "the nine principal studios presented 1086 songs from the singing screen, MGM, Warner Bros. and First National leading." Not inaccurately, she writes: "The major companies bought outright, or acquired shares in, music-publishing concerns." But then, perhaps conflating songs and the generic "photoplay" music that was a holdover from the days of the silent film, she notes:

> In swanky new musical libraries, melody was card-indexed. Scores were classified alphabetically: fight, fire and fury music; cakewalk, college, children, chimes and circus airs. They didn't know that you don't placard music and order it in job-lots: animals, birds, seasons, war.
>
> They found out, though. All that rhythmic din gave us entertainment indigestion. We grew tired of wondering where Sally was, and sick of sunbeams, and ennuye with love defined to the moonlight-on-the-lake area of Rudy Vallee's murmuring glide.[38]

Conflation notwithstanding, the writer reports that lately the numbers of composers employed by the major studios had shrunk drastically:

> Of their fifty tune-setters, MGM retains only a couple. Fox's department of twenty-five has shrunk to a mere handful or less. Paramount's twelve are now three. Pathe holds none of the six once contracted. . . . One day's exodus included fifty option orphans.
>
> The majority returned to New York, a few turned actor, a minority hummed themselves into steady studio jobs.[39]

Those few who found steady studio jobs, the writer notes, were doing extremely well. For example, Erno Rapee, music supervisor at Warner Bros., was on the books for an annual salary of $150,000, and Rudolf Friml, on the composing staff of United Artists, was earning $4,000 per week. Nevertheless, the writer notes, by this point in time Hollywood's once-large cadre of songwriters had been for the most part decimated. According to the writer, George Gershwin, who "received $50,000 for his 'Rhapsody in Blue' number but only recently became personally involved with pictures," was one of the few Broadway composers still working on a film project.[40]

Toward the end of her always amusing and sometimes informative article on the sudden demise, early in 1931, of the music-filled sound film, the writer notes that critics in general objected not to music *per se* but to its treatment. The "presentations were lacking [in] cleverness," she writes, and they featured "a too determined repetition" of musical materials.[41] Nevertheless, she suggests that there is hope for the future. She quotes Victor Schertzinger, a composer who had been involved with silent films since 1915 and who in 1931 was on the staff at RKO:

> Our early attempts were abortive because we did not consider our medium sufficiently. They were as logical as an effort to film a novel unadapted, or a stage play on three sets from one camera position. The new music must be definite screen material, with the same qualities as a good movie story.[42]

And she concludes: "At every studio, an earnest consideration of music's renaissance is going on. [Music] is edging in again, tentatively."[43]

* * *

The entire content of the "Tin Pan Alley Says Good Bye" article, apropos of its headline, has to do with songs. The problem with the previous years' "musical" films centered on the inappropriate use—or over-use—of pop music commodities, the article suggests, and the proposed solution will involve songs better fitted into filmic plots. The article deals not at all with accompanimental music, which was indeed being used, albeit sparingly, in pictures at this time.

Vis-à-vis extra-diegetic music—or what at the time was often called "interpolated" music—an insightful discussion took place in the *Los Angeles Times* a few months before the breezy "Tin Pan Alley Says Good Bye" article appeared. It was prepared not by a feature writer but, rather, by one of the newspaper's film critics. Importantly, it offers not just the critic's own insights but also the opinions of several studio music directors. The writer points out that the song-filled film, for the moment, has gone severely out of fashion. Nevertheless, he says, there is still "the picture with music":

> There is a distinction here. Four musical leaders in Hollywood studios were unanimous, when consulted, in declaring that interpolated music, whether incidental or part of the action, is assuming more importance daily in their respective plants. The trick lies in applying it where it will do the most good.
>
> Music, points out Nathaniel Finston, able general of Paramount's West Coast clef forces, is too much a part of our lives to be ignored in our cinema. He recalls that in those halcyon days when he, along with Hugo Riesenfeld, Erno Rapee, David Mendoza, William Axt, and the late Josiah Zuro were arranging scores for New York's Capitols and Rialtos, these musical accompaniments were regarded as a good 50 per cent of the success of any picture. He asks who can

deny the enhancing power of the scores for such spectacles as "Way Down East," "The Birth of a Nation," "The Big Parade," and all the rest; and adds that all this was forgotten over night with the astounding discovery that voices could be made to come out of the mouths of babes. On that day, he says, the work of twenty years went for naught.

Recovery is only now beginning.[44]

Analyzing the differences between the audience's perception of "interpolated" music and film song, the critic astutely writes:

Summed up, these truths become self-evident:

A majority of filmgoers acknowledge their susceptibility to the influence of music accompaniment. They find it an emotional stimulus, tending to increase reaction to the scenes portrayed on the screen.

But the instant music is made the object of attention, and the visual movement halted for emphasis on the aural, the eye becomes fatigued, the ear conscious that it is listening to a mechanical reproduction.

This, I think, is the whole story of the success and failure of the musical movie.[45]

Significantly, the writer uses the term "underscore"—set off upon its first usage in quotation marks, which suggests the term is relatively new—as a synonym for "interpolated" or accompanimental music. He notes that Finston recently "used a 100 per cent musical 'underscore' for" *Fighting Caravans* and *Rango*.[46] He notes, however, that

[Finston] says that he is not altogether positive that a complete musical underscore is advisable for a talkie, certain episodes lending themselves better to silence; but he is convinced that no music at all is infinitely worse.[47]

The article reports that Warner Bros. and First National, "which have used underscores intermittently in talkies since their inception," will continue to do so. It cites Arthur Franklin, director of music at both studios, to the effect that "the usual 40 per cent underscore will be increased to 60 or 70 per cent in many forthcoming Vitaphones."[48] And it quotes Franklin in a cautionary statement:

We must be careful, however, not to "overload" an audience. As it is, the spectator can no longer relax at a talkie as he used to do in the silent days. It takes greater effort to listen than to look. And we cannot use music that is too familiar, or the hearer will lose track of the picture and concentrate on what [the music's] title is, and where he has heard it before.[49]

Referring to what seems to have been a major point of contention among Hollywood music executives, the author points out that MGM, in particular, "is apparently still opposed to any sort of music which has no 'legitimate' place in the film, believing in a 'literal' interpretation of the action, except in the case of a frankly musical picture like 'Jenny Lind' or 'The Rogue Song.' "[50] Despite MGM's policy, he notes, MGM music executive William Axt "sees no reason why dialogue should not have a musical obbligato." Regarding music that underscores dialogue, he quotes Axt on the importance of orchestration:

> Naturally, people resent an accompaniment that drowns out the dialogue. I know cases of arrangers using woodwinds in the upper register to accompany the actors' voices, when they ought to know that even one flute will do the dirty work. Nobody ever heard of strings in mid-register ruining a speech. It's all a matter of common sense.[51]

The article reports that, along with MGM, the Radio Pictures studio held firmly to the belief that music should *not* be used in films unless it somehow fits "logically" into the plot. In defense of this just announced and apparently rigid policy, the article quotes Radio Pictures music director Max Steiner:

> When music is found in Radio films, it will be secondary to the plot action and the movement of the story itself. Music will be largely incidental, and often atmospheric. It will not come into a picture from some mysterious source (the orchestra pit?) but by some logical, and, if possible, visual means—such as the turning-on of a radio or a phonograph in a scene, or a glimpse of an orchestra or chorus.[52]

Coming from Steiner, this emphasis on exclusively diegetic music is perhaps surprising. Many hands, of course, contributed to the development of the largely extra-diegetic score for the "classical-style" Hollywood film. But posterity would record that this type of score—with most of its music indeed coming from an arguably "mysterious" source quite removed from the world of the film's narrative—was almost single-handedly invented by Steiner. And the breakthrough would happen, according to many summaries of film-music history, within the next year or so.

1932

For all the publicity given to the songwriters' exit from Hollywood, at least some in the industry sustained hope that the once-popular musical film could be revived. Reporting on the movies from the perspective of the East Coast, in September 1931 a newspaper writer cautiously observed: "Musical picture production has been earnestly resumed in Hollywood studios. However, there will not be so many musicals as a year ago, nor will there be even half so much music."[53] With more fanfare, two months later a writer for one of the trade magazines turned out an article that bore the headline "Musical Pictures Are Here Again." It begins:

> A year ago Hollywood would have had a violent attack of the shudders if you had so much as mentioned musical pictures. Especially musical comedies or revues. "Musical pictures are OUT!" the movie magnates chorused. "The public simply won't have 'em. They may revive again in ten or fifteen years. But we doubt it." Everybody doubted it.[54]

But the situation, at least according to the studio publicists, was changing:

> Every single studio in Hollywood—except one—either has a musical picture in production or is getting one ready. And Universal admits that it is just waiting "to see what happens to the others." . . . Musicals, which everybody thought had gone forever, are coming back. In fact, they're here. THIS is the big comeback news of 1931.[55]

There were indeed a few musical films made late in 1931 and throughout 1932, but the "comeback" was hardly momentous. What was truly newsworthy in 1932 and early in 1933, although it was scarcely reported as such, was the convergence of a widespread acceptance of a film-music concept and a technological development that made realization of the concept easily feasible.

The concept—mentioned in the newspaper article quoted at length above, and actually a throwback to the days of the silent film—was that of the "underscore," that is, a musical score usually presented at a volume level *under* that of the dialogue, what today is generally known as extra-diegetic music, what at the time was called not just "underscore" but also accompanimental, interpolated, or background music. The technological development involved the audio console that allowed independently recorded tracks of music, dialogue, and sound effects to be mixed together, at whatever volume levels were deemed appropriate, and without seriously degrading audio quality, *after* editing of a film's visual elements had been completed.

Before the invention of such a console late in 1932, segments of film sound for the most part consisted only of whatever sounds—musical or otherwise—transpired within listening distance of one or more microphones. It was indeed possible to mix phonographically or optically recorded sounds, but this invariably meant playing the various recordings simultaneously over loudspeakers and then re-recording, with a single microphone, the real-time blend. Because the audio results were so poor, this method was rarely attempted. As film historian Barry Salt explains:

> If several microphones were being used to record sound for a shot, their signals were mixed directly before being recorded photographically on the sound negative in the sound camera, in electrical synchronization with the film camera. The mixing of a set of film sound tracks subsequent to their initial recording to give a final combined recording was very rare at the beginning of the thirties; the extra film recording stage introduced a perceptible loss of quality.[56]

Keenly aware of the audio problem, producers in the early years of the sound film focused their attention on dialogue and musical "numbers" that could be recorded in a single "take" within the acoustically optimal environs of the newly invented "sound stage." Thus, Salt further explains, "up to 1932 there was, roughly speaking, either dialogue or music on the sound track, but never both together unless they had been recorded simultaneously. Which they sometimes were."[57] But "by 1933 it was possible to mix a separately recorded music track with the synchronous dialogue track recording after the editing stage without audible loss of sound quality at the extra film recording stage, and from this point on 'background music' came to be used more and more frequently."[58]

That Hollywood was leaning toward "background music" is evidenced by newspaper accounts well in advance of the 1932–3 multi-track mixing console.[59] In June 1931, just a few months after Max Steiner publicly defended Radio Pictures' commitment to use only music that "logically" figured into a film's plot, the *Los Angeles Times* reported that in just six hours "Steiner and a group of musicians produced a studio music library with 10,000 feet of perfectly recorded music." The recorded material "ran practically the entire gamut of human emotions, furnishing thematic music for almost any action that might take place on the screen."[60] Two months later the same newspaper reported that

> "Underscoring," or interpolating musical backgrounds in talking pictures, which is coming more and more into vogue as the art is being perfected, is gradually bringing to the screen music as it was used with the good silent pictures, say musicians in the studios.
>
> Musical phrases chosen for their fitness to the dramatic theme they are to illustrate are "scored" into pictures, very softly so as not to interfere with dialogue, but to furnish a psychological background.[61]

In November 1931 the newspaper ran an interview with Phil L. Ryan, formerly a sales manager at Pathé and at the moment a producer of shorts for Paramount, who summarized the recent history of film music and then prognosticated for the future:

> The first sound subjects (one and two-reelers), more than three years ago, starred such musical celebrities as Giovanni Martinelli, Anna Case and Efrem Zimbalist. The very nature of sound pictures suggested good music, well edited to the demands of the then new medium, as being an integral part of the novel and advanced form of entertainment thrust on us by modern science.
>
> True to past motion-picture tradition, this was grossly overdone, even though it is to be considered that a new art was in the making, and that mistakes would naturally be made. After the musicals had come and gone—after Hollywood had been completely upset and had characteristically adapted herself to the radical change—and after a semblance of understanding had been reached as to what the true field of the talking screen really is, we are back today to the realization that, first, the screen is primarily a motion picture. Second, that, as such, silence is golden—and the basic principle of suspense must be builded [*sic*] on a firm foundation of well-designed sound effects. Third, that the fewer spoken words given the better.
>
> Music is basically the underlying feature or background of all sound. This is a scientific truth. Every sound has its tone and place in the scale. An overdose of anything will ruin a desired effect. Therefore, music is the keynote to the whole secret. Let us be guided accordingly. We do not need to be musicians to understand this.[62]

By early April 1932 the *New York Times* was observing that, after a brief period during which films featured almost no music at all, there now seemed to be two distinctly different scoring strategies at play in Hollywood:

> The cinema rarely does things half way. From the squeaky days of the audible when music was forced into each production with or without reason, pictures

126

overnight would not permit even the lilting warble of birds because "the public was off the song stuff." Again the tide has turned, with music playing a discreet but important part in many of the current productions.

But harmony is used differently than it was at first. It now takes two forms— either it appears as a symphonic or mood score on the sound track, separately or behind the dialogue, or in songs which form a definite part of the story and advance the plot and are spotted at reasonably correct points in the picture.

A dozen or so pictures now being made depend on music in one form or another. Other films with music are awaiting shipment to New York. Other productions are having songs or scores prepared for them.[63]

A sizeable portion of the article is devoted to an interview with Nacio Herb Brown, who reiterated his ideas on the effective use and placement of songs. Describing what he recently did for *A Woman Commands*, a joint production by Pathé and the newly formed RKO (the result of a merger of Radio Pictures with Keith and Orpheum) Brown said: "The best method is to use a short melody that people can remember. This appears early in the picture. Then later it shows up sung by a character. If possible, the tune is used again, even though in an obscure way before the final fade-out."[64]

Regarding what he terms "the symphonic method," the writer is not at all clear, and his list of examples conflates films that indeed feature underscore (MGM's *The Wet Parade*, Universal's *Destry Rides Again*[65]) with films whose music consists largely of songs (Fox's *Delicious* and *Careless Lady*, Paramount's *One Hour with You*). Significantly, though, he calls attention to recent developments at RKO:

> RKO-Radio's "Symphony of Six Million" employs melody to great advantage during some of the most dramatic scenes. A score was prepared by Max Steiner which, at first, was to have run behind all scenes. This was found impractical, but it does background all the dramatic moments of the film. Mr. Steiner has prepared another but different score for "Bird of Paradise." This is Hawaiian music in a more modern and rapid tempo than is usually found in melodies of this type.[66]

Symphony of Six Million had yet to be released at the time the article appeared, but it is possible that the writer was granted a preview screening; *Bird of Paradise* would not be released until late in the summer, so the writer was likely basing his comments on hearsay. In any case, these two films count as important benchmarks in the history of film music. Their plots and settings are not at all alike, and they are the work of two different directors (Gregory La Cava in the case of the Manhattan-based *Symphony of Six Million*, King Vidor in the case of the exotic *Bird of Paradise*). But they have in common something more than their music by Max Steiner. For both films, the executive producer at RKO was David O. Selznick.

* * *

It seems clear that by the middle of 1932 Hollywood in general, doubtless recalling the efficacy of silent-film accompaniment, was recognizing the value of what the *New York Times* writer called "the symphonic method" of underscoring. The precise content of the "symphonic" underscore, however, remained hotly debated.

At least some of the studios that opted for underscoring believed that the material should be drawn largely from well-established concert-hall repertoire. A tongue-in-cheek, but not inaccurate, feature article that ran in the *Los Angeles Times* in early May 1932 observed:

> [W]hether Hollywood is aware of it or not, the studios are going Bach to Beethoven. . . . It would seem . . . that the theme song as such is doomed to luke-warm popularity. . . . And so, with most of the theme song writers returning to New York, studios are adopting a new form of melody—background music which tends to establish the atmosphere of the picture.[67]

Apropos of the article's whimsical headline—"Theme Song Pianissimoed for Bach and Beethoven"—the writer notes that several recent films featured underscores based on classical music. Among the films she mentions are Paramount's *Dr. Jekyll and Mr. Hyde* (music by Herman Hand, but derived from various works of J.S. Bach), the same studio's *Broken Lullabies* (music by W. Franke Harling, based for the most part on Beethoven's "Eroica" Symphony), and Warner Bros.' *The Man Who Played God* (music by Bernhard Kaun, drawn largely from Beethoven's "Moonlight Sonata").

Later that same month, however, another writer for the same newspaper emphasized the studios' increasing use of *original* music. As had been the case in earlier reports, the writer (or his copy editor) sets off the word "underscoring" in quotation marks, suggesting that the term as much as the concept is still fairly new. Under a headline that declares "Film Music Experiences Its Sanest Development—Orchestral Background Finds Niche in Pictures; Original Scores Becoming More Popular," the article begins:

> "Underscoring" of pictures is a new and progressive activity in the motion pictures. It is seeing its sanest development today. Not only are excerpts from published works being used, but more and more original melodies and harmonies are being added to the tapestry of filmy tone.
>
> This optimistic sentiment is vouchsafed by the men in charge of the musical work at the various motion-picture plants of Hollywood. They are making steady headway in securing a place for the orchestral background. Indeed, [the music] often becomes an intimate factor in the scene.[68]

Succinctly and accurately, the writer offers a synopsis of what had transpired, in terms of film music, over the last few years:

> Three stages in the history of the melodious excursion might be described to date:
>
> (1.) The frantic, feverish, frenzied time when everybody went crazy on the subject of music, and little or no discrimination prevailed in its use.
> (2.) The natural follow-up. No music at all.
> (3.) The gradual recovery from the first two eras of insanity. The "creeping in" of music where it really helped.
>
> Mostly, this third stage has been distinguished by the use of the melodic theme as supplementary to the scene. It is a harking back to the days when the theater orchestra accompanied the picture.[69]

The writer makes two important observations on the current state of affairs. He notes, in the first place, that "now the percentage of orchestral backgrounding in pictures is variously estimated at 25 to 50 percent." Then, reflecting on the serious music-licensing issues with which film exhibitors had to deal ever since the formation of ASCAP just before World War I, he notes that

> original music is being much aimed for, provided there is sufficient time allowed for its composition. . . . One thing accomplished by original scores is the avoidance of complications due to the much-entangled foreign copyright laws. It veritably takes a whole legal department to solve the perplexities of obtaining permission to use certain tunes abroad, and some compositions are under an almost absolute ban as applies to motion pictures.[70]

In January 1933 a reporter for the *Los Angeles Times* was suggesting that "classical music," so long as it came from the hands of long-dead composers and thus was free of copyright control, was still favored by most of the Hollywood studios that embraced the idea of underscore:

> Mountains of music, rivers of melody, massive tone effects, huge blocks of vibration dissolving into single-voiced melody which lingers in the memory and increases the sentiment and power of emotion, are used in the modern films. Masters of orchestral and vocal sound, such as Wagner and Tchaikowsky, are now called upon to lend their aid from a bygone generation to the clever musical directors of the Hollywood studios. The film scorers blend these masters so cleverly and add such good composing of their own that the connecting links are never noticed.[71]

But just a few months earlier the same newspaper had commented on why classical music *per se*, quite apart from what selections drawn from this much-lauded and obviously wonderful repertoire might indeed contribute to a film's affect, was being regarded at least by one studio as not at all desirable. The unsigned article quotes composer Max Steiner, who relates specific directives recently given to him by one of RKO's executive producers:

> David O. Selznick came to the conclusion that any music, whether classical or popular, that is known—even if not by name—to the general public, is distracting. He said to me one day:
> "Steiner, when a tune has been heard before, the people in the audience search their memories. They say, 'where did we hear that before? Just what is that melody?'"
> Selznick, who is extremely sensitive musically, also said he thought music should fit the precise action, mood and even words in a screen play, and obviously should be especially composed.[72]

And thus Steiner, who just a year and a half earlier had seemed committed to Radio Pictures' policy that a film should contain no music unless it was "logically" dictated by the plot, was late in 1932 just as committed to RKO's idea that a film could be accompanied aplenty by "illogical" extra-diegetic music so long as that music—however much its impulse and affect had in common with excerpts from the classical symphonic literature—was originally composed.

After *Symphony of Six Million* and *Bird of Paradise*, Steiner provided RKO, at Selznick's behest, with a "symphonic" yet wholly original score for *The Most Dangerous Game* (directed by Richard Connell, released in September 1932). Because they contributed significantly to these films' dramatic impact, Steiner's original "symphonic" scores likely caught the attention of executives at other Hollywood studios. But Steiner's break-through score—the score that solidly established the "symphonic-yet-original" model that Hollywood film music would follow for the next several decades—was the one he concocted early in 1933 for RKO's *King Kong*.[73]

Reporting in advance of the film's release in April 1933, the *Los Angeles Times* quotes Steiner as saying that writing the music for *King Kong* "proved the most difficult job I ever tackled." Quite apart from the problems in making "the music jibe with the unusual sounds made by the [film's] weird animals," Steiner said, composing the music for *King Kong* required an entirely "new technique in score and synchronization."[74]

And this new technique would provide Hollywood—and many of its international imitators—with a model for scoring practice that would sustain itself at least for the next two decades.

Part 3

MUSIC IN THE "CLASSICAL-STYLE" HOLLYWOOD FILM (1933–60)

Chapter 8

THE "GOLDEN AGE" OF
FILM MUSIC, 1933–49

> There is nothing in the world that will make people cry or make
> them laugh as quickly as music. Nothing can take its place in a
> movie. But it must go along with the story to heighten it. Music
> daren't assume first place or it is bad for the film.
>
> Alfred Newman, 1937[1]

The "new technique in score and synchronization"[2] that Max Steiner applied to *King Kong* was not quite the novelty the composer claimed it to be, for by the time of the film's release in March 1933 Steiner—at the behest of producer David O. Selznick—had already provided comparable music for three earlier RKO films. And likely it is for this reason that, despite *King Kong*'s enduring reputation as the film that singularly launched the style of scoring that would prevail at least for the next twenty years, early reviews make no mention at all of the music.[3]

Movie critics who attended the much-touted premieres in New York, Los Angeles, and Washington, D.C., obviously took in the film as much with their ears as with their eyes. They of course wrote excitedly and at length about the film's visual effects, which included not just credible stop-motion animations of giant creatures but also miniatures and rear projections. Significantly, they also paid considerable attention to the various "fantastic" sounds designed by Murray Spivak. Making comparison with 1925's dramatically and visually similar *The Lost World*,[4] one reviewer noted that *King Kong*'s "very goose-fleshy" impact was "magnified by the since perfected qualities of sound,"[5] and a week later he informed readers that "the devices by which the sounds of pre-historic monsters were produced represent new achievements in engineering skill."[6] Another critic, revisiting the film in a Sunday column, commented that the impression made by the animated creatures was "strengthened by the occasional clever use of the microphone. One hears the mammoth ape tearing asunder the jaws of a dinosaurus, and there is also the sound of trees being felled as Kong makes his way through a forest."[7] In the wake of initial reviews, the *Los Angeles Times* offered a news item that explained how the sound of Kong's respirations "was brought to life through breathing sounds made by the lion, modern king of beasts, which were amplified to great volume and lowered many octaves in tone."[8]

But the score, in the first round of reviews from major American newspapers, is consistently overlooked. Indeed, aside from the above-quoted comment that composer Steiner made in advance of the film's release, the only reference to music in the early press coverage of *King Kong* comes in a follow-up interview with the film's director (and

Figure 8.1 Max Steiner. © The Kobal Collection.

recently appointed RKO production chief) Merian C. Cooper. According to Steiner's unpublished autobiography, it was Cooper who pushed—at a time when all of Hollywood had fallen into a financial slump—for an accompanying score made up not of pre-existing "tracks" but of entirely original music, and it was Cooper, against the advice of the studio's accountants, who put up the approximately $50,000 needed to fund fresh recording sessions.[9] It may or may not be that, as Steiner recalled, "*King Kong* was the film that saved RKO from failure."[10] But right from the start *King Kong* was a newsworthy box-office success. Responding to a reporter's questions about what else RKO, under Cooper's leadership, might have in store, Cooper promised a full range of romances, adventures, thrillers, musicals, and serious films that dealt with social issues. Almost as an aside, but certainly apropos of Steiner's contribution to *King Kong*, the reporter noted that Cooper "is strongly in favor of music, and believes it exerts a great emotional influence."[11]

The Classical-Style Hollywood Film

For Hollywood, the severe economic downturn of late 1932 and early 1933—arguably the darkest days of the Great Depression—resulted in the laying off of a large number of studio employees (including musicians) and, in some cases, the cessation of production. But by March 1933—simultaneous not just with the release of RKO's *King Kong* but, more significant, with the first implementations of United States president Franklin D. Roosevelt's "New Deal" policies of widespread financial relief—things looked decidedly brighter. Even before *King Kong*'s momentous West Coast opening, the *Los Angeles Times* noted that the current Hollywood motto seemed to be "the show must go on":

This was the spirit expressed in Hollywood yesterday, despite the imminent threat of a shutdown of the studios which prevailed until a late hour, the producers' association as a body deciding the final issues.

It is an old slogan in the theatrical business that is being tested considerably, but the idea of one group of employees who did not receive their pay checks yesterday was to continue working at all costs, work being the best way of dealing in the future, if not in the actual compensation forthcoming at the moment. It is more than likely that such a theory will become popular in movieland, where the idea of affording entertainment is pre-eminent, and that even despite the assault on the monetary coffers which has gone on so heavily in the past. . . .

Great improvement is anticipated with the issuance of scrip. In fact, even boom times are being talked of.[12]

And toward the end of the month the *New York Times* reported:

Tranquillity reigned this week as studios forgot their pay slashes and other troubles and resumed production activities. Fox, shut down for a week, began shooting again. Thirty companies, a high number, were working on all lots. The biggest upheaval, that of pay cuts, was settled early last week, but this was followed by minor disturbances, including an attempted strike by the scene painters who, making in excess of $50 a week, found themselves subject to slight wage revisions. Finally, every one was relatively happy, however, and the eight-week period during which pay is to be reduced was expected by producers to be limited to five or six weeks, the reports from theatres and financial circles indicating warranted optimism.[13]

Optimism was indeed warranted, and the talked-of boom times came to pass. For individual Americans and their families, there can be no underestimating the hardships imposed by the long-lasting Depression; for institutional Hollywood, there can be no overestimating the bounty of revenue that came its way as a result of providing hard-pressed Americans of all ages, on a regular basis, with escapist entertainment. As film historian Gerald Mast has pointedly observed, whereas in the economically flush 1960s a certain percentage of the American population willingly paid for the experience of particular films, throughout the depressed 1930s a much larger percentage paid, just as willingly, for the experience of "the movies" in general.[14]

By 1935, the eminently lucrative idea of "the movies" had steered Hollywood not just in the direction of well-wrought screenplays enacted by camera-savvy actors and actresses but also toward a panoply of technical innovations that involved lighting, camera housings, microphones, and—important as much for the treatment of dialogue as for musical accompaniments—the complete separation from a film's image track of three different sound tracks (for dialogue, sound effects, and music) each independently controllable in terms of both placement (vis-à-vis the image track) and volume levels.[15] Not just in Hollywood but also in certain European centers of film production, during the second half of the 1930s mechanical innovation and aesthetic development existed in a symbiotic relationship so tight that by and large it is impossible to say which spurred the other. However things might have transpired day-to-day at individual studios, by the end of the decade the global audience for movies was being exposed on a regular basis to something that in general was vastly different from what it had experienced when the fully evolved sound film finally made its debut.

Regarding the situation from a perspective of a quarter century, the French film critic/ theorist André Bazin pointedly observed:

> By 1938 or 1939 the talking film, particularly in France and the United States, had reached a level of classical perfection as a result, on the one hand, of the maturing of different kinds of drama developed in part over the past ten years and in part inherited from the silent film, and, on the other, of the stabilization of technological progress.[16]

In the 1970s, American film scholars began to translate Bazin's concept of a "level of classical perfection" into the notion of a "classical-style" of film production that, while it indeed had international imitators, stemmed largely from Hollywood. In an admirably thorough 1985 book devoted to exploring the style's subtle nuances as much as its obvious characteristics, film historians David Bordwell, Janet Staiger, and Kristin Thompson explain the aptness of the modifier "classical." They remind us that "it was probably . . . Bazin who gave the adjective the most currency," who declared that by 1939 "Hollywood filmmaking had acquired 'all the characteristics of a classical art.'" And thus, they write, "it seems proper to retain the term in English, since the principles which Hollywood claims as its own rely on notions of decorum, proportion, formal harmony, respect for tradition, mimesis, self-effacing craftsmanship, and cool control of the perceiver's response—canons which critics in any medium usually call 'classical.' "[17]

The "classical-style" is richly variegated, to be sure, yet its essence can be easily enough summarized. In their introductory chapter, Bordwell, Staiger, and Thompson define it simply as a style that is "excessively obvious."[18] Embellishing that idea, perhaps with the intention of making sure that the phrase "excessively obvious" is not read as a pejorative, a recent dictionary of film terminology explains that the "classical-style" is a mode of cinematic storytelling whose myriad technical devices serve primarily "to explain, and not obscure, the narrative."[19]

In other words, films in the "classical-style"—which dominated Hollywood production from the late 1930s until the mid 1950s and which has sustained itself, in the face of competition from numerous decidedly non-"classical" styles, up to the present day— are films that in the long run do *not* leave audience members wondering about characters' motivations or the workings of plot devices. Films in the "classical-style" are typically filled with surprise and suspense; unless this were the case, classical-style films—whether their genre be thriller, tear-jerker, western, or screwball comedy—would hardly be entertaining. But sooner or later in the classical-style film the audience is made aware of the relative dramatic weight of almost all that transpires in the plot; by the time the film ends, even audience members whose attention perhaps lapsed know full well not just what has happened but also why and how it happened.

Realization of cinema's classical-style resulted largely from editing. Intriguing scripts and convincing performances by well-directed cast members were of course important to the making of a marketable product. But the classical-style film, quite unlike so many dramatic or comedic feature films from ca. 1931–2, was no mere documentation of a staged play. Whereas the early sound film typically consisted of a relatively few number of extended scenes performed before stationary cameras, the classical-style film tended to be made up of hundreds of brief "shots" pieced together to form a narrative whole. As early as 1933–4—well before the full fruition of cinema's classical-style—actors donned their garb and make-up and went before the cameras to do, perhaps again and again, whatever directors asked of them. In turn, the directors sorted through all the shot footage and selected those relatively few bits that, in their opinion, might contribute to a credible filmic drama. Regardless of its genre, the early sound film was, in essence, an audio-visual recording; in marked contrast, the classical-style film was by and large a meticulously edited construction.

A comparably sharp contrast can be seen in film's treatment of music. In 1930–1, manufacturers of sound films—regardless of their locations—were severely restricted by the limitations of sound-mixing technology. According to stated policies in 1931, the only music to be used in any RKO or MGM film—aside from the fanfare-like music that accompanied the opening credits and the obviously conclusive music that announced "The End"—was music whose presence was logically dictated by the plot. Although this policy was offered to the public as being the result of aesthetic considerations, it remains a fact that in 1931 it was almost impossible to mix recorded music and dialogue without serious degradation of audio quality.

By 1932–3, at least at RKO and the handful of other Hollywood studios that availed themselves of state-of-the-art audio mixers, the earlier limitations no longer applied. Although RKO again publicized its apparently bold new policy vis-à-vis music as

137

something that sprang from aesthetic considerations, it again remains a fact that by this time good-sounding accompanimental music *could* be added to a film whose editing had in all other ways been completed. Doubtless it is no mere coincidence that the proscription against music that had no direct connection with the film's plot began to disappear at the very moment that technology allowed a very different sort of music—illustrative, or emotive, music that seemingly came "from nowhere"—to enter the picture.

* * *

The choices as to which kind of music to use, and how to work the music into a film, were dictated by the directorial thought processes that culminated toward the end of the 1930s in the "excessively obvious" classical-style. With compelling yet absolutely unambiguous storytelling being the goal of this burgeoning cinematic style, extra-diegetic music came increasingly to the fore as directors, in consultation with their editors, applied the "finishing touches" to their filmic constructions.

In some cases, directors from the outset had clear ideas as to how musical underscore might figure into their products. In most cases, decisions as to precisely where extra-diegetic music should enter and exit the soundtrack were made in "spotting sessions" during which directors and composers together viewed a film's completed footage and somehow agreed as to the specific "spots" at which underscore might enter or exit. In his memoir, Max Steiner recalls the "spotting" process:

> I prefer . . . to approach the picture without any prejudice one way or another. So I simply do not read scripts unless it is absolutely necessary, such as when a song is required and it needs prerecording.
>
> The first step, of course, is to run the picture as soon as it is finished. I run it first by myself. I don't want anybody around me at this time, neither the producer nor the director, because they might throw me off with their ideas before I form my own impressions. While I am running the picture, I sit back and decide what kind of a score it requires and make my plans. A few days later, when I have thought it over or, in some rare instances, when I have already thought of a few tunes or themes, I will run the picture with the director, if he so desires. He, and perhaps the producer, will then give me their ideas of what should be done. Their ideas do not always coincide with mine. In this event, I may try to swing them over to my point of view, or it may be that their ideas are better than mine. Eventually, we come to a meeting of minds.[20]

Steiner makes it clear that this was *his* preferred method, and he acknowledges that other composers may well have done things differently. Nevertheless, enough anecdotal accounts have come down to suggest that the "spotting" process Steiner describes—especially in regard to agreements about music being reached only after a film had been otherwise completely edited—was more or less general practice.

The collective decision-making of the musical "spotting session" is consistent with the idea of the classical-style film as an edited construction. As had been the case since the Hollywood studios were first established around the time of World War I, a finished film ca. 1938–9 was the product of many hands. With any given film, doubtless a single individual—likely a producer or a director, but possibly a writer or a stellar actor—

exerted more control than did anyone else. But even the most authoritarian figures could not have functioned unless they were efficient leaders of teams, and the work of even the best filmmaking teams would have been fruitless were it not carefully coordinated with the solid efforts of the studio's technological and commercial departments.

Commenting on what she calls both film music's "golden age" and the "classical age of film composition"—approximately the years 1935 through 1955—Caryl Flinn observes that, not surprisingly, this period "coincides roughly with Hollywood's classical period of production." Glossing on the Bordwell-Staiger-Thompson definition, she notes that the term "classical" "here designates at once a style and a mode of industrial production." Thus "it makes immediate sense," she writes, "that Hollywood's classical age of scoring emerged out of this period of larger economic vitality and gain, and while the latter clearly did not 'cause' the former, it nevertheless provided it with the technologies to stabilize and keep intact an overall coherent style."[21]

Certain technological developments, originating in Hollywood and more or less slow to reach other centers of film production, made the making of classical-style films possible. Certain practicalities of procedure, resulting as much from the organizational hierarchy of studio executives as from technological necessity, made the production of classical-style films increasingly formulaic. And certain marketing strategies—rooted not just in a canny understanding of the American economy in the late 1930s but also, at least for some of the studios, a vertically integrated business structure that allowed for competition-free domestic distribution—made classical-style films extremely profitable.[22]

It is a complex picture, and it would be difficult to say precisely how aesthetics figures into it. Assuming that an "excessively obvious" narrative was indeed the goal of the classical-style Hollywood film, one might wonder: Was the idea something conceived by the sudden coming together of hitherto unknown technologies and marketing strategies in the mid-to-late 1930s? Or was a narrative of this sort something that filmmakers had long sought after? Thinking back to the second and third stages of the silent film—to the period ca. 1914–26, when well-paid musical directors at big-city movie palaces weekly compiled orchestral scores to support the presentation of feature-length films, and before that to the period ca. 1903–14, when lone pianists at nickelodeons lent whatever support they could to the current program of one-reelers—one might ask: Did these musicians completely ignore the narrative content of the films they accompanied, or worse, did they actively seek to obscure it? Common sense dictates that probably they did not. Probably the run-of-the-mill silent-film accompanist, like the run-of-the-mill Hollywood composer at the dawn of classical-style sound film, considered the narrative content of whatever film was at hand and then duly concocted music designed to help make that content at least somewhat—perhaps even excessively—obvious to the audience.

In any case, surely even the youngest of Hollywood producers in the mid 1930s would have remembered that not so long ago accompanimental music regularly, as RKO's Cooper observed in the wake of *King Kong*, "exert[ed] a great emotional influence" on films. After recovering from its short-lived conviction that audiences for sound films were interested primarily in musical "numbers" and its equally short-lived belief that the only music a film could accommodate was music that fit solidly into the plot, Hollywood in general re-embraced the idea that music might indeed serve a film's narrative purposes by offering off-screen "commentary." Following the earlier and obviously successful model, the first wave of "underscored" sound films relied heavily on excerpts from the standard concert-hall repertoire and generic compositions taken directly from the vast libraries of "photoplay" music that so adequately served the needs of musical directors for silent films. Perhaps RKO's competitors saw the wisdom of producer Selznick's 1932 pronouncement that recognizable music, no matter what its source, would likely be perceived by audiences as distracting; perhaps they simply sought to emulate the box-office success of *King Kong* and the other Selznick-produced films that implemented this radical new approach.

Not all the studios responded so quickly to the possibilities of orchestral underscore as did RKO, United Artists, Universal, and Columbia. By the middle of the decade, however, most of Hollywood was open to the idea of plot-rooted source music combined with underscore that was comfortably familiar in its symphonic sound and idiom but which in content was entirely original. By 1938–9—by the time at which, according to Bazin, cinema's "level of classical perfection" had finally been reached—the efficacy of extra-diegetic music was taken for granted. By this time, too, the conventions according to which extra-diegetic music figured into a filmic product were more or less clearly defined.

Music in the Classical-Style Film

Commenting on *The Informer* (RKO, 1935), the music for which composer Max Steiner won the very first Oscar for motion picture scoring, Kathryn Kalinak in a 1992 book attests that the score in many ways "exemplifies the musical conventions of classical film: selective use of nondiegetic music; correspondence between that music and the implied content of the narrative; a high degree of synchronization between music and narrative action; and the use of the leitmotif as a structural framework." The score is also interesting, she writes, "for a practice Steiner himself came to exemplify: the exploitation of musical associations to provide the link between narrative content and musical accompaniment."[23]

A more exhaustive list of the musical conventions, or principles, of the classical-style film is included in the chapter titled "Classical Hollywood Practice: The Model of Max Steiner" (which culminates in a close analysis of Steiner's score for the 1945 *Mildred Pierce*) of Claudia Gorbman's 1987 book on narrative film music. The first item in Gorbman's often-cited seven-point list perhaps seems so obvious that readers might initially wonder why it is even mentioned. "The technical apparatus" by which extra-diegetic music is introduced into a film, Gorbman writes, "must not be visible."[24] On the other hand, the list's second item is deliciously provocative. Indeed, along with getting at the very heart of a matter that was debated by film composers and their critics throughout the era of the classical-style film, the underlying thought provides Gorbman with the title for her book; drawing on an idea introduced by the English poet John Keats in his 1819 "Ode on a Grecian Urn," Gorbman titles her book *Unheard Melodies*.[25]

The source of the classical-style film's extra-diegetic music must be literally invisible,[26] Gorbman writes, but the music itself must only *in effect* be inaudible. In other words, while the music is of course intended to be heard by the audience, it is not—except in rare instances—meant to be heard consciously. To support that view, Gorbman quotes from Leonid Sabaneev's 1935 *Music for the Films: A Handbook for Composer and Conductors*:

In general, music should understand that in the cinema it should nearly always remain in the background: it is, so to speak, a tonal figuration, the "left hand" of the melody on the screen, and it is a bad business when this left hand begins to creep into the foreground and obscure the melody.[27]

The comment from Sabaneev is interesting as much for its content, which would be echoed many times in the next several years, as for its early date and its geographical source. Sabaneev was an esteemed Soviet composer and musicologist who, among other things, served as president of the Soviet Union's Association for Contemporary Music and as music editor for the influential publications *Izvestia* and *Pravda*. Despite his active involvement in Soviet musical life, Sabaneev in fact lived for the most part from 1926 to around 1940 not in his home country but, variously, in France, Germany, England, and the United States.[28] Thus, whereas the filmmakers and composers who together cultivated the Soviet sound film in the 1930s were relatively isolated from developments abroad, Sabaneev had a perspective that was quite international.

Written in Russian and translated by S.W. Pring,[29] Sabaneev's *Music for the Films* is the first of two important books on film music issued in English in the mid 1930s; the other is *Film Music: A Summary of the Characteristic Features of Its History, Aesthetics, Technique, and Possible Developments*, published in translation (from the original German) in 1936 and authored by Kurt London, a composer who taught classes in film music at the Hochschule für Musik in Berlin. Notwithstanding its wealth of theoretical insight and historical information, London's book focuses almost exclusively on the situation in Germany; indeed, as musicologist-composer Fred Steiner[30] notes in his valuable summary of published commentary on music in the early sound film, London "seemed to be completely unaware of developments in Hollywood," and the book "was already outdated when it was issued."[31] Sabaneev's book, on the other hand, is both cosmopolitan in outlook and, in terms of actual practice, quite *au courant*. Significantly, it illuminates several aspects of film music that were contentious in the early years of the classical-style film and which remain contentious today.

As Steiner explains, certain statements by Sabaneev are especially noteworthy on at least two counts:

(1) . . . [Likely] they embody the earliest published specific recommendations to screen composers about the knotty problem of the presence of music vis-à-vis speech and noises on the sound track (a difficulty that has never ceased to trouble composers and directors); and (2), perhaps more importantly, because of Sabaneev's interesting choice of words is his contention that when music is mixed with dialog and sound effects it loses "aesthetic value" and "aesthetic significance." . . . Given that [music's] primary role in motion pictures is to follow and lend support to a series of images of specified lengths and varying content, at the same time it is subject to laws other than cinematic, i.e., the laws of music, which every composer must obey—they certainly cannot be ignored.[32]

Steiner perhaps exaggerates when he claims that the advent of the classical-style film in the mid 1930s marked "the first time musicians had to think seriously about music as a dichotomy,"[33] that is, the first time composers had to weigh purely "musical" needs against "theatrical" needs that their music, according to the terms of its commission, was supposed to serve; surely opera and ballet composers throughout the eighteenth and nineteenth centuries thought seriously about—indeed, struggled with—the same dichotomy. Steiner is correct, though, when he echoes Sabaneev and states that in the years leading up to the classical-style film composers were caught between allegiance to music's traditional values and cinema's "necessary new styles and forms."[34]

In her expansion of the second item on her list of conventions for music in the classical-style film—the convention according to which "music is not meant to be heard consciously" and "should subordinate itself to . . . the primary vehicles of the narrative"[35] (i.e., visuals and dialogue)—Gorbman quotes directly from Sabaneev's 1935 book. Had she chosen to lade her account with citations, she might have included the statement from composer Alfred Newman that serves as an epigraph for this chapter. She might have included, too, this comment from Max Steiner:

> There is a tired old bromide in this business to the effect that a good film score is one you don't hear. What good is it if you don't notice it? However, you might say that the music should be heard but not seen. The danger is that the music can be so bad, or so good, that it distracts and takes away from the action.[36]

Had she so chosen, Gorbman might have filled her account with comments not just from composers but also from studio executives to the effect that music, in films preceding or actually representative of Hollywood's classical-style, needed to be always emotionally potent yet never so ear-catching that it would pull the audience's attention from a film's narrative; indeed, the point comes up again and again in the major American newspapers' occasional reports on the latest thinking on Hollywood film music, and it is sharply honed in almost all of the autobiographies of composers who travailed in Hollywood both during and after the heyday of the classical-style film.[37] But Gorbman, perhaps assuming that film music's desired "inaudibility" is self-explanatory, simply notes that "background" music must be introduced at dramatically appropriate moments and must be stylistically appropriate to the scene at hand before moving on to the other items on her list of principles that govern the use of music in the classical-style film.

By its very presence, she writes, extra-diegetic music in the classical-style film is often a "signifier of emotion itself,"[38] not simply a mimicry of emotions expressed by the film's characters but a clear signal to the audience that the characters are indeed feeling emotions of one sort or another; by way of general examples, Gorbman in her explanatory paragraphs mentions music as an indicator of film characters' response to uncanny or irrational situations, as a sign of romantic interest between male and female characters, and as an emblem for what she terms "epic feeling."[39]

The fourth item in Gorbman's list is labeled "narrative cueing," and this function of music within scores for classical-style films is then divided into "referential/narrative" and "connotative."[40] Extra-diegetic music in the first category, Gorbman writes, marks the beginnings and endings of sections of the filmic narrative, establishes such things as locale or time period or ethnic stereotypes by making reference to pre-existing and fairly well-known music that an audience would likely associate with whatever is being depicted, and in various ways helps an audience to identify with a particular character's momentary "point of view." The almost five pages of explication that Gorbman devotes to "connotative cueing" cover a range of situations so wide that they defy summary here.

But the gist of Gorbman's point is easily enough expressed: by expressing "moods and connotations" that work in conjunction with a film's other elements, "narrative film music 'anchors' the [filmic] image in meaning."[41] In other words, Gorbman seems to be saying, extra-diegetic music in the "excessively obvious" classical-style film not only helps "set the scene" but also informs the audience as to what, in terms of the drama, is *really* going on.

Gorbman's fifth and sixth items deal with music's potential contributions to a classical-style film's structure. On the one hand, the well-timed entrance and exit of underscore often provides continuity between one filmic scene and another. On the other hand, the score that in essence consists of the repetition or variation of just a small number of themes—each of them of course designed to be ear-catching, but associated only with those narrative elements that are central to the film's plot—contributes significantly to a film's sense of unity. The typical well-wrought score for the typical classical-style film, Gorbman summarizes, thus serves the film's structure on scales both small and large.

The seventh and final item is not so clear as the others. Gorbman states that "a given film score may violate any of the principles above, providing the violation is at the service of the other principles,"[42] but her embellishment of this idea amounts to a mere paragraph that, in comparison with the example-filled explications that support the preceding list points, seems short and vague. Deliberately "breaking the rules" would figure importantly into the scoring of films from the period during which the so-called classical-style of production first started to wane (that is, the late 1950s), and it would fairly dominate the musical aesthetics of films both serious and lightweight from the "postmodern" last decades of the twentieth century. For purposes of irony or comedic effect, or simply for the sake of novelty, surely violations of the prevailing norm from time to time figured as well into scores from film music's "golden age," but Gorbman sheds little light on how this might have occurred.

* * *

Gorbman's book on the function of underscore is based on close observation of a great many narrative films (that is, films that tell largely fictional stories, as opposed to documentary films or abstract films). It is a generally estimable book, and since its publication in 1987 its list of "Classical Film Music: Principles of Composing, Mixing, and Editing"[43] has so often been quoted that a browser of the recent film-music literature might be led to imagine that the "seven principles" are somewhere engraved in stone. But Gorbman (who like Flinn and Kalinak approached film music from a formal background not in musicology but in literary criticism) was certainly not the first scholar engaged in so-called film studies[44] to address the role that extra-diegetic music played in classical-style films.

Two years before Gorbman's book was published, the trio of Bordwell, Staiger, and Thompson brought out their monumental *The Classical Hollywood Cinema: Film Style and Production to 1960*. As noted above, and apropos of its title, the book focuses on filmic narrative style and the technical devices that made this style possible. In its early pages, however, it also contains insightful comments on "classical" cinema's use of music.

The book's first music-related passage lays a foundation for Gorbman's point about how a score might lend unity to a film by recycling distinctive themes that within the context of the film become associated with such specific narrative entities as characters, locales, physical objects, or even states of mind. But the passage is not without its problems. While the underlying idea is indeed basic to the technique of scoring for the classical-style film, the discussion unfortunately introduces a term that would bother film-music discourse for the next two decades: it fairly equates the film score's repeated use of themes with the use, in the operas of the nineteenth-century German composer Richard Wagner, of *leitmotivs*.

Translated literally, "Leitmotiv" means "leading motif." The adjective does not mean "chief," as though it described a motif, or theme, that occupies a hierarchical position superior to that of a score's other motifs; rather, it means "directing," and it refers to a musical idea that serves "to guide," or "lead," the listener through the narrative. Bordwell et al. correctly note that accompanists for silent films, and composers for classical-style films, indeed sometimes referred to their themes as *leitmotivs*. In their influential 1985 book, however, they do not question what was clearly a misuse of the German term; indeed—setting the example for the subsequent books by Gorbman (1987), Flinn (1992), and Kalinak (1992)—they write as though "film-score theme" and "*leitmotiv*" were synonyms. Only recently has it been pointed out, by scholars rooted not in literary studies but in musicology, that Wagner's technique (which involved fragmentary motifs capable of being not just developed but also intermixed) differs substantially from the basic Hollywood approach (which involved tune-like musical ideas that were for the most part simply reiterated whenever their associated filmic entities entered the narrative).[45]

Problematic as is their use of the specific term "*leitmotiv*," Bordwell et al. are on the mark with their much-echoed observation that scores for the classical-style film to a certain extent emulated nineteenth-century operatic models by linking recognizable musical ideas to recognizable plot elements. More intriguing—at least in part because the idea is *not* echoed in the follow-up books by Gorbman, Flinn, and Kalinak—they explore the seemingly "privileged" power that music seems to wield in the narratives of both opera and classical-style cinema. In a chapter called "Classical Narration," in a section tellingly headed "Music as Destiny," the authors write:

> Like the opera score, the classical film score enters into a system of narration, endowed with some degree of self-consciousness, a range of knowledge, and a degree of communicativeness. The use of non-diegetic music itself signals the narration's awareness of facing an audience, for the music exists solely for the spectator's benefit. The score of the orchestral forces employed and the symphonic tradition itself create an impersonal wash of sound befitting the unspecific narrator of the classical film. The score can also be said to be omniscient, what Parker Tyler has called "a vocal apparatus of destiny." In the credits sequence, the music can lay out motifs to come, even tagging them to actors' names. During the film, music adheres to classical narration's rule of only allowing glimpses of its omniscience, as when the score anticipates the action by a few moments. . . . As George Antheil puts it, "The characters in a film drama never know what is going to happen to them, but the music always knows."[46]

Further laying foundations for ideas that would be repeated by later writers, Bordwell et al. observe that music in the classical-style film "remains . . . motivated by the story,"

144

that "when dialogue is present, the music must drop out or confine itself to a subdued coloristic background."[47] They also observe that just as complex camerawork comes to the fore whenever dialogue in the classical-style film is minimized, so too "when there is little dialogue ... the music comes into its own as an accompaniment for physical action."[48]

In light of their misleading equating of Wagnerian *leitmotivs* with the classical-style film score's memorable "themes," it is worth noting that Bordwell et al. conclude their brief section on music by pointing out at least one significant way—having to do not so much with music's privileged awareness of a narrative's overall "destiny" as with its ability to penetrate the psyches of a narrative's various characters—in which Hollywood's method veered from Wagner's:

> Since classical narrative turns nearly all anticipations and recollections of story action over to the characters, music must not operate as a completely free-roaming narration. Here is one difference from Wagner's method, which did allow the music to flaunt its omniscience by ironic or prophetic uses of motifs. The Hollywood score, like the classical visual style, seldom includes overt recollections or far-flung anticipations of the action. The music confines itself to a moment-by-moment heightening of the story. Slight anticipations are permitted, but recollections of previous musical material must be motivated by a repetition of situation or by character memory.[49]

None of this—not the adaptation of the basic principles of film scoring as outlined by Gorbman, and certainly not the subtle exploration of music's effect on the psychological aspects of filmic narrative as suggested by Bordwell et al.—happened overnight. Nevertheless, by 1938–9—more or less simultaneous with the American film industry's settling upon the narrative style and mode of production that would eventually be described as "classical"—film music emanating from Hollywood had developed a certain norm. This was not "a prescriptive set of rules for accompaniment," Kalinak writes; rather, it took the form of "a body of conventions which composers drew upon as a resource and a model."[50]

Market-worthy as this body of conventions quickly proved to be, even within the competitive environs of Hollywood there remained plenty of room for experimental deviation and aesthetic argument. Elsewhere in the world—not just in the Soviet Union, where sound-film technology seriously lagged, but also in relatively up-to-date France, Germany, and England, where high concepts of cinematic "art" still outweighed commercial considerations—the musical conventions developed by Hollywood ca. 1938–9 represented both serious temptations and points of ideological/aesthetic resistance. Although they were challenged again and again for various reasons, the Hollywood conventions prevailed; indeed, the musical norm of the classical-style Holly-wood film remains the standard with which film music in general continues to be compared.

Debates over "Inaudibility" and Aesthetic Quality

Even during the formative years of the so-called classical-style, the use of extra-diegetic music in Hollywood had begun to settle into what might be thought of as a "common

Figure 8.2 Russian-born composer Dimitri Tiomkin conducts a 75-piece orchestra while recording the music for director King Vidor's 1946 film, *Duel in the Sun*. A scene from the film, featuring Jennifer Jones and Gregory Peck, plays in the background. (Photo by Hulton Archive/Getty Images.)

practice." The more famous films scored by Max Steiner—*King Kong* (1933), *Of Human Bondage* (1934), *The Informer* (1935)—surely were influential examples. But these are merely the standouts among the more than two-dozen RKO films for which Steiner provided functionally comparable music between 1933 and 1935. And they competed for audience attention with a great many films, also with functionally comparable music, that were being issued by other studios. The list of prestigious films that helped establish the "classical" style of film scoring before Hollywood production in general attained what André Bazin called its "level of classical perfection" might include Paramount's 1934 *Cleopatra* (with music by Rudolph G. Kopp), United Artists' 1935 *The Call of the Wild* (Alfred Newman and Hugo Friedhofer), MGM's 1935 *Mutiny on the Bounty* (Herbert Stothart), Universal's 1935 *The Bride of Frankenstein* (Franz Waxman), Warner Bros.' *The Petrified Forest* (Bernhard Kaun), and Columbia's 1937 *Lost Horizon* (Dimitri Tiomkin). And these, too, are just notable drops in a very large bucket.

The musical norms for what eventually would be known as the classical-style film developed quickly and surely, perhaps at least in part because Hollywood composers ca. 1933–7 were already meeting narrative goals toward which directors, cinematographers, and screen-writers were still striving. But simultaneous with the establishment of these norms there came a load of criticism, voiced as much by composers who struggled within the Hollywood system as by composers who perhaps saw themselves as being above the fray.

The criticism resulted in two ongoing debates. One of them—arguably naïve when considered from the distance of seventy years—centered on the extent to which film music should indeed be, to use Gorbman's term, in effect "inaudible." The other—quite sophisticated, to judge from both the pedigrees of its participants and the general level of its discourse, and not without relevance today—had to do with the purely musical values of the film score as opposed to the values of music written, say, for the concert hall.

A frequent contributor to the debate over film-music aesthetics was Virgil Thomson, an American modernist composer who lived for the most part in Paris between 1925 until 1940 and then, based in New York, from 1940 until 1954 served as music critic for the *New York Herald-Tribune*. Beginning in 1936, Thomson from time to time wrote film music, but with one exception all his scores were for documentaries.[51] But as early as 1933 he was expressing strong opinions about film music.

Thomson's brief 1933 contribution to the journal *Modern Music* seems, on the one hand, peculiarly behind the times in that it celebrates the use in silent film accompaniments of staples from the classical repertoire. On the other hand, Thomson's essay is forward-looking in that, save for a handful of scores by concert-hall composers, it generally discounts original music currently being written for sound films. Thomson of course is commenting from a Parisian perspective, so it is not surprising that he makes note of recent efforts of Arthur Honegger, Jacques Ibert, and Jean Rivier. But even this otherwise commendable music, he writes, does not properly do the job of lending continuity to the "naturally discontinuous medium" of cinema. Thomson summarizes:

> With the exception of [Georges] Auric's music in the court-yard scene of Cocteau's *La Vie d'un Poète*, which is very fine music, I have never heard anything especially written for the films which seemed to me as beautiful and as appropriate as those tremendously dramatic, intimately dramatic (like close-ups), narratively dramatic moments from the symphonies of Beethoven and Mozart that used to envelope us and carry us along through the sorrows of Lillian Gish, the epic adventures of Fred Thompson and of Buck Jones. If any one piece deserves the palm for services to cinematographic art, it is easily, I should say, Schubert's *Unfinished Symphony*, which year in and year out has provided an appropriate dramatic continuity for a larger number of stories than any other single piece classic or modern.[52]

Two years later the same journal featured an article on film music by George Antheil, an American composer who during the 1920s in Paris achieved a reputation as an *enfant terrible* and in 1935 was just beginning a career in Hollywood.[53] Apparently choosing to ignore single-author scores like Steiner's for *King Kong* and *Of Human Bondage*, Antheil writes that most current Hollywood film music takes the form of a "pastiche." "Hollywood" in 1935, he writes, by and large makes music according to "a group formula":

Every studio keeps a staff of seventeen to thirty composers on annual salary. They know nothing about the film till the final cutting day, when it is played over for some or all of them, replayed and stopwatched. Then the work is divided; one man writes war music, a second does the love passages, another is a specialist in nature stuff, and so on. After several days, when they have finished their fractions of music, these are pieced together, played into "soundtrack," stamped with the name of a musical director, and put on the market as an "original score." This usually inept product is exactly the kind of broth to expect from so many minds working at high speed on a single piece.[54]

The pastiche score, Antheil explains, almost by definition lacks musical integrity, and the only way to avoid this problem is to have the scores composed by just one person. Such scores in fact exist, he writes, but all of them come from abroad; he refers specifically to Auric's music for À Nous la Liberté! (1931, French), Ernst Toch's for Karamazov (1930, German), Eugene Goosens's for The Constant Nymph (1934, English), Serge Prokofiev's for Lieutenant Kijé (1933, Soviet), Dmitri Shostakovich's for Odna (1931, Soviet), and Kurt Weill's for Die Dreigroschenoper (1931, German).[55]

Antheil's mention of scores by prestigious European composers doubtless provided ammunition for those who in the ensuing debate would dismiss music by Hollywood "regulars" as being, as if by its very nature, inferior to music by composers experienced in writing for the concert hall or opera house. Yet the overall tone of Antheil's article is not disparaging but optimistic. Antheil notes that for various reasons, not the least of which is the studios' growing awareness that "pastiche" scores often involved the payment of substantial royalties for the use of music that was under copyright, Hollywood seemed to be warming up to the idea of "original scores" written to order, by individuals, for particular films. And this, he concludes, is

an excellent augur for composers. For it becomes obvious even in Hollywood . . . that the best original scores must be written by original composers—in other words that they must be composed. Already feelers are being put out from Hollywood in the direction of one-man scores. Naturally when such scores are tried and prove commercially popular, the mechanical organization of the music departments and studios will be adjusted to new methods of score production. And these will be developed on a sound economic basis as effective for speed and expense as the old ones—perhaps even more so.[56]

Continuing to express optimism, Antheil in 1936—in an article devoted for the most part to extolling the sound practical advice contained in Sabaneev's 1935 Music for the Films: A Handbook for Composer and Conductors—wrote: "The musical departments of our large studios are progressing by leaps and bounds, and the time is not far off when legitimate composers will be able to compose film-scores they need not be ashamed to sign."[57] He sustained the attitude in another article published the same year; significantly, Antheil explained the changes in Hollywood's attitude toward music not just in terms of aesthetics but also in terms of economics:

Within a year's time, a number of composers will, I have no doubt, come to Hollywood, since motion picture producers have found out that better musical scores pay. First of all it is cheaper to write an authentic and exciting musical background than it is to build an equally authentic and exciting background set. [Werner] Janssen's Chinese music lifted at least $50,000 off the budget of *The General Died at Dawn*. When good scores begin to do things like this they talk to Hollywood in its own language—the language of money. Secondly, the great movie publics of the world are gradually being accustomed to better fitting scores—scores that are especially calculated for the needs of each picture and are not dragged out of the pages of Schubert's *Unfinished*. Today a good score is as essential to a production as good photography.[58]

Apropos of Antheil's reference to his sometimes Chinese-sounding music for Paramount's *The General Died at Dawn* (1936), the American-born Werner Janssen wrote a first-person account for the *New York Times* in which he described his experience working on his first feature film.[59] Contrary to what would become typical Hollywood practice, but in keeping with the procedures of many film composers in Europe, Janssen notes that "before I ever saw a scene from [the film] I had heard the music to accompany it." Toward the end of the article he makes apt observations on differences between old-fashioned "melodramatic" film accompaniments and what, in his opinion, seems to be the new Hollywood norm. In many ways, Janssen's conclusions echo the published advice given to silent-film accompanists as early as 1910:

> There are different ways of cueing film music. The old way is episodic. The music announces, or describes, almost every piece of action or flicker of emotion on the screen. So, for example, the girl smiles—and promptly there is a snatch of lilting melody in the violins. She glances out the window toward gathering storm clouds—and suddenly comes a faint rumble of drums. She looks sad— and the flute sings out a doleful tune. And so on it goes, action for action, episode by episode.
>
> I agree with [Paramount music executive] Boris Morros that this way of fitting music and action is weak and may easily become ridiculous. Audiences soon come to the point of anticipating from the music what is about to happen on screen. That is as bad as being able to guess the plot two reels ahead. Music should establish and intensify the mood of an entire scene. It should not constantly veer from this main track to follow little odds and ends of action. Music is the emotional tone, not the detail.[60]

Janssen's *New York Times* piece appeared in August 1936; a few months later the *Los Angeles Times*, apparently deciding that the general public had an interest not just in hearing film music but also in gaining insights into how film music is created, ran an article that included lengthy comments by Franz Waxman. An émigré from Germany, Waxman made his Hollywood debut with Universal's *The Bride of Frankenstein* (1935) and within less than two years scored another dozen and a half films for that studio and for MGM. In the article—from November 1936, while Waxman was still working on his music for *Captains Courageous* (MGM, 1937)—the composer attests to the value of entirely original scores yet notes that adaptations of pre-existing music can still prove useful:

Original composition, not adaptation of others' works, is the answer to film music.

An original score can be fitted much better to film needs, except in cases where a musical production is being transferred bodily to the screen, or where familiar music was first written for, or inspired by, a dramatic production, such as Mendelssohn's "Midsummer Night's Dream" music, or the Tschaikowsky "Romeo and Juliet" overture.

But if I were to adapt Wagner's "Flying Dutchman" score to "Captains Courageous," though both are famous stories of the sea, audiences with a knowledge of music would immediately associate the music with something other than the film.

In "Mutiny on the Bounty" we used adaptations of old English songs, because the picture deals with a particular period in English history and the songs were particularly appropriate. But "Captains Courageous" deals with no great historic period and is not so much national in spirit as it is just a moving story of simple fishermen and their regeneration of a spoiled boy. Our music must fit the action. The inspiration for the score comes from the dynamic strength of the story.[61]

By early 1937, just before the Hollywood film supposedly reached its "level of classical perfection," the situation for composers seemed to be indeed as bright as Antheil had predicted it would be. In his annual report on the state of the American film industry, Will H. Hays—the former postmaster general who since 1922 had been president of the trade association known as the Motion Picture Producers and Distributors of America—declared:

Original scores, written by many of the world's finest composers, are increasingly in use. They pass unrecognized and unheralded, for the most part, and to a degree, quite properly so, for one of the essentials of a fine score is that it be unobtrusive.[62]

Still, there were points of contention. The debate as to how "unobtrusive" film music should really be was occasionally voiced but seemed of little importance—composers who by this time were fairly experienced at writing for Hollywood seemed to know the right mix. On the other hand, the public debate over the aesthetic quality of film music was, at the dawn of Hollywood's classical period, just heating up.

Regarding the situation from a considerable distance, certain music critics—some of whom also happened to be composers—began to declare openly that film music as Hollywood chose to define it was cliché-ridden, derivative, formulaic, and in all other ways simply not very good. At the same time, composers who had collectively struggled to establish the norm for Hollywood's classical-style film began to close ranks against what they perceived as infiltration from the outside.

Antheil, an ambitious yet frustrated composer who would long contend that his expenditure of creative energy on the writing of lucrative film scores kept him from producing symphonies, was perhaps inviting the fight when he boldly stated, in an article from late in 1937, that most of Hollywood's current musical efforts amount to "unmitigated tripe" and suggested that a remedy for this situation might be keen attention paid to film scores by serious music critics in such cities as New York, Boston, and Philadelphia. Antheil speculated that intense aesthetic scrutiny of this sort might well "throw just about half of the present Hollywood 'composers' out of their jobs," but at the same time he granted that Hollywood probably would resist, successfully, with the argument "that our better composers do not understand the needs of the motion picture, that their music is too high-brow." Such an argument, Antheil wrote, would be "sheer poppycock." Nevertheless, it seemed to Antheil a fact that

> many excellent composers have come to Hollywood and returned East again. Scarcely any of them have gotten jobs. While on the other hand, the routine Hollywood composers who have been here many years have grown alarmed at the influx of new men, and have used their influence to sew up every future score available. In other words Hollywood music is, at the present writing, a closed corporation.[63]

Earlier in 1937 Antheil had described how difficult it was for anyone to break into the attractively lucrative business of film scoring, which for composers "with aptitude" paid from "$3,000 to $8,000" per film.[64] Elsewhere in the article, commenting on the building tension between the Hollywood regulars and outsiders, he observed that although "an occasional successful foreign picture will eventually find its director comfortably berthed in Hollywood, . . . as to most foreign musicians—Hollywood is convinced that they are veritable tyros."[65] And tellingly—considering where much of film music's vituperative criticism would soon come from—he noted that Virgil Thomson's score for the previous year's documentary film *The Plow That Broke the Plains* "from the Hollywood point of view [seemed] 'amateurish,' and so Thomson was labeled."[66]

*   *   *

Thomson, likely not pleased that the Hollywood community, as reported by Antheil, considered his music for *The Plow That Broke the Plains* to be "amateurish," struck back in 1939 with a bitter chapter in his book *The State of Music*.

Along with the overall insincerity and low emotional appeal of Hollywood's products, Thomson's concerns included film music's narrative-necessitated lack of continuity, the constant "fading-away and loudening-up" that "contradicts all dynamic variety" that a composer might have written into a score, and the "musical pageantry" that regularly turns naturalistic stories into melodrama.[67] But Thomson attacked what he called "commentary music" for the most part on grounds that were formalistic:

> In order that this commentary be not too prominent, an attempt is made to write it in a neutral style. The style is not really neutral; let us call it, for lack of a better term, pseudo-neutral music. . . . [The composers'] aim is to make music that will be rich in harmonic texture and sumptuous orchestration, but whose melodic material and expressive content will be so vague that nobody will notice it. Such music fulfills its minimum architectonic function of tying together the continuity at the points where it is absolutely necessary that that be done. It is also useful for underlining a bit of humor or a heart throb and for creating fortissimo hubbub at the beginning and end of films, the time when people are

changing their seats. . . . [But] its power of self-effacement is its real virtue. Few persons excepting those of predominantly auditive memory (and these rarely go to the movies) can ever remember anything about the music of serious drama films, even whether there was any or not. It is discreet; it is respectable; it comes and goes without being noticed. It carefully avoids ever making any underlining that might engage it subsequently to a close collaboration with the film story. It retires completely before the speaking voice, no matter how banal a remark that voice may be about to utter. . . . [Yet it] is both architecturally and emotionally inefficient, because music can't be neutral and sumptuous at the same time.[68]

Thomson did not dismiss *all* scores for narrative films. A decade after *The State of Music*, in a newspaper article headlined "Hollywood's Best," he heaped accolades on Aaron Copland's score for Republic's *The Red Pony* (1949), and he offered that "Honegger, Auric, Milhaud, and Sauguet in France, William Walton in England, Kurt Weill in Germany, Prokofiev and Shostakovitch in Soviet Russia have all made film music that was more than a worthy contribution to film drama."[69] The names mentioned by Thomson are worth noting. They are relatively few in number, and they appear again and again in commentaries by critics—some of them, like Thomson, composers who dabbled in film scoring—who passed stern judgment on Hollywood practice.

In the third chapter of his 1939 autobiography *A Smattering of Ignorance*, Oscar Levant—famous both as a jazz pianist and as an interpreter of the keyboard music of George Gershwin, and an occasional contributor of original music for Hollywood films[70]—criticizes the anonymity forced upon the composer by Hollywood's factory-like working conditions (hence the chapter's title, "A Cog in the Wheel"), the musical ignorance of the producers who ultimately have the final say not just about a score's content but also the placement of its segments, the dependence of film music on well-worn clichés, the boldness with which Hollywood composers routinely steal not only ideas but actual material from the works of their concert-hall counterparts, and the general lack of talent among a "vicious circle" of "specialists."[71] Later in the book, Levant mentions Honegger, Auric, Shostakovich, and Prokofiev as non-Americans who have produced especially fine film music; among the noteworthy American composers, he cites only Copland and Thomson.[72]

As already noted, Antheil, in the articles he wrote for *Modern Music* during the 1930s, had praise for film scores by such composers as Auric, Toch, Goosens, Prokofiev, Shostakovich, and Weill. These names come up again in his 1945 autobiography, *Bad Boy of Music*, but throughout the book Antheil focuses critical attention only on film-music regulars, and he concludes pessimistically that "with the exception of Waxman, [Frederick] Hollander, and possibly [Miklós] Rózsa and . . . and [Bernard] Herrmann, not a single composer of new vitality has appeared in Hollywood in years."[73] Two years before Antheil's book was published Ernest Irving, a "pioneer of British film music" who by this time had conducted and/or composed scores for dozens of films,[74] in an article for a prestigious musicological journal was dismissive of American film music in general. But Irving had positive things to say for the film efforts of his countrymen Arnold Bax, Arthur Bliss, Ralph Vaughan Williams, and William Walton, and he noted as well that the film music of Prokofiev, Honegger, and Milhaud "all bears the hall-mark of mastership."[75]

The idea of a film-music "canon"—formulated not by practitioners but for the most part by outside observers—was further solidified in the late 1940s, more or less simultaneous with Thomson's journalistic pronouncements, by the establishment of the College Committee on Film Music, a group of American academics sincerely devoted to study of the genre. Members of the committee included representatives from Queens College, Vassar College, the University of California Press, and the University of Michigan, and the committee's chairman was Dartmouth College music professor Frederick W. Sternfeld. In a 1947 "preliminary report" on the committee's activities, Sternfeld condescendingly dismissed the effects that Hollywood-style film music, in general, seemed to have on audiences:

> However tolerant and capable of real enthusiasm [the] public may be, it needs enlightenment, and the younger generation should have competent instruction. The courageous pioneering of such men as Virgil Thomson, Aaron Copland, George Antheil, [Ralph] Vaughan Williams, George[s] Auric, William Walton, and others, deserves to be encouraged by an intelligent response from teachers and students. As a result, enlightened film directors may be induced to offer more equitable terms of collaboration to their musical associates.[76]

In what might be interpreted as a sensible retreat from an academically hidebound stance, Sternfeld later in 1947—in an article for a musicological journal—lavished praise on a recent film score by a decidedly non-canonic composer (Hugo Friedhofer's music for the Goldwyn Studio's *The Best Years of Our Lives*). He also celebrated the apparent fact that current Hollywood practice not just allowed but, indeed, encouraged composers to indulge freely in modernist idioms that in the concert hall were still regarded, by audiences, with trepidation:

> Hindemith's "secundal" counterpoint, presented in Carnegie Hall as absolute music, receives a cold welcome from a musically unsophisticated audience, but Hindemithian harmonies forming the counterpart of a duel on the screen, as in *The Bandit of Sherwood Forest*, are absorbed with keen emotional enjoyment. Unconsciously, the public has accepted the dissonances and rhythmic complexities of a modern idiom in expressive and illustrative sequences. In fact, the average listener encounters this idiom so much more frequently in the cinema than in concert music that, paradoxically, he is apt to mistake the chicken for the egg. After a performance of a recent symphonic work of one of our distinguished contemporary composers, a layman was induced to remark that it sounded like the movies.[77]

But over the course of the next year Sternfeld seems to have retrenched. The headline assigned to his article in the *New York Times*—"Cinema Scores: A Few Good Ones Give Hope for Future"—expresses the bias. It seems curious that from the perspective of October 1948 Sternfeld finds it necessary to note that Thomson's 1937 score for *The River* is "so substantial that it has been used in at least two subsequent documentaries." Other than that, Sternfeld singles out for praise only Walton's for *Henry V*, Copland's for *Our Town*, and Thomson's for the documentaries *The Plow That Broke the Plains* and *Louisiana Story*, and he notes that "the names of . . . Vaughan Williams, Auric,

153

Milhaud and Honegger" have also "been an asset to the credit lines." He expresses the apparent hope that producers be "far-sighted enough to watch and encourage this trend" in "high-quality" scores, but he concludes that, alas, "in most instances the need for entertainment in countless neighborhood theatres the year around has produced the mediocre and the trite, the safe and the cliché."[78]

More Squabbles

These debates amounted to little. Throughout the initial period of Hollywood's classical-style film—that is, from the last years of the Great Depression, during World War II, and well into the post-war period—production continued unabated, and film-scoring practices by and large held to the conventions described above. For reasons perhaps as much financial as artistic, genuinely prestigious composers continued to be attracted to the possibilities of scoring Hollywood films; Igor Stravinsky, for example, had exploratory conversations with executives at MGM in 1935 and 1940, and between 1938 and 1940 Arnold Schoenberg engaged in discussion with both MGM and Paramount.[79] And for reasons of practicality, which related directly to the profits generated by any given film, Hollywood producers continued to rely on musicians who did not demand "time to wait for inspiration" but, rather, understood full well—and did not complain about—the fact that film music "has to be composed fast and yet prove emotionally telling without getting into the way of dialogue."[80]

The endurance of Hollywood's classical-style film, of course, had very much to do with the fact that the United States benefited hugely from having its film industry *not* disrupted by the war; Hollywood made certain concessions for the sake of the war effort, notably a diversion of energy into products (including government-sponsored documentaries) clearly designed to rally the nation's collective spirit, but in technological terms the war-time situation resulted primarily in economies of cinematography, and Hollywood in general found the war years to be as lucrative as had been the Depression years. Elsewhere, film industries were not so fortunate. In the Axis countries, the cinema was regarded as a potent propaganda tool and thus filmmaking was completely controlled by fascist governments; in the Allied countries of Europe, filmmaking simply struggled to exist. When the war finally ended, in 1945, the once prestigious and internationally influential European film industries—those of victorious England, France, and the Soviet Union as much as those of defeated Germany and Italy—were similarly in a position akin to that of a victim who has barely survived a traumatic accident: certain pre-existing ideals might have been still intact, but the physical apparatus needed to realize those ideals, or new ones that possibly resulted from reflection on the experience, was sorely in need of a long period of recovery.

In marked contrast, in the aftermath of World War II classical-style Hollywood filmmaking simply rolled along as usual. Also rolling along—truly as usual, for the core issues remained the same—were the interrelated squabbles over the extent to which film music should be in effect "inaudible" and the aesthetic "quality" of music for Hollywood feature films as opposed to music for documentaries.

Agenda-laden critics continued to deride Hollywood composers as "musical galley slaves [who] must keep their musical oars going against the time and tide of release dates and dramatic inferiority of whatever picture is assigned to them,"[81] to declare that—with the exception of contributions by the likes of such Europeans as Auric, Honegger, and

Walton and such darlings of the American musical establishment as Copland, Thomson, Paul Bowles, and Marc Blitzstein—"music for the screen" has in general "not been on a much higher level of sophistication than that of the hoarse pianist banging away" in the nickelodeons,[82] that even the best composers typically use their film scores as repositories for "all their discarded tunes, faulty fugues, second-class counterpoint and other waste ideas."[83] In the face of this, Hollywood insiders continued to inform the public that "if you notice the music during a film then we have done a bad job of it" because "your appreciation of music should be subconscious,"[84] that the "melodic successes" of Hollywood are always "secondary to the pictures for which they are designed,"[85] that "much of the music in dramatic scores must be so handled that the audience does not become music-conscious at the expense of dialogue or drama."[86] And apparently objective reporters continued to note that because composing for feature films involves working cooperatively "with a dozen people as important as themselves, composers who have attained a distinctive style find the film medium difficult," that— precisely because they are good collaborators, and flexible in their style—in Hollywood such composers as "Alfred Newman, Max Steiner, Franz Waxman, Morton Gould, Jerome Kern, [Bernard] Herrmann, Nat Shilkret, Edward Ward, Miklos Rosza, Victor Young, Adolph Deutsch, David Raksin, Leo Forbstein, Arthur Lange and [Michel] Michelet . . . get the best pictures to score."[87]

Most of the strong opinions on film music expressed during the 1940s took the form of diatribes or polemics addressed to no one in particular. But at least a few of them had an almost personal touch.

In March 1940, for example, Copland wrote an article for the *New York Times* in which, apparently in reaction to negative reception of the music he had composed for *Of Mice and Men* (United Artists, 1940), he defensively attacked "one of the oldest superstitions in Hollywood"—what he called "an old tradition"—that purports that "the better a motion picture score is, the less attention it attracts. . . . Seriously, I think the principal reason so few people are consciously aware of the music they hear from the screen is that audiences have not yet been fully informed on the subject."[88] A year later, near the conclusion of a scholarly article devoted mostly to an historical survey of film music, dance critic Marian Hannah Winter observed that "Mr. Copland's article . . . unfortunately does not alter the merits of [the critics'] disapproval. It was not a matter of too much or too obtrusive music in 'Of Mice and Men,' but of unperceptive *film music*."[89] Winter opined that the failings of the score for *Of Mice and Men* likely "stem from Copland's apparent conviction that films have no sustained and constant rhythm of their own, and need an evangelical savior in the guise of composer." She noted, nevertheless, that Copland's music for *Our Town* (United Artists, 1940) seemed to be an improvement over *Of Mice and Men*, and she suggested that "probably further work in the medium will temper Copland's lack of restraint and pretentiousness."[90]

Later in the decade Copland, to be sure, had done "further work in the medium"; he had composed music for *The North Star* (Goldwyn, 1943) and for a brief government-sponsored documentary titled *The Cunningham Story* (1945), and early in 1948 he was in Hollywood to score Republic's *The Red Pony*. In a newspaper interview he granted that "movie music has made the public musically more sophisticated," and he said that for proof that film music in general has grown in sophistication one need only "look at some of the present scores, which now imitate the styles of Hindemith, Stravinsky and

Bartók, where once Richard Strauss and Tschaikowsky were the models." Nevertheless, perhaps indeed playing on an "evangelical" theme, he declared:

> The worst feature of most present film music is the kind of orchestral fabric to which the public has become accustomed. If they are not constantly bathed in a certain type of sound they appear to think that something is wrong. We should develop a true movie music style—in the best sense, as we now have operatic and ballet styles. The style should be simplified. It is now too complex, too close to the symphonic style as we know it in the concert hall.[91]

Just a few days after the Copland interview appeared, composer David Raksin—who by this time had worked on more than eighty films in Hollywood—authored a newspaper article that bore the pugnacious headline "Talking Back: A Hollywood Composer States Case for His Craft." Apparently taking aim not just at Copland's comments on Hollywood-style orchestration but also at the "establishment" bias toward music in documentary films, Raksin wrote:

> In the music of documentary films we can hear and see what happens to serious composers when they undertake to write for the screen. Some scores, of course, are first rate. But considering the great freedom of expression allowed the composers of these (in contrast to the Hollywood composers, who must frequently conduct guerilla warfare in the underbrush of contemporary harmony and counterpoint) the percentage of good scores is remarkably small.
>
> I have always felt that it takes a genius to make an orchestra sound bad; apparently some of the documentary boys have what it takes. They sneer openly at our occasional pointing up of visual cues, yet some of their best moments are often more Mickey Mouse than music. And, when they cast loose and write freely, the resulting scores are apt to have a fair share of all the virtues of film music except the indispensable one of relevance.[92]

*　*　*

In 1947 Oxford University Press published the book *Composing for the Films*, officially authored by the German émigré composer Hanns Eisler—and officially related to research Eisler conducted upon receiving a $25,000 grant from the Rockefeller Foundation in 1939—but in all likelihood mostly written by Theodor Adorno.[93] In the book's first chapter, titled "Prejudices and Bad Habits," Eisler (or Adorno) hammers relentlessly on Hollywood music's over-reliance on scores "patched together by means of leitmotifs,"[94] its perennial meeting the requirement of "unobtrusiveness" not "by an approximation of nonmusical sounds but by the use of banal music,"[95] and its penchant for "clichés . . . associated with the mood and content of the picture."[96] Summarizing all that follows this opening chapter, Lawrence Morton in a review aptly notes that "the book is mistitled; for Mr. Eisler's real theme is not film music, but his own indignation at what passes for music making in the studios."[97] Morton, who between 1945 and 1951 contributed a total of nineteen keenly insightful articles on film music to *Hollywood Quarterly* and *The Quarterly Review of Film, Radio and Television*, acknowledges that "all the evils [Eisler] names do exist," but he reminds readers that "they certainly are not universal," and that "there are variations of degree and kind;" apparently shocked at the forcefulness of the condemnations, Morton notes that Eisler's "indictment is so sweeping as to consign to hell fire a number of legitimate practices and an amount of good film music which, in a less Jehovah-like judgment, would be regarded as extenuating."[98] Overall, Morton is respectful of the modernist compositional style that Eisler brought as much to his film scores as to his works for the concert hall; nevertheless, Morton concludes, "it appears that many of Mr. Eisler's objections to today's film music are based less upon its actual failures than upon his desire to promote the twelve-tone aesthetic."[99]

A few years before Morton boldly took issue with the heavy pronouncements of the Eisler/Adorno book, a fascinating debate—involving not just two but three participants —transpired in the pages of the *New York Times*.

The first salvo in this skirmish was fired by Erich Leinsdorf, the highly respected conductor who at the time was music director of the Cleveland Orchestra. Apparently remembering with fondness the pre-1933 days when such studios as RKO and MGM fitted their films only with "source music," Leinsdorf in 1945 complained that nowadays "in so-called realistic pictures one frequently hears an orchestra accompany a scene where absolutely no relation can be established between the music and the pictorial drama," and he was particularly irritated by what he perceived to be the substitution of musical "background" for naturalistic sounds:

> When I see a scene in a railroad terminal with the action centered around the information desk, with the porters running up and down staircases, with people milling about, the sound of a highly romantic piece of music played by a full orchestra is not only absurd but also distracting; it draws the attention of the mind (at least my own) from the actual scene to the music, which is usually too loud, out of place and out of style.[100]

Leinsdorf claimed to be content with orchestral scores that accompanied "pictures of an unrealistic, fantastic nature." But in "realistic" films, he wrote, "the invariably lush sonorities which accompany most emotional scenes are unbearable, because they employ cold-bloodedly devices which have lost their originality, and which are meaningless as used according to a standard pattern."[101] Generally dismayed, Leinsdorf wrote:

> Conclusive proof of the unsatisfactory status of music in the motion picture industry is the fact that some of our modern composers have given up working for pictures, while those who have stayed in Hollywood have subjected them-selves to the demands for standardization and pattern. Typecasting is deadly to a composer, and compulsion to write time and again identical scores for identical stories is bound to result in a lifeless pattern which no ambitious and honest musician will be able to stand for any length of time.[102]

Leinsdorf's article elicited a strong rebuttal from Bernard Herrmann, who in 1945 was still a decade away from his famous relationship with the films of director Alfred Hitchcock but who by this time had nevertheless firmly established Hollywood credentials with his scores for *Citizen Kane* (RKO, 1941), *All That Money Can Buy* (RKO, 1941), *The Magnificent Ambersons* (RKO, 1942), *Jane Eyre* (Twentieth Century-Fox, 1944), and *Hangover Square* (Twentieth Century-Fox, 1945). Herrmann reminds readers of the *New York Times* that Leinsdorf, the week before, "indulged in a favorite sport current among many of our interpretive concert musicians—that of belittling film music."[103] After citing the conductor's contention that film music is almost by definition "subordinate," and that "music in any 'subordinate' place is 'odious' to a musician," Herrmann reminds Leinsdorf that in opera, too, music has long been for the most part subordinate to the needs of drama. Most forcefully, in response to Leinsdorf's suggestion that certain modern composers eschew film work for fear of being typecast, Herrmann states:

> Contrary to all rumor, there is no such thing as the "standardization" of motion-picture music. The only "standard" for film music is that it be dramatic. Perhaps this is something Mr. Leinsdorf does not understand when he deplores the fact that many of our modern composers have given up working for the screen. Might it not be, simply, that these composers, though their talents are of sterling quality, lack the dramatic flair?[104]

Between the disputants stepped Bosley Crowther, the newspaper's veteran movie critic. Interestingly, considering the allusion to Keats that Claudia Gorbman used for the title of her book on music in the narrative film, Crowther's balanced mediation is headlined "Heard Melodies." At the outset of the article, Crowther makes clear that, far from being a musical sophisticate, he is simply an "average Joe." And the Leinsdorf–Herrmann exchange, he says, simply gives him the opportunity to offer some comments that he has long been meaning to make. "The first thing," he writes, is that

> the best test of a musical score of a film is whether the average person is conscious of it. If he's not, then it has merit. If he is—if the incidental music or atmospheric music, as it is called, comes sharply and persistently to attention—then there's something wrong with the score.[105]

Crowther gives numerous examples of music that indeed seems intrusive (the introduction of cliché tunes into scenes, or the underscoring of a conversational scene with music that serves no dramatic purpose). He also gives a few specific examples in which music has been introduced subtly and effectively:

> A literal illustration of a destroyer racing through the water, say, such as the opening sequence of the film "In Which We Serve," is made more effective by a thrilling, soaring musical theme that represents the stimulation of the spirit as one silently observes. In a case of this sort, the music is a commentator on the scene, an accompaniment to the exaltation which the observer inwardly feels. And even a scene such as the fine one at the beginning of "The Purple Heart," in which the "Air Force Song" softly accompanied the American fliers into the hostile courtroom, was considerably helped by the music. It came, as it were, from the audience's heart.[106]

Unfortunately, Crowther never gets around to making a second point. He has merely scratched the surface, he says, of an important topic that surely deserves further attention. In the end, he admits, "we've probably done no more than agitate dispute. But that won't hurt anybody."[107]

Signs of Trouble

Crowther was right. Doubtless it wrinkled the egos of prestigious composers to be collectively identified as "veritable tyros" or to be singled out for having written "amateurish" film scores, and doubtless it bothered at least a few Hollywood regulars to read that their work celebrated "the mediocre and the trite" or to know that the only film music the American and European cultural establishment deemed "masterly" came from the pens of a handful of concert-hall composers whose influence on film scoring was, in the long run, minimal. But public dispute over aesthetic quality and dramatic function did not hurt film music, and it certainly did not hurt the highly profitable industry that made classical-style film music possible.

What hurt Hollywood, but which had little immediate effect on Hollywood film music, was the seemingly star-cross'd coincidence ca. 1948–9 of a number of factors. Only one of these, the sudden feasibility of network television, had directly to do with screen-based entertainment of the sort over which Hollywood for more than three decades had held a monopoly. The others had little to do with cinema *per se* but, rather, with matters sociological, legal, and political. In combination, they dealt Hollywood a serious blow.

Earlier in this chapter it was noted that the Great Depression was a boom time for Hollywood; many Americans hard-pressed to put food on their families' tables nevertheless came up with the relatively inexpensive wherewithal to find escapist solace, week after week, by simply going to "the movies." This trend continued throughout the years of World War II. Film historian Gerald Mast reports that in 1946 Hollywood's gross receipts amounted to $1.7 billion. And 1946, Mast reminds us, was "the peak box-office year in movie history."[108]

From this peak, revenue from Hollywood films plummeted precipitously. "In 1958," Mast writes, "box-office receipts fell below a billion dollars," and "by 1962 receipts had fallen to $900,000,000, slightly more than half the 1946 gross."[109] In the first chapter of his book on American cinema in the 1950s, Peter Lev offers not box-office revenues but weekly attendance figures at American movie theaters between 1940 and 1960. Lev's data come from three sources: the U.S. Department of Commerce and Bureau of Labor Statistics, the U.S. Census Bureau, and the trade organization called the Theatre Owners of America. According to information from the most widely quoted source, the Census Bureau, "weekly attendance dropped from 80 million in 1940 and 90 million in 1946 to 60 million in 1950 and 40 million in 1960." Although the figures from the three sources differ, Lev writes, "the general trend [they show] is the same. Admissions rose from 1940 to 1946, and then dropped fairly rapidly so that by 1956 attendance was down almost 50 percent from the 1946 peak."[110]

At least for a while, the aesthetics of the classical-style Hollywood film—including its convention-based manner of musical accompaniment—endured. But as the United States entered its prosperous post-war period the industry that had long thrived on this style of film, ironically, was in trouble. In March 1949 the *New York Times* ran an interview with the producer who, some seventeen years earlier with his orders to Max Steiner, perhaps had planted the first seeds for the classical-style film score. The article bore the resonant headline: "Films 'Struggle,' Selznick Asserts."[111]

159

Chapter 9

POSTWAR INNOVATIONS AND THE STRUGGLE FOR SURVIVAL, 1949–58

As a film music critic, I am compelled to see about three films a week (or at any rate their respective first halves), but I am not aware of any marked artistic advance in the development from the silent to the sound film and thence to Cinema-Scopic sight and stereophonic sound. It is again a sign of our artistic times—the advance of techniques and physical innovations beyond that which they ought to serve; when you haven't got much to say, you have to "experiment."

Hans Keller, 1954[1]

Addressing participants in the March 1949 fortieth annual conference of the National Board of Review of Motion Pictures, producer David O. Selznick—once an employee of RKO but by this time well-established as the head of his own studio—bluntly reminded his filmmaking colleagues that "the economics of the business have gone very sour" and that movie-makers are "struggling desperately to make ends meet."[2]

As reported in the *New York Times*, Selznick in his grim address to the trade organization did not go into details as to why the American film industry—which had enjoyed uninterrupted financial success since the days of World War I—was suddenly in dire straits. A month earlier, however, the same newspaper noted that Hollywood's troubles resulted at least in part from a "sharp decline in the industry's overseas markets" and, more significant, from "expanding inroads being carved by television" and "the apparent loss of the major [Hollywood] producers' ten-year fight to retain control of their theatre operations."[3]

At the time of the report there were fifty-six commercial television stations operating within the borders of the United States, whereas a year earlier there had been only twenty. In 1950 the stations numbered ninety-eight; in 1954 there were 233 stations, and by 1960 the number had reached 440.[4] The expansion of the broadcasting industry was paralleled by a rise in the manufacture and sale of television sets. In a February 1949 newspaper article headlined "Hollywood in the Television Age," Samuel Goldwyn noted: "There are now 950,000 sets installed, sets are being produced at the rate of 161,000 per month and next year that rate will double."[5] According to the Federal Communications Commission, in 1950 sales of television sets in the United States amounted to more than 7.3 million, and "U.S. TV sales were never less than 5 million in the years 1950–9."[6] Hollywood knew that television was having a negative effect on cinema attendance, but the extent of the effect was unclear. In 1950 Paramount attested that, according to its own survey, families with television sets decreased their cinema attendance not, as had been previously reported, by between 47 and 54 percent but by only 20 to 30 percent; a year later an article in *Variety*, summarizing a survey conducted by Warner Bros., accurately bore the headline: "TV's Impact a Puzzler."[7]

The "sharp decline in [Hollywood's] overseas markets" was attributed largely to squabbles with the film industry in England, which to date had "always been the most important factor in the American film industry's overseas income." As the *New York Times* reported:

> The American film industry began to be deprived of its large revenues from England in 1947 when an "ad valorum" duty of 75 per cent was levied on income of imported films. Some measure of relief was obtained last July with the signing of a four-year pact with the British, whereby Hollywood studios agreed to leave in that country as "blocked sterling" all their sterling revenues from film rentals except for a basic amount of $25,000,000 and an amount equal to what British films earned here.
>
> A new restriction, however, was introduced last October [1948] when England imposed quotas on the playing time to be allowed American films on British screens. This reduced playing time of American films from over 80 per cent to 50 per cent. The latest unfavorable development occurred on Feb. 2 last, when the British Parliament approved a bill creating a national agency to lend money to the country's producers.[8]

Filmmakers in England at this time were truly in need of government support. A March 1949 news item on a planned visit to the United States by representatives of the British film industry noted: "A slow-down in film making has closed three studios in the London area. Between 2,000 and 3,000 film workers have been laid off."[9] More colorfully, a London-based reporter wrote:

> They tell us, those carefree characters who go out and consort with lambs or commune with crocuses, that spring is on the way. Nevertheless, the British film industry is facing the bleakest winter of its history. As we write, eighteen out of our twenty-four studios are closed, and there are idle floors on the remaining six. In recent weeks approximately 2,000 studio employees have been dismissed on grounds of "redundancy," and there are no signs at all that the purge has run its course.[10]

The problem Hollywood faced was not competition with films from England or anywhere else. Rather, the problem had to do with protective economic measures taken by various countries as part of their recovery from the trauma of World War II. Hoping to rebuild their own film industries, a number of countries imposed unusually high tariffs and restrictive quota systems on American imports. Even more troubling to Hollywood, a number of countries passed laws that limited the amount of money that could leave their borders, which meant that a large portion of the cash that Hollywood earned abroad had to stay abroad. Hollywood's quick solution was to bank the money locally and then spend it on productions filmed—at least in part—in whatever countries the "blocked funds" resided. This had no ill effect on American movie stars who happily flew off to shoot "on location," but it had a severe impact on Hollywood's many behind-the-scenes workers. In February 1949, a month before Selznick proclaimed that Hollywood was "struggling desperately to make ends meet," the Hollywood American Federation of Labor Film Council complained publicly about "foreign competition financed by Hollywood capital."[11] Indeed, the group formally requested a government ban on films made in countries that sought to "impound the earnings of American movies":

> The AFL announcement culminates long agitation and frequent complaints by Hollywood labor against the transference of many production projects to Europe by producers anxious to utilize their impounded currency credits. The ban, if it were applied, would halt importation of pictures from virtually every country in Europe, including Great Britain, France and Italy. Behind the AFL move is widespread unemployment in Hollywood, jobs in the film industry last year having fallen 25 per cent below 1940 levels and 33 per cent below 1946 levels.[12]

The third factor that contributed significantly to Hollywood's post-war woes—"the apparent loss of the major producers' ten-year fight to retain control of their theatre operations"—involved a legal dispute that had been sidetracked by the outbreak of World War II. Since the 1920s the largest Hollywood studios had known that distribution of their products could be greatly facilitated, and thus the profits from these products greatly increased, if they simply owned the venues in which their films were exhibited. In such a context, the large studios could maintain complete control over advertisements and run-times for their own films; perhaps more important, they could also severely squelch competition from smaller studios whose real-estate holdings were minimal or nonexistent. As early as 1938 the United States government suspected that this "vertically integrated structure" was monopolistic and thus filed suit.

Revived in 1948, the lawsuit was primarily directed against Paramount, which by this time was not just a major production studio but also the owner—with some 1,450 venues—of "the largest theatre chain in the country."[13] But the suit, officially titled *United States v. Paramount, Inc., et al.* and commonly known as "the Paramount case," involved more studios than just Paramount. Together, the group often identified as the "five major studios"—Paramount, MGM (Loew's), Twentieth Century-Fox, Warner Bros., and RKO—owned approximately 65 percent of the American "first-run" cinemas, and a significant number of "first-run" venues were controlled, if not actually owned, by Columbia, Universal, and United Artists. To make a long and legalistically compli-cated story short, in May 1948 Supreme Court Justice William O. Douglas declared that the suit, by this time much-appealed, should go back to where it originated, the District Court for the Southern District of New York; significantly, Douglas recommended that the studios' cinemas, "to the extent that these acquisitions were the fruits of the monopolistic practices or restraints of trade, . . . should be divested."[14] And so it happened, with the case finally decided on July 25, 1949. Paramount capitulated; MGM, Fox, Warner Bros., and RKO resisted, but only for a while, and within a year all eight of the larger studios had signed consent decrees. Accurately prognosticating, an anonymous business writer for the *New York Times* wrote, in February 1949, that

> Loss of [the major studios'] theatres (which seems certain for all American companies now that Paramount has signed an anti-trust consent decree with the Department of Justice) is expected to cause a sharp reduction in the industry's income and a similarly sharp reduction in the total output of feature films.[15]

Coming as they did almost simultaneously, competition from television, restrictions imposed by overseas governments, and the court-ordered divestiture of its cinematic real estate hit Hollywood hard. But there were still other factors that contributed, ca. 1948–9, to Hollywood's fall from grace.

* * *

One of these was a general feeling, on the part of government agencies and a large part of the American population, that certain persons in Hollywood—and thus by extension certain Hollywood products—were somehow and perhaps dangerously "unpatriotic." The period of Hollywood's "troubles" coincided with the most heated years of the Cold War that the United States fought against communism in all its manifestations; even the slightest connection with leftist thinking was cause for official concern, and Hollywood certainly had its share of leftists.

By coincidence, it was film music composer Hanns Eisler who served as the first high-profile victim of official suspicion. Eisler, who claimed that his politics were simply anti-fascist, never anti-American, had indeed been involved with the socialist movement in Europe during the late 1920s and 1930s, and his brother in fact was a leader of the Communist party in the United States. But Eisler in the 1940s seems to have led a remarkably nonpolitical life; during his California sojourn he associated comfortably with a left-leaning crowd that included Fritz Lang, Bertolt Brecht, Clifford Odets, Harold Clurman, Jean Renoir, Charles Chaplin, and Peter Lorre, but his purpose in Hollywood was simply to earn a living.[16] As is documented by the voluminous file compiled over the course of an intense six-year investigation, the FBI turned up not a shred of evidence to suggest that Eisler was a threat to American security, or even that he had ever been a card-carrying Communist.[17] Eisler nevertheless was eventually deported, and his prolonged and harsh public questioning early in 1947 by the House Un-American Activities Committee in effect marked the start of the government's purge of the motion picture industry. In an attempt to ferret out Hollywood insiders of leftist persuasion, HUAC later in 1947 interviewed more than forty persons involved with filmmaking. Of the nineteen persons named as suspected leftists, ten (Alvah Bessie, Herbert Biberman, Lester Cole, Edward Dmytrik, Ring Lardner Jr., John Howard Lawson, Albert Maltz, Samuel Ornitz, Adrian Scott, and Dalton Trumbo) famously refused to cooperate with the Committee and served prison sentences for contempt; under questioning, the others identified dozens of their colleagues, and the result was the Hollywood "black list" that endured well into the 1950s.

Along with official pressure from the United States government for political reform, Hollywood at this time experienced pressure from a number of groups—among them the American Legion, the Roman Catholic Legion of Decency, the Council of Churches of Christ, and factions within the industry's own Production Code Administration—that throughout the postwar period clamored loudly for reform of films' overall moral content. Along with eventually forcing a strict interpretation of the Motion Picture

Production Code that had been in existence since 1929, these various groups encouraged policing, literally, of films. Hollywood responded not boldly but fearfully, with a sudden output of films carefully designed to offend no one.

As early as September 1949 producer Samuel Goldwyn maintained that "censorship of films is the reason that people in adult age brackets stay out of movie houses in droves." Addressing the annual gathering of the Theatre Owners of America, he railed against "weak-kneed and spineless" producers who have caved in to the demands of "petty, small-minded, single-tracked dirt-sniffers":

> We have permitted ourselves to be frightened to death by the shadow of organized pressure groups whose total membership sometimes represents no more than the half dozen names printed on a letterhead.
>
> What's more, we have taken, lying down, the laws of those States and countless cities which provide for censorship of our business. Ours is the only industry, business, art—call it what you will—in the country which must submit to censorship in advance.
>
> There is no one else who has something to sell, or to show or to say, who must go, hat in hand, to some petty official and say:
> "Please, may I?"[18]

All this—television, foreign embargos, the forced break-up of an allegedly monopolistic distribution system, dark clouds of political and moral suspicion—amounted to a tidal wave of trouble for the American film industry. Possibly some took heart when, late in 1949, newspapers across the United States announced the financial collapse of J. Arthur Rank British, the English conglomerate that had been the sharp spearhead of Hollywood's problems overseas. But a loud headline such as "Rank Failure Held Proof of U.S. Film Superiority"[19] in fact damned with faint praise. With the Rank organization's retreat, Hollywood indeed seemed "to have won its fight for unchallenged world dominance in film making,"[20] yet it remained that the realm over which Hollywood could now exert its sovereignty was a far cry from what had existed since the early 1920s.

Selznick, in his March 1949 address to industry representatives, was quite right in declaring that the audience for films had "drastically changed."[21] At the time, he may or may not have been aware of an industry-commissioned study that just a month earlier concluded that the recent drop in cinema attendance was not due to audience members' "ability to pay" the small price of admission but, rather, simply to a decrease in their "desire to attend theatres."[22] Certainly in the United States, but to a large extent also in Europe, the recovery from World War II involved not just a bounty of well-paying jobs (related to the quick convergence of sophisticated wartime factories to the production of peacetime goods) but also a strong desire, on the part of war-weary ex-soldiers, to settle into some sort of "normal" life. Veterans thus married quickly, and just as quickly—launching the demographic phenomenon commonly known as the Baby Boom—they started to raise families.

At the century's midpoint, American adults could much more easily afford the price of admission to a cinema than had been the case just a few years earlier. Yet they chose, likely for reasons having to do with new family obligations, to stay at home. And Hollywood, little by little, awakened to the apparent fact that Americans in general had simply lost interest in going to "the movies."

Moving Toward Divergence

Film music played curiously into all this. Both internationally and in Hollywood, the nature of film scoring would change markedly during the 1950s. But it was not a matter of the industry as a whole moving, however quickly or slowly, in the same direction.

The sudden shifts in approach that marked the earliest years of the sound film were for the most part triggered by rapid changes in technology; they originated in Hollywood, yet they were imitated in turn throughout the world as soon as the Hollywood-based technology became available. Likewise, the gradual evolution of the classical-style film with its characteristic underscore transpired mostly in Hollywood, and there can be no doubt that it was significantly enabled by 1930s Hollywood technology and production practices; although certain European filmmakers indeed resisted the classical-style film's "excessively obvious" use of music and preferred scores that somehow played "against" filmic action and emotion, just as many, according to whatever erratic pace was afforded them by wartime disruption and postwar recovery, readily adopted the Hollywood aesthetic.

Before the 1950s—indeed, all the way back to the point ca. 1903 when the widely variegated "cinema of attraction" metamorphosed into a more or less consistent "cinema of narrative"—film music at any given moment, in any given place, can be oriented according to one linear and logical progression. Between one filmmaking nation and another, of course, there is seldom an exact correspondence of the precise moments at which this progression involved forward steps. From nation to nation, there are differences in the motivations for these steps; while a small handful of industries indeed instigated shifts in film-music practice, the others simply emulated—in due time, and as their acquisition of the requisite technology allowed—examples that had been market-tested elsewhere. There are differences, too, in the ways that industries around the world spiced their film music with unique nationalistic flavorings.

Although these differences might at first glance seem considerable, from a chronological distance they appear to be localized variations on the same basic themes, each one linked to what came before and after by the same cause-and-effect relationships. Metaphorically speaking, film music flowed along in a single stream, or gave in to a single series of gravitational pulls, or followed a single path. For a variety of reasons—many of them, but not all, related to Hollywood's litany of woes—in the late 1950s the hitherto unified path of film music in general began to diverge. And after this point of divergence the idea of film music "in general" becomes cloudy, indeed.

*   *   *

In its struggle to regain its audience, Hollywood invested heavily in novelties that could not possibly be experienced via the small screens of television sets. Most notable among these—and all emerging ca. 1952–3—were films in wide-screen formats (variously known as CinemaScope, Vistavision, Panavision, Todd-AO) or involving multiple projectors (Cinerama), films with stereoscopic imagery projected onto a single screen (3-D), and films with stereophonic sound.[23] Aware that television broadcasts in color were now possible but equally aware that "color TVs" were still beyond the reach of most Americans, Hollywood at this time converted almost entirely to the production of films in full color.[24] Perhaps most significant, Hollywood, in its effort to compete with

165

the small-scale entertainments offered by television, strove to create products that in one way or another—in terms of their casts, their screenplays, their locales, their scenic effects—were incomparably "large."

Over the course of the decade the number of films made by Hollywood's eight major studios declined, from a peak total of 320 releases in 1951 to a low of 184 in 1960.[25] Many of these releases, however, were far more grandiose than the same studios' offerings of the 1940s. Along with brand new musicals and full-color, wide-screen, star-studded adaptations of Broadway shows,[26] epically proportioned and visually spectacular films such as *The Robe* (Twentieth Century-Fox, 1953), *The Searchers* (Warner Bros., 1956), *Around the World in 80 Days* (United Artists, 1956), *The Ten Commandments* (Paramount, 1956), *The Bridge on the River Kwai* (Columbia, 1957), *The Vikings* (Paramount, 1958), and *Ben-Hur* (MGM, 1959) were, in a way, typical of the period. In all narrative ways, these huge-budget productions were "obvious" to the extreme. That they succeeded handsomely at the box-office owes in no small part to their accompanying music, composed along familiar norms, to be sure, but now writ larger than ever.

On the one hand, then, "excessively obvious" symphonic music of the sort long associated with the classical-style film became more important than ever as Hollywood, in the throes of its depression, struggled to regain its audience. On the other hand, music of quite different sorts began, in the 1950s, to find its way into film scores. The new music—unusual in its sonority and idiom, but not necessarily in the way it served the narratives it supported—was occasionally heard in films made by the major studios but with budgets in most cases considerably lower than what was being lavished on the potential blockbuster hits. More often, the new music was heard in the work of independent producers who likely saw the precarious position of the major studios as an opportunity for succeeding with films that in one way or another veered from apparently hide-bound Hollywood tradition.

Ever since mixing technology first allowed for it, ca. 1932–3, directors as much in Europe as in Hollywood did not hesitate to include in their work such music as seemed appropriate to a particular film's locale, time period, and characters. At least since 1935, film soundtracks fairly teemed with, for example, traditional Irish ballads accompanied only by concertina, revolutionary anthems sung by unruly mobs, or torch songs delivered by inebriated floozies, with tangos and waltzes and polkas, with current hit tunes and excerpts from venerable nineteenth-century sonatas. All of this music meshed comfortably with the goals not just of filmmakers committed to the so-called classical-style but also the goals of filmmakers, most of them European, who in various ways resisted the classical-style conventions. This music, of course, was diegetic, as much a part of the filmic mises-en-scène as were the actors' costumes and manners of speech. And because this music was solidly rooted in whatever fictional worlds the films' characters inhabited, it stood apart from the extra-diegetic "commentary" music that in most cases was just as solidly rooted in the real world inhabited by members of the film's audience.

Before the 1950s, in Europe as well as in Hollywood, there was almost always a clear and deliberate stylistic distinction between diegetic and extra-diegetic music. During the 1950s—in both Hollywood and Europe—this stylistic distinction began to dissolve. From culture to culture reasons for the change differed. In some places—especially in France toward the end of the 1950s—there was a deliberate effort on the part of young filmmakers to break free of norms long established by Hollywood. Elsewhere—most notably in Hollywood itself—the move toward extra-diegetic music that sounded "new" and "different" was largely prodded by the same spur that urged Hollywood in the direction of 3-D and CinemaScope.

Thus, although it functions vis-à-vis the narrative along the lines of classical-style conventions, Alex North's underscore for *A Streetcar Named Desire* (Warner Bros., 1951) draws richly from a "steamy" jazz style that in earlier films would have figured only into diegetic contexts, and the same might be said for Elmer Bernstein's more up-beat jazz-flavored score for *The Man With the Golden Arm* (United Artists, 1955) and Leonard Rosenman's contributions to *Rebel Without a Cause* (Warner Bros., 1955).[27] Jazz flavors similarly dominate the music that Willis Homan and Charles Wolcott wrote for *Blackboard Jungle* (MGM, 1955), but the film earned its enduring place in history not for its in most ways unremarkable underscore but for its extraordinarily bold use, in the title sequence, of Bill Haley and the Comets' recently released recording of the song "Rock Around the Clock."

Although diegetic cowboy songs had been featured aplenty in earlier Hollywood films, Dimitri Tiomkin's score for *High Noon* (United Artists, 1952) broke precedent not just by featuring such a song in the opening credits but also by reprising it throughout the film.[28] Whereas most science-fiction films from the 1950s were low-budget affairs, MGM's 1956 *Forbidden Planet* was a full-color production rich in special effects; its score by Louis and Bebe Barron remains remarkable for many reasons, not the least among them being the simple fact that it was the first feature-film score created entirely by electronic means.[29] The Barrons' electronic music for *Forbidden Planet* was clearly alien to the Hollywood norm, and so—albeit in perhaps not so drastic a way—were the jazzy scores for *A Streetcar Named Desire* et al., the raucous rock 'n' roll music in *Blackboard Jungle*, and the cowboy song in *High Noon*. But what was unusual about all this music was only its sound, not its function vis-à-vis the filmic narrative.

In postwar Hollywood at least some filmmakers used new types of music—usually in ways that were functionally quite conventional—simply in an effort to be, in terms of what they thought their audiences might want to hear, up-to-date. In postwar Europe, many filmmakers used new types of music, and often in new ways, as part of their self-conscious effort to be iconoclastically "modern."

European Influences

The differences in overall narrative style between postwar Hollywood film and its European counterpart are considerable. And they serve to illuminate both the single course that film music, in general, traveled up to its "point of divergence" in the late 1950s and the many courses it took thereafter. To put it simply, if not simplistically, what happened toward the end of the decade was an absorbing by Hollywood of the hitherto resisted European aesthetic. This is not to say that Hollywood's basic approach to filmmaking was displaced; to be sure, this lucrative approach continued comfortably and confidently, but after the 1950s—even within the confines of Hollywood—it was just one approach among many.

Discussing the essential differences between Hollywood and European film in his *Short History of the Movies*, Gerald Mast succinctly observes that in thousands and thousands of films Hollywood has typically opted for one of two endings. In one of them, good triumphs over evil; in the other, a romance is consummated. And both endings are conclusively, incontrovertibly "happy." The Hollywood films before 1960 that do not have "happy endings," Mast writes, are so few that they can almost be counted on one hand. They include D.W. Griffith's *Broken Blossoms* (1919), Erich von Stroheim's *Greed* (1925), Charles Chaplin's *City Lights* (1931), John Ford's *The Grapes of Wrath* (1940), Orson Welles's *Citizen Kane* (1941),[30] John Huston's *The Treasure of the Sierra Madre* (1948), and Billy Wilder's *Sunset Boulevard* (1950), "not a bad group of American films," Mast comments, but nevertheless so exceptional that they easily prove the rule.[31]

Hollywood films with "happy" endings were patronized by plenty of European movie-goers in the postwar years; indeed, as film historians Kristin Thompson and David Bordwell point out early in their chapter on postwar European cinema, by as late as 1953 American films still occupied more than half the screening time in virtually all the European countries.[32] As had been the case before World War II, European directors were not above imitating the Hollywood model and creating "happy ending" films of their own. Many of them realized, however, that a significant portion of their audience desired from the cinema something more than just escapist entertainment. As "European social and intellectual life began to revive" after the war, Thompson and Bordwell write, "artists envisaged the possibility of continuing the modernist tradition founded in the early decades of the century. In a rebuilding Europe, modernism, always promising 'the shock of the new,' became revitalized."[33] Although their book includes detailed sections on film styles distinct to postwar Italy, Spain, France, West Germany, Scandinavia, and England (as well as sections on the postwar cinema of Japan, India, and Latin America), the authors preface those accounts with generalizations.

Starting with the premise that "postwar modernism can be described by three stylistic and formal features," they note that, in the first place, European filmmakers "sought to be more true to life than they considered most [classical-style] filmmakers had been," and "this objective realism" led them toward "episodic, slice-of-life narratives which avoided Hollywood's tight plots." The move toward cinematic realism involved new techniques for camera placement and editing, and new styles of acting that were often seen "as running counter to the rapid, smoothly crafted performances of American cinema." Importantly as it pertains to the use—or non-use—of music, "faithfulness to objective reality could also imply a minute reproduction of the acoustic environment" to the extent that in some films "silence calls attention to small noises."[34]

Along with focusing on objective reality, Thompson and Bordwell write, many postwar European filmmakers focused on realities that, for the films' characters, were subjective. As Hollywood filmmakers had done since the early 1940s, the Europeans drew frequently on the narrative technique of the flashback. But they "plunged still further into characters' minds, revealing dreams, hallucinations, and fantasies."[35]

A third feature that all postwar European "modernist" film has in common is what Thompson and Bordwell call "authorial commentary—the sense that an intelligence outside the film's world is pointing out something about the events we see," the sense that the film's technique and overall style "seems to be suggesting more about the characters than they know or are aware of."[36] This connects with the idea expressed in the 1985 book that Thompson and Bordwell co-authored with Janet Staiger, to the effect that underscore in the classical-style Hollywood film often provides insights into the psychological make-ups of various characters.[37] In the case of the postwar European film, however, the insights resulted from more than simply the treatment of a background theme that had become associated with a particular character; indeed, the "authorial commentary" typically resulted from purely visual matters, and often it spoke most eloquently in scenes in which music played no part whatsoever.

During the 1950s Hollywood was involved in a struggle for survival. It fought a hard battle on the public relations front—the industry as a whole needed desperately to convince both government investigators and moralistic censors that its culture, and thus its products, did *not* do disservice to all that the United States in the postwar years apparently stood for. While independent producers surely rejoiced over the court-mandated break-up of "integrated" structures, the major studios whose monopolies were dissolved for years strained to recover from financial losses. And almost all of Hollywood—until the very end of the decade, when it finally realized that if you can't lick 'em you should join 'em—competed desperately with television.

Through all this, Hollywood's basic strategy was to present audiences with what it had previously delivered, only now bigger, more colorful, and occasionally enhanced with special theatrical gimmicks. What Hollywood, in general, failed to realize was that with its policy of business-as-usual it was alienating an important segment of its potential audience—the segment made up of young adults who were not necessarily, unlike so many of their peers, caught up in new family obligations. Whether or not they had actually been in military service, members of this economically empowered demographic group, like their European contemporaries, found World War II to have been a transforming experience. And with their new sophistication, with their new expectations from life in general, members of this group gradually discovered that "the best films came from Europe." As Gerald Mast explains:

> The films were best not because they often revealed portions of naked bodies together in a bathtub or on a sofa, not because the actors spoke a chic but incomprehensible tongue, not because the films were bathed in obscure, symbolic, pretentious meanings, and not because American audiences had become cultural snobs—as so many chauvinistic American film critics and film executives claimed. The films were best because they raised the same questions in cinematic form that had been raised in the best novels, plays, poems, and philosophical essays of the twentieth century. And the Americans who had become the new movie audience, those who found it easy to leave their television sets, were precisely those who were reading the books.[38]

Debates over "Hollywood" Orchestration

The mid 1950s, clearly, was a period during which film was in flux. Hollywood found itself struggling to sustain both an industrialized mode of production and an overall filmic style in which convention-bound background music, at least since the mid 1930s, had played a significant role. At the same time, the European film industries—crippled by World War II—were starting to make a comeback. Since the inception of the sound film, the European aesthetic had favored the use of music that, instead of simply illustrating what was plainly visible, in various ways enhanced the filmic narrative by somehow playing "against" on-screen action or emotion. As part of a rekindled "modernist" movement, many European directors whole-heartedly re-embraced this

169

aesthetic in their relatively low-budget but psychologically rich postwar films; as part of its effort to retain its core audience, Hollywood issued a raft of big-budget films whose novelty lay mostly in their spectacle. And to its chagrin, Hollywood discovered that at least some American moviegoers actually preferred the European products.

On the eve of World War II, as is well documented by the published attention paid to them in *Modern Music* and daily newspapers, European films with their concomitant music were taken quite seriously by American critics. Upon the war's outbreak, European film production almost ceased to exist, and thus critical writing on film music in the United States focused almost exclusively on what poured forth—for better or worse—from Hollywood. When debates transpired, typically they centered on perceived differences in artistic quality between what was generally known as "Hollywood music"—that is, music written more or less according to convention by composers who earned their livings by scoring Hollywood films—and film music written, arguably with a freer hand, by composers whose names were associated not so much with films as with the concert hall. When champions of the latter position entered the fray, almost always they mentioned as praiseworthy not just a handful of American composers that included Aaron Copland, Werner Janssen, and Virgil Thomson but also such of their European counterparts as William Walton and Ralph Vaughan Williams in England, Georges Auric and Arthur Honegger in France, and Serge Prokofiev and Dmitri Shostakovich in the Soviet Union. Not surprisingly, these debates continued into the 1950s, but now the participants included European critics.

One of the few "Hollywood" composers who, in fact, maintained a busy "concert-hall" career was Miklós Rózsa; by the century's half-way mark Rózsa had not only scored almost sixty feature films but also had to his credit numerous art songs, orchestral works, and pieces for chamber ensemble. Questions from an interviewer in 1952 at first focused on the effects of the rather instant fame Rózsa gained with his use of the electronic instrument called the theremin in his scores for *Spellbound* (1945, Selznick Studios), *The Lost Weekend* (1945, Paramount), and *The Red House* (1947, United Artists), and with Rózsa's generally acknowledged association with films that fell into the category of "psychological dramas."[39] The questions then shifted toward Rózsa's career in general and, finally, toward the composer's thoughts as to how "Hollywood" music was regarded by the musical community at large.

Interestingly, Rózsa suggested that the bias against "Hollywood" music stemmed largely from America's East Coast. There "anything from Hollywood [is described with] a swear word," he told the interviewer. "The reaction to Hollywood music is not so bad, actually, in Europe as in New York and vicinity."[40] That the reaction to Hollywood music in Europe is actually "not so bad" is hardly the impression one might have gained from the volley that transpired just a year earlier between an American writer on film music and several of his European counterparts.

In the spring of 1951 the Los Angeles-based critic Lawrence Morton devoted his column in the journal *Hollywood Quarterly* not to a review of recent film music but to a comparison of remarkably contrasting reports on the previous summer's International Music Congress in Florence, Italy. Morton began:

> There is nothing in the current crop of film scores half so interesting as the discrepancies between Daniele Amfitheatrof's report on the reception given the exhibit of American film music at the International Music Congress at Florence

170

and the reports of the British delegates. "We had a good hand after every entry," wrote Mr. Amfitheatrof, "and prolonged applause, verging on an ovation, at the end of the show." Hans Keller, a British delegate and a critic, this time restrained his penchant for a metaphysical and Freudian vocabulary. Instead he indulged in invective, calling the exhibit a "repellant anthology" and noting that the assembly was composed of "musicians who could hardly be expected to like the stuff." Antony Hopkins, another Briton and a composer, wrote that "the Congress sat in stunned silence while reel after reel of high-powered music was blared out; only Copland's music to *The Red Pony* was vociferously applauded." The day after the exhibition, when Mr. Amfitheatrof had already left for Rome, another British delegate, Benjamin Frankel, took the floor and "attacked in no uncertain terms the bulk of the music we had heard the previous evening," according to Mr. Hopkins. "Heated speeches were made by partisans of both sides," he continued, "but the overwhelming majority supported Frankel in his denunciation."[41]

In his summary of the reports by Keller and Hopkins, Morton noted that the conference's European delegates—along with expressing a general disdain for Hollywood film music—focused negative attention on two main issues. One of these had to do with the virtues of an economy of musical forces, something to which Hollywood composers, according to the reports by the British writers, seemed oblivious. The other concerned the fact that Hollywood composers, quite unlike their European counterparts, typically worked in tandem with teams of orchestrators.

On this last point Morton is especially sensitive, probably at least in part because he, in fact, worked as a Hollywood orchestrator. Indeed, most of his column—and another written a few months later—is devoted to an explanation and defense of Hollywood orchestration practices. The details he offers on this topic are fascinating, but even more fascinating is the response that his column generated when it was reprinted in May 1951 in the British journal *Sight and Sound*.

Morton, continuing his introduction, writes:

> Obviously, strong national passions had been aroused, which, together with a long-standing bias against Hollywood, prevented any discussion of aesthetic matters on an aesthetic level.[42]

Defending his opinion that Hollywood composers in general seem to be not so much artists as artisans, Hopkins (replying in the same *Sight and Sound* issue that carried the reprint of Morton's column) rhetorically asks:

> Who are these people, whose names never seem to appear on any concert programmes? What else have they written; what pages have they placed upon the altar of Art, rather than on the lap of Mammon? When we hear music that so depends on the artifice of the scoring, when we hear page after page of "effects" with no development, no continuity, and little individuality, are we really being so impertinent if we are tempted to doubt the qualifications of the man behind it?[43]

In his August 1951 retort in *The Music Review*, Keller notes that Hopkins simply "protests" against Morton's accusation that European critics have had "a long-standing bias against Hollywood." Not one to mince words, Keller declares that vis-à-vis this bias

> I enthusiastically confess it. My bias has developed from a conscientious study of Hollywood music—the most deadening task a contemporary musician can impose upon himself. Why, now, do I blame Hollywood instead of certain Hollywood composers? The overwhelming majority of Hollywood scores emit such a stench that one is forced to the conclusion that something is basically wrong with this film industry's musico-sociologico-economical set-up.[44]

Then, in his follow-up response in the winter of 1951, Morton grants that Keller's point about there being something "basically wrong" with Hollywood's "musico-sociologico-economical set-up" is one with which he actually agrees. But this is not to say, Morton strongly asserts, that he is a defender of the *status quo*. Perhaps now defending not just "Hollywood" music but also himself, Morton notes that in all his critical writing he has always "condemned mediocrity—which is, I admit, an easy path to virtue." He elaborates:

> Specifically, I have discussed the unfortunate influence of producers and directors whose semi-cultivated tastes invade and oftentimes rule the music departments, the miscasting of composers and the hiring of them on grounds of personal friendships rather than of ability or style, the distortion of sound by engineers who can't let a piece of music "ride" without fiddling with the controls, the pressure of deadlines, the destruction of musical forms and shapes by injudicious cutting, the overemphasis of showmanship, the prevalence of clichés, the absence of experimentation, and so forth. Mr. Keller cannot now maneuver me into defending these evils.[45]

Morton's rant, apparently the last official word in this colorful exchange, goes on to suggest, among other things, that Keller cannot possibly have made a "conscientious study" of the scores for *all* the films (between four and five hundred annually) lately issued by Hollywood, and that Keller perhaps for nationalistic reasons appears to act blissfully ignorant of the British film industry's many "appalling samples of hack work, the exact counterpart of what our Hollywood hacks produce."[46] That neither Keller nor Hopkins responded to Morton's final salvo demonstrates only that the British critics, apparently, found it pointless to persist in a debate for which there could not possibly be an end.

As noted, Morton, in the column in which he first took issue with the European commentators, had a great deal to say about film-music orchestration. He began his diatribe on this sore point by taking issue with Hopkins's comments on French composer Yves Baudrier's music for *Les Maudits* (Speva, 1947):

> It may indeed be true . . . that Baudrier "can do more with one bass clarinet or a string quartet than most Hollywood composers can do with an orchestra of ninety." Aside from the fact that Hollywood composers never have orchestras of ninety (thirty-five to fifty being even above average), while it is the British

who employ the full resources of their great London orchestras—aside from this, it remains to be discovered precisely what Mr. Hopkins means by doing "more." One thing that can't be done with a string quartet is to equal the full sonority of an orchestra *tutti*, a noble and honorable sound that very few composers (even the most fastidious) and very few audiences (even the most snobbish) are quite willing to do without in dramatic music.[47]

But Morton's main purpose was to defend Hollywood's time-proven orchestration practice against what he interpreted as unjust criticism based on ignorance and prejudice. To judge from explanations offered by both Hopkins and Keller in their ripostes, Morton likely misunderstood what had actually been said at the Florence sessions. "The point at issue at the Congress was never one of expressing a lack of confidence in the abilities of the orchestrators," Hopkins wrote; "their technique is unquestionable if at times their taste is not. The finger of suspicion was pointed at the 'composer.' "[48] Similarly, Keller retorted that while Hopkins's speech during the conference possibly created "the impression . . . that Hollywood's orchestrations were the root of most evil," in fact Hopkins's main point was that the orchestrations "are merely the symptoms of a simple though devastating disease."[49]

Morton's account of the orchestrator's work was offered for the sake of educating sparring partners he thought to be sadly benighted. In detailing the relationship between composer and orchestrator, he shed considerable light on a process that had prevailed in Hollywood at least since the mid 1930s and which, by and large, prevails today.

He begins by making it adamantly clear that there are some composers in Hollywood "whose sketches are so complete and so detailed that the orchestrator performs, in effect, the duties of an intelligent copyist." Among these, Morton writes, are Aaron Copland, Adolph Deutsch, Hugo Friedhofer, David Raksin, and Miklós Rózsa. So polished and finished is their work that "no other musical personality has an opportunity to intrude itself upon [the] music." Except in those rare instances when time pressures are extraordinary, "these composers are in fact responsible for every note in their scores."[50]

But composers such as this, Morton, admits, are in the small minority:

> By far the greater number of composers make sketches of varying degrees of roughness. Sometimes the association between a composer and his orchestrator is so intimate and of such long standing that they are in effect two aspects of a single mind. . . . In these cases, if the composers accept the orchestration, criticism can justly make no separation between composition and orchestration, and the music must be evaluated as a unit. For all practical purposes, it would be identical if either of the collaborators had done all the work.
>
> In cases where the composer is totally unable or unwilling to orchestrate his own music, the orchestrator's responsibility is greater and often amounts to composition. He may have to supply inner voices, change harmonies, invent accompaniment patterns, insert counterpoints, and disguise completely the keyboard origin of the music. He may also have to delete great handfuls of cluttering sonority.[51]

Morton grants that critics might well note the difference between a composer who is an "ignorant hack" and a crew of "honest and skilled workmen." But there is no good reason, he insists, why for the sake of music for a commercial marketplace "the inventive musician who lacks craft" should not collaborate with "the capable workman who lacks inventiveness." In a commercial situation, he argues, what should be judged is not the process but only the final output.[52]

Continuing his vehement defense of the orchestrator, Morton makes some observations about idiomatic writing that are as relevant to scoring practices for "excessively obvious" classical-style films today as they were to scores ca. 1950. Referring to recent music created for the concert hall, Morton observes that "much 'modern' orchestration has . . . become 'wrong instrument' orchestration, just as much 'modern music' has become 'wrong note' music."

> Such perversity . . . thrives in the contemporary concert hall where it has been mistaken for a virtue. One is thought to be original if one gives an idiomatic string melody to a trumpet, a flute passage to an E-flat clarinet, a piccolo passage to a glockenspiel. . . . This kind of perversity is little practiced in Hollywood studios, and novelty of effect usually results from a dramatic situation on the screen, the virtuosity of a particular instrumentalist in the studio orchestra, or the special characteristics of the microphone. On the whole, orchestration is remarkably conservative in its intent, for the obvious reason that the music calls for conservatism.[53]

Morton's concluding thought speaks to more than Hollywood orchestration. In sound and style this music called for conservatism because the medium it long served—that is, the classical-style Hollywood film as opposed to European films in general but especially to postwar "modernist" European films—was conservative in all its essence.

New Directions

In February 1952 Thomas Beecham arrived in Los Angeles to lead three concerts with the Los Angeles Philharmonic. Known for his quick wit and barbed tongue, Beecham was met by reporters who by and large were disappointed because the famous British conductor had nothing negative to say, except about film music:

> Some of it's pretty good music, you know. Recording techniques have improved until they provide amazing results. But in movies [music is] not only useless. I think it's highly distracting.[54]

Then, asked if he would prefer movies with no music whatsoever, Beecham remarked:

> Might not be bad—not bad. But I rather fancy a little delicate background. Perhaps just enough to set a mood. Instead, we seem to have trouble deciding whether the music is to accompany the picture—or the picture to accompany the music.[55]

Whereas the unremarkable interview with Beecham had run on page 5 of the *Los Angeles Times*, a report on an angry response from Dimitri Tiomkin appeared the next day on the newspaper's front page. It bore the bold headline: "Film Music Composer Hits Back at Beecham":

Sir Thomas Beecham's condemnation of motion-picture musical scores as "useless" and "highly distracting" yesterday brought a return volley from Dimitri Tiomkin, symphony and motion-picture composer-conductor.

Tiomkin's rebuttal was made via his press agent.

He charged Sir Thomas with being a "chronic sourball indulging in a crusty and hidebound type of thinking that makes music a static rather than a dynamic art."

Specifically, Tiomkin took issue with the great British conductor's opinion that it is ridiculous to have a full symphony sawing away while "some such actress as Lassie disports himself on the screen."

"Had Sir Thomas lived earlier," asserted Tiomkin, obviously warming up, "he could have opposed opera on exactly the same grounds. In fact, even now he could insist it is ridiculous and distracting to have a full symphony sawing away in the pit while an Oklahoma City tenor with an assumed continental name sings an old German song in Italian."

After declaring that background music is as integrated with the screen as it is with opera and ballet, Tiomkin observed:

"Sir Thomas is a superb musician, and his preoccupation with [music] would prove distracting if he sits there all through a movie analyzing the woodwind phrasing or breaking down the orchestration. But this is hardly the average theatergoer's reaction."[56]

And thus continued debates of the sort that had been waged a decade earlier. But in the 1950s press coverage of film music contained at least a few new twists. One of them had to do with the idea, thrown casually to Beecham by an unnamed interviewer, that perhaps films did not really *need* music at all.

In one of his regular columns for *The Music Review*, Hans Keller in November 1952 reported that French composer Georges Auric, who by this time had done some work in the UK,[57] had recently been awarded the prize for film music at the Venice film Biennale. Although full of praise for Auric, Keller could not refrain from noting that all the points Auric made in accepting the award were, in fact, points that Keller himself had been making for some time:

Inter alia, [Auric] maintains that (1) there can no longer be any doubt about the fact that valuable musical works owe their existence to the film . . . ; (2) "the big mistake of early film music" (only early film music?) was to attempt absolute simultaneity of musical expression and filmic movement, as in a cartoon, whereas "in reality" entire scenes, not particular movements, had to be commented upon musically; (3) in most films, there is too much music ("I'm very glad when a French director asks me to fill three quarters of his film with music, but I believe he shouldn't do so"); (4) "the English have a different and very interesting attitude towards film music": [Auric's] quarter of an hour's music for a British film, placed at important junctures, was noticed by everyone, whereas some of his continuous French scores went entirely unnoticed; (5) one can make films without music and indeed will soon do so out of disgust at the exaggerated use of film music.[58]

Six months earlier, Keller had called attention to Pat Jackson's *White Corridors* (Vic, 1951), a British film whose "sound track does not harbour any film music—background, foreground, 'featured,' 'realistic,' 'title,' 'end-title'—whatsoever." Of a film about ethical problems in a hospital, Keller writes, "a musical background would make immediate nonsense, for the essential problem in [the film's] creation is how to avoid, as far as possible, slipping from the realistic level." And instead of nonsense, he continues, *White Corridors* "actually achieves some definite and well-defined poetic realism on the acoustic side *by dint of thematic, indeed, almost musicalized noises.*"[59]

Keller returned to this theme many times, but perhaps most articulately in 1956. In one column from that year, prompted by the absence of underscore and the poignant use of diegetic music in Herbert Wilcox's *My Teenage Daughter* (British Lion/Everest, 1956), he theorized that films aspiring to "naturalism ... will always be able to say more, rather than less, without music."[60] In his next column, triggered by the absence of music of any sort in J. Lee Thompson's courtroom drama *Yield to the Night* (Kenwood, 1956), Keller noted—tellingly—that "music-less sound tracks which respect alike the ethics of naturalism, the craft of film, and the art of music," although "rare and remarkable," are in fact "not quite so rare in this understating country."[61]

It may well have been that, in 1956, filmmakers' deliberate decisions to avoid music were more common in "understating" England than elsewhere. By the end of the decade, the fashion for musical understatement had spread even to Hollywood.

* * *

Just a few months after he publicly "hit back" at Thomas Beecham's casual dismissal of film music, Dimitri Tiomkin was the subject of an article by *Los Angeles Times* film critic Philip K. Scheurer. Tiomkin's own statements add up to sentimental platitude; especially in the face of the industry's competition from television, Tiomkin told the reporter, what film music needs is a "sincere approach, great labor, music written honestly, with thought." Not platitudinous at all, and surely relevant to developments that as early as 1952 were starting to affect Hollywood film-scoring practice, was Scheurer's assessment of recent "breakthroughs" instigated by Tiomkin. "Probably the greatest single accomplishment of Dimitri Tiomkin," Scheuer wrote, "is that he has done away with the trumpet fanfare ('up—full orchestra') which soars over the opening title of nine movies out of ten. As a unique achievement this surpasses even his penning of the 'High Noon Ballad' ('Do Not Forsake Me') which currently is sweeping the country."[62]

In the late 1930s, when Hollywood produced a great many films that combined aspects of the Western and the musical, Tex Ritter—along with Gene Autry and Roy Rogers—had been one of the hybrid genre's leading "singing cowboys."[63] His twangy intonation of "Do Not Forsake Me, Oh My Darlin' " during the title sequence of Fred Zinnemann's *High Noon* doubtless struck a nostalgic chord with certain members of the audience, and, indeed, the song proved to be a hit. But "Do Not Forsake Me, Oh My Darlin' " was certainly not the first song that had a glorious career independent of the film for which it was specifically created. In the earliest days of the sound film, of course, entire screenplays were built around "theme songs" by blue-chip Tin Pan Alley songwriting teams. Recognizing—and promoting—the symbiotic relationship between films and songs, in 1934 the Academy of Motion Picture Arts and Sciences established an award for best song.[64]

A great many classical-style musicals—not adapted from Broadway successes but created for the screen—fairly teemed with songs that, once removed from their filmic contexts, entered the repertoire of pop-music "standards"; familiar examples of such films, all from MGM, include *The Wizard of Oz* (1939), *Meet Me in St. Louis* (1944), *The Harvey Girls* (1946), and *Singin' in the Rain* (1952). The Disney studio's feature-length animated films were not musicals but were nonetheless rich with music, and some of them—*Snow White and the Seven Dwarfs* (1937), *Pinocchio* (1939), *Cinderella* (1950), *Alice in Wonderland* (1951)—contained songs that after their films' initial runs took on long lives of their own. Romantic comedies typically featured songs, at least a few of which—"It's Magic" from *Romance on the High Seas* (Michael Curtiz Productions, 1948), for example, and "Be My Love" from *The Toast of New Orleans* (MGM, 1950)—became popular hits. Even films relatively dark in nature sometimes featured music that, perhaps to the surprise of its composer, found special favor with the general public; fitted with lyrics by Johnny Mercer, David Raksin's theme for Otto Preminger's *Laura* (Twentieth Century-Fox, 1944) quickly acquired "hit" status, and comparable good fortune was granted to themes, in their original instrumental form, concocted by Miklós Rózsa for Alfred Hitchcock's *Spellbound* (Selznick, 1945) and by Anton Karas for Carol Reed's *The Third Man* (British Lion, 1949).[65]

As a film-related hit song, clearly, the ballad that Tiomkin contributed to 1952's *High Noon* was not without precedent. Nevertheless, the effect that this particular song had on nervous Hollywood executives can hardly be underestimated. As Roy M. Prendergast puts it:

> The aesthetic effect on film music was immediate and devastating. Every producer, in order to help assure the financial success of his film, now wanted a film score with a song or instrumental number of a type that would "make the charts." No longer did producers care if the music written for their films was the best possible music for that specific picture; they now wanted music that would sell *away* from the picture. The artistic problems for the composer were obvious. He was now asked to impose a strictly musical form and style, the pop song, onto a film whether it was appropriate to the film or not.[66]

Prendergast perhaps exaggerates when he writes that, with the song for *High Noon*, Tiomkin "unknowingly rang the death knell for intelligent use of music in films."[67] But this sentiment would certainly be echoed by Hollywood "regulars" who later pondered aloud as to why film music in general, toward the end of the decade, experienced a fundamental change.

*   *   *

In 1957 music critics whose orientation was obviously toward the concert hall were still yammering about the aesthetic deficiencies of most film music. The *New York Times*'s Harold C. Schonberg entered the dialogue with a Sunday column prompted by the Capitol label's recent release of three albums of film music drawn from the scores by Mischa Spoliansky for Otto Preminger's *Saint Joan* (Wheel, 1957), by George Antheil for Stanley Kramer's *The Pride and the Passion* (United Artists, 1957), and by Tom Glazer for Elia Kazan's *A Face in the Crowd* (Warner Bros., 1957). Schonberg upheld the high-minded position that had been taken by critics during the previous decade, and he bolstered his argument by citing names that long had been accepted by the classical music establishment as belonging to a film-music "canon." He granted that certain restrictions apply to film scoring. Nevertheless, he wrote,

> Important composers have met the problem and solved it. Prokofieff, Auric, Copland, Thomson, Korngold—all these have written scores that are not only good movie music but good music on any terms. Suites extracted from their movie scores have made the rounds of symphony orchestras the world over. All of which suggests that it takes a good composer to write good music, be it movie music or otherwise; and that if Hollywood wants good movie music it had better think of engaging good composers to write it.[68]

In his introductory paragraph Schonberg easily acknowledges the role that the accompanying score plays in the narrative film:

> Most people, while watching a film, pay no attention to the background music. Film music, generally speaking, is purely functional. It fills in the spaces; it suggests, hints, insinuates. It has been composed by skillful technicians who are almost as much psychologists as composers: men who know all the tricks about underlining a mood in relation to the action on the screen. As presently constituted, films would be unthinkable without music.[69]

And then he makes the mistake so often committed by critics who persist in judging music carefully crafted for one context by standards that apply only to music created for a completely different context:

> But take away the film and let the music stand on its own. Then what? The chances overwhelmingly are that the product suddenly becomes synthetic, a collection of musical banalities and inanities. What may work in a film does not necessarily work elsewhere. Movie music is a highly specialized form and, of course, it has its place. But when an art is specifically concerned with addressing itself to a least common denominator, as do most Hollywood films, the components of that art are going to be played down to the conception of what a mass audience is supposed to like. In comes business, out goes art.[70]

It was certainly true that Hollywood in 1957, as it always had, catered to what it perceived to be "a mass audience." And it is also true that around this time many Hollywood directors—perhaps inspired by the success of Tiomkin's song for *High Noon* but more likely pressured by producers who sought maximal profits from their investments—adjusted their otherwise straightforward screenplays so they could accommodate opportunities for possibly lucrative songs. Even Alfred Hitchcock, a director rarely accused of pandering to "a least common denominator," in his 1956 re-make of *The Man Who Knew Too Much* (Paramount) opted to fit the film not just with a vibrant score by Bernard Herrmann but also with a song (an Oscar-winner, as it turned out) by Jay Livingston and Ray Evans.[71]

Contrary to Schonberg's argument, the presence in filmmaking of "business" considerations can hardly be equated with the exclusion of "art." Indeed, in Hollywood —and to a large extent elsewhere whenever film production was not partially or wholly government-subsidized—it has long been the case that the more or less smooth functioning of filmic "business" has made possible the occasional example of filmic "art." It might even be the case that certain developments in film "art" vis-à-vis music resulted directly from Hollywood's struggle, throughout the 1950s, to keep its "business" in order.

Hollywood's basic strategy in the postwar years was to give audiences what it had successfully given them earlier, only now in bigger and bolder formats to which small-screen black-and-white television, or low-budget European films, could not possibly (or so Hollywood hoped) hold a candle. But some in Hollywood, especially the independent producers who after the court-ordered divestiture of the major studios' exhibition venues came increasingly to the fore, devised an alternative strategy. For reasons that doubtless had much more to do with "business" than with "art," this new strategy involved appealing to audiences with films that arguably were below par in terms of "production values" but which were, in terms of both narrative content and musical accompaniment, either up-to-date or somehow unusual.

As early as the summer of 1954 *Los Angeles Times* film critic Philip K. Scheurer observed, presciently, that "scorers of film music are beginning to reach out in new directions." He remarked that George Antheil's score for *Dementia* (John Parker, 1953) was "played at least in part by a small jazz aggregation." He reminded readers that a simple zither—in marked contrast to a symphony orchestra—had provided the entire underscore for 1949's *The Third Man* and that a harmonica had figured importantly in the scores for the recent *Little Fugitive* and *Genevieve*.[72] Although the director eventually opted for an orchestral score by Bernard Herrmann, Scheuer correctly reported that in 1954 Alfred Hitchcock was at least "mulling the idea of using a piano, solo, throughout his next comedy chiller, 'The Trouble with Harry.'" And he noted that "Leith Stevens has already composed a complete jazz score—'every note, including the main and end titles'—for Filmakers' 'Private Hell 36' and will duplicate the feat for the same outfit's 'Mad at the World,' which deals with juvenile delinquents."[73]

Quite to the point as to the role jazz might play in filmic underscore that hitherto had been dominated by the symphonic idiom, Scheurer quotes Stevens directly:

> I began thinking along those lines with "The Wild One," Marlon Brando's picture about cyclists, in which I incorporated some jazz sequences. However, not all dramatic stories will stand this kind of treatment. "Private Hell 36" does; it's a story about two big-city cops, . . . and jazz works wonders for it.
>
> It's all background music, of course, but it always comes from a legitimate and not an imaginary source—an apartment radio, a jukebox in a bar. A car crashes over a cliff, killing the driver, and out of the deathly silence we hear a jump tune.[74]

The dramatic potency of film music that is not at all "obvious"—the potency that results, for example, from an up-beat "jump tune" intruding upon the "deathly silence" that enshrouds a tragic scene—was not lost to Scheurer. He had been a music-lover since the days of the silent film; during his long career he paid more attention than did most

179

film critics to scores he perceived innovative and/or of high quality, and after his retirement on at least two occasions he returned to the pages of the *Los Angeles Times* to reminisce about film music's history.[75] In the late summer of 1958, still reporting full-time on Hollywood, he was confidently positioned to challenge comments on film music offered by one of his colleagues.

The retort was triggered by remarks made by the newspaper's music critic, Albert Goldberg, in a general column on August 31, 1958. Goldberg's first item was a negative criticism of Dmitri Shostakovich's Symphony No. 11, which he had recently heard via a two-LP recording by the Houston Symphony Orchestra under the direction of Leopold Stokowski (Capitol PBR 8448):

> It makes the composer's interminable Seventh Symphony, the "Leningrad," seem like a masterpiece in comparison, and if this is the best Russia's principal composer can produce it gives a new status to Hollywood film scores, which it closely resembles.[76]

And this prompted Goldberg to expand on what he felt to be the problem with film music in general. Echoing an opinion that the *New York Times* music critic had expressed just a year before, Goldberg wrote:

> Speaking of movie music, one could not avoid being struck in the recent TV releases of Greta Garbo's "Anna Christie" and "As You Desire Me" with the difference in practice when those films were made some 20 years ago and now.
>
> "Anna Christie" had music only under the introductory credits, virtually none at all during the progress of the play or under the dialogue. "As You Desire Me" had only brief snatches of music where it was apropos. The players were on their own to create mood and character through the spoken dialogue only, and what a relief it was to hear the lines as one hears them in a theater without the intrusion of second-rate incidental music.
>
> In comparison to these early films we found the incessant din of the commercial, cliché-ridden score that accompanies Hemingway's "The Old Man and the Sea" completely distracting. We are willing to leave evaluation of the cinematic merits of the picture to our knowledgeable colleague Philip K. Scheuer, but as a music critic we felt that what might have been a notable artistic unity was destroyed by so much and such commonplace music. Granted that writing music for films is a highly specialized business, it still seems a pity that Hollywood does not avail itself of the services of ranking contemporary composers.[77]

In the next day's editions Scheuer took strong exception to what Goldberg had written about Tiomkin's music for *The Old Man and the Sea* (Warner Bros., 1958). Perhaps commenting on the basis of something he heard from Goldberg in the course of conversation, Scheuer notes that this is a film Goldberg said he saw and admired. And thus he argues:

> I don't see how he could separate the Dimitri Tiomkin score from it. The two seemed to me integral. In such a motion picture, with stretches of silence broken

only by the monotone of narrator Spencer Tracy, the music surely contributes 50% to the illusion.[78]

Then, instead of continuing his own argument, Scheuer simply cites an explanatory article on film music (in the *Juilliard Review*) by UCLA faculty member Walter H. Rubsamen. Scheuer writes that Rubsamen divides film music roughly into two categories: background music and music that is somehow part of the action. It is clear, however, that Rubsamen's second category does not include music that nowadays would be called diegetic music or "source music." Rather, he refers to underscore that somehow "becomes pictorial." And this type of music he sub-divides into five classifications:

(1) The imitation by musical means of such sounds as animal cries, the roar of an airplane motor or the whistling of the wind; (2) the transfer of a visual or psychological impression to one that is audible; (3) music that reflects certain phenomena in our physical make-up; (4) special melodies or types of music that call forth specific associations in the minds of the audience; and (5) music that deviates from the norm of instrumental sound in order to depict abnormal states of mind, the supernatural or the mysterious.[79]

Notable examples in which these various classifications of film music are demonstrated, Scheurer writes, include Alfred Hitchcock's *Rebecca* (Selznick, 1940; music by Franz Waxman), Billy Wilder's *The Lost Weekend* (Paramount, 1945; Miklós Rózsa), Carol Reed's *The Third Man* (British Lion, 1949; Anton Karas), Elia Kazan's *A Streetcar Named Desire* (Warner Bros., 1951; Alex North), John Ford's *The Quiet Man* (Republic, 1952: Victor Young), and Fred Zinnemann's *From Here to Eternity* (Columbia, 1953; George Duning).

Just a week after the polite and presumably pre-planned exchange with his colleague Albert Goldberg, Scheuer wrote another article in which, largely through quoted comments from composer Ernest Gold, he illuminates the new path that film music in general would soon take.

Scheuer's job, of course, was to deliver critiques on the latest releases from Hollywood and elsewhere and to report, whenever he thought it appropriate, on what he perceived to be industry trends. He wrote not from the perspective of an historian but, obviously, from that of a day-to-day journalist. At this time, André Bazin's idea that Hollywood production ca. 1938–9 had reached a level of "classical perfection" was just being formulated; almost three decades would pass before Bordwell et al., looking back, defined the classical-style Hollywood film as a product in which every element, vis-à-vis the narrative, contributed to a product that was "excessively obvious," and it would be longer than that before theorists such as Gorbman, Flinn, and Kalinak would write at length about how extra-diegetic music regularly served the needs of "excessively obvious" filmic narratives. Oblivious to all this future theorizing, Scheuer in 1958 simply noted that at least some composers and directors in Hollywood were starting to believe that background music could contribute to a film by making certain aspects of the narrative not obvious at all.

For an example of current ideas, he quotes a letter from Gold, whom he identifies as "one of the 'serious' composers who music critic Albert Goldberg believes should be giving attention to motion pictures." To establish Gold's credentials, Scheuer notes that "he has written two symphonies, a piano concerto and chamber music and is musical director of the Santa Barbara Symphony"; he fails to mention that by this time Gold already had at least twenty scores for feature films to his credit, but he does acknowledge that Gold had recently composed the music for Stanley Kramer's film *The Defiant Ones* (United Artists, 1958).

In his letter, Gold takes issue in general with the "oversimplification" offered the previous week by the UCLA professor and, in particular, with the professor's idea of "pictorial" music. He makes the point:

> What is already visible should not be duplicated by the sound track. Music can demonstrate inner processes taking place in the characters, elucidate relationships between them and—most important—throw its weight with or against a character in order to sway the point of equilibrium of a scene.[80]

Then Gold offers a hypothetical illustration:

> Suppose a scene shows a man who had committed a crime . . . rushing down a street to right the wrong. . . . If we accompany such a scene with music communicating the man's remorse, his sudden feeling of compassion for another human being, we will throw the feeling of the audience with the man and they will root for him. The same scene accompanied by music that would take no note of the man at all but would stress the surroundings (music floating out of a bar or depicting the busy city that extends far beyond the actually visible street) will throw the sympathy of the audience AGAINST the man.
>
> They will sense the futility of one man trying to work a near miracle in a big beehive of activity where people are preoccupied with their own lives, and he cannot expect support from anyone. His failure will seem inevitable or his success doubly unexpected.[81]

Gold concludes by citing an example of an "unusual approach to music" taken in *The Defiant Ones*. Significantly, he notes that the idea for this approach was suggested not by him but by the film's director:

> The story deals basically with two opposing groups: the two defiant convicts (Tony Curtis and Sidney Poitier) that have escaped and the posse trying to track them down. In one of the early posse scenes a character (Carl Switzer) is established who carries a portable radio on which he plays the most raucous rock 'n' roll music. From that scene on, ALL scenes dealing with the posse were accompanied by rock 'n' roll even though the music had no more than a casual and purely physical connection with the contents of those scenes.
>
> Its value lay primarily in the effect it had on the scenes dealing with the convicts, which contained no music whatsoever. The sudden stark silence and the naturalistic sound effects were made more eloquent and the plight of the convicts more terrifying by the sudden withdrawal of music. The value of the music lay not in its presence in the film's most meaningful scenes but in its absence.[82]

Labor Pains

As Hans Keller and Georges Auric early in the 1950s had suggested would increasingly be the case in European films, by the end of the decade even in Hollywood music was making its presence known—thus strengthening its dramatic importance—by being present not nearly so often as it had been in the classical-style film. But in Hollywood in 1958 the idea of "absent music" was more than just an aesthetic conceit on the part of certain forward-looking directors and composers. As the result of a bitter labor dispute, for much of that year music was quite literally absent from filmmaking.

Being a well-organized and fairly powerful labor union, the American Federation of Musicians (AFM) had long had a contentious relationship with the film studios that regularly employed its Southern California members. In May 1944 the union's president, James C. Petrillo, arrived in Los Angeles and blustered that he was going to straighten out, once and for all, the situation for the "500 or 600 of my boys" who earn their livings "by getting work in the picture production studios here." Petrillo declared:

> Well, the studios, they're going to take on a minimum of so many and keep them on all year around. That is, if the producers do what I want them to do. We are negotiating a contract now. We've never had an individual one of our own before.
>
> I'll say this, we negotiated for some time in New York and now we're here to finish it if we can and they're friendly. We want a one-year contract, each studio to keep a staff of so many musicians. So far we've gotten along fine with the producers. They've been co-operative and reasonable and I think everything's going to be all right.[83]

Everything, indeed, turned out to be "all right." The Hollywood studios in 1944 knew that orchestral accompaniments were as important to their products as were good screenplays and star-studded casts; they also knew—from observing the effect of the AFM's still on-going ban, for the sake of increasing work for radio musicians, on the making of commercial recordings[84]—how forceful a Petrillo edict could be. And so they readily complied.

For the studio musicians, the contract was surely a boon. In May 1948 *Los Angeles Times* music critic Albert Goldberg wrote an article in which he attempted to explain the considerable turnover in personnel experienced by the Los Angeles Philharmonic since the appointment, in 1943, of music director Alfred Wallenstein. Defending Wallenstein's musicianship as well as his abilities as a leader, Goldberg noted:

> When Wallenstein took over the orchestra in 1943 the minimum wage scale was $70 a week, and at the same time the movie studios, by Petrillo edict, were expanding their orchestras. On a basis of 52 weeks a year as opposed to the Philharmonic's 22-week season the studios were able to offer competent musicians several times the amount they were earning in the Philharmonic, and naturally many accepted.[85]

More pertinent to what was transpiring in Hollywood, two months later the *New York Times*'s Hollywood reporter wrote, in anticipation of a new contract between the

AFM and the studios: "It is expected here that the question of how many of the union's members the motion-picture companies must keep on their payrolls will cause sharp division."[86]

> Under the terms of the prevailing agreement between the producers and the A.F. of M., which was entered into two years ago and is due to expire at the end of this month, no major studio is permitted to carry fewer than thirty-five musicians on its staff and some are required to keep as many as fifty constantly in their employ. These men receive an annual minimum wage of approximately $7,000 a year. This is figured on the basis of a minimum ten-hour work-week at $13 an hour and double time for two weeks' vacation. No other union group on the movie lots has a similar pact guaranteeing a minimum annual wage.
>
> Under present conditions in the industry and in view of the fact that, according to the producers, the studios are overstaffed with musicians, it is understood that they will press for relief in the contract negotiations about to start. What they will ask, it is said, is a return to the employment of a comparatively small nucleus of instrumentalists through the year, with the addition from time to time of such players as are needed.[87]

However much the studios felt they might be overstaffed with musicians, they nevertheless again complied with the union's demands. On August 26, 1948, the existing contract was extended for yet another year. The contract linked the AFM with the eight "major" Hollywood studios (MGM, Paramount, Twentieth Century-Fox, RKO, Republic, Warner Bros., Universal, and Columbia). According to the labor reporter for the *New York Times*, "five hundred regularly employed musicians are covered by the agreements. Their wage rate remains at $13.30 an hour, with a minimum of three hours' work on each call."[88]

After five more one-year extensions of the contract, in January 1954 the AFM signed a four-year pact with the "major" Hollywood studios, which by this time were reduced to six (MGM, Columbia, Warner Bros., Universal-International, Paramount, and Twentieth Century-Fox). The agreement covered between 500 and 700 musicians and included a 5 percent wage increase (up from $106.70 per week).[89] Separate contracts, according to newspaper reports, were to be negotiated with RKO and Republic.

As the four-year contract approached its expiration date, in January 1958, the AFM naturally asked for more concessions. To the union's surprise, this time around there was resistance from the major Hollywood studios (which again numbered eight, now including Disney and Allied Artists). And so on February 20 the AFM's Los Angeles Local 47—by this time second in size only to the New York Local 802, and with an estimated 1,200 musicians working in the film industry—declared a strike against the Hollywood studios. The studios showed no signs of capitulation; although the labor action had been instigated by the union, in effect it was a lockout that lasted five months.

Girded for battle, Hollywood simply looked abroad for its scoring needs. Bernard Herrmann's music for Alfred Hitchcock's *Vertigo* (Paramount, 1958) and Leigh Harline's music for Philip Dunne's *Ten North Frederick* (Twentieth Century-Fox, 1958), for example, were recorded not in Hollywood but in London. According to Herman D. Kenin, who had recently succeeded Petrillo as AFM president, "both studios sent the films outside the United States for their musical scoring" as part of "an odious effort to defeat a lawful strike by resort to cheap foreign labor."[90] And thus both films found their exhibiting theaters in at least twenty American cities picketed by AFM members.

In April 1958 the independent studio Samuel Goldwyn Productions signed "an interim agreement" with the AFM, and newspapers reported that the union and some twenty other independent studios were on the verge of signing similar agreements.[91] But by late June the AFM and the major studios had still not come to terms. The *Los Angeles Times* reported that Kenin and Charles Boren, labor vice-president of the Association of Motion Picture Producers, were discussing the possibilities of having film scores recorded by union members but in areas of southern California outside the jurisdiction of Local 47. And this, in turn, triggered a heated response from the leader of a "splinter" organization that had been formed just a few months earlier. Cecil F. Read, a studio trumpet player and chairman of the new Musicians Guild of America (MGA), said the AFM's "dump Hollywood" proposal was

> a desperate attempt to frighten 1200 studio musicians with a loss of employment. It is foolish to propose the scoring of films outside Los Angeles, where 95% of the musicians employed by the studios for 30 years have lived and worked.
>
> This is the familiar "run-away" shop—a notorious anti-labor device. For Kenin to suggest such a maneuver is disgraceful, although not surprising in view of the AFM's past record of callous disregard of the welfare of professional musicians.[92]

The musicians' strike ended on July 12, 1958, with the major studios reaching a tentative agreement not with the AFM but, rather, with the MGA. According to the announcement by the Los Angeles office of the National Labor Relations Board, the MGA "won a bargaining representation election by a vote of 580 to 484." This meant that finally, in the opinion of the *New York Times* labor reporter, "the American Federation of Musicians' thirty-year monopoly in the film industry ended."[93]

AFM president Kenin immediately pointed out that "labor's history has shown that even short-lived technical victories, won by irresponsible splinter groups such as Cecil Read's guild, wind up in catastrophe for those who have followed the path of division."[94] A month later Eliot Daniel, president of the AFM's Los Angeles Local 47, called the contract between the Musicians' Guild of America and the studios "a tremendous sellout," an agreement that "sacrifices the right to job security and guaranteed employment [and] surrenders the musician's rights in the product he produces."[95] To which Guild chairman Read responded: "The agreement with the motion-picture producers negotiated by the M.G.A. represents the first positive action of musicians to reverse the Petrillo policies of the A.F.M. which in the past decade have almost destroyed employment opportunities for motion-picture and television-film musicians."[96]

*   *   *

The tentative agreement between the MGA and the major studios, and eventually with the independent studios as well, meant that musicians would soon be back at work in Hollywood. But the conditions of the final agreement, not reached until late August 1958, meant that the term "Hollywood music"—as used by Hans Keller and

Lawrence Morton in their trans-Atlantic debate early in the decade—would soon be all but meaningless.

Under the old pact with the AFM, the major studios had no choice but to hire "contract orchestras ranging in number from 50 at MGM, Warners and Fox to 45 at Paramount and 36 at Columbia and Universal. The wage scale was $48.21 per musician per three-hour recording session."[97] The new agreement with the MGA provided musicians with higher pay, but the pay was now determined by "variable wage rates according to the number of musicians called for every three-hour recording session."[98] Specifically, the scale offered musicians $55 for a three-hour session that involved an ensemble of thirty-five or more players, $57.74 for a session involving between thirty and thirty-four players, $60.50 for a session involving between twenty-four and twenty-nine players, and $63.25 for a session involving twenty-three players or less.[99] Certain musicians indeed stood to gain considerably from the MGA agreement. But the studios gained as well, for they no longer had to engage—or, at least, pay for, whether they used it or not—a full orchestra for every recording session.

In early September 1958 the *Los Angeles Times* reported:

> Under terms of a new three-year contract with the Musicians Guild of America, 20th Century-Fox studio yesterday called seven musicians for a prerecording session on a Pat Boone picture.[100]

The article bore the headline "Musicians Get First Film Jobs Since Feb. 20." For some this was good news, but for "Hollywood music" it was handwriting on the wall.

Part 4

FILM MUSIC IN
THE POST-CLASSIC PERIOD
(1958–2008)

Chapter 10

A "NEW WAVE"
OF FILM MUSIC, 1958–78

The whole style of film-making has changed, but many of the older guys haven't bridged the gap creatively or technically.

The idea is not to bombard the audience and beat them down with sound, not to fill the screen with as much music as there is picture. Composers have learned to save it for the right moments and make them count. . . .

Music is a more potent force in society than it ever was before, and therefore it's a more potent force in the making of films. The young producers are much more aware of this. Some them aren't yet aware how it works, but they know how it should work.

Jerry Goldsmith, 1967[1]

When the labor issues between Hollywood musicians and both the major and independent studios were finally resolved late in 1958, "Hollywood music" as it had come to be known and often disparaged would largely be a thing of the past. This is not to say that an end had come to scores that were at the same time consistently symphonic in both sound and idiom and in terms of function firmly aligned with the "obvious" narrative goals of the so-called classical-style film. Throughout the 1960s plenty of such scores were used, not just in Hollywood but also in Europe, and they have continued to be used right up to the present day. Indeed, in the late 1970s they were so much in evidence that it is now commonplace to identify that period with the style's "revival."[2]

But the term "revival" is misleading, for in order for something to be revived it must first be dead or, at least for a while, quite dormant. Since reaching its maturity in Hollywood ca. 1938–9, the classical-style score has never been dead or dormant; it has never been completely displaced. Since the late 1950s, however, this type of score has shared the spotlight, so to speak, with film music that either in whole or in part sounds not at all symphonic. It has shared the spotlight, too, with scores that in various ways serve the purposes of films whose content, design, and purpose—likewise, in whole or in part—is hardly in keeping with classical-style narrative. Before the late 1950s, "Hollywood music" in both form and function had a more or less uniform essence, so much so that it could be thought of as a musico-theatrical genre; after this point, music in Hollywood films, as in films from elsewhere, manifest itself in so many different ways that the idea of a single genre becomes untenable. To borrow from the autobiographical statement that the American poet Walt Whitman made in his 1855 *Leaves of Grass*, the broad concept of film music in general since the late 1950s has been "large, [it] contain[s] multitudes."

189

For audience members of the time, the film-music equivalent of a "Cambrian explosion" of styles likely proved entertaining or, at the very least, interesting; box-office records show that the early 1960s was the period during which the European film industries at last demonstrated full recovery from their war-inflicted injuries and also the period during which Hollywood finally emerged from its postwar "years of groping."[3] For today's film-music scholars, the sudden proliferation of scores that veered from the existing Hollywood and European norms has provided a rich bounty of stimulation; indeed, it seems that the most vigorous recent articles and essays on film music focus on examples—sometimes complete scores but more often selected diegetic, or "quasi-diegetic," bits of scores—that somehow violate established conventions, and it seems that in most cases the roots of the "deviant" approaches are located in the innovations of the late 1950s and early '60s. For at least some of the composers who had long invested their energies in a 'traditional' approach to film music, however, the innovations ca. 1960 amounted to disaster.

Crass Commercialism?

"The beginning of the end of the golden age of film music," composer Elmer Bernstein wrote in 1972, was signaled by "two innocent events in the early and middle Fifties." The first of these, Bernstein claimed, was

> the extraordinary success of the title song by Dimitri Tiomkin for the 1952 motion picture *High Noon*. How fresh and exciting that main title seemed then! But the free advertising resulting from the song—not to mention the enormous money that the song itself made—led to an instant demand by movie producers for similar title songs in almost every picture that followed. Lyric writers were beset with such problems as setting titles like *The Revolt of Mamie Stover* to music and the situation rapidly became ridiculous. But the commercial attitude has remained: To hell with the score—let's get that title song on the charts![4]

The second "innocent event," Bernstein suggested, was

> the success of my own *Man with the Golden Arm* in 1955, which was compounded by Henry Mancini's TV success with *Peter Gunn*. With the commercial bonanza of these "pop" sounds in two perfectly *legitimate* situations—my score was not a jazz score, but a score in which jazz elements were incorporated toward the end of creating [a] specific atmosphere for that particular film—producers quickly began to transform film composing from a serious art into a pop art and recently into pop garbage.[5]

These strong words appear in an article in *High Fidelity* magazine that carries the headline "What Ever Happened to Great Movie Music?" Insofar as it represents the author's sentiment, the headline is apt, for there can be no doubt that Bernstein at this time felt that something had "happened" to film music and that the results were far from "great." In his opening paragraph Bernstein writes that he finds it "inconceivable" that the sophisticated art of film scoring

> has in such a short time degenerated into a bleakness of various electronic noises and generally futile attempts to "make the pop Top 40 charts." Today the trend

is most obviously to the nonscore, the song form, and General Electric. It appears that the king is dead and the court jester has been installed in his place.[6]

Even more pessimistically, he concludes:

> The quality of film scores is being strangled by the search for effect, for "new sounds" without content and form on the part of the artist, and by avarice on the part of the producer. Today the once proud art of film scoring has turned into a sound, a sensation, or hopefully a hit. How ironic that in an era in which music enjoys its greatest popularity as an art, film producers are demonstrating the greatest ignorance of the use of music in films since the beginning of that medium's history.[7]

Among veteran Hollywood composers, Bernstein was not alone in expressing bitter resentment. In an article that eventually bore a headline very similar to the one that announced Bernstein's, David Raksin railed against what he took to be the film industry's new-found ignorance toward film music and its pandering to youthful audiences.

Raksin's essay was first published in *Variety* in May 1974 but is better known in the slightly revised version—titled "Whatever Became of Movie Music?"—that appeared in the inaugural issue of a Bernstein-sponsored newsletter called *Film Music Notebook*. Friendly with young persons through his teaching activities at both the University of Southern California and the University of California, Los Angeles, Raksin acknowledges that he has nothing against either rock/pop music in itself or, significantly, its use in films. Indeed, he cites three recent films in which such music very effectively makes up the entirety of the score: Dennis Hopper's *Easy Rider* (Columbia, 1969), Peter Bogdanovich's *The Last Picture Show* (Columbia, 1971), and George Lucas's *American Graffiti* (Universal, 1973).[8] And he confesses to feeling "absurdly virtuous" whenever he asks his students if they can even imagine these particular films, all of which feature narratives populated almost solely by characters contemporaneous with the soundtrack selections, "with any other kind of music." "The fact is," Raksin writes, "that the music in those films was just what it should have been." But, he continues,

> I do not find this to be equally true of all films in which such music is used. For unless we are willing to concede that what is essentially the music of the young is appropriate to *all* of the aspects of human experience with which films are concerned, we must ask what it is doing on the soundtracks of pictures that deal with other times and generations, other lives. It is one thing to appreciate the freshness and naiveté of pop music and quite another to accept it as inevitable no matter what the subject at hand—and still another to realize that the choice is often made for reasons that have little to do with the film itself.[9]

It is on the subject of the "reasons" for popular music's infiltration into film scores that Raksin is most vociferous. He identifies three of them that to him, apparently, are most painful:

> One: to sell recordings—and incidentally to garner publicity for the picture. Two: to appeal to the "demographically defined" audience, which is a symbolic

unit conceived as an object of condescension. Three (and to my mind saddest of all): because so many directors and producers, having acquired their skills and reputations at the price of becoming elderly, suddenly find themselves aliens in the land of the young; tormented by fear of not being "with it," they are tragically susceptible to the brainwashing of the Music-Biz types.[10]

Raksin concludes with a rhetorical question: "What is one to think of men of taste and experience who can be persuaded that the difference between a good picture and a bad one is a 'now' score that is 'where it's at'?" But in his opening salvo he has already given the answer: "It should be news to no one that many people believe the Industry has been plundered, ruined by incompetence and left to twist slowly in the wind by men whose principal interests—whatever they may be—do not lie in film-making."[11]

Raksin and Bernstein both suggest that popular music's rise to the fore in film scores during the 1960s owes primarily to ignorance, bad taste, and crass commercialism on the part of both filmmakers and film producers. This is debatable; indeed, there seem to be plenty of good reasons—purely aesthetic as well as generally cultural—why jazz, rock, and other vernacular styles entered so forcefully into filmmaking at this time. What is not debatable is that such music, in conjunction with its use in films, sometimes did prove to be extraordinarily lucrative.

In May 1966 *New York Times* film critic Vincent Canby reported that "the sound-track album for 'A Hard Day's Night,' the first feature film starring the Beatles, has so far made a profit estimated at $2 million for United Artists Corporation. This is more than three times the cost of the film itself ($550,000) and explains why film companies today place such emphasis on their music-publishing subsidiaries." Canby also reported that Michael Stewart, president of United Artists' music division, told him that Marlboro Cigarettes recently paid "a sum which runs well into six figures" to use several bars of Elmer Bernstein's music for *The Magnificent Seven* in a radio-television advertising campaign, and that the studio had recently turned down an offer of $200,000 for use of the song "Never On Sunday" because it had become a "standard" that earned between $60,000 and $100,000 annually.[12]

Two months earlier composer Bernard Herrmann, who for more than a decade had been famously involved with the films of Alfred Hitchcock, was fired by the director in the midst of a recording session of music that Herrmann had written for *Torn Curtain* (Universal, 1966).[13] Numerous accounts, all fairly well documented, suggest that the break-up was triggered by Herrmann's ignoring of Hitchcock's specific instructions regarding the treatment of the film's murder sequence but actually was the inevitable climax of a long-standing clash of egos.[14] Yet rumors circulated to the effect that Herrmann's dismissal had to with his refusal to compose the pop-flavored orchestral score requested by studio executives; ten years after the fact Herrmann claimed that his parting words to Hitchcock were: "Look, Hitch, you can't outrun your own shadow. And you don't make pop pictures. What do you want with me? I don't write pop scores."[15]

In any case, in February 1968 Herrmann voiced a general complaint:

Pictures have become a promotional gimmick for music publishers and recording companies. I can't understand how you can make a sophisticated film, then proceed to the lowest common denominator in the score, which will turn out to be rubbish.[16]

Another loud complaint that year came from Elmer Bernstein, who—as newly elected chairman of the Academy of Motion Picture Arts and Sciences' music branch—argued that the system by which the organization granted awards for music was sorely in need of reform. As early as 1931 William Axt noted that Hollywood was still trying to figure out what to do with music that was not in the form of a Tin Pan Alley song and quipped that most producers "still cannot tell a songwriter from a composer."[17] Perhaps with Axt's remark in mind, *Los Angeles Times* music critic Martin Bernheimer, putting Bernstein's complaint in context, explained: "Hollywood has not yet made a clear distinction between a song writer, a score composer and an arranger."[18] As a result, Bernstein said, Academy Awards were more and more often going to scores based on just a single tune:

> They are the easy winners. With help from record companies and publishers who capitalize on title-song profit sharing, and from studios that welcome the free publicity from allied media. Some of the most simple-minded scores have a way of winning. We don't know yet how to fight industry cynicism, but we aren't oblivious to the problem either.[19]

For Bernstein, Herrmann, Raksin, and many others who had contributed richly to the music for classical-style films, "the problem" irritatingly persisted. For most studio executives, the only "problem" was the reluctance of veteran composers to jump onto what clearly seemed to be a smooth-rolling bandwagon. And this "problem" could easily be ignored, for in Hollywood in the late 1960s and early '70s there were plenty of creative musicians willing to give the studios exactly what they wanted.

Contemporaneous with Raksin's eulogy for traditional film music, a New York journalist recalled that one of the songs that Paul Simon and Art Garfunkle wrote for *The Graduate* (United Artists, 1967), "Mrs. Robinson," had—as a single—sold more than a million copies, and that sales of the film's soundtrack album numbered almost two million. He also noted impressive sales figures for soundtrack albums derived from *Easy Rider*, *The Last of Sheila* (Warner Bros., 1973), and *The Way We Were* (Columbia, 1973).[20] Reporting accurately, but not without a hint of sarcasm, he added:

> Nowadays, before a script is completed, producers study Cashbox magazine to see who's Number One. "Their thinking is, 'Let's get whoever sold 17 million records last year,'" sighs one publicist who's sat through many moody music sessions. When the film is completed, disk jockeys receive glossy promotion kits and private screenings. "Gee, kids, I saw a great flick last night . . . and here's your favorite . . . singing his own title song. . . ." *That's* the kind of music producers want to hear.[21]

* * *

As musicologist Julie Hubbert has recently observed, the gist of Bernstein's and Raksin's diatribes has long been accepted as a gospel-like truth. "No doubt as a result of the invective these two composers used in describing the invasion of pop and rock music in early 1970s film music," she writes, "their perspective was immediately echoed in the film and film-music literature."[22]

To support this claim, Hubbert refers to Gerald Mast, whose *A Short History of the Movies* was in fact published a year in advance of Bernstein's essay. Observing the scene from the perspective of 1971, Mast actually had quite a bit to say about why film music had lately changed, and little of it has to do with ignorance or commercialism on the part of filmmakers. In the course of his analysis, however, Mast did make the generalized statement that Hubbert quotes: "Gone is the old principle of studio scoring—to underscore a scene with music that increases the action's emotional impact without making the viewer aware of the music's existence. In new films there is little of this kind of background music."[23]

Hubbert does not mention Irwin Bazelon, whose 1975 *Knowing the Score: Notes on Film Music* contains a chapter titled "A Short History"—the chapter is only twenty-one pages in length, yet a full quarter of it is taken up with a colorful rant about how much recent film music, driven by "the American money rhythm" and written by composers with "a special talent for being able to identify with the film industry" but "having no set cultural values," has lately contributed to "today's ear pollution."[24] She does, however, cite Roy M. Prendergast, whose 1977 *Film Music: A Neglected Art* was one of the first books of recent decades to approach the entire topic of film music from an historical point of view. In ways that will be addressed below, Prendergast takes issue with Mast over his stated reasons as to why film music, in effect, "changed its tune" in the 1960s. But again Hubbert quotes only the generalization:

> The change reshaping current film music, [Prendergast] asserted, was being brought about by a new set of pop music "conventions and clichés," a new practice "as stereotyped in manner as its Strauss-symphonic counterpart in the 1930s and 1940s—only that Strauss is now replaced by the pop, and the symphonic by the Fender bass." The new sound of film music, [Prendergast] continued, was shaped not only by unmusical executives but by directors, too, who "are as unaware as they always have been—perhaps even more so because of their youth—of the potential of music in films."[25]

Possibly Hubbert emphasizes Mast's and Prendergast's generalizations about the "new" sound of film music, at the expense of their discussion as to how this "new" sound came to be, for the sake of better positioning her own argument. The thrust of her 2003 article, after all, is that the shift in film music involved something more than Hollywood's perennial attraction toward potentially lucrative "hit" songs and its natural interest in wooing audiences with up-to date 'pop' sounds. But even if Hubbert deliberately downplays ideas expressed well in advance of her own, she is not incorrect in stating:

> Composers and historians working in the 1970s [e.g., Bernstein, Raksin, Mast, and Prendergast] have not been the only ones to propose this assessment of film music. To a large degree, this theory—that film music of the early 1970s featured primarily pop music and that this shift in tastes was being motivated by the commercialization of film music—is one that has found a solid place in current film and film-music histories as well.[26]

Nor is she incorrect in observing that recently "several film historians have begun to see the early 1970s' fascination with pop and rock music not as the beginning but rather the middle of a long history of . . . studio commercialism." Hubbert notes that Jeff Smith, in his 1998 *The Sounds of Commerce: Marketing Popular Film Music*, "sees anticipations of the early 1970s pop-music phenomenon in the movie theme song bonanza of the 1950s" that began with *Blackboard Jungle* (MGM, 1955). She notes, too, that Alexander Doty ten years earlier had rooted "1970s music practice" in the so-called teen-pics and "Elvis Presley movies" that during the late 1950s and early '60s "were specifically aimed at exploiting the new musical tastes of the youth market."[27]

She fails to remind her readers, however, that during the early years of the sound film, ca. 1930-1, Hollywood had been fairly obsessed with linking its products to marketable "theme songs," and that even during the nickelodeon period there existed a financially cozy relationship between film producers and Tin Pan Alley music publishers. During the 1960s and early '70s there was indeed, as Hubbert writes, a "complicated 'synergy' of film, television, and radio media marketing strategies by studio executives,"[28] between filmmakers and the producers of commercial music. In fact, a complicated synergy involving music publishers had been a feature of filmmaking almost from the very start.

In his often-quoted article from 1972, Bernstein writes that certain events of the 1950s "signaled" the beginning of the end of what has often been described as the "golden age" of film music. To his credit, Bernstein does not suggest that these events—the enormous popularity of Dimitri Tiomkin's song for 1952's *High Noon*, the success of his own jazz-based score for 1955's *The Man with the Golden Arm*—in any way caused film music's "golden age" to pass. The examples that Bernstein cites were indeed signals, mere harbingers, of drastically new approaches to film music that in the 1960s doubtless would have been taken, regardless of precedent, by Hollywood and European filmmakers alike.

The commercialism so loudly decried by Bazelon, Bernstein, and Raksin surely figured into film music's sudden transformation. But there was more to it than that.

Changing Times

Since the start of the nickelodeon period film music had "played" not just to the narrative needs of the on-screen picture but also to the aesthetic needs, and expectations, of its audiences. Whether sounded by lone pianists or large orchestras, accompaniments for silent films tended to consist of steady streams of generic action-illustrating or mood-setting music mixed with supposedly meaningful quotations drawn from a classical/popular repertoire with which most audience members, it was assumed, were familiar.

At least in Hollywood, for a long while accompaniments for sound films worked the same way. The industry, of course, had to work through its obsession first with musical "numbers" and then with ubiquitous "theme songs," and after that it had to get over its insistence that all music in films be somehow integrated into the plot. Because they remembered what had worked so well during silent film's heyday, filmmakers in the early 1930s reverted to scores that featured well-known classical music. Within just a few years they abandoned the use of music that audience members might actually recognize, on the grounds that such music would be distracting. Instead, they encouraged composers to write scores that were entirely original in terms of content but at the same time—in terms of sound, idiom, and affect—were remarkably similar to the orchestral music to which patrons, in general, had grown accustomed.

European filmmakers in practice, and highbrow critics in theory, took exception to the musical conventions that ca. 1938-9 solidified in tandem with the production techniques and narrative approach of the so-called classical-style Hollywood film. Exceptions notwithstanding, thanks to Hollywood's overwhelming screen dominance even the least educated persons in the smallest cities throughout the world came to regard "Hollywood music" as the norm. This norm readily incorporated modernist devices, especially in films whose plots involved science-fiction and psychological deviance, yet its expressive essence remained firmly rooted in the symphonic and operatic literature of the late nineteenth century. Instead of seeming old-fashioned, however, "Hollywood music" for most moviegoers in the 1940s and '50s was very much music of the times.

In the 1960s, as the lyrics of a song by Bob Dylan have it, "the times, they [were] a-changing."

*   *   *

In September 1960, twenty-three persons connected with American filmmaking, each staunchly independent and thus not much prone to memberships, met in New York and formally established an organization to promote what they called the New American Cinema. Their "First Statement" began with an international rallying cry:

> In the course of the past three years we have been witnessing the spontaneous growth of a new generation of filmmakers—the Free Cinema in England, the Nouvelle Vague in France, the young movements in Poland, Italy, and Russia, and, in this country, the work of Lionel Rogosin, John Cassavetes, Alfred Leslie, Robert Frank, Edward Bland, Bert Stern, and the Sanders brothers.
>
> The official cinema all over the world is running out of breath. It is morally corrupt, aesthetically obsolete, thematically superficial, temperamentally boring. Even the seemingly worthwhile films, those that lay claim to high moral and aesthetic standards and have been accepted as such by critics and the public alike, reveal the decay of the Product Film. The very slickness of their execution has become a perversion covering the falsity of their themes, their lack of sensitivity, their lack of style.
>
> If the New American Cinema has until now been an unconscious and sporadic manifestation, we feel the time has come to join together. There are many of us—the movement is reaching significant proportions—and we know what needs to be destroyed and what we stand for.[29]

The rest of the manifesto had to do mostly with the group's anti-censorship stance and its resolve to seek new, presumably more equitable, means of financing and distribution. There is no comment on how music might figure into the New American Cinema, nor is there much discussion of music in the pages of *Film Culture*, the periodical that independent director Jonas Mekas founded in 1955 and which throughout the 1960s was the main platform for the group's commentary on its own work. From the last paragraph of the manifesto, however, one can almost imagine how the New American cinema would sound. Announcing its intention to unite with like-minded filmmakers in France, Italy, Russia, Poland, and England, the group declares:

> As they, we have had enough of the Big Lie in life and in the arts. As they, we are not only for the New Cinema: we are also for the New Man. As they,

we are for art, but not at the expense of life. We don't want false, polished, slick films—we prefer them rough, unpolished, but alive; we don't want rosy films—we want them the color of blood.[30]

Films representative of the New American Cinema perhaps metaphorically were "the color of blood," but literally they were often shot in black-and-white, and this was the case, too, for comparable "new wave" films from France, Italy, and England. The reasons for this were to a certain extent budgetary: no matter what country they were in, independent filmmakers of "new wave" persuasion simply did not have access to the production processes of Hollywood and other participants in the international "official cinema." But the prime reasons for the overall look of "new wave" film were aesthetic and political.

The 1960s witnessed, to use the clichéd phrases, a sexual revolution and a rising drug culture, the women's liberation movement and the Hippie movement, the "British invasion" of American pop music and eventually the dominance of serious "rock" music over care-free rock 'n' roll. The decade's enduring icons include the Apollo moon landing and the Woodstock festival. Among its many driving forces, surely the most potent was wide-spread opposition, at least by young adults, to the United States' ever-escalating military involvement in Vietnam. As one cultural historian puts is, "for radical student movements in London, Paris and Tokyo as well as Berkeley, Kent State and Washington, Vietnam was indeed a symbol—of American corruption, interventionism and neo-imperialism— a symbol so potent as to inspire bloody demonstrations around the globe."[31]

Interviewed in the 1990s, former *Village Voice* film critic Andrew Sarris recalled that American "new wave" filmmaking in the '60s had been very much concerned with "the underground aspect, the covert aspect, the revolutionary aspect." Some participants in the movement, he said, were "genuinely underground" and indeed had "subversive ideas of one type or another." Most of them, however, engaged only in what he called "the second underground thing":

> It was the perception that a great many things that were considered dis-reputable, grubby, cheap, vulgar, were really much more interesting than that. And that there was something underneath all of this. The process of getting underneath is basically an intellectual process. It's a high-art process. It's not fandom. It's not just undisciplined enthusiasm. It's overturning something. And I think my generation, the people with whom I identify critically, people at *Cahiers [du Cinéma]*, people at *Movie*, were in their different ways over-throwing a very pious, proper, socially conscious, socially responsible—but really socially conservative—establishment, mostly a critical establishment.[32]

Italian filmmakers involved in the "new wave" movement (e.g., Federico Fellini, Michelangelo Antonioni, Luchino Visconti) sometimes used pre-existing and eminently recognizable music in bizarrely iconoclastic ways. In general, though, they maintained the clear distinction between source music and "musical commentary" that had been established with Italy's neo-realist films of the 1950s. As Richard Dyer has aptly noted, in the earlier films

> People . . . sing, play and dance and listen to folk songs, popular hits, jazz and snatches of opera. Yet these forms of music rarely appear in the background

197

music, which runs the stylistic gamut of concert music from mid-romanticism to early modernism. This discrepancy could just be conventional . . ., but it is a gap with bitter implications for a movement presumed to be about creating a cinema genuinely expressive of ordinary people's reality.[33]

And in the adventurous Italian films of the '60s this "gap"—with implications that by this time were perhaps not so much "bitter" as simply intriguing—tended to remain open.

Adventurous films from England, on the other hand, strove for a gap-free consistency. Vis-à-vis politics, the "small but influential body of films" (by, for example, Lindsay Anderson, Karel Reisz, and Tony Richardson) that resulted from Britain's catching the "new wave" likely carried a more potent charge than films coming from any other country. "British New Wave cinema," Jeffrey Richards has noted, "was born out of the social and cultural upheaval of the late 1950s that embraced the death of the empire, the rise of working-class affluence, the emergence of a distinctive youth culture and the revival of the intellectual left."[34] The British movement was clearly influenced, as was the New American Cinema, by the French Nouvelle Vague, "which preferred location-shooting to studio work, natural lighting to formal lighting and a fragmented impressionist approach to traditional linear narrative." But what distinguished British

Figure 10.1 Franck Purcel conducting the music for Frederico Fellini's 1955 *La Strada* with Giulietta Masina. March 1955. © LAPI/Roger-Viollet/The Image Works.

"new wave" films from their international counterparts was their pervasive darkness. Their common characteristics, Richards writes, were their dreary "northern locations," their "black and white photography," and—perhaps most striking—their "melancholy jazz scores."[35]

Jazz figured into French films as well, but it was not always melancholy, and it shared space with a great many other types of music. Rarely in the generally realistic work of the Nouvelle Vague directors, however, did music function—as it often in did contemporaneous films from Italy and England—as underscore. In France during the 1950s, critics for the journal *Cahiers du Cinéma* fairly worshipped Hollywood's approach to filmmaking. It was in a column for *Cahiers* that André Bazin first explored the idea that filmmaking in Hollywood, and arguably also in France, had ca. 1938–9 reached a level of "classical perfection." It was in columns for *Cahiers*, too, that Jean-Luc Godard and François Truffaut—film critics long before they became filmmakers—cultivated their much-celebrated "politiques des auteurs" theory that suggested that at least some films, no matter how subject they might have been to industrial processes, nevertheless stand apart from the crowd as the stylistically recognizable work of certain directorial "authors."

Godard's 1961 *Une Femme est une femme* indeed features extra-diegetic music, by Michel Legrand. But it comes in the form of a stylized homage, exaggerated "to the point of caricatured musical punctuation of some of the spoken dialogue,"[36] to the "Hollywood music" that surely remained beloved by Godard and his colleagues but which was now considered, at least for their own purposes, to be outdated. More typical of the Nouvelle Vague's *cinéma vérité* are bits and pieces of music—some of them composed especially for the film at hand, most of them drawn from a wide variety of pre-existing sources—that drift in and out of on-screen narratives in unpredictable patterns not unlike those that mark the appearance of music in the lives of real people. Occasionally such music is unambiguously meaningful. Far more often the music just "happens," apparently bearing no message at all; if meaning is indeed attached to such "random" or "accidental" music, it likely stems as much from the audience member as from the director. Commenting specifically on Godard's 1962 *Vivre sa vie*, but with important implications for the function of music in a great many recent films, Craig Sinclair writes:

> Music is employed as a floating signifier, freed of the chains of signification.... The experiencer is now the source of textual power and can rewrite not just the signifier but also the very presence of the signified itself. This music is intra-textually malleable and descriptive but perhaps only for the writerly pleasure of the experiencer, not the readerly passiveness of the viewer.[37]

All of this—the Italian idea that there could comfortably be a stylistic "gap" between diegetic music and extra-digetic musical "commentary," the British idea that grittily realistic films warranted appropriately "melancholy" underscores, the French idea that the "meaning" of at least some film music might lay largely in the ears of the beholder—percolated into the work of the defiantly independent filmmakers who had banded together to launch the New American Cinema. Eventually it percolated into Hollywood. This was in part because mainstream producers liked—or simply wished to appropriate—what they heard in films made outside the system; it was also in part because some of the "new wave" filmmakers, after successes on the fringe, had actually become part of the establishment. In 1960 Peter Bogdanovich, at the time a film critic for *Esquire* magazine, was among those who signed the "First Statement" of the New American Cinema Group; ten years later he was directing *The Last Picture Show*.[38]

* * *

Bogdanovich, Julie Hubbert convincingly argues, used vintage popular songs in *The Last Picture Show* not for the sake of capitalizing on the music's commercial appeal but for the sake of making the film—in the manner of the French *cinéma vérité* and the Italian neo-realist movement—seem more life-like. Indeed, the main point of her article is to suggest that while much of Hollywood indeed embraced popular music in the hopes of generating a hit song, a small but significant element looked to popular music of all sorts for reasons that were purely artistic. "In a very audible way," she writes,

> The vérité-ists' conceptualization of musical realism affected a wide range of films of the early 1970s, films as disparate in subject matter as Peter Bogdanovich's *The Last Picture Show* (1971), Martin Scorsese's *Mean Streets* (1973), George Lucas's *American Graffiti* (1973), and Sidney Lumet's *Dog Day Afternoon* (1975). What unites many of these important films from the early 1970s, even more than a new realistic look, in fact, is a new realistic sound, the dramatic absence of nondiegetic music and the striking imposition of the vérité-ists' mandate of "source music only."[39]

Gerald Mast published his *A Short History of the Movies* in 1971, before the Hollywood version of *cinéma vérité* became fashionable. He had recently observed, in films made by pioneers of the New American Cinema movement, a trend toward realism. But he also observed another trend, both in independent productions and in their Hollywood counterparts, that affected the use of music in films at least as much as did arguably crass commercialism and arguably pure vérité-ism.

Concentrating on Hollywood, Mast notes that musicals, classical-style films with traditional underscores, and "films that conscientiously seek the industry's 'G' rating" were made throughout the 1960s. But, he notes, "each year's most discussed, most important American films do not receive the 'G' rating." He asks: "What has produced this new cinema?" And then he lists four causes: Hollywood's very real economic need for products in one way or another "sensational" enough to draw potential audience members away from their television sets; the stylistic influence of "new wave" French and Italian filmmakers; the gradual infiltration into Hollywood of "underground" aesthetics; and the general change in "sexual and social values" of the "new American film audiences."[40]

Citing such examples as *Bonnie and Clyde* (Warner Bros., 1967), *Cool Hand Luke* (Warner Bros., 1967), *Easy Rider* (Columbia, 1969), and *Butch Cassidy and the Sundance Kid* (Twentieth Century-Fox, 1969), Mast argues that, for all their innovations, the new films remain "as subservient to convention and cliché" as were most American films of previous decades. Perhaps still riding a moralistic hobbyhorse, he identifies one of the conventions as a propensity for "protagonists [who] are social misfits, deviates, or outlaws." Then, switching to aesthetics, he notes a second convention that seems to fly in the face of vérité-ism:

The new American cinema does not ask to be taken as reality but constantly announces that it is artificial. Rather than effacing the film's artfulness, as [Ernst] Lubitsch, or [John] Ford, or [Howard] Hawks intentionally did, the new directors throw in as many cinematic tricks as possible, which both intensify the film's moods and remind the audience that it is watching a film. Slow motion, freeze-frames, jump-cutting, mixtures of black-and-white and color are all standard, indeed obligatory tricks of the trade.[41]

There are "consequences" of this "deliberate artificiality," Mast writes. One of them is "an emotional power in the visual assaults of the medium itself," with the result that audience members respond "not just to story and people but to the physical stimulation of eye and ear for its own sake." Another is an "emphasis of the films as emotional metaphors rather than as literal stories," with all the "film trickery . . . totally destroy[ing] the definitions of time and space, of now and then, of reality and fantasy, purposely emphasizing emotional continuity at the expense of linear continuity."[42] Still another consequence of the new American cinema's self-conscious artifice—significantly —has to do with the treatment of a film's aural elements:

The new films play as trickily with sound as they do with images. . . . If there is to be music it must be either clearly motivated (i.e., playing on a radio or record player nearby) or deliberately artificial (a song on the sound track that exists specifically to be noticed and plays either in harmony or in counterpoint with the sequence's visuals). In *Butch Cassidy and the Sundance Kid* (1969), the story stops for an idyllic ride on a bicycle accompanied by a pleasant Burt Bacharach rock tune. In *Medium Cool* ([Paramount,] 1969), the patriotic speeches and songs inside the Democratic Convention hall accompany the riots between students and police in Grant Park. Some sequences in the new films distort sound purposely; others are completely silent, contrasting with the other sequences of song or noise.[43]

Mast concludes his perceptive comments on film music with a bromide, a simple statement to the effect that creators of rock music and jazz were ca. 1969–70 more favored in Hollywood than were old-school composers such as Alfred Newman, Miklós Rózsa, and Max Steiner.

As noted earlier, Roy M. Prendergast, in his 1977 *Film Music: A Neglected Art*, quibbles with Mast. The rebuttal has not at all to do with Mast's bottom-line conclusion that various forms of popular music had lately superseded classical-style orchestral scoring. Rather, Prendergast's carping focuses on Mast's arguably astute observations that, on one hand, the new Hollywood revels in artifice and "emphasiz[es] emotional continuity at the expense of linear continuity" and that, on another hand, the interest of certain filmmakers in sonic "realism" was, in the context of the 1960s, relatively new. Regarding vérité-ist directors who insisted that their soundtracks feature only diegetic music, Prendergast, who had included a sixteen-page chapter on music in the early sound film in the first part of his book, notes:

If this observation sounds familiar to the reader it is because this attitude of music "clearly motivated" is the same one held in the infancy of sound. American cinema has, musically, experienced an aesthetic regression.[44]

Mast had differentiated between "clearly motivated" music and music whose use was "deliberately artificial," but Prendergast conflates the ideas and accuses Mast of contradicting himself. "One is immediately tempted to surmise," he writes, "that if the new American cinema does not ask to be taken as reality then the 'unreal' aspect of dramatic music on a sound track should not be bothersome." After directly quoting Mast's comment on the new Hollywood films' favoring of a non-linear approach to narrative, Prendergast responds: "Film music has almost always been nonlinear, which apparently makes it a perfect match for today's American film. Music in films continues to be as misunderstood as it ever was."[45]

Prendergast's *non sequitur* is curmudgeonly. Clearly, Bazelon, Bernstein, and Raksin were not the only ones who, as composer Jerry Goldsmith put it in the interview quoted in this chapter's epigraph, had not "bridged the gap."

A Rich Variety

Remembering the sense of urgency that fueled many of the cultural changes in both Europe and the United States during the 1960s, veteran film critic Andrew Sarris granted that the times had indeed been revolutionary. He recalled: "It's like when rock music came in, people said, 'Well, what's new about that?' Well, what's new about it is that it just completely overturned everything else. It ended pop music in the way it had been; it destroyed it." And there was destruction as well, he admitted, in the world of filmmaking:

> The nouvelle vague did a lot of damage, the *Cahiers* people did a lot of damage, I did a lot of damage. You can't make an omelette without breaking a lot of eggs, and a lot of eggs were broken, a lot of eggs that didn't deserve to be broken, not that completely. Now I feel I want to return to film history everything that we dislodged.[46]

Sarris offered his comments from a perspective that postdates the "new wave" "damage" by thirty years, and likely his bittersweet regrets had not much to do with how music, in particular, was treated by vanguard filmmakers in the 1960s. As early as the mid 1970s, however, commentators who paid attention to film music were noticing changes in Hollywood that suggested an industry-wide desire to reinstall something valuable that—amidst the previous decade's simultaneous cravings for, on the one hand, sonic "realism" and, on the other hand, income- and publicity-generating hit songs— had perhaps been "dislodged."

Nostalgia might have played a part in this. At the suggestion of executive R. Peter Munves, RCA Records in 1972 had launched a series of fresh recordings of "classic film scores" by composers such as Erich Wolfgang Korngold, Alfred Newman, and Max Steiner.[47] Within a few years recordings of "classic" film scores were being released by Delos, Entr'acte, and the Elmer Bernstein Film Music Collection Club, and a newspaper reported that "several Japanese and European record companies have begun reissuing original sound tracks no longer in print by the parent U.S. companies, usually with remastered sound."[48] In July 1976 *Washington Post* film critic Tom Shales penned a column about the recent popularity not of the latest and perhaps "hippest" soundtrack albums but, rather, of albums devoted to scores from film music's "golden age." "Where is Old Hollywood?" he asked. In response to his rhetorical question, he answered:

It is everywhere. New Hollywood can't escape it. Television alone reminds us nightly in shows both late and late-late that many qualities within easy grasp of the old Hollywood are impossibly beyond the new. Movie nostalgia has become more than a disposition; it has turned into an industry, but beneath what seems to be just a grass-was-greener longing for anything previous to now, there is the fact that Old Hollywood had powers and capacities that very nearly were magical. . . .

You don't have to see old movies to realize the distinctions. You can just hear them. The best new movie music albums released in recent weeks are almost invariably records of old movie music. When the major studios maintained vast music departments, they produced music proportionate to the size of the screen and the enormity of the myths; it had style, melody, lushness, and it also had *importance*.[49]

Shales was speaking only for himself when he remarked that, to his ears, old-style film scores had had a certain *gravitas,* an "importance," that seemed to be lacking in the music contained on a great many "soundtrack albums" generated by recent films. Freelance writer Thomas Maremaa likely spoke for Hollywood in general when he wrote, four months earlier, on what he perceived to be the start of an overall shift in film-music practice.

The article includes a fairly thorough summary of Hollywood practice since the early years of the sound film, but this anecdote-rich account comes after Maremaa has made his main point. Probably it was only for reasons of space that editors at the *Los Angeles Times*, where the article was reprinted four weeks after its original appearance in the *New York Times*, lopped off the last 250 or so words, in which the author offers a pithy conclusion that applies not just to film music in the mid 1970s but also to film music in our own time. It seems strange, though—because they generally gave prominent play even to the most speculative reports on developments in one of their most financially robust local industries—that the Los Angeles editors emphasized the article's retrospective content at the expense of its pointed observations on the current state of affairs. On its introductory page and on the first of its two "jump" pages, the West Coast version of the article bore the headline "Movie Music Down through the Decades," and on the second "jump" page it was labeled simply "Movie Music through the Ages."[50] The East Coast editors, who understood that Maremaa's purpose was to comment on the here and now, aptly headlined the article "The Sound of Movie Music."

Maremaa begins with a few paragraphs that remind readers of, on the one hand, the dramatic effectiveness of authentic-sounding songs lately heard in Robert Altman's *Nashville* (Paramount, 1975) and *Buffalo Bill and the Indians* (De Laurentiis,1976),[51] and, on the other hand, the extraordinary commercial success that Marvin Hamlisch achieved in 1973 both with his song-centered original score for *The Way We Were* (Columbia) and his adaptations of vintage ragtime music by Scott Joplin for *The Sting* (Universal). Then he gets right to the point:

Audiences have changed and so has movie music: Audiences in the '60s, demanding greater realism, tended to reject the artificial use of music in pictures. Music had to come from an authentic "source"—one that the audience could see or identify, such as a band or a jukebox—it couldn't be superimposed on the action. Some film makers even went so far as to discard the main title music altogether, though there was still pressure on a composer to write a hit song or a theme that could in turn be made into a hit soundtrack. Music was at best something that a film maker used sparingly in a picture, and with great caution, so as not to spoil the realism or appear too blatantly commercial.

Yet what audiences rejected just a few years back as unrealistic is precisely what they want all over again. They want music to work on them, to wipe them out, and that is what the new movie music is all about.[52]

Maremaa notes that there was now—in 1976—more music being written in Hollywood than ever before, "due mainly to the insatiable appetite of television where the fear of silence is almost pathological." He also notes that, probably because of Hollywood's increased involvement with television, fewer feature films are being made. Notwithstanding the impact that director Stanley Kubrick made with his use of pre-exiting avant-garde music by Hungarian composer György Ligeti in *2001: A Space Odyssey* (MGM, 1968), Maremaa maintains that "fewer producers are willing to gamble on music of the post-Schoenberg idiom because, they maintain, the public isn't ready for it. So movie music has remained pretty much firmly rooted in the late 19th-century idiom of Wagner, Strauss and Mahler."[53]

Vis-à-vis this, he quotes John Williams, whose score for Steven Spielberg's *Jaws* (Universal, 1975) likely signaled film music's turning point:

> This is a regressive and in many ways decadent period in movie scoring. Yet it's exciting to a lot of composers because it affords them the opportunity of working with a large orchestra, painting with a big brush. Nevertheless, we have to be humble when measured against the great period of romantic film scoring in the '30s and '40s.[54]

Williams's acknowledgement of his forebears is worth noting, for there is no denying the similarity—in scope, idiom, and function—between his contribution to *Jaws* and the scores from film music's "golden age." Indeed, Meremaa centers his entire article on the *Jaws* score, which utilized an 80-piece orchestra and featured not even a whiff of a song. And Meremaa is not the only critic in the first half of 1976 to single out Williams as a bellwether of a renewed interest in classical-style film music. Tom Shales, in his review of soundtrack recordings, observes that along with albums of "golden age" scores there were at least a few samplings of new music worthy of praise. He mentions, for example, a recent disc that featured Henry Mancini leading the London Symphony in performances of music by a variety of film-music composers,[55] and he calls particular attention to the excerpts from Williams's scores for *Jaws*, *Earthquake* (Universal, 1974), and *The Towering Inferno* (Twentieth Century-Fox, 1974). Shales writes:

> Williams has been highly instrumental in trying to bring back to the movies the full symphonic score, with all its potentials for pleasurable manipulation and its intimations of life larger than life. This was an important part of what we got from the movies once, and there are many signs that many us want it back again.[56]

* * *

Meremaa's article was clearly an optimistic celebration of the "new" sound of film music that in many ways was actually film music's "old" sound, albeit now in spiffier

Figure 10.2 John Barry and Bryan Forbes. © The Kobal Collection.

orchestral and sonic garb. But the article's conclusion contained a sobering reminder that very little in the film industry, and especially in Hollywood, ever happened for artistic reasons alone:

> Composers, of course, are just as vulnerable to the fads of the industry as anyone else. The symphonic sound, for example, will continue as long as the movies in which it's used make money. Once they don't, producers will demand something different musically.[57]

Apparently meeting producers' needs to satisfy what they perceived to be the audience's needs, and thus satisfying the need to make money, the "symphonic sound" continued. Along with providing the music for *Jaws*, Williams during this period composed high-impact orchestral scores for other films in a variety of genres.[58] And he was not alone in cultivating the symphonic sound. Ca. 1975–6, music comparable in style and overall effect was also being written by, among others, John Barry,[59] Maurice Jarre,[60] and Jerry Goldsmith.[61]

The second 1977 film for which Williams composed the music was George Lucas's *Star Wars* (Twentieth Century-Fox/Lucasfilm) and the third was Spielberg's *Close Encounters of the Third Kind* (Columbia); the second 1978 film to feature a score by Williams was Richard Donner's *Superman* (Alexander Salkind).[62] At least in part due to the potency of Williams's music, all three of these films were tremendously successful at the box office. For all intents and purposes, this trio of films blazed the trail for film music's future, but not just because of the content of Williams's scores. The breakthrough had to do as well with the means by which the music—and also the films' dialogue and a wide variety of sound effects—was presented.

Star Wars was the first film to feature through its entirety a new technology developed by British-born electrical engineer Ray Dolby.[63] Dolby, after undergraduate training at Stanford and Ph.D. studies at Cambridge, in 1965 set up a company that at first was dedicated to perfecting a "noise-reduction" system that significantly decreased the amount of "hiss" inherent in recordings made with, or reproduced by, machines that involved magnetic tape. In the early 1970s Dolby began exploring ways by which "noise" might be similarly reduced in film soundtracks that, since the introduction of two-channel stereophonic sound in the early 1950s, involved magnetic recording as well as reproduction. By the mid 1970s, Dolby had come up with a relatively inexpensive method by which *all* filmic sound could be not just presented in a relatively noise-free way but also—significantly—separated into more channels than the earlier binaural systems had allowed.

Dolby Laboratories, Inc., was headquartered in the San Francisco Bay Area. Following university study in Southern California and completion of his first two films,[64] Lucas likewise based himself in the Bay Area as he worked on his next project. "Like the other Bay Area filmmakers," writes film historian Peter Biskind, "Lucas had always been interested in sound." And so Lucas, after learning about the new technology and realizing how it might be applied to his own directorial concerns, "over Fox's objections . . . insisted on using Dolby Stereo" in *Star Wars*.[65]

Star Wars was more than just another instant hit. It was a film whose lucrative exhibition depended crucially, as had been the case in 1927 with *The Jazz Singer*, on theaters having the necessary reproduction equipment licensed and installed. In order to capitalize on the film's extraordinary popularity, in cities around the world theaters that had never before "played stereo were [now] forced to do it if they wanted *Star Wars*." Thus, according to sound designer/editor Walter Murch, "*Star Wars* was the can opener that made people realize not only the effect of sound, but the effect that good sound had at the box office."[66]

In his recent book on the effect that Dolby had on filmmaking in general, Gianluca Sergi suggests that "Dolby's achievement goes considerably further than a technological shake-up. In the 1970s and early 1980s, Dolby achieved nothing less than a comprehensive industry-wide transformation, from studio attitudes to sound, filtering through to filmmakers' creative use of sound and audience expectations."[67] But in an earlier essay Sergi reminds us, pointedly, that celebration of Dolby Stereo ca. 1977 should not cause us to minimize the sincere attempts that engineers had long been making to deliver to movie audiences the best sound possible. Before the advent of Dolby Stereo, he writes, film sound's most nagging problem stemmed not from the studios but from the theaters. The loudspeakers in most theaters had a limited frequency range; very loud sounds, or complex mixes of sound, typically resulted in distortion, and so "to avoid a cacophony" filmmakers "tended to give aural priority to music and the human voice."[68] In the 1950s and 1960s there were indeed notable achievements in theatrical sound reproduction, but invariably these involved "special" installations. "The differences between then and now," Sergi notes, lie largely in the combination of standards of production and reproduction. Where with a film like *Spartacus* (1960) full stereo sound reproduction was possible with only a handful of (extremely expensive) 70 mm road-show prints in a handful of first-run cinemas, the soundtrack on *Star Wars* (1977) could be reproduced to high standards in most theatres thanks to the cheaper and more flexible Dolby system.[69]

Star Wars, which opened in May 1977, featured four-channel sound on 35 mm film. Opening seven months later, *Close Encounters of the Third Kind* featured four-channel sound in combination with subwoofers that enhanced the power and clarity of low-frequency sounds. *Superman*, opening in December 1978, featured subwoofers and sound in five channels, including one whose audio content played only from speakers in the rear of the theater. Since exhibition of these three hugely popular films required installation of the proper sound system, by the end of the decade Dolby-equipped venues had become the norm. This resulted, of course, in huge profits for Dolby Laboratories, Inc. It also resulted, among filmmakers, in a new "confidence" and "willingness to experiment."[70]

Writing in 1978 even before the release of the "surround-sound" *Superman*, Charles Schreger commented on what seemed to be an exciting new symbiosis:

> With sound as with image, of course, it takes a collaborative art to convince us that a movie is life, and it takes modern technology to make the art possible. Was it the availability of complex sound equipment that sparked Hollywood's fascination with high-quality sound on film? Or did a few daring directors have a vision (or hear voices) and then seek out the hardware and soundmen to help them realize it? Whatever the answer, the short list of sound-conscious directors comprises a baker's dozen of some of the industry's most successful, esteemed, and adventurous talents. In alphabetical order: Robert Altman, Michael Cimino, Francis Coppola, Milos Forman, Philip Kaufman, Stanley Kubrick, George Lucas, Terr[ence] Malick, Alan J. Pakula, Ken Russell, Martin Scorsese, Jerzy Skolimowski, Steven Spielberg.[71]

In regarding the work of these and other "sound-conscious directors," of which in the ensuing decades there would be many, one might be tempted to think that their exploration of Dolby technology focused largely on the clear projection of subtly spoken dialogue and, more obviously, on the three-dimensional presentation of diegetic noise that ranges from aural stimuli so quiet that in earlier films (or in real life) they would go almost unnoticed to the loudest possible quasi-realistic crashes and explosions. For reasons as much commercial as artistic, filmmakers since the late 1970s have indeed exploited the Dolby technology's capacity to make "spectacular" their products' dialogue and sound effects. But the technology was applied as well—for better or worse—to music.

* * *

Early in the 1970s *New York Times* music critic Harold C. Schonberg penned a column on film music in which, surprisingly, he relaxed his stance. Instead of referring to his own archly conservative opinions of the previous decade, he used as his "straw man" a bromide-filled article on film music that Igor Stravinsky had contributed a quarter-century before to the journal *Musical Digest*. Apparently having gone to the movies and "seen the light," and prompted by recent exposure to Ken Russell's arguably ridiculous biographical treatment of Tchaikovsky in *The Music Lovers* (United Artists/Rossfilms, 1970), Schonberg wrote:

> There have been considerable changes in the format of movie music since [Stravinsky's 1946 article], especially in the last few years. Film composers no longer are tied to the sweet gush of sound that was de rigueur in the old days. ... The cinema is now taken much more seriously by intellectuals as an art form. Composers are granted infinitely more latitude, and have been experimenting enthusiastically with every avant-garde device—serialism and electronic music very much included. Suddenly film music has become a little more than wallpaper, and if most of it still remains pretty feeble, there is that small percentage where creative musical minds are working with creative directors.[72]

Late in the '70s, after Dolby technology had made its considerable impact, *Los Angeles Times* film critic Charles Champlin offered a synopsis of how film music had evolved over the decades:

> Watching today a movie like "Wuthering Heights" [1939], you realize how the musical fashion changed. That one had music (by Alfred Newman, and wonderful) for everything—standing up, sitting down, opening drawers, putting on hats. Silence, sudden and unexpected, became its own kind of musical accent.
>
> Postwar, the music grew jazzier and smaller (the earlier Henry Mancini influence) and less, to the point at which some movies have no music at all.
>
> The disaster films, whatever their other claims on history, can be said to have given mock-Mahler and other symphonic sounds a new lease on celluloid life, and John Williams's growling basses at the start of "Jaws" had as much bite as the shark itself, maybe more.
>
> A rich variety, and a close suiting of the musical form to the story content, is the current fashion, so far as I can hear. The present mode includes all those identical wistful ballads, indistinguishable as currants, behind the opening and closing credits, but you can't have everything.[73]

Wistful ballads behind opening and closing credits, often in combination with classical-style symphonic underscores and vérité-istic samples of pre-existing music from a great many genres, would remain the fashion. The driving forces perhaps have been largely commercial, but to a certain extent they have been artistic as well. In any case, since the 1970s—but especially since the advent of Dolby sound technology—it seems that more than a few "creative musical minds" have been working closely with "creative [film] directors." In terms of film music as it might be broadly defined, the result has indeed been "a rich variety."

Chapter 11

ECLECTICISM, 1978–2001

I detest contemporary scoring and dubbing in cinema. Film music as an art took a deep plunge when Dolby stereo hit. Stereo has the capacity to make orchestral music sound big and beautiful and more expansive, but it also can make sound effects sound four times as big. That began the era of sound effects over music. It's easier to let sound effects be big and just jump out and do everything than it is to let music do the same thing.

Danny Elfman, 1990[1]

Involving reproduction equipment that was relatively inexpensive for exhibitors to license and install, Dolby Stereo soon enough became the norm for market-oriented filmmakers. Its spread was not so endemic as had been that of the Western Electric amplification system that initiated the era of the sound film. With no alternatives except to continue showing silent films, all theater owners who wanted to remain in business in the 1927–30 period were in effect compelled to adopt the Western Electric system; Dolby was optional, a requirement only for those theater owners who wished to capitalize on "blockbuster" hits.

Many of the films from the 1980s and '90s that aspired to "blockbuster" status fell into the category of the "action film." One of the goals of directors who used Dolby was clarity of sound, but another goal—perhaps the prime goal—was that the sound be noticed. Subwoofers in movie theaters surely enhanced the fidelity of film scores, but what they contributed in terms of lending definition to low-register orchestral sonorities was negligible compared with the quasi-realistic presence they gave to thunderous sound effects. The loudspeakers installed at the rear of the theaters were seldom used for a soundtrack's extra-diegetic music; when experiencing live performances of music, after all, one normally takes in sounds that come only from the direction in which one's head is turned. But the rear speakers, in combination with the subwoofers, were ideal for providing filmgoers with aural stimuli that helped them feel as though they were actually in the midst of, for example, storms at sea, creature-filled jungles, and fierce battles.

Naturally, filmmakers who sought to take advantage of the capabilities of the new technology were attracted to projects that allowed them to fill their audience's ears with a wide range of loud, three-dimensional sound effects. This resulted in a great many films that in one way or another featured action; it also resulted in a great many films whose action was supported by music. Studios in the Dolby era continued to lard their products with pop songs in the hope that the songs would generate both publicity and income; indeed, cultivation of the "soundtrack album" only intensified during the twentieth century's last two decades. But up-to-date pop songs—or vintage oldies, or moody jazz—would hardly do to illustrate automobile chases, spaceship attacks, and the like. For this, filmmakers *en masse* tended to rely on orchestral underscores in spirit and content not much different from what Max Steiner had provided for the original version of *King Kong*.

Writing in 1938, George Antheil complained about Hollywood's insistence on asking composers for "music that ties up inanely with every bit of the picture's action." "In fact," Antheil wrote, "Hollywoodian music is 'action-crazy.'" To be sure, Antheil complained even more about what he called the "European method of scoring," by which music

> plays so completely "against" the film to which it is "set," that one cannot imagine why it was placed there, except, perhaps, for the very good reason that the film composer had an octet, a symphony, and a couple of string quartets tucked away, and so decided that this sound track was as good an occasion to get them heard as any other.[2]

"Certainly," he concluded, such music "is not the movie music of the future, any more than the ridiculous 'action music' of present day Hollywood is the movie music of the future."[3]

Had "the future" been frozen in the 1960s, when film music tended as much toward "realism" as toward blatant commercialism and "deliberate artificiality," posterity might have proven Antheil's predictions to be more or less on the mark. But time did not stand still. Dolby sound, and the THX specifications developed in 1982,[4] were novelties that mainstream filmmakers in Hollywood and elsewhere hungrily wished to exploit. In large part inspired by the contributions that John Williams's scores for *Star Wars*, *Close Encounters of the Third Kind*, and *Superman* made to the box-office of those films, it seems that in the early 1980s "Hollywoodian music" was again quite "action-crazy."

A "Pitched Battle"?

For composers able to turn out action-filled orchestral scores that could accompany Dolby-powered crashes and explosions, the 1980s were indeed boom times. But not all directors were as sensitive to the dramatic needs of action films as were George Lucas and Steven Spielberg, who for all their interest in state-of-the-art technology nevertheless maintained strong affinities with the conventions—musical and otherwise—of classical-style filmmaking. Other directors used orchestral music not in a thematic way, as did Lucas and Spielberg throughout their films, but simply as a means to boost the excitement level of action scenes, as a churning affective backdrop noticeable only during slight gaps in the foregrounded battery of sound effects.

The scores may have been orchestral, but that did not automatically put them on a par with scores from film music's "golden age." Vis-à-vis the generic quality of such music, Elmer Bernstein complained bitterly:

The art of film scoring is in dire danger today, the greatest it's faced. The problem is one of pure ignorance. To the studios, film music is just a sort of wallpaper. If they don't like what they bought, they just paint over it.

In the days when studios had music heads like John Green at MGM and Alfred Newman at Fox, composers had people who would fight for them if necessary, who would educate the executives. Today, the composer has no one to protect him. It's a very disturbing situation.[5]

The idea that scores could be replaced rather at the last minute was not new to the film industry. In Hollywood, Alfred Hitchcock famously dropped Bernard Herrmann's music for *Torn Curtain* (1966) in favor of music by John Addison; in England, Stanley Kubrick abandoned the orchestral score that Alex North had written for *2001: A Space Odyssey* (1968) and used instead an assortment of pre-existing compositions.[6] Indeed, the practice dates back to the late 1930s, when producers such as David O. Selznick regularly commissioned "back-up" scores in case the music by the first-choice composer somehow failed to please.[7]

In the mid 1980s, however, it seemed that the practice of last-minute substitution was becoming more widespread. The Bernstein quotation appeared in a *Los Angeles Times* article headlined "Movie Music: Is It Becoming Hit or Miss?" The writer noted that director Ivan Reitman had replaced portions of Bernstein's orchestral score for *Ghostbusters* (Columbia, 1984) with pop songs, that Walter Hill had replaced James

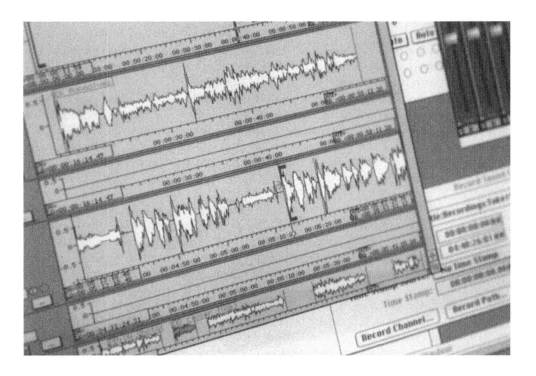

Figure 11.1 A computer screen shows a soundtrack being digitally edited on a Sonic Solutions system at Silver Linings Audio studio. © Corbis.

Horner's modernist percussion music for *Streets of Fire* (Universal, 1984) with blues-flavored music by Ry Cooder, and that Ridley Scott had replaced Jerry Goldsmith's orchestral score for *Legend* (Universal, 1985) with electronic music by the German art-rock ensemble Tangerine Dream.

Goldsmith's score for *Legend* was "probably one of the best he's done," Scott told the reporter, but as the film started to be "toughened up" the original music started to seem "too sweet."[8] Scott insisted that the decisions to alter the tone of the film and to request an entirely new score were entirely his own. According to an insider at Universal, however, the idea for a new score originated with the president of Universal's music department, and the decision was made for reasons not just practical but also "commercial." "Goldsmith is naturally frustrated by the rejection of his 'Legend' score, but he doesn't consider himself a victim. 'I think the real victim is the picture,' he said."[9]

However strong, Goldsmith's opinion as to how dramatic films were being "victimized" by pop-music scores is, after all, only an opinion. It is fact, however, that in the early 1980s commercial interests figured importantly in how the major Hollywood studios regarded music.

In April 1981 a former editor for *Billboard* magazine thought it quite remarkable that both Universal and Paramount now "have as heads of their music departments executives whose backgrounds are steeped in rock and pop music." Indeed, he wrote, there is at the moment "a growing platoon of music executives now involved in films, which would insure the growth of contemporary scores." He quotes Jay Lawton, music executive at Disney: "Contemporary music will come to the fore because of its popularity and because it's been a good ticket draw." He also quotes Harry Lojewski, head of music at MGM since 1972, who said that the studios currently look to the public to "make a judgment as to how much rock, country or middle-of-the-road music is in films. The industry is constantly monitoring the audience, what records are selling and who the major record acts are."[10]

The film studios' interest in which musical performers were "hot" would only grow keener as the decade rolled along. Along with witnessing the resurgence of the symphonic film score in action films, the 1980s also witnessed an extraordinary number of mergers of corporations that hitherto had been involved primarily either with music or with film. In a recent book on the commercial synergy between music and film, Pauline Reay writes:

> The only studios that were able to withstand threats to their music divisions were Universal and Warner Bros. During the 1980s four companies, Warner Communications Inc. (WCI), Gulf+Western (Paramount), Disney and MCA (Universal) dominated film production and distribution, and all of these companies had diversified with interests in publishing and music. A second tier of companies also had interests in related areas: MGM/UA, Columbia and Twentieth Century-Fox.
>
> Soon a new wave of mergers began: Sony bought the CBS Record Group in 1986 and Columbia Pictures in 1989 in order to have a software library to use with its new equipment, one version of synergy. Rupert Murdoch's News Corporation bought Twentieth Century-Fox in 1985, Warner Communications merged with Time Inc. in 1989 to become the world's largest media conglomerate, and Matsushita bought MCA (Universal) in 1990.[11]

The merger activity of the 1980s calls to mind what happened in the early years of the Great Depression, when prosperous Hollywood studios—convinced that the success of the new sound films might be directly proportional to the amount of musical "numbers" they featured—in an instant bought the entire holdings of financially strapped New York music publishers. But the stakes, in the 1980s, were enormously higher. Ca. 1929–30 the inclusion in a film of an already popular song was likely to contribute to that film's success, and a film whose success was based largely on the box-office appeal of blue-chip stars could likewise trigger sales for printed or recorded versions of brand new songs. Ca. 1985 the filmic use of popular music had little to do with benefits that might be gained—before or after a film's release—from individual songs. Rather, it concerned entire albums of songs, the rewards from which could be considerable.

A "feeding frenzy" has broken out in Hollywood as a result of the studios' "search for profitable sound tracks," the *Los Angeles Times* reported in October 1986. "This year alone, 13 of Billboard's Top Pop Albums came from films. But for every 'Top Gun' or 'Stand By Me' (now rapidly climbing the charts) there have been dozens of failures like 'Out of Bounds' and 'Howard the Duck.' Yet the hunt for the right musical chemistry and the battle for the potentially impressive revenues continue at full tilt. In 1985 alone, 10 sound-track singles made Billboard's year-end Hot 100 singles chart and in 1986 a whopping 13 sound-track LPs have already landed on the Top Pop Albums list."[12]

The writer notes that

> Sound-track deals are among the most complicated in the movie business. While the music component is usually less than 5% of [a film's] total budget, there is often a mountain of paper work to divide the album revenues. According to entertainment attorney Lionel S. Sobel, 47 separate contracts were made to cover the nine original songs on the enormously successful "Flashdance" sound track. (There would have been more if the producers had opted for existing music rather than original material.)
>
> Typically, the studio provides a hefty advance (anywhere from $75,000 to as much as $1 million) for the production costs of the album in exchange for a royalty (typically 16% to 22%) on the record sales and a share in the publishing revenues (sheet-music sales and fees paid for the performance of the songs by other artists). But as these albums have become more and more successful, the relationships between the record companies and the movie studios are growing increasingly strained as they each try to maximize their pieces of the profit pie.[13]

Continuing the gustatory metaphor, he quotes Dave Anderle, director of film music for A & M Records:

> The rush to jump into the sound-track bonanza has produced some predictable side effects. Both sides [the record companies and the movie studios] became gluttons. A lot of sound tracks have been produced that should never have been done and a lot of film companies came to the record companies looking for music that should never have been there.[14]

One important result of the film industry's urgent interest in potentially lucrative pop songs was the creation of a new "character" in the filmmaking process. Ever since

1917, when the United States Supreme Court finally upheld the right of members of the American Society of Composers, Authors and Publishers to collect revenues from movie theaters that used ASCAP-controlled work in accompaniments for silent films, film exhibitors and filmmakers had been cautious about the use of music that was not originally composed, as "work for hire," by their own employees. Even in the early days of the sound film the studios had on staff persons whose job it was to make sure that every bit of pre-existing music in a soundtrack had been properly cleared for use; if the music were not in the public domain or an example of license-free "photoplay" music, it needed to be officially obtained through negotiations with whomever controlled the music's copyright.

The "music supervisor," as such a person was usually called, up until the 1960s performed work that was largely administrative, its prime function being to support the decisions of a film's composer and director by ensuring that those decisions were, in fact, legally acceptable. With the use of popular music in soundtracks on the rise, in the 1960s the work of the music supervisor changed markedly. In his 1998 book on the role of popular music in film, Jeff Smith explains:

> Over time, the music supervisor's duties would come to include the creation of a music budget, the supervision of various licensing arrangements, the negotiation of deals with composers and songwriters, and the safeguarding of the production company's publishing interests. Yet while the position is largely an administrative one, music supervisors also participate in a number of decisions that shape the overall concept of a score. The music supervisor's input is typically sought for such things as spotting sessions, the selection of preexisting musical materials, the organization of prerecords, the screening of dailies, and the preparation of "temp tracks."
> . . . Once the score's concept is agreed upon by the filmmaker, distributor and record company, then the music supervisor will assist in providing suitable composers, songwriters and recording artists to match that concept. In doing so, the music supervisor operates with an eye toward budget considerations, the promotional value of various musical materials, and the dramatic appropriateness of the score's concept.[15]

It may be that "the role [of the music supervisor] still has no definitive meaning and can vary enormously"[16] from studio to studio and, within a studio, from project to project. Yet is seems clear that in at least some cases the music supervisor, having a significant say as to the "dramatic appropriateness" of a particular song or even an entire score, has taken on artistic responsibilities that during film music's "golden age" would have belonged almost exclusively to the composer.

*   *   *

Writing at the end of the decade, *New York Times* pop music critic Stephen Holden—doubtless mindful of the complaints lately voiced by Elmer Bernstein and other members of the film-music community's old guard—observed that "for years many in the film industry have worried that the rise of the pop compilation might spell the demise of the traditional score." Importantly, he added: "But it hasn't happened; nor is it likely to. Artistically, the late '80s are a very healthy period for movie music."[17]

Holden's article is a succinct account of Hollywood film music since the late 1970s, notable as much for its detailed information as for its optimistic yet unprejudiced point of view. It begins with a vivid description of the music featured in Tim Burton's recently released *Batman* (Warner Bros., 1989):

> The film's noisy soundtrack presents a pitched battle between the two strains of music that have accompanied movies since the dawn of the sound era: one derived from high culture, the other from pop. The majority of the film's score is loud, post-Wagnerian action music composed by Danny Elfman. Sly, subterranean funk songs by Prince make up the rest.
>
> Until recently, movie directors, in choosing the music for a potential block-buster, tended to opt either for music like Mr. Elfman's, composed of carefully edited orchestral cues, or for compilations of prerecorded pop tunes like Prince's contributions. When both approaches were used in the same movie, pop tunes were typically tacked on to the credits, while the main body was composed of musical fragments synchronized with the images. In adapting both approaches at once, "Batman" spawned enough original music to prompt Warner Bros. Records to release two separate "Batman" albums. Prince's nine-song soundtrack—a product of the cross-marketing mentality that has infected Hollywood since "Saturday Night Fever"—is soaring on the charts, and an album of the music by Mr. Elfman is scheduled for release next month.[18]

The fact that the *Batman* soundtrack gave almost equal time to two very different, seemingly incompatible, types of music was in itself remarkable. At the same time, Holden noted, it was just another sign that film music was becoming "more pluralistic in style than ever before." As examples, Holden cited John Williams's "muscular symphonic score" for Steven Spielberg's *Indiana Jones and the Last Crusade* (Lucasfilm, 1989), the "up-to-the-minute collection of potential hit singles" used in Ivan Reitman's *Ghostbusters II* (Columbia, 1989), a combination of rap and jazz in Spike Lee's *Do the Right Thing* (40 Acres and a Mule Filmworks, 1989), and—from the previous year— Peter Gabriel's "art-rock ... world-music suite" for Martin Scorsese's *The Last Temptation of Christ* (Cineplex-Odeon,1988).[19]

Holden puts pop music's infiltration of Hollywood into keen perspective:

> It is only in the last decade that pop-rock music, by its sheer saturation of movies, has finally dissipated much of the lingering resentment felt by Holly-wood's old-guard musical establishment at the intrusion of rock.
>
> Especially in the late 1960s, when a generation of performers lacking academic musical credentials began invading Hollywood sound studios, the field of movie music became embattled. The soundtracks for "The Graduate" (1967) with songs by Simon and Garfunkle, and "Easy Rider" (1969), the first major movie hit with a multi-artist rock compilation, brought the generation gap to Hollywood movie music, just as the films did to the screen.
>
> The dust finally began to settle when a younger generation of directors ascended to power, led by Steven Spielberg and George Lucas. Mr. Spielberg

and Mr. Lucas had both grown up with rock music . . ., but they both also maintained a keen appreciation for the musical showmanship of the past.[20]

In his survey of pop music in films, Holden notes how Richard Lester's *A Hard Day's Night* (United Artists, 1964), which featured the British pop group The Beatles, "presaged the music-video era with its jump-cutting and very loose organization of action around the songs." But "it wasn't until 1978, when the soundtrack for 'Saturday Night Fever' became the best-selling album in history . . ., that movie producers and record executives recognized the full economic potential of cross-marketing movies with records."[21] And

> from that moment, the race was on in the record industry to create blockbuster soundtrack albums for potential hit movies. The albums for "Urban Cowboy," "Flashdance," "Footloose," "Beverly Hills Cop," "Top Gun," "Cocktail," "Dirty Dancing" and "Beaches" are among the many soundtracks that have sold in the millions. But with these hits, movies, television, home video and records—even lunch boxes—all began to become adjuncts of one another in a regulated chain of products. Merchandising, movies and music became inseparable.[22]

In contrast to journalists who had sympathetically interviewed veteran film composers such as Bernstein and Goldsmith throughout the 1980s, Holden—perhaps because his basic stance was that of a pop music critic—had no problem whatsoever with the merchandising of music and everything else connected with the film industry. He seemed to understand instinctively that filmmaking right from the start had been an enterprise largely commercial in nature, that films whose participants consciously aspired to the status of "artist" were in a very small minority, that it was the successful marketing of mainstream film that made possible the occasional manifestation of mainstream film as art.

* * *

Holden's 1989 article is noteworthy because it is one of the first clear expressions of an attitude that would characterize film music up to the present time. The attitude, which celebrates pluralism and eclecticism, is not without controversy. Among some scholars who engage seriously with the topic, there continues to be a "pitched battle" not just over what constitutes "good" film music or its opposite but, indeed, over what *is* film music. A faction still argues that film music, by definition, is music composed specifically for the sake of supporting, in extra-diegetic fashion, a film's narrative content; others argue that film music, also by definition, is simply whatever music happens to occur in the course of a film.

As famously delineated in 1987 by Claudia Gorbman[23] and as embellished by numerous other writers both before and since, the musical "conventions" of the classical-style film of course provide students of any film music with a useful basis of comparison. It should be remembered, though, that never were these "conventions" carved in stone. As is obvious from her more recent writings,[24] Gorbman would be the first to remind film-music conservatives that her listed "conventions" apply only to films made at a certain time by studios of a certain stature that generally followed procedures that, at that time, were appropriate to their perceived commercial needs. At other times, before and after the heyday of the classical-style Hollywood film, filmmakers' commercial needs would be different. And so filmmakers, responding always less to aesthetic dictum than to the possibilities of the marketplace, varied their approaches to film music.

The approach generally taken during the "golden age" of film music established a "grand symphonic tradition" to which John Williams was indeed, as Holden notes, "the most distinguished successor." But surely there were other approaches, in principle just as valid, to the problem—by 1989 almost a century old—of how to enliven a film with musical accompaniment. In the late 1980s as much as in the nickelodeon period and in the early years of the sound film, these approaches involved not just original underscore that perhaps in "inaudible" ways stirred an audience's emotions but also deliberately ear-catching up-to-date musical "numbers" and symbol-laden vintage music with which a large portion of the audience, presumably, would have some affinity. In terms of the variety of music it listed, a late 1980s "cue sheet"—a document that, for legal purposes, specified the provenance of every bit of music used in a film—would have been not much different from the merely suggestive "cue sheets" published in tandem with the release of one-reel silent films ca. 1909–10.

To be sure, Holden celebrates "traditional scoring," by which he means specially composed extra-diegetic music that services a filmic narrative in all the ways enumerated in Gorbman's list of classical-style conventions. He notes, though, that in 1989 "traditional scoring" entailed not just the familiar sonorities of the symphony orchestra but also "melodramatic synthesizer effects" of the sort invented a decade earlier by composer Giorgio Moroder for Alan Perker's *Midnight Express* (Casablanca Filmworks, 1978) and the "moody, new-age-influenced" sounds that "trumpeter and electronic impressionist" Mark Isham more recently applied to Alan Rudolph's *Trouble in Mind* (Pfeiffer/Blocker, 1985) and *The Moderns* (Nelson Entertainment, 1988).

"Good movie music," Holden writes, embraces all of this. It ranges from intelligently used pop songs to "modern symphonic action music," from "the tingly electronic music of the contemporary horror movie to the sleek pop-jazz of sophisticated comedies," and it certainly includes scores such as Peter Gabriel's for *The Last Temptation of Christ* in which the "warring strains of symphonic and pop film music" seem to have been merged into a hybrid style that is neither the one nor the other but which, significantly, "has characteristics of both."

As a professional journalist assigned to the "pop music" beat of a national newspaper, Holden—perhaps for no reason other than the quotidian need to fill an allotted column space—was simply putting in his two cents' worth about how popular music in its various guises had lately been affecting film scores. His summary statement, in any case, is profoundly relevant to the consideration of the whole of film music in the 1990s and beyond. No matter what its genre, Holden reminds us, film music is "what seduces us to hop on to a celluloid magic carpet and take a ride to a place where sound and image, dream and reality, meet and momentarily merge."

"Ultimately in film music," he concludes, "what's good is what works."[25]

The "Postmodern" in Film Music

What works in a fast-paced adventure such as Steven Spielberg's *Indiana Jones and the Temple of Doom* (Paramount/Lucasfilm, 1984) is a traditional symphonic score that craftily blends "action music," "mood music," "scene-setting music," and cliché-based "symbolic music" of the sort that characterized silent-film features as well as films of the early "classical" period and which would, doubtless to the posthumous chagrin of Antheil and other critics ca. 1938, prove to be a significant component of "the movie music of the future." What works in a dark science-fiction thriller like James Cameron's *The Terminator* (Orion/Hemdale/Pacific Western, 1984) is an accompaniment that frightfully *suggests* the future by means of state-of-the-art sound effects that sometimes come across as cyborg-generated noise and at other times as components of a modernist percussive score. And what works in a comedy such as Robert Zemeckis's *Back to the Future* (Universal, 1985) is "action music" and "mood music" aplenty mixed with an array of pop music, presented diegetically and otherwise, that represents the various time periods in which the story is set.

That these very different approaches to film music all seemed to "work" is not simply a matter of opinion. All three of the above-mentioned films either belonged to or spawned highly successful series of films, and in the case of all three series the use of music has remained more or less consistent.[26] The producers of one series or another felt no particular need to "change their tune" just because others were doing well by doing things differently. In the highly competitive film marketplace of the mid 1980s, clearly there was room—so far as music was concerned—for variety.

The period during which these films were made, and during which their diversity of film music flourished, coincides with the introduction into intellectual parlance of the term "postmodern."[27] "Postmodern" soon enough become *the* buzzword of the next decade and a half, popping up in discussions whose topics ranged across the full scope of human activity without ever having a definition upon which more than just a handful of persons could even momentarily agree. The prefix implies that the "postmodern" is something—a societal condition, a collective attitude—that somehow came after whatever is meant by the term "modern," but it has never been clear if the relationship between the two concepts is reactionary or simply chronological. Following the lead of a great many writers and dignifying the buzzword with a suffix that suggests an ideology, philosopher Terry Eagleton observes that "postmodern*ism* is such a portmanteau phenomenon that anything you assert of one piece of it is almost bound to be untrue of another."[28]

For all that, at least a few characteristics seem to be common to almost all manifestations of what serious writers in the 1980s and '90s—regardless of their political, psychological, or artistic agendas—say fall into the large and loose category of the "postmodern."[29]

One of these has to do with a cessation, in the minds of both producers and consumers, of the idea of "historical flow." Hitherto, but especially early in the twentieth century when Western culture in general was in the throes of the "modernist" movement, intellectual/artistic products tended to be judged as either adventurously moving forward or, in conservative resistance, dragging their feet. In the "postmodern" period, that dichotomy seemed to be as irrelevant as the very idea—crucial to modernist thinking, but now, apparently, quite passé—of the historical "timeline."

Another generally agreed upon characteristic of the "postmodern" has to do with its apparently freewheeling plurality of both style and content. In the past, of course, a great many works of art—whether literary, musical, or visual—had enriched themselves by making reference to their predecessors. From Homer to Shakespeare to William Butler

Yeats (and their painterly and musical equivalents), references to the work of past "masters" were almost always deliberate; whether obvious direct quotations or subtle allusions, the references seemed—upon critical scrutiny—to be purposeful and meaningful. In marked contrast, according to Frederic Jameson, "postmodern" artworks seemed to be characterized by a "complacent eclecticism" that "randomly and without principle but with gusto cannibalize[d] all the . . . styles of the past and combine[d] them in over-stimulating ensembles."[30]

Jameson early in his seminal article mentions music and film almost in the same breath. In an "enumeration" of manifestations that is admittedly "empirical, chaotic, and heterogeneous," he says that "the postmodern" includes:

> Andy Warhol and pop art, but also photorealism, and beyond it, the "new expressionism"; the moment, in music, of John Cage, but also the synthesis of classical and "popular" styles found in composers like Phil Glass and Terry Riley, and also punk and new wave rock (the Beatles and the Stones now standing as the high-modernist moment of that more recent and rapidly evolving tradition); in film, Godard, post-Godard, and experimental cinema and video, but also a whole new type of commercial film.[31]

This new type of film is something Jameson calls "the nostalgia film." He grants that "nostalgia" may not be "an altogether satisfactory word for [audiences'] fascination" with bits of a real or imagined past. Nevertheless, the word "directs our attention to what is a culturally far more generalized manifestation of the process in commercial art and taste," a process by which "the whole issue of pastiche" is restructured and projected "onto a collective and social level, where the desperate attempt to appropriate a missing past is now refracted through the iron law of fashion change and the emergent ideology of the generation."[32]

Issue has been taken with Jameson's thoughts on the "nostalgia film," perhaps most notably by Barbara Creed, who points out their lack of attention to feminist theory.[33] Lacking or not, Jameson's ideas on the implications of pastiche remain relevant to the study of recent film and, with it, recent film music. It seems interesting that Jameson, who first approached the concept of "the postmodern" from the standpoint of an economics-oriented critic of architecture, has focused so much of his attention on film. Indeed, he deals quite specifically with film in two later books, *Signatures of the Visible* (1990) and *The Geopolitical Aesthetic* (1992). His summary view, according to Michael Walsh, is that

> Film has two histories: one for the silent film, in which there is a progression from realism to modernism, then a truncation with the introduction of sound. This begins the process over from scratch, moving from an interlocking system of classical Hollywood genres (realism) to the modernism which comes to the fore in both practice and criticism (auteurism) in the 1950s with the end of the classical studio film, to full postmodernism, which emerges after the 1960s [to] exploit the cultural conditions of postwar late capitalism.[34]

It was in the midst of this on-going second progression that film and film music found themselves in the 1980s and '90s. Aided by postwar capitalism that enabled independent companies to generate blockbuster hits as big as any attempted by the major studios, and long emancipated from an industrial system that once had fostered particular genres and styles of narrative, filmmakers in the postmodern era were encouraged—for reasons as much commercial as artistic—to take chances. For music, they used whatever seemed to "work" for the product at hand, sometimes holding to a particular idiom that had deep roots in the past, sometime comfortably mixing styles that in earlier decades likely would have been heard as unimaginably incompatible.

The eclecticism of "pastiche" scores perhaps was not so complacent as Jameson suggested, but it was nevertheless unprecedented in its variety. Often accompanying narratives that reveled in fragmentation and discontinuity, the pastiche scores presented audience members with a bounty of possible meanings. And in keeping with one of the prime characteristics of "the postmodern" as it manifests itself in music, many of these scores located their multiple meanings not in the music itself but in the minds of its perceivers.[35]

*　*　*

Musical meaning located in the minds of its individual perceivers is a central topic of Anahid Kassabian's 2001 book on contemporary Hollywood film music. Kassabian distinguishes, significantly, between the effects on moviegoers of music that is specially composed for a film and pre-existing music that is somehow used in a film. With both types of music, she writes, audience members form what she terms "identifications."

In the case of well-crafted original music, which regardless of its idiom is likely to support a modern narrative in much the same ways that "golden age" scores served the narratives of classical-style films, audiences for the most part easily accept whatever messages the music conveys. Although for the filmgoer the actual content of such music itself is entirely new, the tradition to which the music belongs—the tradition on which, for its meaningfulness, the music crucially depends—certainly is not. By buying a ticket for a film that features a tradition-rooted score, the patron in effect enters into a contract by which he or she agrees to suspend disbelief for a few hours and to be drawn into whatever "socially and historically unfamiliar positions" the film proposes. Perhaps because they involve the filmgoer's quite willing surrender to the score's psychologically manipulative force, Kassabian describes such relationships between listeners and composed scores as "assimilating identifications."[36]

Quite a different relationship typically exists, Kassabian writes, between listeners and compiled scores—that is, scores that consist largely not of original music but of pre-existing music with which most audience members, in advance of their entering the movie theater, are likely to be at least to a certain extent familiar. Especially when they entail popular songs, Kassabian writes, "compiled scores ... can operate quite differently" from composed scores:

> With their wide range of complete songs used just as they are heard on the radio, they bring the immediate threat of history. Most people in the movie theater, even on opening day, have probably heard at least a few of the songs before, whether the score is made up of oldies or new releases. Airplay for the songs may serve as good advertising for the film, but it means that perceivers bring external associations with the songs into their engagements with the film.

A score that offers assimilating identifications is much harder to construct from such songs. More often, compiled scores offer what I call *affiliating identifications*, and they operate quite differently from composed scores. These ties depend on histories forged outside the film scene, and they allow for a fair bit of mobility within it. If offers of assimilating identifications try to narrow the psychic field, then offers of affiliating identifications open it wide. This difference is, to my mind, at the heart of filmgoers' relationships to contemporary film music.[37]

Verbally awkward though it might be, Kassabian's concept of "identifications" that are for the most part "assimilating" or "affiliating" remains at the heart of thinking that regards many film scores from the 1980s and 1990s as examples of the postmodern. While Kassabian herself avoids the buzzword, Ronald Rodman—in one of the essays that constitute a 2006 anthology on the use of pre-existing music in film—uses it explicitly when referring to Kassabian's book, and his observations even allude to Jameson's idea that both of cinema's "two histories" reached a point of modernism. Summarizing primarily the books of Gorbman and Kalinak, but also those of Prendergast and Bazelon, Rodman explains:

> The authors present classical Hollywood films scores as art works in the modernist tradition, because most film composers of the 1930s and 1940s considered themselves heirs to the tradition of musical modernism, especially through the tradition of opera. In this tradition, classical film scores are original art works that draw upon the style of nineteenth-century Romanticism to produce works that are unique to each film.[38]

Rodman notes that "a second practice"—i.e., the compilation score—also exists, and that in fact it dates back to the nickelodeon period of silent film. Along with the continuing traditions of the originally composed score, this practice has evolved in the late twentieth century into "the 'popular music' score, featuring a pastiche of popular songs by various artists." Introducing an essay that focuses on Quentin Tarantino's *Pulp Fiction* (A Band Apart, 1994) and Danny Boyle's *Trainspotting* (Channel Four Films, 1996), both of which use scores made up entirely of pre-existing songs, he writes:

> In these films, the popular song scores may be viewed as "postmodern," in that they decentre the role of the unique musical work, and draw upon discourses around the musical work such as style and celebrity. While operating in this new postmodernist practice, however, popular song scores in these films also continue to function as modernist musical artifacts, in similar ways to Gorbman's and Kalinak's classical Hollywood film score model, but the model now operates on different semiotic planes.[39]

Kassabian was not the first to suggest that filmmakers' penchant for pop music in the 1980s and 1990s might have been spurred by more than simply commercial considerations. Most of Jeff Smith's 1998 *The Sounds of Commerce* indeed deals primarily with the ways in which compilation scores added to the market value of films, but scattered throughout the book are comments about how various songs lend meaning, more or less

221

obviously, to filmic narratives. And in 1999 Hilary Lapedis published an article that contrasts the postmodern function of popular music in film not just with the classical-style film score but with the supposedly "autonomous" compositions that represented musical modernism in concert halls through most of the twentieth century.

In Lapedis's case, the films studied in detail are Lawrence Kasdan's *The Big Chill* (Columbia, 1983), which uses songs from the '60s to underscore a get-together of adults who came of age during those years, and Robert Zemeckis's *Forrest Gump* (Paramount, 1994), which uses popular songs from a range of decades (along with original music by Alan Silvestri) to illustrate the life story of the title character. But in her introduction Lapedis concerns herself with the widespread phenomenon of using popular music in film:

> [The] commodification of pop music does not completely explain the explosion of its use in mainstream cinema. Obviously, the economic concerns of a multinational industry, both cinema and music, are paramount, and this new phenomenon has clearly opened up a new market for soundtrack sales, but it is the *effect* of the shifting relationship of pop music to image that is interesting— how pop music in its three-minute form has affected the narrative structure of mainstream cinema, and how the emergence of the pop video in all its manifestations has changed both the way that music works with image and the way in which audiences read visual/musical texts.[40]

Later she makes the point that the simple fact that *because* such songs are "popular," because they are already familiar to members of a film's audience, by definition they trigger a collection of responses in type different from those that might be triggered by original scores:

> Pop songs in films use pop's own emotional conventions and, in so doing, place those films in a much wider context of popular culture than would be the case with a traditional score. Contrary, therefore, to Schoenberg's view that "music should never drag a meaning around with it" and Eisler's description of "abstract art par excellence," pop music, while having an existence separate from the visual system, nevertheless possesses its own codified meanings and associations. These meanings are drawn from shared conventions of musical meaning that are then associated with the visual system to which they are harnessed.[41]

* * *

Most of the above paragraphs have dealt with the semiotic potential, within the context of the "postmodern" film score, of the pop song. But pre-existing music used in films— not solely for the purpose of helping to publicize the film or to profit from sales of soundtrack albums but at least in part for the purpose for adding to the film's semiotic resonance—is hardly limited to that single genre.

Postmodern culture, writes Pauline Reay, has been described as "a culture of 'intertextuality'—rather than original cultural production there is cultural production born out of other cultural production."[42] In such a production-conscious culture, it is not surprising that film music itself has often been the object of film music's "post-modern" borrowings. As early as 1978 director John Carpenter cannily featured in his *Halloween* (Compass International) a terrifying segment in which a killer stalks a house while inside children sit in front of a television watching a scene—accompanied by appropriately creepy music—from the 1956 *Forbidden Planet*. More recently, romantically smitten characters in Nora Ephron's *Sleepless in Seattle* (TriStar, 1993) visibly react to Hugo Friedhofer's extra-diegetic music for the 1957 *An Affair to Remember*, and in Martin Scorsese's *The Departed* (Warner Bros., 2006) an apparently guilt-ridden protagonist meditates in front of a television set on which plays a Steiner-scored scene from the 1935 *The Informer*. In a twist on intertextual referencing, Peter Jackson's remake of *King Kong* (Big Primate Pictures, 2005) appropriates some of Steiner's quasi-diegetic "island music" from the 1933 original film but presents it not by way of a film clip but as diegetic music performed by a Broadway pit orchestra.[43]

Because it is so prevalent, popular music in film has generated more commentary in recent years than any other form of "borrowed" music.[44] The essays that make up the first half of the 2006 anthology *Changing Tunes: The Use of Pre-Existing Music in Film*,[45] however, all deal with film scores whose "borrowings" come mostly from opera or the classical concert-hall repertoire. And in the introduction to a more recent anthology with a similar focus—*Beyond the Soundtrack: Representing Music in Cinema*—the editors note that "classical music looms rather large, a welcome surprise in the age of its cultural retrenchment."[46]

On the Upswing

The reference to classical music's cultural retrenchment doubtless has to do with the genre's apparently ailing career. Inspired by changes in radio programming, a severe drop-off in the sales of recordings, and dwindling attendance at concerts, journalists and authors since the mid 1990s—especially in the United States but also in England—have been penning obituaries for classical music.[47] But classical music, of course, has not disappeared. And one of the places where it seems to thrive is the cinema.

In July 1987 *New York Times* music critic Donal Henahan wrote a column in which he rescinds his earlier judgment on Swedish director Bo Widerberg's extensive use of Mozart's Piano Concerto No. 21 in the film *Elvira Madigan* (Europa Film, 1967). Henahan confessed that when the recording of the "Elvira Madigan Concerto" was released in the wake of the film he felt that the piece had been "brutalized . . . in the pursuit of cinematic gain." Twenty years later, he felt that "the choice of music was clairvoyantly right. The innocent sentimentality of the film was both tempered and refined by the pathos of the Mozart melody, with its pained, throbbing accompaniment."[48]

Henahan admits:

> It still bothers me when certain deeply cherished pieces of music are merged with visual images in such a way that the sounds take on a filmmaker's specific meanings, thereby depriving me of my own—or at any rate trying to. In that respect, Ingmar Bergman has a lot to answer for in the next world. I can't pinpoint which of his films to blame, but whenever I hear a recording of [Pablo] Casals playing a Bach [cello] suite, I am trapped in a dark room with a morbidly depressed woman.[49]

But he also admits that this extreme negative reaction has, for him, lately become more the exception than the rule. He notes the use of music by György Ligeti and Richard Strauss, among others, in Stanley Kubrick's *2001: A Space Odyssey* (MGM, 1968), of lengthy excerpts from Mahler's Symphony No. 5 in Luchino Visconti's *Death in Venice* (Warner Bros./Alfa, 1971), and of vintage recordings by opera tenor Enrico Caruso in Werner Herzog's *Fitzcarraldo* (Herzog/ProjectFilmproduction, 1982). And as a result of exposure to these and other musically "intelligent" films, he writes, "I have found my own righteous disdain softening in recent years."[50]

It may be that Henahan's personal disdain toward the use of classical music in films had softened. It may be, too, that film critics of postmodern persuasion, and audience members in general, were becoming increasingly appreciative of film music's rich eclecticism. Nevertheless, throughout the 1980s and 1990s there was still plenty of resentment, or at least skepticism, directed toward film music in general.

* * *

Interviewed in March 1986 in advance of his being named winner of the Academy of Motion Picture Arts and Sciences' first "special" Oscar for a composer, Alex North, then age 75, recalled that in the 1950s film composers were sometimes encouraged to be adventurous. His impression was that, in terms of their attitudes toward scoring, directors of the mid 1980s were far less daring than had been their predecessors. "Fear is a problem with film music and films," he said. "People want to be conventional, and there's more commercialism today."[51]

North's comments seem generous when compared with those offered four years later by Elmer Bernstein. Interviewed in Ireland, where he was doing on-location scoring for Jim Sheridan's *The Field* (Granada, 1990), the veteran composer said:

> I think there's less understanding of the function of film music now than there was 30 years ago, and much more fear of music on the part of young directors. Music comes at the end of the process as a sort of odd stranger, and there's no question that the film changes when the music goes into it.
>
> Some young directors are totally thrown by that, and very many of them don't seem to have a great feel for music at all. They think music is something you just kind of slap on a film like wallpaper. But if you're going to have music in a film at all, you have to understand that it's going to change the film, by pointing things up, supporting things, toning things down. It's going to do something. And therefore, the director really has to be ready to make it a part of the process.[52]

As had been the case since the late 1960s, commercialism still figured into the debate. While soundtrack albums "have been big business for a long time," their popularity, according to a 1995 report in the *New York Times*, seems lately to have surged. In a sidebar, the writer noted: "In a recent week, the Billboard album chart contained 20 movie soundtracks. The fastest-rising album on the charts was the soundtrack from 'Clueless'; songs from soundtracks also topped the adult-contemporary and modern-rock radio charts."[53]

As a result of music in films, wealth was steadily flowing in the direction of the studios. But in the main article the writer pointedly observed that "film composers who write the instrumental scores that are often the music most crucial to a movie aren't really sharing in the good times.... Nearly every notable composer now has stories of impossible deadlines, music drowned out by deafening sound effects, scores rejected for capricious reasons or pop songs substituted for scores."[54] And he included an observation from film composer Thomas Newman—son and nephew, respectively, of film-music legends Lionel and Alfred Newman—that fans of "golden age" film music might find downright depressing:

> It's not that composers get less respect than we used to. It's just that there's no interest in what we do. Post-production is a psychologically desperate time, and that's when the composer comes in. There's only a small amount of time for you to prove that you have good ideas. If they tell you, "We need to put a song here because such-and-such record company has advanced us so many hundred thousand dollars," there's nothing you can do about it. In those cases it doesn't matter if it's not a good idea; it's a marketing tool and an opportunity to jump on a bandwagon.[55]

And then there is the telling comment that Jerry Goldsmith made in November 1997. At this time Goldsmith was 68, a full three decades beyond the point at which he dared say—as is quoted in the epigraph for the previous chapter—that "many of the older guys" in film music still "haven't bridged the gap creatively or technically."

The comment appears in a *New York Times* article headlined "In Hollywood, Discord on What Makes Music." As its headline suggests, the article focuses not on film music's recent accomplishments but on remembrances of things past. Preparing the reader for what will be a litany of complaints not just from Goldsmith but also—as might have been expected—from Elmer Bernstein and David Raksin, the writer at the outset states: "At a time when loose collections of pop songs increasingly displace integrated orchestral scores in motion pictures, it makes sense that composers and cinéphiles alike are nostalgically looking back to an era when film music was a vibrant and respected art."[56]

But there seems to be more than nostalgia at the root of Goldsmith's remark. Goldsmith perhaps feigns optimism when he says that "filmmaking is a cyclical thing" and, therefore, the current trend will not necessarily be the trend of the future. But there is no hiding his disdain when he declares that at the moment the world of filmmaking features "a preponderance of dilettantes and sophomoric people." As a result, he says, "now is certainly not the greatest time for film music."[57]

* * *

Even as veteran Hollywood composers were collectively ruing the demise of classical-style film music, critics who approached the cinema not as insiders but simply as audience members were voicing the idea that film music was as interesting as it had ever been.

As noted earlier, *New York Times* pop music critic Stephen Holden wrote in July 1989 that "artistically, the late '80s are a very healthy period for movie music."[58] Six months

225

Figure 11.2 Composer John Corigliano holds his Oscar for Best Original Score for *The Red Violin* at the 72nd Annual Academy Awards in Los Angeles March 26, 2000. © Hector Mata/AFP/Getty Images.

later Holden remained of the same opinion. The purpose of the newer column was to compare Elliot Goldenthal's "sparse" and "original and esoteric" score for Gus Van Sant's *Drugstore Cowboys* (Avenue Pictures, 1989) with John Williams's "inflated" score—yet another example of the "old-time Hollywood movie music tradition brought up to date"—for Oliver Stone's *Born on the Fourth of July* (UIP/Ixtlan, 1989). Quibbles over details aside, Holden noted that "at least for the moment, the mating of movies with would-be pop hits has lost its novelty" and that "meanwhile, fully composed scores that once seemed like an endangered species continue to hold their own comparatively modest position in the marketplace." In any case, he wrote, "the quality of film music" in general seems to be "on the upswing."[59]

The upswing, at least in the minds of some critics, continued through the decade. In April 2001, when commentators in many fields were celebrating the dawn of a new millennium by reviewing the distant as well as the immediate past, musicologist David Schiff observed that in both that year and the year before the Academy Award for best original film score had gone to an individual who was neither a film-music regular nor a pop musician but, rather, a composer whose career was solidly rooted in the world of the concert hall.

Granted, the films that accommodated the award-winning films did not originate in Hollywood: François Girard's *The Red Violin* (Channel Four Films, 1999), which featured a score by John Corigliano, was a French production, and Ang Lee's *Crouching Tiger, Hidden Dragon* (Asia Union Film, 2000), which featured music by Tan Dun, was made in Hong Kong. Still, it was Hollywood that awarded the prizes, not for best scores in foreign films but for best scores, period. And this, Schiff wrote, seemed cause for celebration:

> While cynics claim that this is the film industry's way of advertising its high-art pretensions, Hollywood may really be ahead of New York in acknowledging that the opposition between film music and concert music is a phantom of the last century.[60]

Chapter 12

EPILOGUE, 2001–8

> We will argue for a more inclusive definition of the term "film music" than that proposed in previous publications. In our view, film music is one component of a spectrum of sound that includes the musical score, ambient sound, dialogue, sound effects, and silence. The functions of these constituent elements often overlap or interact with one another. . . . In the absence of a composed musical score, other elements (e.g. ambient sound) can function similarly to music, providing dynamically shifting and structurally meaningful sound to propel the narrative forward.
>
> Scott Lipscomb and David Tolchinsky, 2005[1]

The previous chapter made reference to George Antheil's determined comment, from 1938, to the effect that neither the "ridiculous 'action music' of present day Hollywood" nor the "European method of scoring" that has music playing "completely 'against' the film" could possibly be "the movie music of the future."[2]

But "action music" has never been far from action-packed films wherever they have been made, and especially since the advent of Dolby sound in the late 1970s it has been endemic to films aspiring to the status of the "blockbuster" hit. At least since the early 1960s, when the modernist "new wave" swept over film industries worldwide, likewise endemic has been music that somehow plays "against" on-screen action or emotion. Crucial to filmmaking in the last half-century has been what Eisenstein and his Soviet colleagues in 1928 called "contrapuntal" or "asynchronous" music, what French theorist Michel Chion in the 1980s called "anempathetic" music,[3] what British musicologist Nicholas Cook in the late 1990s described as music that "contradicts" or "contests" the filmic image.[4] To be sure, a fair amount of film music in recent years has held to classical-style conventions and helped make "excessively obvious" all that was transpiring in the filmic narrative. But at the same time—and often within the context of a single film—a good deal of film music has been, vis-à-vis the narrative, not at all obvious. As Kay Dickinson has noted, deliberate "mismatches" between music and image, "off-kilter" combinations of sound and action that are "clashing" and perhaps purposefully "dis-orienting," are in recent films quite the norm.[5] Clearly, posterity proved Antheil wrong.

But perhaps posterity proved right another prognostication offered at around the same time. Like Antheil in Hollywood, the Australian-born composer Arthur Benjamin in London was of the opinion that film music, even as international cinema was entering into its period of "classical perfection," was still in its infancy. Writing in 1937 in *The Musical Times*, Benjamin quoted from an article by art critic Louis le Sidaner that had recently appeared in the *Mercure de France*. It was all well and good that esteemed French artists such as Ibert and Honegger at the moment were providing films with "incidental" music composed "according to classical procedure," Le Sidaner had observed. But the "true cinematographic music of the future" will likely involve other elements, such as

> the noise of flowing water; the grinding of carriage wheels; the stridency of a policeman's whistle; the languorous voice of a "vamp"; the chug-chug of a motor; the irregular tic-tac of a typewriter; the barking of a dog; even silence; a man sneezing; church bells; the caustic laugh of a "boulevardier"; the cry of a child who suffers or is frightened; the song of the nightingale; the grunts of a pig or the tender murmur of happy lovers. Up till now we have hardly touched on these things.[6]

*   *   *

That in 1937 these things had been "hardly touched on" is debatable. Considering the theories of Eisenstein et al. as to how sonic elements might figure into film montage, or the differences between the "*film sonore*" and the mere "*film parlant*" as described by French director René Clair, it seems that at least some filmmakers even in the earliest days of the sound film were indeed thinking about how "the noise of flowing water," etc., might figure into a soundtrack not for the sake of conjuring an illusion of reality but, rather, for the sake of creating affect in much the same way that extra-diegetic music does.

It is likewise debatable, of course, that the calculated use of sound effects really does constitute a sort of "cinematographic music." What is not debatable is that since the early 1970s—perhaps beginning with the contributions that Walter Murch made to George Lucas's 1971 *THX 1138*—the role of the sound designer has been coming increasingly to the fore, and that serious-minded critics more and more are regarding the work of at least certain sound designers as, indeed, a form of music.

In his 1983 book *All American Music: Composition in the Late Twentieth Century*, John Rockwell, a music critic for the *New York Times*, described Murch's soundtrack for *THX 1138* as

> a floating cloud of realistic and electronically altered or generated effects. The characters in the film are narcotized robots who move dreamily through a dehumanized world of electronic gadgetry, disembodied voices and computer-controlled appliances. The sonic ambience is subtly grating, distorted, metallic, on edge. . . . The sound score both echoes and evokes the visual images, often suggesting things that we do not actually see and leaving it to the viewer to imagine effects Murch does not bother to supply. They are rarely missed,

so potent is the power of audio-visual suggestion; when they are, the loss contributes to the sense of disorientation. The result is fully the equal of any similar collage score by a practicing electronic-music composer, with additional coherence provided by the imagery. It is a piece of electronic music-theater by Lucas and Murch together. It is, in short, opera; the soundtrack is music and Murch is a composer.[7]

Similarly arguing that diegetic sound effects can indeed be organized in musical fashion by filmmakers and heard, as music, by audience members, an essay from 2003 points to examples of industrial noise and insect chirping in Terrence Malick's *Days of Heaven* (Paramount, 1978) and the sound of wind, grass, and water in the same director's *The Thin Red Line* (Fox 2000 Pictures, 1999).[8] Forestalling resistance from readers for whom filmic sound effects by definition fall into a category all their own, the author quotes the American avant-garde composer John Cage. In the same year in which Arthur Benjamin quoted Louis le Sidaner's comment on the "true cinematographic music of the future," Cage wrote: "If this word 'music' is sacred and reserved for eighteenth- and nineteenth-century instruments, we can substitute a more meaningful term: organization of sound."[9]

Another essay from 2003, by Anahid Kassabian, describes a scene from Tarsem Singh's *The Cell* (Avery Pix, 2000)[10] that features first the sounds of "a cash register, a baby crying, birds, the distorted sounds of a baptism, [and] machine sounds" and then "extremely distorted sounds matched by surreal images." Referring to the 'conventions' of the classical-style film score as familiarly outlined by Claudia Gorbman, Kassabian writes:

> This is neither music nor not music, but rather a textural use of sound that disregards most, if not all, of the "laws" of classic Hollywood film-scoring technique. The sound music is foregrounded for attention, not "inaudible" as is standard. It is not a signifier of emotion, nor does it provide continuity or unity. It is not subordinate to the narrative or the visuals, but on par with them in creating an affective world. *The Cell* initiates a soundtrack of the unconscious, where the familiar boundaries recede in favour of a different logic.[11]

In contrast to the standard filmic illusion, Kassabian explains, "*The Cell* actively strives to break that illusion, to mismatch visual and aural position by using a range of techniques such as sound close-ups to signify perceived rather than objective sound."[12] The same might be said for films written and/or directed by Ethan and Joel Coen (for example, *The Big Lebowski*, 1998; *Intolerable Cruelty*, 2003; the "Tuileries" segment of *Paris, je t'aime*, 2006; and *No Country for Old Men*, 2007), the recent films of David Lynch (*Dumbland*, 2002; *Darkened Room*, 2002; and *Inland Empire*, 2006), and the various "Matrix" films written and directed by Andy and Larry Wachowski (*The Matrix*, 1999; *The Matrix Reloaded*, 2003; *The Matrix: Revolutions*, 2003).[13] At least to a certain extent, it might also be said for Joe Wright's *Atonement* (Working Title Films, 2007), a British film in which a more or less conventional Academy Award-winning score by Dario Marianelli indeed plays in tandem, during the opening credits, with "the irregular tic-tac of a typewriter."

230

Definitions?

A view of "cinematographic music" that takes in all manner of diegetic noise stands in marked contrast to the conservative definition of film music proposed by William H. Rosar in his editorial for the 2002 inaugural issue of the *Journal of Film Music*.

Rosar correctly observes that for decades the film industry used the term "film music" almost exclusively to denote instrumental music that was composed specifically for the sake of accompanying, in extra-diegetic fashion, a particular film. For Rosar, this is an "essential definition" that identifies film music's unique characteristic, and it differs hugely from a "functional definition" that merely identifies the various uses to which music of all sorts has been put in films. Rosar goes so far as to argue that "the *essence* of film music [has come] to be thought of as a compositional technique, or style in the broadest sense," and that "despite all its stylistic variability throughout the decades— whether the often cited 'late Romantic' style or passing trends in musical fashion—there was and remains a film music sound, elusive though it may be to define."[14]

Lamenting the "verbal muddle" created by writers who apply the term "film music" to all music that occurs in films, Rosar states that the term "has come to have two definitions that are *incommensurable*. If writers cannot agree on the meaning of film music as a term we obviously face a fundamental problem in defining the field to which the term applies."[15] He notes that as early 1980 the German musicologist Helga de la Motte-Haber "was evidently aware of the semantic problem and proposed that in German *Film-Musik* be used to denote music in films from the standpoint of function (i.e., music in films), and that *Filmmusik* be reserved for film music as a musical genre."[16] But he admits that "it is probably too late to institute this usage in English now, because film music as a synonym for music in films has become established in some circles, and once a term has come to be used in a more general way it is difficult to restrict its meaning."[17]

Attempting to pinpoint the problem, Rosar writes:

> At the heart of the matter then there would seem to be—implicitly if not explicitly—a *genuine dispute* rather than merely a *verbal dispute* underlying the two definitions of film music, because there are those who would insist that there is—or should be—only one definition of film music, whether it be the *essential* one or the *functional* one. Probably never the twain shall meet, because there is no compelling reason—other than clarity—to abandon either usage, except where verbal confusion results from using both senses of the term in the same context. . . .[18]

Yet Rosar grants that the dispute, even if it is not merely verbal but genuine, need not necessarily be a bad thing. At least, he concludes his "Prolegomena to the Study of Film Music" by quoting historian Carlo Ginzburg on the potentially fruitful dialogue that sometimes emerges when scholars trained in very different fields—for example, scholars rooted in, on the one hand, musicology and, on the other hand, in film studies—engage in conversation on a topic of mutual interest. Interviewed in 1986, Ginzburg said:

> If you have conflicting results, you have a real interdisciplinary work. I think that a lot of interdisciplinary work is dull in effect because you start off with the

assumption that both disciplines can be mingled peacefully, which is not true. The conflict is much more interesting.[19]

* * *

Conflict is indeed more interesting than simple agreement. Yet if true conflict exists among today's scholars of film music, it tends to surface only when a partisan of one ideological camp or another adamantly insists on narrow definitions. Most people in the interdisciplinary field know full well the difference between music composed specifically for a film and music borrowed from somewhere and used either as source music or as underscore. Most people know, too, the difference between diegetic music and extra-diegetic music, and they realize that while the distinctions between the two are as often blurred as they are clear-cut the dichotomy nevertheless serves as a useful starting point for discussion. And most people know that what once were basic stylistic differences between treatment of music in Hollywood films and their European counterparts have, in the new century, all but ceased to exist.

In the introduction to their recent anthology on music in European films, Miguel Mera and David Burnand remind us that

> The prevalent argument that European cinema is threatened by the external power of Hollywood is in reality much more complicated than polarized studies would initially suggest. Given the increased ease of communications, the processes of globalization, and the intricate nature of film financing, the fluency between European and Hollywood film is a vital feature of both industries and cultures. Morley and Robbins believe that the boundaries are blurred and that "America is now part of a European cultural repertoire, part of European identity." The growth of Euro-American cinema could be viewed as a confirmation of America's cultural dominance. . . . However, one might equally argue that Europe is an essential part of Hollywood's cultural identity.[20]

Responding to this book, Stan Link seconds the motion that differences between European and Hollywood styles are today mostly a remembrance of things past. "The question of what constitutes 'European film music' is at least partially framed in the position of its reception. How do Europe, Hollywood and others *read* 'Europe' and 'Hollywood'? . . . Perhaps the spirit of European difference and identity is merely a phantasm, the desire for which in fact acknowledges its non-existence or death."[21]

A recent book that explores the differences between Hollywood and European approaches to film music is Annette Davison's *Hollywood Theory, Non-Hollywood Practice*, but even here the idea that non-Hollywood filmmakers "turned to the soundtrack (as well as the organization of narrative, camerawork, and so on) as a possible means of critiquing, or resisting, classical Hollywood" is limited to films of the 1980s and 1990s.[22] In the twenty-first century, critique seems to come as much from within Hollywood as without. And what is resisted is simply a norm, perhaps once rooted in a certain place but nowadays as internationally ubiquitous as Starbuck's coffee shops.

Reviewing Davison's book, James Buhler has noted that the breakdown of distinctions between Hollywood and non-Hollywood theory/practice is paralleled by a breakdown of distinctions between the roles of the various persons who might contribute to all that, today, might be considered to fall under the rubric "film music":

> Indeed, as sound effects grow ever more musical—with sound engineers (sometimes trained as composers) sampling sounds, digitally processing them, or creating sounds synthetically and playing them into the effects track using electronic keyboards—and as composers draw more and more on the resources of the synthesizer and other elements of electro-acoustic music, the division of labour between the music and sound departments grows ever less distinct. In many respects, it is not so much the division of labour per se, but rather the overlapping responsibilities to which this division of labour gives rise that pose the greater challenge to building an aesthetically convincing soundtrack.[23]

Indeed, what matters is the extent to which the soundtrack is, indeed, aesthetically convincing. The contemporary film soundtrack is likely to contain music both diegetic and extra-diegetic, both original and borrowed, playing "with" the action as well as "against" it. It is likely, too, to contain dialogue and sound effects obviously musical or not. However one parses all that sonic content, and no matter where one draws the line between what is and what might not actually be film music, it is the *complete* soundtrack—composed, compiled, compound, complex—that makes the aural effect/affect on the audience member.

In a recent book on films that warrant attention simply because of the way they *sound*, Australian critic Philip Brophy writes:

> Clearly, the soundtrack is a chimera of the cinema. It is sound *and* noise; noise *and* music; music *and* speech. At no point can it be distilled into a form which allows us to safely state its essential quality. The soundtrack is a world caught in eternal disequilibrium by two meta-forces: *films scores*—the commissioned composition of music for specific scenes—and *sound design*—the conceptualisation of how dialogue, sound effects and atmospheres are edited and mixed to provide the sound for a scene. Despite the many existing ways in which critics and practitioners tend to *separate* the two forces, they continue to combine according to a unique, mutative and hermetic logic—little of which conforms to literary models, operatic figures, painterly diagrams or photographic allusions. In order to accept this inability of sound and music to be essenced from each other, one has to think with one's ears.[24]

Summary

One of the main themes of *Film Music: A History* has been the idea that for its first six decades, from its murky origins ca. 1895 up to the mid 1950s, the music that accompanied motion pictures at any given time was somehow "of a piece." The precise nature of this music and its function within the context of the films it serviced changed over the years. Sometimes the changes were slow and gradual; sometimes—most notably in the period 1929–33, when filmmakers anxiously attempted to come to grips with the possibilities of the new sound film—the changes were extreme and occurred with breathtaking rapidity. But when the changes happened they affected, to a large extent, virtually all of what at any moment fell into the large category of film music.

Always, during these first sixty or so years, film music followed a linear path. Around the world there were differences in the speed with which the path was traveled and also—often for the explicit purpose of asserting nationalistic identities in the face of a burgeoning Hollywood hegemony of style—in the "style" of the travel. Nevertheless, and notwithstanding culturally determined nuances, the travel took place along a single path. The twists and turns of this path were many, but all of them were logically determined by socio/technological/economic developments that manifested themselves locally in a myriad unique ways but which in the long run turned out to be more or less the same.

Thus it is possible to generalize about film music during these first six decades, to think of film music "in general." But in the 1950s—when Hollywood's fortunes waned and postwar European cinema's waxed— the path of film music "in general" approached a point of divergence. It may well be, as Elmer Bernstein argued in his article for *High Fidelity* magazine, that the end of Hollywood's "golden age" of film music was signaled by the unexpected popularity of Dimitri Tiomkin's hit song for *High Noon* in 1952 and, three years later, of Bernstein's own jazz-flavored score for *The Man with the Golden Arm*. But there were other factors that contributed, in the late 1950s and especially in the socially turbulent '60s, to the "splitting" of film music's hitherto singular path.

These included:

- labor actions in Hollywood that had the effect of freeing the major studios from what had almost been an "obligation" to use large orchestras;
- a trend throughout the 1950s, motivated especially by the American film industry's urgent need to compete with television, in epic-scale films fitted with appropriately grand symphonic scores performed by very large orchestras;
- another trend, motivated by the same reason, to experiment with sonic novelties (stereo, surround-sound) that could only be experienced in a theatrical venue;
- a growing interest on the part of mainstream Hollywood filmmakers in the long-standing European practice of employing extra-diegetic music that somehow played "against" the on-screen action and emotion, not for the sake of obscuring an otherwise "obvious" classical-style narrative but for the sake of enriching it;
- the rise in the late 1950s—especially in France, Italy, and England—of a "new wave" of filmmaking that countered prevailing film-music customs in ways that ranged from using background music seemingly chosen at random to using no music at all;
- a comparable rise, in the 1960s, of a "new American cinema" that began as an "underground" movement but which soon enough infiltrated Hollywood and which sometimes featured *only* plot-motivated diegetic music and at other times indulged, spectacularly, in extra-diegetic music whose application to the on-screen situation was deliberately artificial;
- the realization by serious filmmakers both in and out of the cinema establishment that the credibility of an "obvious" filmic narrative might be strengthened if the accompanying music followed classical-style conventions yet was in a style (for example, jazz, or rock 'n' roll, or rock) contemporaneous with the film's subject matter;

- the simultaneous realization, perhaps not so much by filmmakers as by the studios that financed their efforts, that potential "hit songs" included in a film score could not only generate considerable publicity for the film but also, if cleverly packaged in so-called soundtrack albums, generate income quite apart from what the film might earn at the box-office.

Regarded in terms of the idea that film music—or music in film, or music simply associated with film exhibition—for its first six decades had been more or less all "of a piece," the factors listed above suggest a shredding of the fabric that had formerly been film music's international norm. Vis-à-vis the idea that for sixty years film music "in general" had followed a single path, the listed factors suggest forks in the road.

A Final Metaphor

For historians, such metaphors have longed proved useful for illuminating the specific moments at which a once unified development split into different directions. But shredded fabrics, crossroads, and other reality-based metaphors seem not to apply to what actually has happened with film music over the last three decades. Regarding the situation of film music that has held since the early 1980s, the best metaphor that comes to mind is one of a phenomenon that probably is not to be found anywhere on earth but which—perhaps with the help of carefully engineered tectonic shifts—nevertheless *could* exist.

Imagine a river that over many miles has accepted the in-put of various tributaries and mixed it equitably into a strong-flowing mainstream. Imagine that this river, which is sometimes frothy and sometimes gentle, reaches an obstruction that causes it to split into, say, a "north" branch and a "south" branch. Imagine that both of these branches similarly branch and then branch again, the result being that a river once known by a single famous name has now become a large number of rivulets whose names are known only to the locals. To imagine such a river is not difficult, for some waterways in fact do work this way. But in real-life examples such as the United States' Mississippi River, Brazil's Amazon, and Egypt's Nile, such repeated divergence of divergences results sooner or later in a delta, a formation in which the energy of a once-deep river is dissipated into countless relatively shallow dribbles.

But now imagine—and this will take imagination, indeed—a situation in which the various branches and sub-branches, instead of losing force, actually *gain* in momentum. Imagine that they have meandered through very different geological regions, in the process picking up natural silts, or perhaps pollutants, that cause the water of each branch to have a distinct make-up. Imagine, too, that instead of moving farther and farther apart, as would happen in the real world, the branches eventually converge. What normally would have been an energy-dissipating delta becomes, in this imaginary world, a strength-gathering basin; with the branches now serving as tributaries, once again there is a real river. This second incarnation of the river could perhaps be just as potent as had been its predecessor, and geographers might decide to call it by the same name. But the old and new rivers would hardly be identical. Analyzing water from upstream, a hydraulic chemist might well conclude: "Yes, this is indeed a sample, drawn at a certain location on a certain date, from what is generally known as The Old River, and it is in all ways consistent with our expectations." Analyzing water from downstream, the same chemist might say: "This particular sample definitely features elements unique to this or that tributary, but its specific components match up not at all with other samples drawn from The New River at the same place and the same time."

The river continues to flow, all the while picking up new components yet now and then reverting—usually because a filmmaker wants to make a "nostalgic" effect—to a state that existed at some point in the past. For the person seriously interested in film music, there is simply no telling what lies beyond the river's next bend. For the music-oriented filmgoer who fancies exploring, every new film is an adventure.

NOTES

Preface

1   Oscar Levant, *A Smattering of Ignorance* (New York: Doubleday, Doran & Co., 1939), 111.

2   For a comprehensive bibliography of recent writing on film music, see Robynn J. Stilwell, "Music in Films: A Critical Review of Literature, 1980–96," *The Journal of Film Music* 1, no. 1 (2002), 19–61.

3   French and German books that deal with the history of film music include Alain Lacombe's *La musique de film* (Paris: F. Van de Velde, 1979), Wolfgang Thiel's *Filmmusik in Geschichte und Gegenwart* (Berlin: Henschelverlag, 1981); Michel Chion's *La musique au cinéma* (Paris: Fayard, 1995), and Anselm C. Kreuzer's *Filmmusik: Geschichte und Analyse 2.—Erweiterte und überarbeitete Auflage* (Berlin: Peter Lang, 2003). At the time of this writing, I am aware that Mervyn Cooke is writing a history of film music soon to be published by Cambridge University Press.

4   Among the most impressive of these studies are Charles Merrell Berg, *An Investigation of the Motives and Realization of Music to Accompany the American Silent Film, 1896–1927* (New York: Arno Press, 1976); Martin Miller Marks, *Music and the Silent Film: Contexts and Case Studies, 1895–1924* (New York and Oxford: Oxford University Press, 1997); Gillian B. Anderson, "The Presentation of Silent Films, or, Music as Anaesthesia," *The Journal of Musicology* 5, no. 2 (Spring 1987); Rick Altman, "The Silence of the Silents," *The Musical Quarterly* 80, no. 4 (Winter 1996); and Rick Altman, *Silent Film Sound* (New York: Columbia University Press, 2004).

5   Despite their promising titles, Russell Lack's *Twenty-Four Frames Under: A Buried History of Film Music* (London: Quartet Books, 1997); Laurence E. MacDonald's *The Invisible Art of Film Music: A Comprehensive History* (Lanham, Maryland: Ardsley House, 1998); and Roger Hickman's *Reel Music: Exploring 100 Years of Film Music* (New York: W.W. Norton, 2005) are devoted primarily to case studies and explorations of the aesthetics of film music. Earlier books that address the history of film music during the "silent" period, but only briefly, include Hanns Eisler and Theodor W. Adorno's *Composing for the Films* (Oxford: Oxford University Press, 1947), Roger Manvell and John Huntley's *The Technique of Film Music* (London: Focal Press, 1957), Irwin Bazelon's *Knowing the Score: Notes on Film Music* (New York: Arco, 1975), Mark Evans's *Soundtrack: The Music of the Movies* (New York: Hopkinson and Blake, 1975), and Roy M. Prendergast's *Film Music: A Neglected Art* (New York: W.W. Norton, 1977). Among the more recent books whose historical overviews seem to brush over music in film's 'silent' period are Royal S. Brown's *Overtones and Undertones: Reading Film Music* (Berkeley: University of California Press, 1994), Tatiana Egorova's *Soviet Film Music* (London: Routledge, 1997), Larry M. Timm's *The Soul of Cinema: An Appreciation of Film Music* (Needham Heights, Maryland: Prentice-Hall, 1998), and Pauline Reay's *Music in Film: Soundtracks and Synergy* (London: Wallflower Press, 2004).

6   In Constance Garnett's translation of *War and Peace* for the 1931 Modern Library edition, the source quotation, from chapter eight of part II, is: "If the will of man were free, that

is, if every man could act as he chose, the whole of history would be a tissue of disconnected accidents."

7   Donald J. Grout, *A Short History of Opera* (New York: Columbia University Press, 1947), xii.

8   Early examples include Arthur Elson, *A History of Opera* (Boston: L.C. Page, 1906) and Percy A. Scholes, *A Miniature History of Opera* (Oxford: Oxford University Press, 1931). More recent examples include Thomas Matthews, *The Splendid Art: A History of the Opera* (New York: Crowell-Collier, 1970), Leslie Orrey, *A Concise History of Opera* (New York: Scribner's, 1972), Joseph Wechsberg, *Opera: An Entertaining, Lively Commentary on the Colorful History of the Opera* (New York: Macmillan, 1972), Henry Sutherland Edwards, *History of the Opera: From Monteverdi to Donizetti* (New York: Da Capo, 1977), and Burton D. Fisher, *A History of Opera: Milestones and Metamorphoses* (Miami: Opera Journeys Publishing, 2003). Recent anthologies that similarly deal not so much with the history of opera as the history of operatic music include Stanley Sadie, ed., *History of Opera* (New York: Norton, 1990) and Roger Parker, ed. *The Oxford History of Opera* (New York: Oxford University Press, 1996).

9   Recent interdisciplinary monographs on opera include Anselm Gerhard, trans. by Mary Whittall, *The Urbanization of Opera: Music Theater in Paris in the Nineteenth Century* (Chicago: University of Chicago Press, 2000), Jane Fulcher, *The Nation's Image: French Grand Opera as Politics and Politicized Art* (Cambridge: Cambridge University Press, 2002), Ruth Bereson, *The Operatic State: Cultural Policy and the Opera House* (London: Routledge, 2002), Downing A. Thomas, *Aesthetics of Opera in the Ancien Régime, 1647–1785* (Cambridge: Cambridge University Press, 2003), Susan Rutherford, *The Prima Donna and Opera, 1815–1930* (Cambridge: Cambridge University Press, 2006), Aubrey S. Garlington, *Society, Culture and Opera in Florence, 1814–30: Dilettantes in an "Earthly Paradise"* (Aldershot: Ashgate, 2006), and Camille Crittenden, *Johann Strauss and Vienna: Operetta and the Politics of Popular Culture* (Cambridge: Cambridge University Press, 2006).

10 The articles that appeared in *The Journal of Interdisciplinary History* 36, nos. 3–4, as a result of a 2004 conference at Princeton are Wendy Heller, "Poppea's Legacy: The Julio-Claudians on the Venetian Stage"; Ellen Rosand, "Seventeenth-Century Venetian Opera as *Fondamente nuove*"; Dennis Romano, "Why Opera? The Politics of an Emerging Genre"; Edward Muir, "Why Venice? Venetian Society and the Success of Early Opera"; James H. Johnson, "The Myth of Venice in Nineteenth-Century Opera"; William Weber, "Redefining the Status of Opera: London and Leipzig, 1800–48"; Mary Ann Smart, "A Stroll in the Piazza and a Night at the Opera"; Thomas S. Grey, "Opera in the Age of Revolution"; Michael C. Tusa, "Cosmopolitanism and the National Opera: Weber's *Der Freischütz*"; John A. Davis, "Opera and Absolutism in Restoration Italy, 1815–60"; Paul Monod, "The Politics of Handel's Early London Operas, 1711–18"; Ellen T. Harris, "With Eyes on the East and Ears on the West: Handel's Orientalist Operas"; Mauro Calcagno, "Censoring *Eliogabalo* in Seventeenth-Century Venice"; Jane Fulcher, "French Identity in Flux: The Triumph of Honegger's *Antigone*"; Lewis Lockwood, "Beethoven's *Leonore* and *Fidelio*"; and Richard Crawford, "Where Did *Porgy and Bess* Come From?"

11 The Brown, Evans, and Prendergast books mentioned in footnote 5 contain a bounty of biographical material. Biographies can also be found in Tony Thomas's *Music for the Movies* (South Brunswick, New Jersey: Barnes, 1973), Christopher Palmer's *The Composer in Hollywood* (New York and London: Marion Boyars, 1990), William Darby and Jack Du Bois's *American Film Composers, Techniques, Trends, 1915–90* (Jefferson, North Carolina: McFarland & Co., 1990), Michael Schelle's *The Score: Interviews with Film Composers* (Los Angeles: Silman-James, 1999), and David Morgan's *Knowing the Score: Film Composers Talk about the Art, Craft, Blood, Sweat, and Tears of Writing for Cinema* (New York: Harper, 2000).

12 Very thorough analyses of particular film scores make up Scarecrow Press's new series of Film Score Guides; to date the films covered are *The English Patient, Batman, The Good, the Bad, and the Ugly, Forbidden Planet, The Ghost and Mrs. Muir, The Ice Storm,* and *The Adventures of Robin Hood*. Shorter analyses are contained in Claudia Gorbman's

Unheard Melodies: Narrative Film Music (*Zéro de conduite, Sous les toits de Paris,* and *Hangover Square*) and Kathryn Kalinak's *Settling the Score: Music and the Classical Hollywood Film* (Madison: University of Wisconsin Press, 1992) (*The Informer, The Magnificent Ambersons,* and *Laura*). In addition, analyses of individual film scores can be found in *The Journal of Film Music, Cinema Journal,* and other scholarly periodicals.

Chapter 1

1   Kurt London, *Film Music: A Summary of the Characteristic Features of Its History, Aesthetics, Technique, and Possible Developments,* trans. Eric S. Bensinger (London: Faber & Faber Ltd., 1936), 80.

2   Since the late 1980s the academic press has issued a steady trickle of monographs and textbooks that deal not only with film music's history but also with its fundamental aesthetic and musico-dramatic theory. In the same period, English-language music journals have gradually opened their pages to scholarly articles having to do with film music; 2003 witnessed the launch of *The Journal of Film Music,* and in 2007 two more journals—the similarly titled *Music and the Moving Image* and *Music, Sound, and the Moving Image*—made their debuts. Since 1989 American universities have sponsored more than a dozen and a half Ph.D. dissertations or D.M.A. theses devoted at least in part to film music. Indicative of the genre's new acceptability in academe, recent announcements for positions in musicology have listed film music almost as often as American vernacular music and so-called world music among subjects that prospective candidates might be asked to teach.

3   George Antheil, *Bad Boy of Music* (Garden City, N.Y.: Doubleday, 1945; reprint, Hollywood: Samuel French, 1990) and Oscar Levant, *A Smattering of Ignorance* (New York: Doubleday, Doran & Co., 1940). After *A Smattering of Ignorance,* Levant wrote two more autobiographies: *The Memoirs of an Amnesiac* (New York: G.P. Putnam's Sons, 1965) and *The Unimportance of Being Oscar* (New York: Putnam, 1968).

4   Between 1935 and 1957 Antheil provided scores for twenty-five feature films and three documentaries; for the complete list, see Clifford McCarty, *Film Composers in America: A Filmography, 1911–70,* 2d ed. (Oxford: Oxford University Press, 2000), 26. Between 1930 and 1942 Levant was involved—sometimes only as co-composer—with just five feature-length films. Along with the 1942 documentary *Fellow Americans,* McCarty (190) lists *Leathernecking* (1930), *Crime Without Passion* (1934), *Nothing Sacred* (1937), and *Made for Each Other* (1939) as Levant's only film-music credits; from both Levant's auto-biography (*A Smattering of Ignorance,* 117–19) and manuscripts held at the University of Southern California, however, it is clear that Levant also composed the operatic music for the 1936 *Charlie Chan at the Opera.*

5   Thomson composed music for the documentary films *The Plow that Broke the Plains* (1936), *The River* (1937), and *The Spanish Earth* (1937), but he was never involved in the Hollywood scene. While Thomson often alluded disparagingly to commercial film music during his tenure (1940–54) as music critic for the *New York Herald Tribune,* his most potent diatribe was an essay ("How to Write a Piece, or Functional Design in Music") included in the 1939 *The State of Music* (New York: Morrow, 1939) and reprinted in *A Virgil Thomson Reader,* ed. John Rockwell (Boston: Houghton Mifflin Company, 1981): 150–4.

6   André Bazin, "The Evolution of the Language of Cinema," in *What Is Cinema?* vol. 1, trans. Hugh Gray (Berkeley: University of California Press, 1967), 30.

7   Antheil, 294.

8   Levant, *A Smattering of Ignorance,* 90.

9   Thomson, 155.

10 See David Burnand, "Reasons Why Film Music Is Held in Low Regard: A British Perspective," in *Brio* 39, no. 1 (Spring–Summer 2002): 26–32; and Bernd Wefelmeyer, "Musik zweiter Klasse? Musik zum Film: Eine Standortbestimmung" ("Second-class Music? Film Music: Where It Stands"), in *Das Orchester* 51, no. 2 (February 2003): 16–21.

11 James Buhler and David Neumeyer, review of Caryl Flinn's *Strains of Utopia: Gender, Nostalgia, and Hollywood Film Music* (Princeton: Princeton University Press, 1992) and

Kathryn Kalinak's *Settling the Score: Music and the Classical Hollywood Film* (Madison: University of Wisconsin Press, 1992). *Journal of the American Musicological Society* 47, no. 2 (Summer 1994): 364–85. For an illuminating account of how the modernist ideology came to be, at least in the United States academic community, see Patrick McCreless, "Rethinking Contemporary Music Theory," in *Keeping Score: Music, Disciplinarity, Culture*, edited by David Schwartz, Anahid Kassabian, and Lawrence Siegel (Charlottesville: University Press of Virginia, 1997), 13–53.

12   The view that music should be autonomous was expressed on both sides of the Atlantic; in the 1950s it was the representative ideology, for example, of Milton Babbitt in the United States, Pierre Boulez in France, and Karlheinz Stockhausen in Germany. For an eloquent discourse on the subject, see Leonard B. Meyer, *Emotion and Meaning in Music* (Chicago: University of Chicago Press, 1956).

13   John Huntley, *British Film Music* (London: Skelton Robinson, 1947), 209–10.

14   Ernest Irving, "Music in Films," *Music & Letters*, 24 (1943), 227.

15   Ibid., 233.

16   Hanns Eisler, *Composing for the Films* (London: Oxford University Press, 1947), 9. When the book was first published only Eisler was listed as an author. In a postscript for the 1969 German edition (*Komposition für den filmen*), Adorno explains that he withdrew his name because he "did not seek to become a martyr" in "the [political] scandal" in which Eisler, in 1947, was involved. See *Composing for the Films*, revised edition (Freeport, N.Y.: Books for Libraries Press, 1971), 167. For details on Eisler's six-year investigation by the Federal Bureau of Investigation, and his eventual deportation in 1948, see James Wierzbicki, "Sour Notes: Hanns Eisler and the FBI," in *Modernism on File: Writers, Artists, and the FBI, 1920–50*, ed. Claire A. Culleton and Karen Leick (New York: Palgrave Macmillan, 2008): 197–219.

To this day, the authorship of the book—that is, how much of it came from Adorno, how much from Eisler—remains problematic. For discussions, see Eberhardt Klemm's introduction to the 1969 German edition; James Buhler and David Neumeyer, review of Caryl Flinn's *Strains of Utopia: Gender, Nostalgia, and Hollywood Film Music* and Kathryn Kalinak's *Settling the Score: Music and the Classical Hollywood Film, Journal of the American Musicological Society* 47, no. 2 (Summer 1994), 369–70; and Martin Hufner, "*Composing for the Films* (1947): Adorno, Eisler, and the Sociology of Music," *Historical Journal of Film, Radio and Television* 18, no. 4 (October 1998), 535–40.

17   Ibid., 9–10.

18   The Hollywood feature films for which Eisler provided music are *Hangmen Also Die* (1942), *None But the Lonely Heart* (1944), *Jealousy* (1945), *The Spanish Main* (1945), *A Scandal in Paris* (1946), *Deadline at Dawn* (1946), *Woman on the Beach* (1947), and *So Well Remembered* (1947). For critical commentary on Eisler's Hollywood film music, see Claudia Gorbman, "Hanns Eisler in Hollywood," *Screen* 32 (1991): 272–85; Jürgen Schebera, "Die Filmkomponist Hanns Eisler," in *Hanns Eisler der Zeitgenosse: Positionen-Perspektiven Materialen zu den Eisler-Festen 1994/95*, ed. Günter Mayer, 41–59, (Leipzig: VEB Deutscher Verlag für Musik, 1997); Horst Weber, "Eisler as Hollywood Film Composer, 1942–8," *Historical Journal of Film, Radio and Television* 18, no. 4 (October 1998): 561–6; Jürgen Schebera, "*Hangmen Also Die* (1943): Hollywood's Brecht-Eisler Collaboration," *Journal of Film, Radio and Television* 18, no. 4 (October 1998): 567–73; Gerd Gemünden, "Brecht in Hollywood: *Hangmen Also Die* and the Anti-Nazi Film," *The Drama Review* 43, no. 4 (Winter 1999): 65–76; and Sally Bick, "Political Ironies: Hanns Eisler in Hollywood and Behind the Iron Curtain," *Acta Musicologica* 75, no. 1 (2003): 65–84.

19   Prendergast, *Film Music: A Neglected Art*, 3.

20   Along with the Oscar Levant and George Antheil autobiographies already noted, see, for example, Dimitri Tiomkin (with Prosper Buranelli), *Please Don't Hate Me* (New York: Doubleday and Company, 1959); Miklós Rózsa, *Double Life: The Autobiography of Miklós Rózsa* (New York: Hippocrene Books, 1982); Henry Mancini, *Did They Mention the Music?* (Chicago: Contemporary Books, 1989); and André Previn, *No Minor Chords: My Days in Hollywood* (New York: Doubleday, 1991).

21 See footnote 10.

22 For example, *Music from the Movies, Soundtrack!, Scoretime!*, and *Film Score Monthly.*

23 Claudia Gorbman, *Unheard Melodies: Narrative Film Music. Unheard Melodies*, which stems from the author's dissertation in media studies, ranks high in bibliographies because it was the first book in a long while to treat film music in a rigorously theoretical and thoroughly researched manner. As had been the case in the 1930s and then again in the years following World War II, throughout the 1980s serious attention was indeed being paid to film music, but the results of the scholarship appeared only in specialized journals. See, for example, Royal S. Brown, "Herrmann, Hitchcock, and the Music of the Irrational," *Cinema Journal* 21, no. 2 (Spring 1982); William Rosar, "Music for the Monsters," *Quarterly Journal of the Library of Congress* 40, no. 4 (Fall 1983); and Simon Frith, "Mood Music: An Inquiry into Narrative Film Music," *Screen* 25, no. 3 (May–June 1984). An essay containing the seed of Gorbman's book was included in *Yale French Studies* 60, no. 1 (1980), a special issue devoted entirely to film music and sound.

24 Laurence E. MacDonald, *The Invisible Art of Film Music* (Lanham, Md: Ardsley House, 1998).

25 Larry M. Timm, *The Soul of Cinema: An Appreciation of Film Music* (Needham Heights, Mass: Pearson Custom Publishing, 1998) (rev. ed., Upper Saddle River, N.J.: Prentice Hall, 2003).

26 Along with the short documentaries *The City* (1939) and *The Cunningham Story* (1945), Copland's film credits include the Hollywood feature films *Of Mice and Men* (1940), *Our Town* (1940), *The North Star* (1943), *The Red Pony* (1949), *The Heiress* (1949), and *Something Wild* (1961). Copland's *What to Listen for in Music* was first published by McGraw-Hill in 1939. The "Film Music" chapter, which makes reference to the scores for *The Red Pony* and *The Heiress*, was included in the 1957 second edition.

27 Quoted in Nat Shapiro, ed., *An Encyclopedia of Quotations about Music* (New York: Doubleday, 1978), 318, and Derek Walton, ed., *The Wordsworth Dictionary of Musical Quotations* (Hertfordshire: Wordsworth Editions, 1994), 266.

28 Federico Fellini, in Federico Fellini (with Tony Guerra), *Fellini on Fellini* (New York: Dalacorte, 1976), quoted in Nat Shapiro, ed., *An Encyclopedia of Quotations about Music* (New York: Doubleday, 1978), 319.

29 In the United States, the three most important trade magazines were *The Film Index, Moving Picture News*, and *Moving Picture World.*

30 In 1936 and 1937, for example, George Antheil wrote a column titled "On the Hollywood Front" for the journal *Modern Music.* Several European film journals were founded at around this time—for example, *Bianco e nero, Sight and Sound*, and *Cinema Quarterly*—and frequently they contained articles on music.

31 Beginning in 1946 and continuing into the early 1950s, Lawrence Morton contributed articles on film music to *Film Music Notes, Hollywood Quarterly*, and *The Quarterly of Film, Radio, and Television.* During the same period, Frederick W. Sternfeld wrote on film music for both *Hollywood Quarterly* and *The Musical Quarterly.* Throughout the 1950s, Everett Helm wrote on film music for *The Quarterly of Film, Radio, and Television, The Musical Quarterly*, and *The Musical Times*, and Hans Keller—whose writing on film music are now collected in *Film Music and Beyond: Writings on Music and the Screen, 1946–59*, ed. Christopher Wintle (London: Plumbago Books, 2006)—contributed importantly to *Tempo, Music Review, The Musical Times*, and other British journals.

32 A landmark event in the renewal of scholarly interest in film music was the publication of *Yale French Studies* 60 (1980), a special issue devoted entirely to explorations of film music and sound. Along with key articles by Christian Metz, Rick Altman, Mary Ann Doane, Douglas Gomery, Alan Williams, David Bordwell, Philip Rosen, Nick Browne, and Annette Insdorf, the issue contained an article by Claudia Gorbman ("Narrative Film Music") that led to her seminal 1987 *Unheard Melodies* book. The already noted books by Caryl Flinn (1992), Kathryn Kalinak (1992), and Royal S. Brown (1994), as well as Anahid Kassabian's *Hearing Film: Tracking Identifications in Contemporary Hollywood Film Music* (London: Routledge, 2000), similarly stem from the tradition of literary criticism.

33   A conference titled "Sound, Music and the Moving Image" was held at the University of London in September 2007, and conferences titled "Music and the Moving Image" have lately taken place at the University of California, Santa Barbara (January 2006) and at New York University (May 2007 and June 2008). Stanford University hosted a conference titled "Reviewing the Canon: Borrowed Music in Films" in May 2003. Two years earlier film music conferences took place at New York University ("Music/Image in Film and Multimedia," June 2001) and the University of Colorado ("Hollywood Musicals and Music in Hollywood," July 2001); a special issue of the journal *American Music* (22, no. 1 (Spring 2004)) contained articles based on papers presented at these two conferences. In addition to these specialized events, sessions devoted to film music have been included since 2000 in the agendas of annual meetings of the Society for Cinema and Media Studies, The Society for American Music, and the American Musicological Society.

34   *The Journal of Film Music* began publication in 2002. A journal called *Music and the Moving Image*—a spin-off of the May 2007 conference at New York University—debuted early in 2008, and the London conference similarly launched a journal called *Music, Sound, and the Moving Image*.

35   Articles on film music have lately been published in the *Journal of the American Musicological Society, American Music, Journal of the Society for American Music, The Musical Quarterly*, and *Acta Musicologica*; likewise, articles on film music appear from time to time in *Cinema Journal, Camera Obscura, Velvet Light Trap, The Journal of Popular Film and Television, Philosophy and Film*, et al.

36   Exceptions to the generalization include Katherine Spring's "Pop Go the Warner Bros., et al.: Hollywood's Marketing of Popular Songs During the Transition to Sound," scheduled to be published in *Cinema Journal* in 2008, and my own "The Hollywood Career of Gershwin's *Second Rhapsody*," *Journal of the American Musicological Society* 60, no. 1 (Spring 2007).

37   In Kurt London's 1936 *Film Music*, for example, and in various writings from the 1930s—anthologized in *Film Sound: Theory and Practice*, ed. Elisabeth Weis and John Belton (New York: Columbia University Press, 1985)—by Rudolph Arnheim, Béla Balázs Alberto Cavalcanti, and Siegfried Kracauer.

38   Anahid Kassabian's 2000 *Hearing Film* is devoted almost entirely to this topic. More discussion of the widely varied "meaning" of extant music in films can be found in the essays contained in Phil Powrie and Robynn Stillwell, eds., *Changing Tunes: The Use of Pre-Existing Music in Film* (Aldershot: Ashgate, 2006); Jeongwon Joe and Theresa Rose, eds., *Between Opera and Cinema* (London: Routledge, 2001); and Daniel Goldmark, Lawrence Kramer, and Richard Leppert, eds., *Beyond the Soundtrack: Representing Music in Cinema* (Berkeley: University of California Press, 2007).

39   For an especially provocative and insightful essay on the "blurring," see Robynn J. Stilwell, "The Fantastical Gap between Diegetic and Nondiegetic," in *Beyond the Soundtrack: Representing Muic in Cinema*, ed. Daniel Goldmark, Lawrence Kramer, and Richard Leppert (Berkeley: University of California Press, 2007), 184–202.

40   Richard Taruskin, "Speed Bumps" (review of *The Cambridge History of Nineteenth-Century Music*, ed. Jim Samson, (Cambridge: Cambridge University Press, 2001) and *The Cambridge History of Twentieth-Century Music* (Cambridge: Cambridge University Press, 2004)), *19th-Century Music* 29, no. 2 (2005), 187.

41   Webster's *Ninth New Collegiate Dictionary*, s.v. "history" (New York: Merriam-Webster Inc., 1984). 572.

42   *The Compact Edition of the Oxford English Dictionary*, s.v. "history" (Oxford: Oxford University Press, 1971), vol. II, 305–6.

43   The origin of this familiar cliché, nowadays used as an admonition to "get to the point," remains unknown. It seems to derive from the parlance of nickelodeon-period (i.e., 1903–11) film directors who felt that the interest of audiences possibly bored by character development could be rekindled instantly by quick cuts to action (typically "chase") sequences. Some etymologists, however, have argued that the phrase derives from jargon related to the printing industry in the eighteenth century, when a small frame containing units of type was called a "phrase" and the large frame that contained all of a page's

"phrases" was called a "chase"; in this context, the admonition to "cut to the chase" meant that a complete page was ready for printing.

44   The article "The End of History?" appeared in the summer of 1989 in the journal *The National Interest*; the book is *The End of History and the Last Man* (New York: Free Press, 1992).

Chapter 2

1   Quoted in Emmanuelle Toulet, *Birth of the Motion Picture*, trans. Susan Emanuel (New York: Harry N. Abrams, 1995), 130.

2   Hanns Eisler [and Theodor Adorno], *Composing for the Films* (New York: Oxford University Press, 1947), 51. Repr. Freeport, N.Y.: Books for Libraries Press, 1971.

3   Richard Crangle, " 'Next Slide Please': The Lantern Lecture in Britain, 1890–1910," in *The Sounds of Early Cinema*, ed. Richard Abel and Rick Altman (Bloomington: Indiana University Press, 2001), 46. Crangle attributes the "bricolage" idea to Michael Chanan, *The Dream That Kicks: The Prehistory and Early Years of the Cinema in Britain* (London: Routledge and Kegan Paul, 1980), 51–3.

4   Gerald Mast, *A Short History of the Movies* (New York: Pegasus, 1971), 23–4.

5   Louis Lumière, quoted in Toulet, 40.

6   The German priest-inventor Athanasius Kircher first proposed a "magic lantern" in 1646.

7   Larry M. Timm, *The Soul of Cinema: An Appreciation of Film Music* (Upper Saddle River, N.J.: Prentice Hall, 2003), 57. Timm gives no source for his information.

8   The films were titled, respectively, *La Sortie d'Usine, Le Repas de bébé, L'Arroseur arrosée, Leçon de Bicyclette, La Partie d'Ecarté, Bataille de Femmes*, and *L'Arrivée d'un train à la Ciotat*.

9   Martin Miller Marks, *Music and the Silent Film: Contexts and Case Studies, 1895–1924* (New York and Oxford: Oxford University Press, 1997), n. 2, 222.

10   Marks, 3. Emphasis mine.

11   Toulet, 16.

12   The pianist was Emile Maraval, who performed on a Gaveau instrument. Referring to a printed program mentioned in David Robinson, "Music of the Shadows/Musica delle ombre: The Use of Musical Accompaniment with Silent Films, 1896–1936," *Griffithiana* 38/39 (October 1990), 22, Marks (n. 31, 249) notes that Maraval was identified as a "pianiste-compositeur."

13   The information comes from Cecil Hepworth, who in his autobiographical *Came the Dawn: Memories of a Film Pioneer* (London: Phoenix House, 1951) cites a statement from one Birt Acres. See Roger Manvell and John Huntley, *The Technique of Film Music* (London: Focal Press, 1957), 17.

14   Manvel and Huntley, 17. Marks (31) mentions an Empire Theatre playbill, dated March 9, 1896, that declares that as part of the entertainment "a selection of music will be performed under the direction of Mr. George Byng."

15   Similar to the Cinématographe, the Vitascope was manufactured by Edison after being developed—as the Phantoscope—by C. Francis Jenkins and Thomas Armat and licensed to Norman Raff and Frank Gammon.

16   Charles Musser, *Before the Nickelodeon: Edwin S. Porter and the Edison Manufacturing Company* (Berkeley: University of California Press, 1991), 60–2.

17   Toulet, 20–1.

18   Along with Marks's *Music and the Silent Film*, the most thorough studies are Rick Altman's "The Silence of the Silents," *The Musical Quarterly* 80, no. 4 (Winter 1996) and *Silent Film Sound* (New York: Columbia University Press, 2004).

19   *New York Herald*, April 24, 1896. Quoted in Musser, 61–2.

20   Altman, "The Silence of the Silents," 659.

21   Charles Merrell Berg, *An Investigation of the Motives for and Realization of Music to Accompany the American Silent Film, 1896–1927* (New York: Arno Press, 1976), 24. Originally a Ph.D. dissertation, University of Iowa, 1973.

22 Respectively, the descriptions come from an article by Harvey Brougham in the November 1920 issue of *Overland Monthly* (82); an article by Stuart Fletcher in the June 1929 issue of *Sackbut* (374); the entry on film music, by Wilfred H. Mellers, in the 1954 edition of *Grove's Dictionary of Music and Musicians* (vol. 3, 103); an article by Dorothy M. Richardson in the August 1927 issue of *Close Up* (60); Louis Levy's 1948 book *Music for the Movies* (7); and Ernest Lindgren's 1963 book *The Art of Film Music* (137).

23 Quoted in Toulet, 130.

24 Quoted in Toulet, 15.

25 Quoted in Toulet, 133.

26 Quoted in Paul F. Boller, Jr., "The Sound of Silents," *American Heritage* 36, no. 5 (August–September 1985), 99. Statements supportive of the Thalberg quip—from film director Alberto Cavalcanti, theater organist Gaylord Carter, and film/film-music scholars Allardyce Nicoll, Kevin Brownlow, Charles Berg, Raymond Fielding, Douglas Gomery, Charles Hofmann, Gillian Anderson, Norman King, George Pratt, and André Gaudreault—are cited by Altman, "The Silence of the Silents," 657–8.

27 Toulet, 50. For more details, see Stephen Bottomore, "An International Survey of Sound Effects in Early Cinema," *Film History* 11, no. 4 (1999), 485–98.

28 *Philadelphia Record*, August 11, 1896. Quoted in Charles Musser, *The Emergence of Cinema: The American Screen to 1907* (New York: Scribner's, 1990), 178.

29 *Providence Journal*, September 7, 1896. Quoted in Altman, *Silent Film Sound*, 86.

30 Ibid.

31 *Providence Evening Times*, September 9, 1896. Quoted in Altman, *Silent Film Sound*, 86.

32 "A Lantern Entertainment Well Worth a Visit," *The Optical Magic Lantern Journal and Photographic Enlarger* 10 (November 1899), 143. Quoted in Joseph H. North, *The Early Development of the Motion Picture, 1887–1909* (New York: Arno Press, 1973), 75.

33 *Providence Journal*, September 7, 1896. Quoted in Altman, *Silent Film Sound*, 86.

34 *New York Times*, October 21, 1896. Quoted in Kemp R. Niver, *Biograph Bulletins, 1896–1908* (Los Angeles: Locare Research Group, 1971), 14.

35 Kemp R. Niver, *Klaw and Erlanger: Famous Plays in Pictures* (London: Renovare, 1985), 11.

36 *New York World*, February 27, 1898. Quoted in Altman, *Silent Film Sound*, 87.

37 Henry V. Hopwood, "Living Pictures," *Optician and Photographic Trades Review* (1899), 231.

38 See A. Nicholas Vardac, *Stage to Screen* (New York: Benjamin Blom, 1968) and Anne Dhu Shapiro, "Action Music in American Pantomime and Melodrama, 1730–1913," *American Music* 2, no. 4 (Winter 1984): 49–72.

39 The references are to Monteverdi's 1609 *L'Orfeo*, Mozart's 1786 *The Marriage of Figaro*, and Puccini's 1896 *La bohème*, but these, of course, are just a few of the operas in which theatrically potent "underscore" plays an important dramatic role.

40 Cecil M. Hepworth, *Came the Dawn: Memories of a Film Pioneer* (London: Phoenix House, 1951), 31–2. The passage is quoted in Manville and Huntley, 16; Marks, *Music and the Silent Film*, 28–9; Russell Lack, *Twenty-four Frames Under: A Buried History of Film Music* (London: Quartet Books, 1997), 11; and Altman, *Silent Film Sound*, 204.

41 "On observa combine le musicien a suivi de près le 'découpage' de la pantomime d'Émile Reynaud." Quoted in translation by Marks, *Music and the Silent Film*, 29.

42 Marks, *Music and the Silent Film*, 32. Marks's discussion (31–48) of the Skladanowsky materials includes four facsimiles of instrumental parts and a ten-page transcription of an orchestral "Polka."

43 Marks, *Music and the Silent Film*, 247.

44 Enduringly famous for his 1902 *A Trip to the Moon*, Méliès made his film debut in 1896 with *A Game of Cards*. After the Lumière brothers denied him access to their equipment, Méliès produced his films with the Theatrograph developed in England by R.W. Paul.

45 There is no record as to how music might have figured into the presentation of *Un homme de têtes*. It seems worth noting, however, that after the protagonist "grows" a fourth head he picks up a banjo and engages his other heads in what appears to be a sing-along chorus.

46 L.H. Robbins, "The Magical Pageant of the Films," *New York Times*, May 7, 1933.

47   Mordaunt Hall, "The Screen: The Old and the New," *New York Times*, January 28, 1927.
48   "The Screen: Motion Picture History," *New York Times*, January 20, 1923.
49   "Notes Written on the Screen," *New York Times*, February 25, 1917.
50   "Quiet Week at the Theatres," *New York Times*, December 20, 1903.
51   Edison catalogue synopsis for *The Great Train Robbery*, 1903.
52   Mast, 50–1.
53   Under the heading "Vaudeville," the December 20, 1903 *New York Times* column that announces the "biograph" premiere of *The Great Train Robbery* lists rosters that include, along with numerous human performers, motion pictures projected by means of the vitagraph, the kalatechnoscope, the kinetograph, and the deweyscope.
54   Altman, *Silent Film Sound*, 103.
55   John Belton, *American Cinema/American Culture* (New York: McGraw-Hill, Inc., 1994), 10.
56   James Lastra, *Sound Technology and the American Cinema: Perception, Representation, Modernity* (New York: Columbia University Press, 2000), 97.
57   Timm, *The Soul of Cinema: An Appreciation of Film Music* (Upper Saddle River, N.J.: Prentice-Hall, 2003).

Chapter 3

1   Joseph Medill Patterson, "The Nickelodeons: the Poor Man's Elementary Course in the Drama," *The Saturday Evening Post*, November 23, 1907, 11.
2   Tom Gunning, "The Cinema of Attraction: Early Film, Its Spectator and the Avant-Garde," *Wide Angle* 8, nos. 3–4 (1986): 63–70, and "'Now You See It, Now You Don't': The Temporality of the Cinema of Attractions," *Velvet Light Trap* 32 (Fall 1993): 4.
3   For a largely pictorial history of the nickelodeon, see O. David Bowers, *Nickelodeon Theatres and Their Music* (London: Vestal Press, 1999).
4   Patterson, 10.
5   Barton W. Currie, "The Nickel Madness," *Harper's Weekly*, August 24, 1907, 1246.
6   Ibid. For more statistics, see Ben Singer, "Manhattan Nickelodeons: New Data on Audiences and Exhibitors," in *The Silent Cinema Reader*, Lee Grieveson and Peter Krämer, eds., 119–33 (London: Routledge, 2004).
7   Patterson, 10.
8   Raymond B. Fosdick, *Report on Motion Picture Theatres of Greater New York*, March 22, 1911, 1.
9   Patterson, 11.
10   Currie, 1246.
11   Patterson, 10.
12   Currie, 1246.
13   Patterson, 10.
14   Quoted in Lary May, *Screening Out the Past: The Birth of Mass Culture and the Motion Picture Industry* (New York and Oxford: Oxford University Press, 1980), 36.
15   "The character of the attendance varies with the locality, but, whatever the locality, children make up about thirty-three percent of the crowds." Patterson, 11.
16   Gerald Mast, *A Short History of the Movies* (New York: Pegasus, 1971), 57.
17   The Méliès and Pathé companies had been founded in France, but by 1908 they were producing films in the United States.
18   Mast, 58–9.
19   Currie, 1246.
20   Rick Altman, *Silent Film Sound* (New York: Columbia University Press, 2004), 240.
21   Mast, 57.
22   The first such column, titled "Playing the Pictures," appeared under the by-line of Clyde Martin in *Film Index* on October 8, 1910. Clarence E. Sinn's "Music for the Picture" column debuted in *Moving Picture World* debuted on November 26, 1910, and early in 1912 *Moving Picture News* started to run comments on film music—variously labeled "Our Music Page," "Our Music Column," "The Musician and the Picture," "Music and

the Picture," and "Picture Music"—by C.W. Long and Ernst L. Luz. The first audience-oriented film magazine in the United States was *Motion Picture Story*, first published in February 1911. This was followed in 1912 by *Photoplay*, a periodical whose circulation surged in 1914 when its editorship was taken over by James Quirk.

23 *Moving Picture World*, July 27, 1912, 321.
24 Roger Manvell and John Huntley, *The Technique of Film Music* (London and New York: Focal Press, 1957), 18–9. The anecdote comes from Louis Levy, *Music for the Movies* (London: Sampson Low, 1948), 12.
25 *New York Dramatic Mirror*, October 9, 1909.
26 Clarence E. Sinn, "Music for the Picture," *Moving Picture World*, November 26, 1910, 1227.
27 Max Winkler, *A Penny from Heaven* (New York: Appleton-Century-Crofts, 1951), 168–9. An excerpt from the autobiography appeared, under the title "The Origin of Film Music," in *Films in Review* 2, no. 34 (December 1951). Royal S. Brown, who quotes the anecdote in his *Overtones and Undertones: Reading Film Music* (Berkeley: University of California Press, 1994), notes (354) that Winkler's memory seems to have been faulty, for the film *War Brides* was not made until 1916.
28 James Lastra, *Sound Technology and the Modern Cinema: Perception, Representation, Modernity* (New York: Columbia University Press, 2000), 112.
29 *New York Dramatic Mirror*, October 9, 1909.
30 Sinn, "Music for the Picture," *Moving Picture World*, March 27, 1915, 1917.
31 The illustrations are reproduced on p. 680 and p. 684, respectively, of Rick Altman's "The Silence of the Silents," *The Musical Quarterly* 80, no. 4 (Winter 1996).
32 Louis Reeves Harrison, "Jackass Music," *Moving Picture World*, January 21, 1911, 125.
33 Altman, *Silent Film Sound*, 241.
34 Samuel L. Rothapfel, "Management of the Theater," *Moving Picture World*, April 9, 1910, 548.
35 Clyde Martin, "Playing the Pictures," *Film Index*, December 10, 1910, 5.
36 H.L. Barnhart, "Orchestral Music in Pictures," *Film Index*, May 20, 1911, 15.
37 Eugene A. Ahren, *What and How to Play for Pictures* (Twin Falls, Idaho: Newsprint, 1913), 12.
38 Sinn, "Music for the Pictures," *Moving Picture World*, December 20, 1913, 1396.
39 Sinn, "Music for the Picture," *Moving Picture World*, November 26, 1910, 1227.
40 "Incidental Music for Edison Pictures." *Edison Kinetogram*, September 15, 1909, 12–13. Reproduced in Charles Merrell Berg, *An Investigation of the Motives and Realization of Music to Accompany the American Silent Film, 1896–1927* (New York: Arno Press, 1976), 103.
41 Ibid.
42 Ibid.
43 Recommended in the music cues for *Why Girls Leave Home*, the song "Home! Sweet Home!"—with music by Henry Rowley Bishop and words by John Howard Payne—dates from an 1823 London production titled *Clari*. The suggested "Incidental Music for Edison Pictures" listed in the September 15, 1909 issue of the *Edison Kinetogram* also includes, for a short film titled *A Knight for a Night*, the song "He's a Jolly Good Fellow."
44 Twenty-five pieces, all bearing generic titles, were listed in an 1883 Carl Fischer catalogue under the label "New York Theatre Orchestra Melodramatic Music." For more on how music was used in melodrama, see John Fell, "Dissolves by Gaslight: Antecedents to the Motion Picture in Nineteenth-Century Melodrama," *Film Quarterly* 23, no. 3 (Spring 1970): 22–34; and Anne Dhu Shapiro, "Action Music in American Pantomime and Melodrama, 1730–1913," *American Music* 2, no. 4 (Winter 1984): 49–72. For actual examples of music used in melodrama, see David Mayer and Matthew Scott, *Four Bars of "Agit": Incidental Music for Victorian and Edwardian Melodrama* (London: Samuel French, 1983).
45 *Edison Kinetogram*, December 15, 1909. Quoted in Altman, *Silent Film Sound*, 252. Gounod's *Faust* dates from 1859.

46 Music cues for *Frankenstein*, quoted in Charles Hoffmann, *Sounds for Silents* (New York: DBS Publications, 1970), 14–15.

47 *Der Freischütz* premiered at Berlin's Schauspielhaus in June 1821; two years later, when Weber visited Vienna, he found the city "reacting against his music in the wake of several *Freischütz* parodies." Philipp Spitta and John Warrack, "Weber, Carl Maria von," in *The New Grove Dictionary of Music and Musicians* (1980), vol. 20, 247. Wagner's *Lohengrin* dates from 1850. While the lyrics for "Annie Laurie" date from early in the eighteenth century, the popular melody was written by Alicia Anne Scott (née Spottiswoode) in the 1840s.

48 Balfe's opera was premiered in London in 1843. Rubinstein's Op. 3—a pair of "Melodies" in the keys of F and B—dates from 1852.

49 Sinn, "Music for the Picture," *Moving Picture World*, September 23, 1911, 872. Reproduced in Berg, 105.

50 The music recommended for the opening scene is probably the 1906 song "Martinique," by William Lorraine and Otto Langey, and the music identified as "La Cinquantine" (for Part I, scene 8) is probably the 1892 "La Cinquintaine"—also known as "The Golden Wedding"—by a team identified only as Gabriel and Marie. The music suggested for Part I, scene 12, is clearly the segment labeled "Reverie" in the score for *The Roses' Honeymoon* (words by Paul West, music by John W. Bratton) that opened on Broadway in 1903. The 'reverie' suggested for Part II, scene 10, is perhaps the song "Heart's Ease" that was published as early as 1651 in John Playford's *The English Dancing Master*; the tune, which is mentioned by name in the Shakespeare play (Act IV, scene 5), had long been popular as an accompaniment for contra-dancing. The "reverie" suggested for the film's Part II, scene 8, remains unclear, but in all likelihood it is *not* the 1908 song "Shine On, Harvest Moon" by Jack Norworth and Nora Bayes.

51 Ernst Luz, "Musical Plots," *Moving Picture News*, October 9, 1912, 20. Reproduced in Berg, 106.

52 Not much remembered today, Franz von Blon (1861–1945) was an Austrian-born composer well-known early in the twentieth century for such marches as *Unter dem Siegesbanner*, *Die Wacht am Rhein*, *Heil Europa!*, and *Kaiser-Parade*.

53 "Music Suggestions for *The Blind Miner*, *Vitagraph Bulletin*, January 17–February 1, 1912, 10. The various misspellings—of *Träumerei*, Schumann, and *Tannhäuser*—are original. Quoted in Altman, *Silent Film Sound*, 266.

54 Bert Ennis, "Music Cues—Without the Aid of Riesenfeld—in 1910," unpublished typescript, quoted in Hofmann, *Sounds for Silents*, 18–19.

55 Gillian B. Anderson, "The Presentation of Silent Films, or, Music as Anaesthesia," *The Journal of Musicology* 5, no. 2 (Spring 1987), 284.

56 *Encore*, January 1904. Quoted in Russell Lack, *Twenty-Four Frames Under* (London: Quartet Books, 1997), 28.

57 Marks, *Music and the Silent Film*, 51.

58 During his lifetime Saint-Saëns attempted to suppress performances of *The Carnival of the Animals* (scored for two pianos and chamber ensemble) except for the section titled "The Swan." Without opus number, the piece was published one year after the composer's death in 1921, and it remains his best-known work.

59 Titled *L'Assassinat du Duc le Guise: Tableaux histoire*, the piano reduction of Saint-Saens's music was published in 1908 by A. Durand & Fils. Le Borne's *L'Empreinte: Mimodrame en 11 tableaux* was published in 1908 by Mathot; Berardi's *Le Secret de Myrto: Poème musicale* was published in 1909 by Hegel.

60 Although the published orchestral score indeed calls for only strings, piano, and harmonium, the score used for the film showing included oboe, flute, clarinet, bassoon, and horn. In addition, an arrangement of the score for violin, 'cello, and piano, with optional clarinet and bassoon, was made by R. Branga in 1925. See Marks, *Music and the Silent Film*, 253.

61 The complete film is discussed by Pierre Jenn and Michel Nagard in "L'Assassinat du Duc de Guise (1908)," *L'Avant-scène cinéma* 334 (November 1984): 57–72. A truncated version was circulated in the United States in 1909. See Marks, *Music and the Silent Film*, 252.

62   Lack, *Twenty-Four Frames Under*, 29.
63   Roger Manvell and John Huntley, *The Technique of Film Music* (London: Focal Press, 1957), 18. With remarkable fidelity, the statement is echoed in James Harding's *Saint-Saëns and His Circle* (London: Chapman and Hall, 1965): "The suite . . . consists of an introduction and five tableaux, with each part meticulously cued for the action of the film" (204).
64   Marks, *Music and the Silent Film*, 52.
65   Ibid.
66   Marks, *Music and the Silent Film*, 53.
67   Royal S. Brown, *Overtones and Undertones: Reading Film Music* (Berkeley: University of California Press, 1994), 53.
68   Ibid.
69   Adolphe Brisson, "Chronique théâtrale," *Le Temps*, November 23, 1908, 1.
70   Marks, *Music and the Silent Film*, 52.
71   Ibid.
72   The co-directors (Charles Le Bargy and André Calmettes) were prominent actors, most of the cast members were affiliated either with the Comédie française or the Maison de Molière, and the author of the screenplay (Henry Lavedan) was a member of L'Académie française. For more on the film's credits, see Marks, *Music and the Silent Film*, 50–1.
73   Both Marks and Altman note that newspaper accounts and catalogue references make no mention of music. See Marks, *Music and the Silent Film*, 64; Altman, "The Silence of the Silents," 651; and Altman, *Silent Film Sound*, 205.
74   *L'Arlésienne* preceded *L'Assassinat* by a month; the other films had their Paris premieres early in 1909.
75   Altman, *Silent Film Sound*, 252.
76   Marks, *Music and the Silent Film*, 64.
77   *Edison Kinetogram*, December 15, 1909. Quoted in Altman, *Silent Film Sound*, 252.
78   Advertisement in *Moving Picture World*, December 28, 1907, 704. Quoted in Altman, *Silent Film Sound*, 251.
79   Marks, *Music and the Silent Film*, 189–94.
80   *Moving Picture World*, December 21, 1909, 5. Quoted in Marks, *Music and the Silent Film*, 191.
81   *Catalogue of Copyright Entries*, May 13, 1913. Quoted in Marks, *Music and the Silent Film*, 191.
82   *Moving Picture World*, June 13, 1914, 12. Quoted in Marks, *Music and the Silent Film*, 194. Although Ildebrando Pizzetti received the commission for *Cabiria* and wrote the film's "Sinfonia del Fuoco," most of the music seems to have been composed by Pizzetti's student Manlio Mazza. See Marks, 103–8.
83   Advertisement in *Motion Picture World*, June 29, 1912, 1241. Quoted in Altman, *Silent Film Sound*, 254.
84   Altman, *Silent Film Sound*, 254–5.
85   Marks, *Music and the Silent Film*, 83, 84.
86   Marks, *Music and the Silent Film*, 84. Emphasis original. Marks's treatment of Simon's music for *An Arabian Tragedy* includes reproductions of three of the score's pages.
87   "Playing the Pictures," *Film Index*, February 18, 1911, 12. Quoted in Altman, *Silent Film Sound*, 257.
88   "Music for Pictures," *Moving Picture Weekly*, October 19, 1912, 235. Quoted in Marks, *Music and the Silent Film*, 86.
89   "Music for Pictures," *Moving Picture Weekly*, June 7, 1913, 1020. Quoted in Marks, *Music and the Silent Film*, 88.
90   Clarence E. Sinn, "Music for the Pictures," *Moving Picture World*, November 26, 1910, 1227.
91   Eugene A. Ahern, *What and How to Play for Pictures*, 34–5.
92   Eugene Platzman, *F.B. Haviland's Moving Picture Pianist's Album* (New York: Haviland, 1911), title page.
93   H.S. Fuld, "Fitting the Words of a Song to the Picture," *Moving Picture News*, December 5, 1914, 114.

94   The first nationwide American copyright law had been enacted in 1787, but it was not until 1831 that a revised copyright law would apply to musical compositions.
95   So called because the sound of multiple pianists "plugging" music publishers' latest wares called to mind the noise of tin pans being banged together, Tin Pan Alley was never an actual place. Apparently the term was coined by songwriter Monroe H. Rosenfeld in the 1890s, when music publishers were centered on New York's East 14th Street, and then was popularized after the industry moved, around the turn of the century, to West 28th Street. See H. Wiley Hitchcock, "Tin Pan Alley," in *The New Grove Dictionary of American Music* (London and New York: Macmillan, 1986), vol. IV, 396.
96   Altman, *Silent Film Sound*, 267.
97   The test case involved Victor Herbert, one of ASCAP's founders, suing Shanley's Broadway Restaurant for unlicensed use of the title song from his 1913 operetta *Sweethearts*. Herbert lost the case, but the decision was reversed by the Supreme Court.
98   Dennis Sharp, *The Picture Palace and Other Buildings for Movies* (London: Hugh Evelyn, 1969), 70.
99   Quoted in Belton, 16.
100 For more on the development of the large theaters, see—along with Sharp—Ben M. Hall, *The Best Remaining Seats: The Story of the Golden Age of the Movie Palace* (New York: Bramhall House, 1961); Robert B. Harmon, *Perspectives on a Vanishing Species in Architecture: The Movie Palace, A Selected Bibliography* (Monticello, Ill.: Vance Bibliographies, 1981); Edwin Heathcote, *Cinema Builders* (Chichester: Academy Press, 2001); Janna Jones, *The Southern Movie Palace: Rise, Fall, and Resurrection* (Gainesville, Fla.: University Press of Florida, 2003); Ross Melnick and Andreas Fuchs, *Cinema Treasures: a New Look at Classic Movie Theaters* (St. Paul, Minn.: Motorbooks International, 2004); David Naylor, *American Picture Palaces: The Architecture of Fantasy* (New York: Van Nostrand Rheinhold, 1981); and Michael Putnam, *Silent Screens: The Decline and Transformation of the American Movie Theater* (Baltimore: Johns Hopkins University Press, 2000).
101 The first so-called theater organ—that is, a traditional pipe organ combined with a variety of sound-effects devices—was the Hope-Jones Unit Orchestra manufactured in 1910 by the Rudolf Wurlitzer Company.
102 The distributors formed the General Film Company. For nickelodeon operators, the license that allowed them access to MPPC films distributed by GFC agents cost two dollars a week. See Mast, 58.
103 Belton, 64.

Chapter 4

1   Max Winkler, *A Penney from Heaven* (New York: Appleton-Century-Crofts, 1951), 236.
2   Altman, *Silent Film Sound* (New York: Columbia University Press, 2004), 243.
3   Altman argues that in the 1910–12 period Gounod's "Ave Maria," Mendelssohn's "Spring Song," Rubinstein's "Melody in F," Schumann's "Träumerei," Tosti's "Goodbye," Weber's "The Storm" (from *Der Freischütz*), the "Sextette" from Donizetti's *Lucia da Lammermoor*, the "Berceuse" from Godard's *Jocelyn*, the "Barcarolle" from Offenbach's *Tales of Hoffmann*, the "Overture" and "Waltz" from von Suppé's *Poet and Peasant*, the "Triumphal March" from Verdi's *Aïda*, and the "Pilgrims' Chorus" from Wagner's *Tannhäuser*—along with various wedding marches and funeral marches by Chopin, Mendelssohn, and Wagner—constitute "very much the totality of the common repertory on which trade press columnists and other musical suggestion compilers felt they could depend." Altman, *Silent Film Sound*, 267.
4   Winkler, 171–3.
5   Universal had been founded in 1912 by Carl Laemmle.
6   Winkler, 174–5.
7   Winkler, 175.
8   Frank A. Edson, "The Movies," *Metronome*, April 1915, 38.
9   Altman (*Silent Film Sound*, 427) notes that Winkler's name first appears in Sinn's "Music for the Picture" column, *Moving Picture Weekly*, July 31, 1915, 827. Two months later he was named in Edson's "The Movies" column, *Metronome*, September 1915, 18.

10 Little is known of Berg's background. Winkler (238) refers to him as "Sam Berg" and writes that "Berg was, I believe, of English descent" (239).
11 The advertisement is reproduced in Altman, *Silent Film Sound*, 350.
12 Martin M. Marks, *Music and the Silent Film: Contexts and Case Studies, 1895–1924* (Oxford: Oxford University Press, 1997), 68.
13 Altman, *Silent Film Sound*, 258. As grounds for comparison, Altman mentions Carl Fischer's 1883 *New York Theatre Orchestra Melodramatic Music*, which contains works with such titles as "Battle," "Rustic," "Hunting Piece," and "Storm Tempest," and he notes that "shortly after the turn of the century, Fischer distributed several 'Theatrical Budgets' by L.O. De Witt and an annual *Dramatic Music* volume with compositions by Theodore Bendix and arrangements by the period's most prolific descriptive music composer, Theodore Moses-Tobani" (258). Older examples of music for melodrama can be found in David Mayer and Matthew Scott, *Four Bars of "Agit": Incidental Music for Victorian and Edwardian Melodrama* (London: Samuel French, 1983).
14 Advertisement in *Moving Picture Weekly*, October 1, 1910; reproduced in Marks, *Music for the Silent Films*, 70.
15 Advertisement in *Moving Picture Weekly*, July 2, 1910: 36; reproduced in Marks, *Music for the Silent Film*, 69.
16 Advertisement in *Moving Picture Weekly*, October 1, 1910: 815; reproduced in Marks, *Music for the Silent Film*, 70.
17 Title page of *F.B. Haviland's Moving Picture Pianist's Album* and advertisement in *Moving Picture News*, September 2, 1911: 30; quoted in Altman, *Silent Film Sound*, 259.
18 Advertisement from back cover of Lyle B. True, *How and What to Play for Pictures: A Manual and Guide for Pianists* (San Francisco: The Music Supply Co., 1914); quoted in Altman, *Silent Film Sound*, 259.
19 Advertisement from an unnumbered page of an undated *Carl Fischer Analytical Orchestral Guide*, quoted in Altman, *Silent Film Sound*, 259.
20 Altman, *Silent Film Sound*, 261.
21 Ibid., *Silent Film Sound*, 261.
22 G.H. Clutsam, Metzler's *Original Cinema Music, No. 1* (London: Metzler & Co., 1914), preface.
23 Advertisement in *Motion Picture News*, November 13, 1915, 160; reproduced in Altman, *Silent Film Sound*, 356. The albums in the Photo Play series are the *A.B.C. Dramatic Set* (1915–20), the three-volume *A.B.C. Feature Photo-Play Edition* (1917–19), the *A.B.C. Photo Play Concert Edition* (1918), and the *Luz Feature Photo Play Edition* (1919).
24 "Foreword," quoted in Marks, "Film Music: The Material, Literature, and Present State of Research," 317.
25 The pieces were also issued in arrangements, by Richard Tourbié, for piano-violin-cello trio and for large and small orchestra.
26 Roger Manvell and John Huntley, *The Technique of Film Music* (London: Focal Press, 1957), 22.
27 Kurt London, *Film Music* (London: Faber and Faber, 1936), 54.
28 *Motion Picture Moods* was reprinted in 1974 by the Arno Press (New York).
29 Originally published by Belwin, Rapee's *Encyclopedia* was reprinted by the Arno Press (New York) in 1970.
30 Erno Rapee, *Encyclopedia of Music for Pictures* (New York: Belwin, 1925), 25.
31 Altman, *Silent Film Sound*, 368.
32 The Milano Film Company's 1911 five-reel *Dante's Inferno* came with a piano score—based on Boito's opera *Mefistofole*—by Raffaele Caravaglios, and Italia's 1914 twelve-reel *Cabiria* featured an orchestral score by Ildebrando Pizzetti and Manlio Mazza.
33 The American composers for *Homer's Odyssey, Quo Vadis?, The Last Days of Pompeii, Antony and Cleopatra*, and *Spartacus* were, respectively, Edgar Selden, Cecil Copping. Palmer Clark, George Colburn, and Modest Altschuler.
34 Marks, *Music and the Silent Film*, 105.
35 Joseph Carl Breil, "Moving Pictures of the Past and Present," *Metronome*, 1916. Quoted in Marks, *Music and the Silent Film*, 105.

36 Breil, "Original Music in Cabiria"; letter dated July 21, 1914, and printed (n.d.) in the *Pacific Coast Musical Review*. Quoted in Marks, *Music and the Silent Film*, 105.

37 These were *Camille, Mme. Sans-Gêne,* and *Queen Elizabeth*. The first two were distributed in the United States by French-American; the third, a four-reel film starring Sarah Bernhardt, was distributed by Famous Players.

38 These were *The Prisoner of Zenda, Tess of the D'Ubervilles,* and *In the Bishop's Carriage*. Clifford McCarty cites an article from *Motion Picture News,* April 1, 1922, that credits Breil with a total of ten scores for Famous Players films from 1913. Clifford McCarty, *Film Composers in America: A Filmography, 1911–79* (Oxford: Oxford University Press, 2000), 51.

39 Program for Clune's Auditorium, May 24, 1915. Reproduced in Marks, *Music and the Silent Film,* 134.

40 Grace Kingsley, "At the Stage Door," *Los Angeles Times,* February 8, 1915, part 3, 4.

41 For more on the film's still controversial content, see Linda Williams, "Race, Melodrama, and *The Birth of a Nation* (1915)," in *The Silent Cinema Reader,* Lee Grieveson and Peter Krämer, eds., 242–53 (London: Routledge, 2004).

42 *Chicago Examiner,* July 18, 1915. Quoted in Russell Lack, *Twenty-Four Frames Under: A Buried History of Film Music* (London: Quartet Books, 1997), 35.

43 Along with a narrative account of Breil's score, Marks in a series of appendices offers a detailed breakdown of the score's component materials. See Marks, *Music and the Silent Film,* 109–66 and 199–218.

44 Many musical reference books, including the venerable *Harvard Dictionary of Music,* state that the German term "leitmotif" ("leading motif") was coined by Wagner. In his entry on "leitmotif" for the 1980 *New Grove Dictionary of Music and Musicians* (Volume 10, 644), John Warrack writes that the term was first used in F.W. Jähns's 1871 *Carl Maria von Weber in seinem Werken*. Along with Weber, other composers who made use of the idea in advance of Wagner are Mozart, Grétry, Méhul, Spohr, Hoffmann, Marschner, Lortzing, and Schumann. See Warrack, 644–5.

45 The relevant pages of the score, in piano reduction, are reproduced in Marks, *Music and the Silent Film,* 116–8.

46 Manvell and Huntley, *The Technique of Film Music,* 21.

47 Manvell and Huntley, 21–2.

48 Marks, *Music and the Silent Film,* 142–3.

49 Manvell and Huntley, 22.

50 Despite newspaper reports that some of the music for *The Birth of a Nation* was to be penned by Griffith, the director's role seems to have been entirely advisory. See Marks, *Music and the Silent Film,* 139–41.

51 Roy Aitken, with A.P. Nelson, *"The Birth of a Nation" Story* (Middleburg, Va.: Delinger, 1965), 51.

52 Lillian Gish, with Ann Pinchot, *The Movies, Mr. Griffith, and Me* (Englewood Cliffs, N.J.: Prentice-Hall, 1969), 152.

53 Lack, 34.

54 William Darby and Jack Du Bois, *American Film Music: Major Composers, Techniques, Trends, 1915–90* (Jefferson, N.C.: McFarland & Company, 1990), 3.

55 Marks, *Music for Silent Films,* 143.

56 Gerald Mast, *A Short History of the Movies* (New York: Pegasus, 1971), 81–81.

57 Lack, 36.

58 Charles Merrell Berg, *An Investigation of the Motives for and Realization of Music to Accompany the American Silent Film, 1896–1927* (New York: Arno Press, 1976), 150.

59 These included, along with the Italian epics, Universal's *Traffic in Souls* and *Where Are My Children?* and a travelogue based on an expedition to the South Pole.

60 Fred., "Road Show Pictures to Date," *Variety,* December 29, 1926, 14.

61 Ibid.

62 "6 Road-Show Films' History," *Variety,* February 1, 1928, 9.

63 George Beynon, "Demand the Best in Cue Sheets," *Moving Picture World,* March 16, 1918, 1513. Quoted in Altman, *Silent Film Sound,* 353.

64 M.M. Hansford, "Music and the Motion Picture," *Metronome*, September 1919, 86. Quoted in Altman, *Silent Film Sound*, 353.
65 Winkler, 235.
66 Altman, *Silent Film Sound*, 353.
67 Berg, 154.
68 Winkler, 237.
69 Altman, *Silent Film Sound*, 354.
70 Berg, *An Investigation*, 156–8.
71 Horace Fuld, "Exhibiting the Picture," *New York Dramatic Mirror*, January 14, 1914, 54.
72 "How Music Is Made to Fit the Film," *Literary Digest*, January 26, 1918, 58.
73 Harold Vincent Milligan, "Look, Listen and Thrill!" *Woman's Home Companion*, July 1920, 13.
74 Winkler, 235–6.
75 Winkler, 236.
76 Winkler, 237.
77 Hugo Riesenfeld, "Music and the Motion Pictures," *Annals of the American Academy of Political and Social Science*, November 1926, 60.
78 Riesenfeld, 61.
79 Riesenfeld, 62.
80 Riesenfeld, 61.
81 Ibid.

Chapter 5

1 Quoted in "Who's Who in the Film Game," *The Nickelodeon* 4, no. 3 (August 1, 1910), 64.
2 Ibid.
3 See Chapter 3, pp. 36.
4 "Who's Who in the Film Game," 64.
5 An account of the restored "Dickson Experimental Sound Film," presented in June 1998 as part of the Domitor conference in Washington, D.C., is offered by Patrick Loughney in "Domitor Witnesses the First Complete Public Presentation of the [*Dickson Experimental Sound Film*] in the Twentieth Century," in *The Sounds of Early Cinema*, ed. Richard Abel and Rick Altman (Bloomington: Indiana University Press, 2001): 215–19.
6 Photographs taken ca. 1895 at Kinetoscope parlors show patrons pressing their faces to the peephole while wearing earpieces that look very much like the "buds" familiar to today's iPod users.
7 W.K.L. Dickson and Antonia Dickson, *The History of the Kinetograph, Kinetoscope, and Kineto-phonograph* (New York: Albert Bunn, 1895), 8. Quoted in Loughney, 216.
8 In *The Coming of Sound* (New York and London: Routledge, 2005), film historian Douglas Gomery states emphatically that the idea that Dickson in 1889 successfully demonstrated a kineto-phonograph is "a myth" that has been "repeated in the standard literature" (159, note 3). Edison's first successful linkage of recorded sound and motion picture, Gomery writes, did not come until the earphone-equipped Kinetoscope products of 1895, but "the machines did not become popular enough to justify the extra expense," and the project was soon abandoned (24–5).
9 Citing a vintage book on sound film—Harold B. Franklin's *Sound Motion Pictures* (Garden City, N.Y.: Doubleday, Doran & Co., 1929)—Rosalind Rogoff notes that an 1892 system called the Chronophotophone involved 'magic lantern' slide projections accompanied by a phonograph. Rosalind Rogoff, "Edison's Dream: A Brief History of the Kinetophone," *Cinema Journal* 15, no. 2 (Spring 1976), 59.
10 Tom Gunning, "Doing for the Eye What the Phonograph Does for the Ear," in *The Sounds of Early Cinema*, Richard Abel and Rick Altman, eds. (Bloomington: Indiana University Press, 2001), 13. Without explanation, Gunning gives both 1880 and 1886 as the novel's dates; in his 2000 *Sound Technology and the American Cinema* (New York: Columbia

University Press), James Lastra states that the novel was begun in 1878, completed in 1886, and published in 1889 (18 and 225, note 7).

In discussions of film history, the first mention of *L'Eve future* seems to have been by André Bazin in a 1946 review of Georges Sadoul's *Histoire génerale du cinéma*, revised as "The Myth of Total Cinema" and included in the 1967 collection *What Is Cinema?* Along with *L'Eve future*, Gunning in his own survey of literary origins of "myths of total cinema" also mentions Jules Verne's 1892 *Le château des Carpathes* and—because of its characters' fascination with the idea of disembodied sound—the American novelist Charles Brockden Brown's 1799 *Wieland, or the Transformation.*

11 Benjamin's landmark essay "The Work of Art in the Age of Mechanical Reproduction" first appeared in 1936 in the *Zeitschrift für Sozialforschung*. Translated by Harry Zohn, it is included in Benjamin's *Illuminations: Essays and Reflections* (New York: Harcourt Brace Jovanovich, 1968), 217–51. The essay's sections xi, xii, and xiii deal in some detail with the sound film.

12 Quoted in Scott Eyman, *The Speed of Sound: Hollywood and the Talkie Revolution, 1926–30* (New York: Simon & Schuster, 1997), 26.

13 Ibid.

14 "Reserved His Decision," *New York Times*, June 20, 1895, 6.

15 Ibid. The report continues: "[The magistrate] seemed very much interested in it, and when he had got enough of it, he gave way for the learned counsel in court to satisfy their curiosity by a peep into the marvelous machine."

16 Fuller (1862–1928) began her career as a burlesque and circus dancer. She became famous ca. 1890 for dances involving costumes of flowing silk and multi-colored lighting effects.

17 Various sources say that the 1900 Paris Exposition featured such devices, but only Gaumont's Chronophone is named.

18 The concept of phonograph horns "powered" by compressed air originated in England with Charles Parson's 1902 Auxetophone.

19 For an account of the friction between Gaumont's Chronophone attractions and the Parisian cabaret/theater culture ca. 1905, see Edouard Arnoldy, trans. Franck Le Gac and Wendy Schubring, "The Event and the Series: The Decline of *Cafés-Concerts*, the Failure of Gaumont's Chronophone, and the Birth of Cinema as an Art," in *The Sounds of Early Cinema*, 57–65.

20 "The Drama—Players, Playhouses, Gossip of the Stage," *New York Times*, July 12, 1908, III1. An earlier report in the same newspaper, from June 18, 1908 (II5), advises: "'Lohengrin,' 'Lakme' and 'Orpheus' are the operatic exceprts delivered at Fischer's Chronophone Theater this week."

21 Arnoldy, "The Event and the Series," 59.

22 For a summary of Gaumont's stated reasons for his abandonment of the Chronophone, see *Moving Picture World*, March 27, 1909, 362, and 369.

23 The audio recordings were made at the Columbia Records facility; the video recordings were made in a studio space on the top floor of Daly's Theater at 30th Street and Broadway. *Moving Picture World*, April 25, 1908, 369–70.

24 *Moving Picture World*, March 20, 1909, 328.

25 Eyman, *The Speed of Sound*, 28.

26 Whereas most nickelodeon-era films cost distributors ten or eleven cents per foot, the Cameraphone products were priced as high as twenty cents per foot. Gomery, *The Coming of Sound*, 26.

27 "The Nation-Wide Wave of Moving Pictures," *New York Times*, January 3, 1909, SM10. The Cameraphone photograph, one of five photographs that accompany the unsigned article, clearly depicts an audio recording. With an acoustic horn featured prominently in the right foreground of a casually cluttered room, it shows a half-dozen men in shirts and ties apparently singing at the behest of a man who, one presumes, serves as their conductor. Why the singers, in what looks to be an audio-only recording session, are all raising their right arms remains a mystery.

28 "Bankruptcy Notices," *New York Times*, August 19, 1909, 13.

29 "American Cinephone Shown," *New York Times*, February 25, 1910, 7.

30   *Moving Picture World*, August 20, 1910, 415.
31   For details on many of these, see Rick Altman, *Silent Film Sound* (New York: Columbia University Press, 2004), 158–75.
32   The Edison quotation at the head of this chapter is drawn from a trade-press article prompted by the Kinetophone demonstrations.
33   "Motion Pictures Are Made to Talk," *New York Times*, August 27, 1910, 8.
34   "Edison's Latest Invention," *Los Angeles Times*, August 28, 1910, 19.
35   "Edison in a New Triumph," *Chicago Daily Tribune*, August 27, 1910, 5.
36   "New York Applauds the Talking Picture," *New York Times*, February 18, 1913, 3.
37   Ibid.
38   Hector Alliott, "'Siren' Pleases Great Crowd/Carroll McComas Shines in Comedy at Mason/'Witching Hour' Second Week at Morosco/Edison Kinetophone a Success at the Orpheum," *Los Angeles Times*, March 18, 1913, III1.
39   "The Kinetophone," *New York Times*, January 5, 1913, 16.
40   "Tries Out Kinetophone," *Los Angeles Times*, January 3, 1913, 11.
41   Percy Hammond, "Edison the Headline in Two Theaters," *Chicago Daily Tribune*, February 20, 1913, 14.
42   Ibid.
43   For details, see *Moving Picture World*, June 28, 1913, 1347.
44   Rogoff, "Edison's Dream: A Brief History of the Kinetophone," 61.
45   Gomery, *The Coming of Sound*, 27.
46   In a long endnote affixed to the "Films That Talk" chapter of his *Silent Film Sound* (409–10), Altman cites a number of period sources that specify the Kinetophone's "listening" range.
47   Eyman, *The Speed of Sound*, 35.
48   "Dehumanizing the Stage," *Current Opinion*, April 4, 1913, 297–8 (quoting an article first published in the *New York Dramatic Mirror*).
49   This is not to say that producers of early sound-films did not occasionally attempt longer projects. Edison issued at least two four-reel Kinetophone films (see Altman, *Silent Film Sound*, 175), and the Vivaphone Company exhibited a multi-reel, multi-disc version of *Faust* that lasted forty-six minutes (see Rogoff, "Edison's Dream," 66).
50   Epes Winthrop Sargent, "Photoplaywright," *Moving Picture World*, March 1, 1913, 881.
51   Headline in *Variety*, March 1913, quoted in Eyman, 35.
52   Douglas Gomery, "The Coming of Sound: Technological Changes in the American Film Industry," in *Film Sound: Theory and Practice*, 7.
53   "Motion Picture Men Sued as a Trust," *New York Times*, August 17, 1912, 6.
54   "Orders Movie Trust to Be Broken Up," *New York Times*, October 2, 1915, 17.
55   Numerous recent books detail the early years of the Hollywood film industry. See, for example, Eileen Bowser, *The Transformation of Cinema, 1907–15* (New York: Charles Scribner's Sons, 1990); John Bengston, *Silent Echoes: Discovering Early Hollywood through the Films of Buster Keaton* (Santa Monica: Santa Monica Press, 2000); and Joel W. Finler, *The Hollywood Story* (London: Wallflower Press, 2003). One of the earliest, and most thorough, accounts is Clifford M. Zierer, "Hollywood—World Center of Motion Picture Production," *Annals of the American Academy of Political and Social Science*, 254 (November 1947), 12–17.
56   Robert Grau, *The Theatre of Science* (New York: Broadway Publishing Co, 1914), 350.
57   "Motion Picture Men Sued as a Trust."
58   Austin C. Lescarboura, *Behind the Motion Picture Screen* (New York: Scientific American Publishing Company, 1921). Quoted in Eyman, 37.
59   Donald Crafton, in *The Talkies: American Cinema's Transition to Sound, 1926–31* (Berkeley: University of California Press, 1997), states that Lauste was a native of England (51). Scott Eyman, in *The Speed of Sound*, writes that Lauste was born, in 1856, in the Montmartre district of Paris (30).
60   Crafton, *The Talkies*, 31. For more on this, see Gerald F.J. Tyne, *Saga of the Vacuum Tube* (Indianapolis: Sams, 1977).
61   Gomery, *The Coming of Sound*, 31–2.

62 Leo Enticknap, "De Forest Phonofilms: A Reappraisal," *Early Popular Visual Culture* 4, no. 3 (November 2006), 277. The de Forest comment, quoted by Enticknap, is from p. 676 of a typewritten manuscript archived at History San Jose in San Jose, California.

63 Details on developments at Western Electric and at Bell Laboratories, an AT&T division founded in 1924, are given in Frank H. Lovette and Stanley Watkins, "Twenty Years of Talking Movies," *Bell Telephone Magazine*, Summer 1946: 84–9.

64 Quoted in Eyman, *The Speed of Sound*, 43.

Chapter 6

1 William Fox, quoted in "Another New Miracle—William Fox, Now Owner of Roxy Theatre, Predicts Talking Photoplays," *New York Times*, April 3, 1927, X7.

2 Enticknap, "De Forest Phonofilms: A Reappraisal," 273. Enticknap explores this idea more thoroughly in pp. 89–119 of his *Moving Image Technology: From Zoetrope to Digital* (London: Wallflower Press, 2005).

3 Gomery, *The Coming of Sound*, 36. The first two sets of brackets are Gomery's; the third set of brackets is added. Both quotations derive from depositions given in conjunction with legal proceedings that took place in 1937. For exact sources, see Gomery, 160, notes 48 and 49.

4 Ron Hutchinson, "The Vitaphone Project: Answering Harry Warner's Question: 'Who the Hell Wants to Hear Actors Talk?'" *Film History* 14, no. 1 (2002), 40. Hutchinson does not give the source of the quotation.

5 Mordaunt Hall, "Vitaphone Stirs as Talking Movie," *New York Times*, August 7, 1926, 6. Hutchinson (41) suggests that Smeck's performance involved not guitar but banjo, and Gomery (38) suggests it involved both banjo and harmonica.

6 Ibid.

7 After working as a conductor for Broadway shows, in 1921 Axt joined the music staff of New York's Capitol Theatre. One his first original film scores, in that year, was for the revival of D.W. Griffith's *The Birth of a Nation*. Later, with Mendoza, Axt created scores for such 'road show' films as *The Sea Hawk* (First National, 1924), *The Big Parade* (MGM, 1925), and *Ben-Hur* (MGM, 1925). Orchestration of the *Don Juan* score, as had been the case with *The Big Parade* and *Ben-Hur*, was by Maurice Baron. The opening credits of *Don Juan* say that the accompaniment is performed by the New York Philharmonic; an unsigned October 24, 1926 report in the *Los Angeles Times* ("Science Endows Silent Drama with Voice," B6) attributes the conducting to Hadley, but this statement seems based only on supposition; considering Axt's extensive experience as a film accompanist, it is far more likely that Axt, not Hadley, did the conducting.

8 Hall, "Vitaphone Stirs as Talking Movie."

9 "Demand Royalties on Vitaphone Songs," *New York Times*, August 24, 1926, 19.

10 "May Settle on Royalties—Vitaphone Dispute Likely Not to Go into Court," *New York Times*, August 25, 1926, 19.

11 "Warner Bros. Market Hit," *Los Angeles Times*, August 26, 1926, 14.

12 According to the printed program (reproduced in Crafton, *The Talkies*, 84), the music was "by Herman Heller, assisted by Maurice Baron, Fred Heff and Dr. Edward Kilenyi." Clifford McCarty, in his generally reliable *Film Composers in America: A Filmography, 1911–70* (Oxford: Oxford University Press, 2000), credits the score only to Baron (35).

13 Harry Warner, quoted by Herbert Moulton in "Silent Drama Is Audible—Vitaphone May Revolutionize Screen Technique Through Demand for Good Speaking Voice," *Los Angeles Times*, September 12, 1926, C17.

14 "Projection Jottings," *New York Times*, April 24, 1927, X5.

15 Grace Kingsley, "Al Jolson Signs with Warners," *Los Angeles Times*, May 26, 1927, A8.

16 After *The Better 'Ole*, other Warner Bros. Vitaphone features were *When A Man Loves* (November 1926, music by Henry Hadley), *Old San Francisco* (June 22, 1927, music by Hugo Riesenfeld), and *The First Auto Race* (June 28, 1927).

17 In part an original composition and in part a pastiche of familiar musical tropes, the score is the work of Louis Silvers.

18   In two of these cases, the spoken words amount to asides likely improvised by Jolson in the course of delivery of songs. In one case, however, a single spoken word—an angry "stop!" voiced by the father of the title character—is obviously scripted.

19   The character of the jazz singer's father, a cantor, sings the "Kol Nidre" and a mourning song called "Yahrzeit Licht." Just before the climactic scene, Jolson's character also sings the "Kol Nidre." Early in the film, before the character of Jackie Rabinowitz leaves home in order to pursue a stage career under the name Jack Robin, the audience witnesses a child actor miming his way—rather poorly—through fictional saloon performances of "My Gal Sal" and "Waiting for the Robert E. Lee."

20   Alan Williams, "Historical and Theoretical Issues in the Coming of Recorded Sound to the Cinema," in *Sound Theory/Sound Practice*, ed. Rick Altman (London: Routledge, 1992), 130.

21   Quoted in A. Scott Berg, *Goldwyn: A Biography* (New York: Knopf, 1989), 173.

22   James W. Elliott, "Studios Spend Millions in Talkie Construction," *Los Angeles Times*, August 5, 1928, E1.

23   Ibid., E2.

24   Alan Williams, "Historical and Theoretical Issues in the Coming of Recorded Sound to the Cinema," in *Sound Theory/Sound Practice*, ed. Rick Altman (London: Routledge, 1992), 132–3.

25   Ibid., 133.

26   Samuel Goldwyn, quoted by Mordaunt Hall in "Goldwyn Urges Caution," *New York Times*, August 5, 1928, 96.

27   John MacCormac, "Sight and Sound," *New York Times*, June 24, 1928, X3.

28   Ibid.

29   Ibid.

30   *Film-Kurier* 172, July 20, 1928. Available on-line at www.filmportal.de. No translator is named.

31   S.M. Eisenstein, V.I. Pudovkin, and G.V, Alexandrov, "A Statement," trans. Jay Leyda, in *Film Sound: Theory and Practice*, Elisabeth Weis and John Belton, eds. (New York: Columbia University Press, 1985), 83. The "Statement" was first published in the Leningrad magazine *Novij Lef* on August 5, 1928.

32   Ibid., 83–5. Emphases original.

33   Translator Jay Leyda maintains that the "Statement" is largely "of historic interest" and that it had little impact, in fact, on Soviet films in the early 1930s. See Jay Leyda, *Kino* (New York: Collier Books, 1973), 279. Kristin Thompson argues that the only truly "countrapuntal" Soviet films were Dziga Vertov's 1931 *Enthusiasm* and Vsevolod Pudovkin's 1933 *Deserter*. Nevertheless, Thompson writes, "sound-image disjunction" is found at least to a certain extent in such Soviet films as *Alone, Deserter, Enthusiasm, The Road to Life, Outskirts, The Great Consoler, Lieutenant Kizhe, Revolt of the Fishermen,* and *Three Songs of Lenin*. See Kristin Thompson, "Early Sound Counterpoint," *Yale French Studies* 60 (1980), 116–17.

34   For a collection of his often politically charged work, see *The Compound Cinema: Selected Film Writings of Harry Alan Potamkin*, Lewis Jacobs, ed. (New York: Teachers College Press, 1977).

35   Harry Alan Potamkin, "Music and the Movies," *The Musical Quarterly* 15, no. 2 (April 1929), 295–6.

36   René Clair, "The Art of Sound," trans. Vera Traill, in *Film Sound: Theory and Practice*, Elisabeth Weis and John Belton, eds. (New York: Columbia University Press, 1985), 92. Weis and Belton do not give the source of the Clair piece, and they suggest—as do other anthologists and citers—that "The Art of Sound" was originally written as an essay. According to Richard Barrios in *A Song in the Dark; The Birth of the Musical Film* (Oxford: Oxford University Press, 1995), 68, it was originally "a letter home." The document first appeared in print in Clair's *Réflexion faite. Notes pour servir à l'histoire de l'art cinématographique de 1920 à 1951* (Paris: Gallimard, 1951); the English version dates from 1953, when the entire book was translated by Traill as *Reflections on Cinema* (London: Kimber, 1953).

37   Ibid., 93–4.

38   Ibid., 94–5.

39   Ibid., 92.

40   Ibid.

41   Des O'Rawe, "The Great Secret: Silence, Cinema and Modernism," *Screen* 47, no. 4 (Winter 2006), 399.

42   Aaron Sultanik, *Film: A Modern Art* (Cranbury, N.J.: Cornwall Books, 1986), 60.

43   The term "silent sound film" likely was coined by Noël Carroll in "Lang, Pabst, and Sound," *Ciné-Tracts* 2, no. 1 (Fall 1978): 15–23. Under the title "Lang and Pabst: Paradigms for Early Sound Practice," the article appears in *Film Sound: Theory and Practice*, ed. Elisabeth Weis and John Belton, 265–76 (New York: Columbia University Press, 1985).

44   This should not to be confused with Georg Wilhelm Pabst's 1930 *Westfront 1918*, a silent film that was not retrofitted with sound until 1935.

45   Regarding Hitchcock's *Blackmail*, for example, see John Belton, "Awkward Transitions: Hitchcock's *Blackmail* and the Dynamics of Early Film Sound," *Musical Quarterly* 83, no. 2 (1999): 227–46; and Charles Barr, "*Blackmail*: Silent and Sound," *Sight and Sound* 52, no. 2 (1983): 189–93; and chapter 2, ("First Experiments with Sound: *Blackmail* and *Murder*," pp. 28–62) of Elisabeth Weis's *The Silent Scream: Hitchcock's Soundtrack* (Rutherford, N.J.: Farleigh Dickinson University Press, 1982). Regarding Vertov's *Entuziazm* and other early Soviet sound films, see Kristin Thompson, "Early Sound Counterpoint," *Yale French Studies* 60 (1980): 115–40; regarding von Sternberg's *Der Blaue Engel*, see Geoffrey Wagner, "*The Blue Angel*: A Reconsideration," *The Quarterly Review of Film, Radio and Television* 6, no. 1 (Autumn 1951): 48–53. Regarding Milestone's *All Quiet on the Western Front*, see John Whiteclay Chamber II, "*All Quiet on the Western Front* (1930): The Antiwar Film and the Image of the First World War," *Historical Journal of Film, Radio and Television* 14, no. 4 (1994): 377–411. Regarding the early sound films of René Clair, see R.C. Dale, "A Clash of Intelligences: Sound vs. Image in Rene Clair's 'A nous, la liberté,'" *The French Review* 38, no. 5 (April 1965): 637–44; Lucy Fischer, "René Clair, *Le Million*, and the Coming of Sound." *Cinema Journal* 16, no. 2 (Spring 1977): 34–50; Dudley Andrew, "Sound in France: The Origins of a Native School." *Yale French Studies* 60 (1980): 94–114; chapter 7 ("Music and Sound Space in *Sous les toits de Paris*," pp. 140–50) of Claudia Gorbman's *Unheard Melodies: Narrative Film Music* (Bloomington: Indiana University Press, 1987); and Michel Marie, "'Let's Sing It One More Time': René Clair's *Sous les toits de Paris*," in *French Film: Texts and Contexts*, ed. Susan Hayward and Ginette Vincendeau (London: Routledge, 1990): 51–65.

46   The praises of these films, and others of similar persuasion, were generously sung in the journal called *Close Up*. For examples of contemporaneous criticism, see the writings anthologized in *Close Up, 1927–33: Cinema and Modernism*, ed. James Donald, Anne Friedberg, and Laura Marcus (London: Cassell, 1998).

47   Ernest Marshall, "London Film Notes—Good and Bad Points of 'Blackmail,' Britain's First Talking Feature," *New York Times*, August 11, 1929, X5.

48   "Talkie Development," *New York Times*, August 14, 1929, 14.

49   "Britain's First Talking Film," *New York Times*, October 7, 1929, 29. In the context of the newspaper's coverage of films, this review is something of an anomaly. The norm was for reviews to be signed and to appear immediately after a film's opening; this review is not signed, and it followed *Blackmail*'s New York premiere—at the Selwyn Theater on September 20, 1929—by more than two weeks.

50   Mordaunt Hall, "The Screen—A French Audible Production," *New York Times*, December 16, 1930, 36.

51   Kenneth MacGowan, "When the Talkies Came to Hollywood," *The Quarterly of Film, Radio and Television* 10, no. 3 (Spring 1956), 288.

52   Mordaunt Hall, "Movietone Shown in the Fox Studio," *New York Times*, January 6, 1927, 27.

53   Norbert Lusk, "'Movietone' Is Given Showing," *Los Angeles Times*, May 8, 1927, 17.

54 The music for Fox's *Mother Knows Best* was composed by William Kernell, Erno Rapee, and S.L. Rothafel.
55 The music for *Steamboat Willie* was compiled by Disney animator Wilfred Jackson. *Steamboat Willie* was not the first animated cartoon to feature synchronized recorded sound; the Phonofilm technology had been applied to Max Fleischer's "Song Car-Tune" series since 1924. For more on music in early animated cartoons, see Daniel Goldmark, *Tunes for 'Toons: Music and the Hollywood Cartoon* (Berkeley: University of California Press, 2005), 10–21; and Ross Care, "Make Walt's Music: Music for Disney Animation, 1928–67," in *The Cartoon Music Book*, ed. Daniel Goldmark and Yuval Taylor (Chicago: A Cappella Books, 2002), 21–36.
56 Mordaunt Hall, "The Screen," *New York Times*, November 19, 1928, 16.
57 "Big Film Producers Adopt 'Movietone,'" *New York Times*, May 16, 1928, 27. The article notes that First National Pictures, Universal, and Keith-Albee-Orpheum will soon adopt the Movietone technology.
58 Preston J. Hubbard, "Synchronized Sound and Movie-House Musicians, 1926–9," *American Music 3*, no. 4 (Winter 1985), 433. As sources for his quotations, Hubbard cites articles that appeared in *Variety* on June 13, 1928, and in the *New York Times* on July 15 and July 30, 1928.
59 M.B., "'Talking Films Bettered"/"Sound Films Are Improved," *Los Angeles Times*, December 25, 1927, C17, C21.
60 Hubbard, "Synchronized Sound and Movie-House Musicians, 1926–9," 433. Emphasis added.
61 Hubbard, 438.
62 *Variety*, August 15, 1928; paraphrased in Hubbard, 435.
63 E.I. Sponable, "Historical Development of Sound Films," a paper presented at the annual meeting of the Society of Motion Picture Editors (SMPE) in Hollywood on October 22, 1946. Sponable, an engineer importantly involved in the development of sound-film technology, stated that in December 1929 "there were 234 different types of theater sound equipments in use" and that "most of these, produced by the independents, were for sound-on disc." He also stated that by this time "the total number of theaters equipped for sound of all makes in the United States was 8,741." Of these installations, he stated, "ERPI and RCA [which manufactured the equipment] had provided 4,393."
64 Gomery, *The Coming of Sound*, 92.
65 Ibid.
66 Kenneth MacGowan, "The Coming of Sound to the Screen," *The Quarterly of Film, Radio and Television* 10, no. 2 (Winter 1955), 145. MacGowan draws his figures from the *Film Daily Year Book* for 1929.
67 "Musical Unemployment," *New York Times*, February 28, 1930, A4.
68 Film historian Douglas Gomery, in *The Coming of Sound*, writes: "Beginning in September 1930 talkies had taken over the movie industry, with the silent film rendered instantly obsolete" (87). But Gomery also notes that throughout 1930 "almost one-fourth of all theaters in the United States still could present only silent films" (92); all of these were small theaters in small towns, and the reason for their not converting to sound had nothing to do with aesthetics but simply with the fact in the depressed economic climate they could not afford the cost of conversion. "As late as January 1931," Gomery writes, "some 2.6 percent of the [still] open theaters continued to present only silent films. . . . It took until 1935 to eliminate silent film theaters as they simply closed" (ibid.).
69 "Americans May Pay Paris Piper," *Los Angeles Times*, September 22, 1930, 4. For cultural historians, the report is likely especially interesting because it speculates that American musicians working in Paris feared retaliation. The report says: "At least 80 per cent of the music to which revelers dance in the Montmartre cabarets is furnished by American jazz bands, most of the players being Negroes. They were on the job as usual tonight but all are frankly apprehensive as to whether they will be allowed to continue working in France."
70 Gomery, *The Coming of Sound*, 109.
71 Emily Thompson, "Wiring the World: Acoustical Engineers and the Empire of Sound in the Motion Picture Industry, 1927–30," in *Hearing Cultures: Essays on Sound, Listening and Modernity*, ed. Veit Erlmann (Oxford: Berg, 2006), 191–2.

72   Rachael Low, *The History of the British Film, 1918–29* (Oxford: Routledge, 1997), 203–5.

73   Peter Jelavich, *Berlin Alexanderplatz: Radio, Film, and the Death of Weimar Culture* (Berkeley: University of California Press, 2006), 215–16.

74   Reinhold Wagenleitner, trans. Diana M. Wolf, *Coca-Colonization and the Cold War: The Cultural Mission of the United States in Austria after the Second World War* (Chapel Hill: University of North Carolina Press, 1994), 253.

75   Colin G. Crisp, *The Classic French Cinema, 1930–60* (Bloomington: Indiana University Press, 1997), 102–3.

76   See James Chapman, *Cinemas of the World: Film and Society from 1895 to the Present* (London: Reaktion Books, 2003).

77   Marek Haltof, *Polish National Cinema* (New York and Oxford: Berghahn Books, 2002), 24.

78   Eric Reade, *History and Heartburn: The Saga of Australian Film, 1896–1978* (East Brunswick, N.J.: Associated University Presses, 1979), 79–80.

79   Peter Kenez, *Cinema and Soviet Society from the Revolution to the Death of Stalin* (London and New York: I.B. Tauris, 2001), 121–4; Tatiana K. Egorova, *Soviet Film Music: An Historical Survey*, trans. Tatiana A. Ganf and Natalia A. Egunova (Amsterdam: Harwood Academic Publishers, 1997), 3–18.

80   For more on the function of the *bunraku*-style narrator, or *benshi*, in conjunction with Japanese sound films, see Jeffrey A. Dym, "*Benshi* and the Introduction of Motion Pictures to Japan," *Monumenta Nipponica* 55, no. 4 (Winter 2000): 509–36; and Freda Freiberg, "The Transition to Sound in Japan," in *History on/and/in Film*, ed. Tom O'Regan and Brian Shoesmith, 76–80 (Perth: History & Film Association of Australia, 1987).

81   Noël Burch, *To the Distant Observer: Form and Meaning in the Japanese Cinema* (Berkeley: University of California Press, 1979), 145–6; Joseph L. Anderson and Donald Richie, *The Japanese Film: Art and Industry*, second edition (Princeton: Princeton University Press, 1982), 77.

82   Linda Lai, "Hong Kong Cinema in the 1930s: Docility, Social Hygiene, Pleasure-Seeking and the Consolidation of the Film Industry," *Screening the Past* 11 (November 2000).

83   Ashish Rajadhyaksha and Paul Willemen, *BFI Encyclopedia of Indian Cinema*, revised edition (Oxford and New York: BFI/Oxford University Press, 2002), 254–60; Stephen Putnam Hughes, "Music in the Age of Mechanical Reproduction: Drama, Gramophone, and the Beginnings of Tamil Cinema," *Journal of Asian Studies* 66, no. 1 (February 2007): 3–34. For valuable comments on the introduction of popular song into India's early sound films, see Peter Manuel, "Popular Music in India: 1901–86," *Popular Music* 7, no. 2 (May 1988): 158–62.

84   Arthur Knight, *The Liveliest Art: A Panoramic History of the Movies* (New York: Macmillan, 1957), 188–9.

85   Charles O'Brien, *Cinema's Conversion to Sound: Technology and Film Style in France and the U.S.* (Bloomington: Indiana University Press, 2005), 39.

Chapter 7

1   William Axt, quoted in Philip K. Scheuer, "Musical Picture Quietly Undergoes Renaissance," *Los Angeles Times*, February 22, 1931, B20.

2   Kristin Thompson, *Exporting Entertainment: America in the World Film Market, 1907–34* (London: British Film Institute, 1985), 219–21.

3   Ibid., 164.

4   Douglas Gomery, "Economic Struggle and Hollywood Imperialism: Europe Converts to Sound," in *Film Sound: Theory and Practice*, Elisabeth Weis and John Belton, eds. (New York: Columbia University Press, 1985), 27.

5   For a detailed and intriguing account on the production of what in the American industry were known as FLVs (foreign language versions), see Nataša Ďurovičová, "Translating America: the Hollywood Multilinguals 1929–33," in *Sound Theory/Sound Practice*, ed. Rick Altman (London: Routledge, 1992), 138–53.

6   For more on the political intricacies of "dubbing" during the early years of the sound film, see Antje Ascheid, "Speaking Tongues: Voice Dubbing in Cinema as Cultural Ventriloquism," *The Velvet Light Trap* 40 (Fall 1997): 32–41; and Agnieszka Szarkowska, "The Power of Film Translation," *Translation Journal* 9, no. 2 (April 2005), available online at http://accurapid.com/journal/32film.htm.

7   Rié Kitada, "L'exploitation et la réception des films à Laussanne (Suisse) au moment du passage de muet au parlant: Une histoire de la naissance des sous-tites et du doublage," *CineMagaziNet! Online Research Journal of Cinema* 4 (September 8, 2000), 18.

8   Anna Sofia Rossholm, *Reproducing Languages, Translating Bodies: Approaches to Speech, Translation and Cultural Identity in Early European Sound Film* (Stockholm: Almqvist & Wiksell International. 2006), 107.

9   Quoted in Eyman, 332.

10 Béla Balázs, *Theory of the Film: Character and Growth of a New Art*, trans. Edith Bone (London: Dennis Dobson Ltd., 1952), 227. Balázs, who lived from 1884 until 1949, wrote the book in Hungarian (as *Filmkultúra*); the English translation was its first publication.

11 Joseph M. Schenck, "Millions in Celluloid—An Industrial Survey of Motion Pictures," *Los Angeles Times*, January 2, 1930, D14.

12 Ibid.

13 Ibid.

14 Crafton, *The Talkies*, 5. Crafton refers to the "short but persuasive" chapter, titled "The Introduction of Sound" and apparently authored by Bordwell alone, in Bordwell's, Janet Staiger's, and Kristin Thompson's *The Classical Hollywood Cinema: Film Style and Mode of Production to 1960* (New York: Columbia University Press, 1985). Similar statements, with reference to Bordwell, can be found in Douglas Gomery's *The Coming of Sound* (139) and Charles O'Brien's *Cinema's Conversion to Sound* (51–2).

15 For details on Warner Bros.' acquisition of music publishing companies, see Crafton, *The Talkies*, 195–6.

16 Muriel Babcock, "Tin Pan Alley Invades Town," *Los Angeles Times*, December 9, 1928, C13 and C24.

17 Production costs were only $280,000.

18 "Background of Melody Now Passe," *Los Angeles Times*, March 3, 1929, C33.

19 Ibid.

20 "Sound Pictures Often Use 60,000 Sheets of Music," *Los Angeles Times*, March 3, 1929, C27.

21 David Mendoza, "The Theme Song," *American Hebrew*, March 15, 1929, 124.

22 "Sound Pictures Often Use 60,000 Sheets of Music," C27.

23 Muriel Babcock, "Picture Music Trend Viewed," *Los Angeles Times*, July 7, 1929, 17.

24 Philip K. Scheuer, "Classics May Go to Screen—Present Trend to Light Music Passing Phase," *Los Angeles Times*, August 18, 1929, 13.

25 Ibid.

26 Ibid.

27 Edwin Schallert, "Screen Music Made by Rule," *Los Angeles Times*, December 8, 1929, 21.

28 Nathaniel Finston, quoted in Schallert, "Screen Music Made by Rule," 21.

29 Schallert, "Screen Music Made by Rule," 21.

30 *The Vagabond King* was based on Rudolf Friml's 1925 operetta of the same title. Friml of course remained the primary composer, but the film also includes music by W. Franke Harling, John Leipold, Oscar Potoker, Herman Hand, and Max Terr.

31 Ludwig Berger, quoted in Philip K. Scheuer, "Orchestrated Actor Latest," *Los Angeles Times*, March 2, 1930, B11–12.

32 For figures on film production in 1929 and 1930, see Patrick Robertson, *Film Facts* (New York: Billboard Books, 2001), 17; and Kenneth MacGowan, "The Coming of Sound to the Screen," *The Quarterly of Film, Radio and Television* 10, no. 2 (Winter 1955), 145. For detailed information on early Hollywood musicals, see Jane Feuer, *The Hollywood Musical* (Bloomington: Indiana University Press, 1993), and Thomas S. Hischak, *Through the Screen Door: What Happened to the Broadway Musical When It Went to Hollywood* (Lanham, Md.: Scarecrow Press, 2004). For a generally accepted definition of "musical," see Rick Altman, *The American Film Musical* (Bloomington: Indiana University Press, 1987).

33 Robert Crawford, quoted in "Talking Films Bring Music to Masses," *Los Angeles Times*, May 4, 1930, B11.
34 Ibid.
35 "Writers of Film Music Optimistic," *Los Angeles Times*, September 21, 1930, B11.
36 In 1931 there were 501 films, of which eleven were "musical"; of the 489 films released in 1932, only ten were "musical."
37 Myrtle Gebhart, "Tin Pan Alley Says Good Bye," *Los Angeles Times*, May 10, 1931, K9.
38 Ibid.
39 Ibid.
40 Gershwin's project, for the Fox studio, was *Delicious*. Released in December 1931, *Delicious* featured not only songs by Gershwin and his lyricist brother, Ira, but also a truncated version of his purely instrumental *Second Rhapsody for Piano and Orchestra*. For details on how the *Rhapsody* was adapted for use in the film, see James Wierzbicki, "The Hollywood Career of Gershwin's Second Rhapsody," *Journal of the American Musicological Society* 60, no. 1 (Spring 2007): 133–86.
   The fee of $50,000—confirmed by Gershwin scholars Charles Schwartz (*Gershwin: His Life & Music* (New York: Da Capo Press, 1973), 89) and Edward Jablonski (*Gershwin* (New York: Doubleday, 1987), 140)—was paid by Universal for use of the *Rhapsody in Blue* in the 1930 film *The King of Jazz*. A year before Universal's biographical treatment of band-leader Paul Whiteman went into production, however, newspaper readers were informed that "the largest offer ever made a song writer took place when Fox, negotiating with George Gershwin, reportedly offered him $100,000 for his 'Rhapsody in Blue.'" See Muriel Babcock, "Tin Pan Alley Invades Town," *Los Angeles Times*, December 9, 1928, C13.
41 Gebhart, "Tin Pan Alley Says Good Bye."
42 Victor Schertzinger, quoted in Gebhart, "Tin Pan Alley Says Good Bye."
43 Gebhart, ibid.
44 Philip K. Scheuer, "Musical Picture Quietly Undergoes Renaissance," *Los Angeles Times*, February 22, 1931, B9.
45 Ibid.
46 Both films were released early in 1931. The score for *Fighting Caravans* was primarily the work of John Leipold, with additional music by Max Bergunker, Emil Bierman, A. Cousminer, Karl Hajos, Herman Hand, Emil Hilb, Sigmund Krumgold, and Oscar Potoker. The score for *Rango* was primarily by Hajos, with additional music by Bergunker, Gerard Carbonara, Hand, W. Franke Harling, Krumgold, Leipold, and George Steiner. See Clifford McCarty, *Film Composers in America: A Filmography, 1911–70* (Oxford: Oxford University Press, 2000), 186 and 125.
47 Scheuer, "Musical Picture Quietly Undergoes Renaissance," B9 and B20.
48 Ibid. B20.
49 Ibid.
50 MGM's *Jenny Lind* was a 1931 re-release, for European markets only, of its 1930 *A Lady's Morals*; offered as a starring vehicle for opera singer Grace Moore, it featured an operetta-style score by William Axt, with additional music drawn from the studio's library of "stock" recordings. Released in 1930, MGM's *The Rogue Song* was a comparable vehicle for tenor Lawrence Tibbett loosely based on Franz Lehár's 1910 operetta *Zigeunerliebe* ("Gypsy Love"); along with Lehár melodies and "stock" recordings, the score features original music by Axt and, to a small extent, Dimitri Tiomkin. See McCarty, 30, and *Halliwell's Film Guide*, eighth edition, ed. John Walker (London: HarperCollins, 1991), 951.
51 William Axt, quoted in Scheuer, "Musical Picture Quietly Undergoes Renaissance," B20.
52 Max Steiner, quoted in Scheuer, "Musical Picture Quietly Undergoes Renaissance," B20.
53 "Musical Pictures Again to be Vogue," *Washington Post*, September 7, 1931, 3.
54 Helen Louise Walker, "Musical Pictures Are Here Again," *Motion Picture Magazine*, November 1931, 53.
55 Ibid., 52.
56 Barry Salt, "Film Style and Technology in the Thirties," in *Film Sound: Theory and Practice*, ed. Elisabeth Weis and John Belton (New York: Columbia University Press, 1985), 42;

the article originally appeared in *Film Quarterly* 30, no. 1 (Autumn 1976). As examples of films whose post-production mix of music and dialogue resulted in seriously degraded sound quality, Salt cites the Laurel and Hardy comedies from 1931–2.

57 Salt, "Film Style and Technology in the Thirties," 43.
58 Ibid.
59 The console had four channels, each equipped with a single rotary pontentiometer and an on/off switch. See Maxwell Steer, "A Brief History of Film Dubbing" (1995), available online at http://msteer.co.uk/analytical/jfilmdubbing1.html.
60 "Music Library Provided on Short Notice," *Los Angeles Times*, June 28, 1931, B13.
61 "Screen Music Being Aided by 'Underscoring,'" *Los Angeles Times*, August 16, 1931, 28.
62 Phil L. Ryan, quoted in "Dominant Position for Films' Music Forecast," *Los Angeles Times*, November 29, 1931, B13.
63 Chapin Hall, "Hollywood Turns to Music in Films," *New York Times*, April 3, 1932, X4.
64 Nacio Herb Brown, quoted in Hall, "Hollywood Turns to Music in Films."
65 Originally produced by Universal in 1932 (starring Tom Mix and with music by Hugo Riesenfeld and Heinz Roemheld), *Destry Rides Again* was re-made by the same studio (with James Stewart in the title role and music by Frank Skinner) in 1939.
66 Hall, "Hollywood Turns to Music in Films."
67 Mary Mayer, "Theme Song Pianissimoed for Bach and Beethoven," *Los Angeles Times*, May 1, 1932, B13–14.
68 Edwin Schallert, "Film Music Experiences Its Sanest Development," *Los Angeles Times*, May 22, 1932, B16.
69 Ibid.
70 Ibid.
71 Isabel Morse Jones, "Studio Music-Makers Set Out for New Achievement," *Los Angeles Times*, January 29, 1933, A2.
72 "Classical Composers Banished from Films," *Los Angeles Times*, October 16, 1932, B10.
73 *King Kong* was released on April 7, 1933. The directors were Merion C. Cooper and Earnest B. Schoedsack; again, the executive producer was David O. Selznick.
74 "Large Band Assembled for Cinema," *Los Angeles Times*, March 8, 1933, A7.

Chapter 8

1 Alfred Newman, quoted in Isabel Morse Jones, "Emotional Power of Music Revealed," *Los Angeles Times*, June 20, 1937, C9.
2 "Large Band Assembled for Cinema," *Los Angeles Times*, March 8, 1933, A7.
3 For commentary on Steiner's music for *King Kong*, see Peter Franklin, "*King Kong* and Film on Music: Out of the Fog," in *Film Music: Critical Approaches*, ed. K.J. Donnelly (New York: Continuum, 2001), 88–102.
4 Based on the same-titled novel by Arthur Conan Doyle, First National's *The Lost World* featured, as did *King Kong*, stop-motion animations of prehistoric creatures. *The Lost World* was a silent film; music for the New York premiere was composed by Cecil Copping, and the release of the film coincided with publication of a "title song" with music by Rudolf Friml and lyrics by Harry B. Smith.
5 Nelson C. Bell, "About the Show Shops," *Washington Post*, March 13, 1033, 14.
6 Nelson C. Bell, "About the Show Shops," *Washington Post*, March 20, 1933, 14. The devices, Bell wrote, included "a machine to create the sibilant roar of the tyrannosaurus" that "occupied about 500 cubic feet of space" and, for "the cataclysmic commotion caused by King Kong's triumphant beating upon his chest," a "sound box 20 by 25 feet in size."
7 Mordaunt Hall, "A Journalist at Large: Lee Tracy's Admirable Acting in 'Clear All Wires'—A Prehistoric Ape," *New York Times*, March 12, 1933, X3.
8 "Lion Proxy for Kong in Sound," *Los Angeles Times*, April 2, 1933, A3.
9 A portion of Steiner's memoir is reproduced in Tony Thomas, *Film Score: A View from the Podium* (South Brunswick, N.J.: A.S. Barnes & Co., 1979), 75–81. Details on the recording sessions—including the size of the orchestra (forty-six players)—are contained in Fred Steiner's liner notes for the Southern Cross recording (SCCD 901) of the *King Kong* score.

10   Max Steiner, unpublished autobiography, quoted in Thomas, *Film Score*, 77.

11   "Thriller 'King Kong' Presages Follows-Up," *Los Angeles Times*, March 19, 1933, A3.

12   Edwin Schallert, "Show Goes on in Hollywood," *Los Angeles Times*, March 8, 1933, A7.

13   "Pictures and Players in Hollywood: Thirty Companies Busy in Various Studios," *New York Times*, March 26, 1933, X3.

14   Gerald Mast, *A Short History of the Movies* (New York: Pegasus, 1971), 272. Mast notes that whereas in 1968 weekly attendance at American movie theaters totaled approximately twenty million, weekly attendance in 1939 was close to eighty million.

15   For a detailed account of technological developments in the mid 1930s, see David Bordwell and Kristin Thompson, "Technological Change and Classical Film Style," in *Grand Design: Hollywood as a Modern Business Enterprise, 1930–9*, ed. Tino Balio (Berkeley: University of California Press, 1995), 109–41.

16   André Bazin, "The Evolution of the Language of Cinema," in *What Is Cinema?* vol. 1, trans. Hugh Gray (Berkeley: University of California Press, 1967), 30.

17   David Bordwell, Janet Staiger, and Kristin Thompson, *The Classical Hollywood Cinema: Film Style and Production to 1960* (London: Routledge & Kegan Paul, 1985), 3–4.

18   Ibid., 1.

19   Susan Hayward, *Cinema Studies: The Key Concepts* (London: Routledge, 2000), 64.

20   Steiner, unpublished autobiography, quoted in Thomas, *Film Score*, 79.

21   Caryl Flinn, "The Most Romantic Art of All: Music in the Classical Hollywood Cinema," *Cinema Journal* 29, no. 4 (Summer 1990), 35. It was only upon the 1992 publication of her book *Strains of Utopia: Gender, Nostalgia, and Hollywood Film Music* that Flinn adopted the spelling of her given name as cited here. Before 1992, she used the given name "Carol."

22   For an insightful account of Hollywood production and marketing practices that developed simultaneous with the classical-style film, see chapter four, "Feeding the Maw of Exhibition," of Tino Balio's *Grand Design: Hollywood as a Modern Business Enterprise, 1930–9* (Berkeley: University of California Press, 1993): 73–107.

23   Kathryn Kalinak, *Settling the Score: Music and the Classical Hollywood Film* (Madison: University of Wisconsin Press, 1992), 113. Using the same film as the basis of her study, Kalinak furthers her argument in "Max Steiner and the Classical Hollywood Film Score: An Analysis of *The Informer*," in *Film Music 1*, ed. Clifford McCarty (Los Angeles: Film Music Society, 1998): 123–42.

24   Claudia Gorbman, *Unheard Melodies: Narrative Film Music* (Bloomington: Indiana University Press, 1987), 73.

25   Gorbman quotes Keats in her epigraph: "Heard melodies are sweet, but those unheard/Are sweeter; therefore, ye soft pipes, play on. . . ."

26   The point is subtler than it first might seem. In a two-page embellishment of this point, Gorbman merely alludes to the fact that among early sound films there are indeed primitive examples in which cables and shadows of overhead microphones are within the camera's view, and she refers not at all to silent film or to opera, during the presentation of which the source of extra-diegetic music would be plainly visible to any audience member who chose to look not at the stage but at the orchestra pit. Most of Gorbman's discussion involves classical-style films in which diegetic music from an on-screen source (for example, a café ensemble somehow metamorphoses into extra-diegetic music whose source (typically a symphony orchestra) remains off-screen. Gorbman also briefly discusses cases in which, for comic effect, the relationship between "visible" diegetic music and "invisible" extra-diegetic music is deliberately inverted. In this regard, she mentions directors Mel Brooks and Woody Allen but cites only Brooks's *Blazing Saddles* (1974), in the course of which a suitably "western"-sounding underscore is shown to be coming, in fact, from Count Basie's jazz band. Brooks's 1977 *High Anxiety* features a comparable scene in which a sudden burst of tension-filled symphonic music is "shown" to be coming from a bus carrying a touring orchestra; likewise, Allen's 1971 *Bananas* features a scene in which apparently extra-diegetic music suggestive of a reverie is "shown" to be coming from a harpist who had been practicing in a hotel closet.

263

27 Leonid Sabaneev (trans. S.W. Pring), *Music for the Films: A Handbook for Composer and Conductors* (London: Pitman, 1935), 22.

28 Rita McAllister, "Sabaneyev, Leonid Leonidovich," in *The New Grove Dictionary of Music and Musicians* (London and New York: Macmillan, 1980), volume XVI, 363–4.

29 Apparently based in Glasgow, S.W. Pring between 1929 and the early 1940s translated from Russian numerous articles for such publications as *The Musical Quarterly*, *Music & Letters*, and *The Musical Times*.

30 Fred Steiner, who earned his Ph.D. in musicology at the University of Southern California with a dissertation on the scoring practices of Alfred Newman, wrote music for numerous films and for such television series as *The Twilight Zone*, *Gunsmoke*, and *Star Trek*. He is no relation to the film composer Max Steiner.

31 Fred Steiner, "What Were Musicians Saying about Movie Music during the First Decade of Sound? A Symposium of Selected Writings," in *Film Music I*, ed. by Clifford McCarty (Los Angeles: The Film Music Society, 1989), 94.

32 Fred Steiner, ibid., 91–2.

33 Ibid., 92.

34 Ibid.

35 Gorbman, *Unheard Melodies*, 73.

36 Max Steiner, unpublished autobiography, quoted in Thomas, *Film Score*, 81.

37 These include, in chronological order of publication, Oscar Levant's *A Smattering of Ignorance* (1939), George Antheil's *Bad Boy of Music* (1945), Dimitri Tiomkin's *Please Don't Hate Me* (1959), Miklós Rózsa's *Double Life: The Autobiography of Miklós Rózsa* (1982), Henry Mancini's *Did They Mention the Music?* (1989), and André Previn's *No Minor Chords: My Days in Hollywood* (1991).

38 Gorbman, *Unheard Melodies*, 73.

39 Ibid., 81.

40 Ibid., 73.

41 Ibid., 84.

42 Ibid., 73.

43 Ibid.

44 Curiously, neither "film studies" nor "cinema studies" is defined in the admirably thorough dictionary-like *Cinema Studies: The Key Concepts*, ed. Susan Hayward (London: Routledge, 2000). In one form or the other the term seems to have sprung up in American and UK universities in the 1980s, and almost always the courses or programs linked to the term were originally based in departments of literary criticism.

45 See, for example, Scott D. Paulin, "Richard Wagner and the Fantasy of Cinematic Unity: The Idea of the *Gesamtkunstwerk* in the History and Theory of Film Music," in *Music and Cinema*, ed. James Buhler, Caryl Flinn, and David Neumeyer (Hanover: Wesleyan University Press, 2000): 58–84; Justin London, "Leitmotifs and Musical Reference in the Classical Film Score," in *Music and Cinema*: 85–96; and Peter Franklin, "The Boy on the Train, or Bad Symphonies and Good Movies: The Revealing Error of the 'Symphonic Score,'" in *Beyond the Soundtrack: Representing Music in Cinema*, ed. Daniel Goldmark, Lawrence Kramer, and Richard Leppert (Berkeley: University of California Press, 2007): 13–26.

46 Bordwell et al., *The Classical Hollywood Cinema*, 34. The quotation from Parker Tyler comes from *The Hollywood Hallucination* (New York: Simon & Schuster, 1970), 155; the quotation from George Antheil comes from Lawrence Morton, "An Interview with George Antheil," *Film Music Notes* 10, no. 1 (September–October 1950), 5.

47 Ibid.

48 Ibid.

49 Ibid., 35.

50 Kalinak, *Settling the Score*, xiv.

51 Thomson's only feature-film project involved *The Goddess*, a 1958 Columbia film based loosely on the life of Marilyn Monroe. The documentary films for which Thomson wrote music are *The Plow That Broke the Plains* (1936), *The Spanish Earth* (1937, with Marc Blitzstein), *The River* (1937), *Tuesday in November* (1945), *Louisiana Story* (1948), *Power*

Among Men (1959) and *Voyage to America* (1964). For more on Thomson's music for documentaries, see Neil Lerner, "The Politics of Polyphony in Selected Documentary Film Scores by Virgil Thomson and Aaron Copland," in *Film Music 2: History, Theory, Practice*, ed. Claudia Gorbman and Warren M. Sherk (Los Angeles: Film Music Society, 2004): 1–25.

52 Virgil Thomson, "A Little About Movie Music," *Modern Music* 10, no. 4 (May–June 1933), 189. Along the Schubert symphony, Thomson singles out Dvořák's "New World" Symphony and Wagner's *Tristan und Isolde* as having adequately served the needs of recent dramatic films.

53 Antheil achieved long-lasting notoriety with his 1926 *Ballet mécanique*; with an orchestra that included siren, amplified piano, electric bells, and airplane propellers, *Ballet mécanique* was originally intended to accompany a silent film by Fernand Léger, but synchronization problems prevented this plan from ever being realized. Antheil began his Hollywood career by writing music for Paramount's *Once in a Blue Moon* (1935) and *The Plainsman* (1937); the last of his two dozen or so film scores, completed two years before his death in 1959, were for Columbia's *The Young Don't Cry* and United Artists' *The Pride and the Passion*.

54 George Antheil, "Composers in Movieland," *Modern Music* 12, no. 2 (January–February 1935), 63.

55 Weill's music for *Die Dreigroschenoper* is not so much a film score as simply an adaptation—for G.W. Pabst's filmed production—of the music from the same-titled 1928 operetta.

56 Antheil, "Composers in Movieland," 64.

57 George Antheil, "Good Russian Advice about Movie Music," *Modern Music* 13, no. 4 (May–June 1936), 55.

58 George Antheil, "On the Hollywood Front," *Modern Music* 14, no. 1 (November–December 1936), 47.

59 Throughout his career, Janssen was known more as a conductor than a composer. According to Clifford McCarty's *Film Composers in America* (149), between 1936 and 1958 Janssen wrote music for only a dozen Hollywood feature films; Gustave Reese's article on Janssen in the 1986 edition of *The New Grove Dictionary of American Music* (Vol. II, 533) indicates that Janssen's film scores, including music for documentaries, number more than forty-five.

60 Werner Janssen, "Scoring for the Screen," *New York Times*, August 23, 1936, X4.

61 Franz Waxman, quoted in "Original Scores for Film Music Urged by Waxman," *Los Angeles Times*, November 1, 1936, C5. The mention of *A Midsummer Night's Dream* doubtless refers to the 1935 Warner Bros. version of the Shakespeare play, with Mendelssohn's well-known incidental music adapted by Erich Wolfgang Korngold. The reference to Tchaikovsky's *Romeo and Juliet* overture likely is to MGM's 1936 film of that title, which features a Tchaikovsky-based score by Herbert Stothart, and not to the 1933 Warner Bros. cartoon version of the Romeo and Juliet story, part of the studio's Terrytoon series, with music by Philip A Scheib.

62 Will H. Hays, quoted in Frank S. Nugent, "The Cinema Wields the Baton," *New York Times*, April 11, 1937, 175.

63 George Antheil, "On the Hollywood Front," *Modern Music* 15, no. 1 (November–December 1937), 48–9.

64 George Antheil, "Breaking into the Movies," *Modern Music* 14, no. 2 (January–February 1937), 86.

65 Ibid., 83.

66 Ibid.

67 Virgil Thomson, "How to Write a Piece, or Functional Design in Music," from *The State of Music* (orig. New York: Morrow, 1939), reprinted in *A Virgil Thomson Reader*, ed. John Rockwell (Boston: Houghton Mifflin Company, 1981), 150–4.

68 Ibid. (in *A Virgil Thomson Reader*), 155.

69 Virgil Thomson, "Hollywood's Best," *New York Herald-Tribune*, April 10, 1949, reprinted in *A Virgil Thomson Reader* (Boston: Houghton Mifflin Company, 1981), 325.

70   Between 1930 and 1942 Levant was involved—sometimes only as co-composer—with just five feature-length films. McCarty's *Film Composers in America* (190) lists *Leathernecking* (1930), *Crime Without Passion* (1934), *Nothing Sacred* (1937), *Made for Each Other* (1939), and the documentary *Fellow Americans* (1942) as Levant's only film-music credits. From the autobiography biography cited below (117–19), however, it is clear that Levant also composed the opera sequence for the 1936 *Charlie Chan at the Opera*.

71   Oscar Levant, *A Smattering of Ignorance* (New York: Doubleday, Doran & Co., 1939), 88–90.

72   Ibid., 141–4.

73   George Antheil, *Bad Boy of Music* (Garden City, N.Y.: Doubleday, 1945), 315–16.

74   John Huntley, *British Film Music* (London: Skelton Robinson, 1947), 209–10.

75   Ernest Irving, "Music in Films," *Music & Letters*, 24 (1943), 229.

76   Frederick W. Sternfeld, "Preliminary Report on Film Music," *Hollywood Quarterly* 2, no. 3 (April 1947), 300.

77   Frederick W. Sternfeld, "Music and the Feature Films," *The Musical Quarterly* 33, no. 4 (October 1947), 517–18. *The Bandit of Sherwood Forest* (Columbia, 1946) features a score by Friedhofer.

78   Frederick W. Sternfeld, "Cinema Scores: A Few Good Ones Give Hope for Future," *New York Times*, October 10, 1948, X7.

79   For details on these discussions, especially on the patently ridiculous demands these composers made for both remuneration and scheduling, see William H. Rosar, "Stravinsky and MGM," in *Film Music I*, 109–22, ed. Clifford McCarty (Los Angeles: The Film Music Society, 1989); and Sabine M. Feisst, "Arnold Schoenberg and the Cinematic Art, *The Musical Quarterly* 83, no. 1 (Spring 1999), 93–113.

80   Bruno David Ussher, "Composing for Films," *New York Times*, January 28, 1940, X7.

81   Bruno David Ussher, "Composing for the Movies," *New York Times*, August 18, 1940, 110.

82   Theodore Strauss, "Music to See By," *New York Times*, April 27, 1941, X5.

83   Irving, "Music in Films," 233.

84   Louis Lipstone, musical director at Paramount, quoted in "Music Educators Learn About Film Melody-Making," *Los Angeles Times*, April 5, 1940, A12. The newspaper article reported on presentations by various Hollywood figures at the Music Educators National Conference.

85   Max Steiner, quoted in ibid.

86   Herbert Stothart, "Film Music through the Years," *New York Times*, December 7, 1941, X8.

87   Isabel Morse Jones, "Composers for Films Seek Light," *Los Angeles Times*, January 14, 1945, B1. Among composers who write high-quality music but nonetheless get relatively few films to score, Jones mentions "Erich Korngold, Aaron Copland, Hanns Eisler, Werner Janssen, George Antheil, Louis Gruenberg, William Grant Still, Richard Hageman, Ernst Toch [and] Alexander Tansman."

88   Aaron Copland, "The Aims of Music for Films," *New York Times*, March 10, 1940, 158.

89   Marian Hannah Winter, "The Function of Music in Sound Film," *The Musical Quarterly* 27, no. 2 (April 1941), 163–4. Emphases original.

90   Ibid.

91   Aaron Copland, quoted in Albert Goldberg, "The Sounding Board: Copland, Film Scores, and Critics," *Los Angeles Times*, February 15, 1948, C6.

92   David Raksin, "Talking Back: A Hollywood Composer States Case for His Craft," *New York Times*, February 20, 1949, X7.

93   See note 34 in the "Introduction" for *Film Music: A History*.

94   Hanns Eisler, *Composing for the Films* (London: Oxford University Press, 1947), 4.

95   Ibid., 10.

96   Ibid., 12.

97   Lawrence Morton, "Hanns Eisler: Composer and Critic," *Hollywood Review* 3, no. 2 (Winter 1947–8), 208–9.

98   Ibid., 209.

99 Ibid., 210. The "twelve-tone aesthetic" refers to the so-called serial musical technique devised in the 1920s by Eisler's teacher Arnold Schoenberg. According to this archly modernistic technique, the entirety of a musical composition—not just its melodies but also its harmonies and counterpoint—could stem from permutations of a single series of pitches that entailed, without repetition, all twelve tones of the chromatic scale.

100 Erich Leinsdorf, "Music and the Screen," *New York Times*, June 17, 1945, X3.

101 Ibid.

102 Ibid.

103 Bernard Herrmann, "Music in Films—A Rebuttal," *New York Times*, June 24, 1945, 27.

104 Ibid.

105 Bosley Crowther, "Heard Melodies: Some Comments by a Strictly Average Listener on the Uses of Film Music," *New York Times*, June 24, 1945, 25.

106 Ibid.

107 Ibid.

108 Mast, *A Short History of the Movies*, 315.

109 Ibid.

110 Peter Lev, *The Fifties: Transforming the Screen, 1950–9* (Berkeley: University of California Press, 2003), 6.

111 "Films 'Struggle,' Selznick Asserts," *New York Times*, March 31, 1949, 30.

Chapter 9

1 Hans Keller, "*West of Zanzibar*: Some Problems of Film Music," *Musical Opinion* 77 (July 1954), 585.

2 "Films 'Struggle,' Selznick Asserts," *New York Times*, March 31, 1949, 30.

3 "Movie Crisis Laid to Video Inroads And Dwindling of Foreign Market," *New York Times*, February 27, 1949, F1.

4 Peter Lev, *The Fifties: Transforming the Screen, 1950–9* (Berkeley: University of California Press, 2003), 9. Lev's figures, in turn, come from the Federal Communications Commission as reported in Christopher R. Sterling and Timothy R. Haight, *The Mass Media: Aspen Institute guide to Communication Industry Trends* (New York: Praeger, 1978), 49.

5 Samuel Goldwyn, "Hollywood in the Television Age," *New York Times*, February 13, 1949, SM15.

6 Lev, ibid. Lev gets the figures from Sterling and Haight, *The Mass Media*, 361.

7 "20–30% Family B.O. Cut Via Home TV," *Variety*, February 15, 1950, and "TV's Impact a Puzzler," *Variety* March 22, 1951. Both cited in Lev, 9.

8 "Movie Crisis Laid to Video Inroads And Dwindling of Foreign Market," ibid.

9 "To Discuss Film Problem," *New York Times*, March 10, 1949, 35.

10 C.A. Lejeune, "Bleak Outlook for British Film Producers," *New York Times*, March 13, 1949, X5.

11 Thomas Brady, "Hollywood Protest," *New York Times*, February 20, 1949, X5.

12 "AFL Film Council Seeks Import Ban," *New York Times*, February 15, 1949, 28.

13 Thomas M. Pryor, "Ten Years Later—Movie Anti-Trust Action Draws to Close," *New York Times*, March 6, 1949, X5.

14 William O. Douglas, quoted in Charles Hurd, "Film Booking Issue Ordered Reopened," *New York Times*, May 4, 1948, 1.

15 "Movie Crisis Laid to Video Inroads And Dwindling of Foreign Market," *New York Times*, February 27, 1949, F1. For details on the lawsuit and its effects, see Arthur De Vany and Henry McMillan, "Was the Antitrust Action that Broke Up the Movie Studios Good for the Movies? Evidence from the Stock Market." *American Law and Economics Review* 6, no. 1 (2004): 135–53; and J.C. Strick, "The Economics of the Motion Picture Industry: A Survey," *Philosophy of the Social Sciences* 8, no. 4 (December 1978): 406–17.

16 The Hollywood feature films for which Eisler provided music are *Hangmen Also Die* (1942), *None But the Lonely Heart* (1944), *Jealousy* (1945), *The Spanish Main* (1945); *A Scandal in Paris* (1946), *Deadline at Dawn* (1946), *Woman on the Beach* (1947), and *So Well Remembered* (1947). Most of these are middle-of-the-road genre pieces, but the first

two—in keeping with the spirit of the times—feature screenplays strongly supportive of the Allies' war effort.

17 For a detailed account of the FBI's investigation of Eisler, see James Wierzbicki, "Sour Notes: Hanns Eisler and the FBI," in *Modernism on File: Writers, Artists, and the FBI, 1920–50*, 197–219, ed. Claire A. Culleton and Karen Leick (New York: Palgrave Macmillan, 2008).

18 Samuel Goldwyn, quoted in "Sam Goldwyn Hits at Film Censorship," *Los Angeles Times*, September 15, 1949, A1.

19 *Los Angeles Times*, November 8, 1949, 23.

20 "British Film Battle Won by Hollywood," *Los Angeles Times*, November 7, 1949, 25.

21 David O. Selznick, quoted in "Films 'Struggle,' Selznick Asserts."

22 Arno Johnson, chief of J. Walter Thompson, Research and Statistical Branch, quoted in "Film Study Shows Small Drop in '48," *New York Times*, February 23, 1949, 30.

23 As early as 1937 Bell Laboratories had successfully demonstrated the possibilities of films with stereophonic sound. See "New Sound Effects Achieved in Film," *New York Times*, October 12, 1937, 27. Ca. 1938–41 MGM and Twentieth Century-Fox experimented with, but did not release, stereophonic soundtracks. The Disney studio used three-channel stereophonic sound in its 1940 *Fantasia*, but this version was realizable only in specially equipped theaters, and so most audiences experienced the film with a monaural remix. For more on the muse of music in *Fantasia*, see Mark Clague, "Playing in 'Toon: Walt Disney's *Fantasia* (1940) and the Imagineering of Classical Music," *American Music* 22, no. 1 (Spring 2004): 91–109.

24 Motion pictures in color date back to 1908, when Charles Urban demonstrated the results of a process he called Kinemacolor; the Technicolor Corporation was founded in 1917 and its method was used at least occasionally by almost all the large Hollywood studios. By 1933 Technicolor had perfected the visually credible three-color process with which viewers today are familiar, but the process was expensive and thus reserved, until the 1950s, for films in one way or another deemed "special."

25 Lev, *The Fifties: Transforming the Screen, 1950–9*, 303.

26 Among the more famous original musicals are *An American in Paris* (MGM, 1951), *Singin' in the Rain* (MGM, 1952), *Funny Face* (Paramount, 1957), and *Gigi* (MGM, 1958). The adaptations include *Kiss Me, Kate* (MGM, 1953), *Kismet* (MGM, 1955), *Oklahoma!* (Magna, 1955), *Guys and Dolls* (Goldwyn, 1955), *Carousel* (Twentieth Century-Fox, 1956), *The King and I* (Twentieth Century-Fox, 1956), *Silk Stockings* (MGM, 1957), *South Pacific* (Magna, 1958), and *Damn Yankees* (Warner Bros., 1958).

27 For more on the filmic use of both jazz-flavored music and actual jazz during the 1950s, see Martin Williams, "Jazz in the Movies," a 1967 essay that is anthologized both in *Film Music: From Violins to Video*, ed. James Limbacher (Metuchen, N.J.: Scarecrow Press, 1974), 42–4, and in Martin Williams, *Jazz in Its Time* (Oxford: Oxford University Press, 1991), 17–21. Also see Krin Gabbard, *Black Magic: White Hollywood and African American Culture* (Rutgers: Rutgers University Press, 2004) and David Butler, *Jazz Noir: Listening to Music from "Phantom Lady" to "The Last Seduction"* (London: Praeger, 2002).

28 For commentary on Tiomkin's music for *High Noon*, see Neil Lerner, " 'Look at That Big Hand Move Along': Clocks, Containment, and Music in *High Noon*," *South Atlantic Quarterly* 104, no. 1 (2005): 151–73.

29 For commentary on the electronic music for *Forbidden Planet*, see Rebecca Leydon, "*Forbidden Planet*: Effects and Affects in the Electro Avant Garde," in *Off the Planet: Music, Sound and Science Fiction Cinema*, ed. Philip Hayward (Eastleigh, UK: John Libbey Publishing, 2004), 61–76; and James Wierzbicki, *Louis and Bebe Barron's "Forbidden Planet"* (Lanham, Md.: Scarecrow Press, 2005).

30 For commentary on Bernard Herrmann's music for *Citizen Kane*, see Hanjörg Pauli, "Bernard Herrmanns Musik zu *Citizen Kane*," *Disssonance* 26 (November 1990): 12–18; and William H. Rosar, "The *Dies Irae* in *Citizen Kane*: Musical Hermeneutics Applied to Film Music," in *Film Music: Critical Approaches*, ed. K.J. Donnelly (New York: Continuum, 2001), 103–16.

31 Gerald Mast, *A Short History of the Movies* (New York: Pegasus, 1971), 337.
32 Kristin Thompson and David Bordwell, *Film History: An Introduction* (New York: McGraw-Hill, 1994), 408.
33 Ibid., 412.
34 Ibid., 412–13.
35 Ibid., 413.
36 Ibid.
37 See chapter seven, note 48.
38 Mast, *A Short History of the Movies*, 336.
39 For more on the theremin and its role in "psychological" Hollywood films from the late 1940s, before its appropriation by composers for science-fiction films in the 1950s, see James Wierzbicki, "Weird Vibrations: How the Theremin Gave Musical Voice to Hollywood's Extraterrestrial 'Others,'" *Journal of Popular Film and Television* 30 (2002): 125–35. Along with the theremin-flavored films, the Rózsa-scored "psychological dramas" mentioned in the interview include *Double Indemnity* (1944, Paramount), *The Strange Love of Martha Ivers* (1946, Paramount), *The Killers* (1946, Universal), *Brute Force* (1947, Universal), and *The Secret Behind the Door* (1948, Universal).
40 Miklós Rózsa, quoted in Philip K. Scheuer, "Invisible Strings of Dr. Rózsa's Theremin Bring Audible Acclaim," *Los Angeles Times*, December 7, 1952, D1 and D3.
41 Lawrence Morton, "Film Music of the Quarter," *Hollywood Quarterly* 5, no. 3 (Spring 1951), 282. The report by Hollywood composer Amfitheatrof was titled *Italy: Music and Films* and appeared in the form of a newsletter issued in late 1950 by the Academy of Motion Picture Arts and Sciences. Keller's report on the conference appeared in *The Music Review* in August 1950; in the same month Hopkins's report appeared in *Sight and Sound*.
42 Ibid., 283.
43 Antony Hopkins, "Film Music," *Sight and Sound* (May 1951), quoted in Hans Keller, "Hollywood Orchestrators: The Dragon Shows His Teeth," *The Music Review* 12, no. 3 (August 1951). The Keller article is reprinted in Hans Keller, *Film Music and Beyond: Writings on Music and the Screen, 1946–59*, ed. Christopher Wintle (London: Plumbago Books, 2006): 41–6; in the anthology, the quoted Hopkins passage appears on p. 45.
44 Hans Keller, "Hollywood Orchestrators: The Dragon Shows His Teeth," *The Music Review* 12, no. 3 (August 1951), 222. The entire article is reprinted in Keller, Hans. *Film Music and Beyond: Writings on Music and the Screen, 1946–59*, ed. Christopher Wintle (London: Plumbago Books, 2006): 41–6; in the anthology, the quoted passage is found on pp. 42–3.
45 Lawrence Morton, "Composing, Orchestration, and Criticizing," *The Quarterly of Film, Radio and Television* 6, no. 2 (Winter 1951), 193. Upon the launch of its sixth volume in the autumn of 1951, the *Hollywood Quarterly* changed its name to *The Quarterly of Film, Radio and Television*.
46 Ibid., 205.
47 Morton, "Film Music of the Quarter" (Spring 1951), 283–4.
48 Hopkins, "Film Music," quoted in Keller, "Hollywood Orchestrators," in *Film Music and Beyond*, 45.
49 Keller, "Hollywood Orchestrators," in *Film Music and Beyond*, 44.
50 Morton, ibid., 285–6.
51 Ibid., 286.
52 Ibid., 286–7.
53 Ibid., 287–8.
54 Thomas Beecham, quoted in "Beecham Arrives Minus Acid Speech," *Los Angeles Times*, February 27, 1952, 5.
55 Ibid.
56 "Film Music Composer Hits Back at Beecham," *Los Angeles Times*, February 28, 1952, A1.
57 In England, Auric had scored Charles Crichton's *Hue and Cry* (Ealing, 1947), Alexander Mackendrick's *Whiskey Galore* (Ealing, 1948; released in the United States as *Tight Little Island*), Crichton's *The Lavender Hill Mob* (Ealing, 1951), Henry Cornelius's *The Galloping Major* (British Lion, 1951), and John Huston's *Moulin Rouge* (Romulus, 1952).

58 Hans Keller, "World Review," *The Music Review* 13, no. 4 (November 1952), 310.
59 Hans Keller, "Noisy Music and Musical Noise," *The Music Review* 13, no. 2 (May 1952), 138–9. Emphases original.
60 Hans Keller, "Alwyn—Benjamin—Black" The Music Review 17, no. 3 (August 1956), 255.
61 Hans Keller, "No Music—Malcolm Arnold—Benjamin Frankel," *The Music Review* 17, no. 4 (November 1956), 337.
62 Philip K. Scheurer, "Tiomkin Soft-Pedals Fortissimo Fanfare in Film Music Scores," *Los Angeles Times*, August 17, 1952, D1.
63 For a study on the genre, see Peter Stanfield, *Horse Opera: The Strange History of the 1930s Singing Cowboy* (Urbana: University of Illinois Press, 2002).
64 Until 1941 a song was eligible for the Academy Award simply if it had been used in a film during the previous year; since 1941 the award has gone only to original songs written specifically for use in a film. Between 1941 and 1952—when Tiomkin and lyricist Ned Washington won for "Do Not Forsake Me, Oh My Darlin'"—the award-winning songs were composer Jerome Kern's and lyricist Oscar Hammerstein II's "The Last Time I Saw Paris" (from *Lady Be Good*), Irving Berlin's "White Christmas" (from *Holiday Inn*), Harry Warren's and Mack Gordon's "You'll Never Know" (from *Hello, Frisco, Hello*), Jimmy Van Heusen's and Johnny Burke's "Swinging on a Star" (from *Going My Way*), Richard Rodgers's and Oscar Hammerstein II's "It Might as Well Be Spring" (from *State Fair*), Harry Warren's and Johnny Mercer's "On the Atchison, Topeka and the Santa Fe" (from *The Harvey Girls*), Allie Wrubel's and Leo Robin's "Zip-a-Dee-Doo-Dah" (from *Song of the South*), Jay Livingston's and Ray Evans's "Buttons and Bows" (from *The Paleface*), Frank Loesser's "Baby, It's Cold Outside" (from *Neptune's Daughter*), Jay Livingston's and Ray Evans's "Mona Lisa" (from *Captain Carey, U.S.A.*), and Hoagy Carmichael's and Johnny Mercer's "In the Cool, Cool, Cool of the Evening" (from *Here Comes the Groom*).
65 Rózsa's music circulated in 1946 as an orchestral work titled *Spellbound Concerto*; the original version featured, as did the film score, a theremin, and the alternate version featured a solo piano. Karas was a zither player who before *The Third Man* had worked only in Viennese cafés; released as a single in the spring of 1950, his "Third Man Theme" held the number one position on the Billboard chart for eleven weeks.
66 Roy M. Prendergast, *Film Music: A Neglected Art* (New York: W.W. Norton, 1977), 103. Emphasis original.
67 Ibid., 102.
68 Harold C. Schonberg, "Records: Background Music for Films," *New York Times*, July 14, 1957, 88.
69 Ibid.
70 Ibid.
71 The song, performed in the film by Doris Day and later a major hit, was "Que Sera, Sera." For more on the song, and on the 1956 film's re-use of the cantata that Arthur Benjamin composed for the 1934 original version, see James Wierzbicki, "Grand Illusion: The 'Storm Cloud' Music in Hitchcock's *The Man Who Knew Too Much*," *Journal of Film Music* 1, nos. 2–3 (Fall–Winter 2003): 217–38. Also see Murray Pomerance, "Finding Release: 'Storm Clouds' and *The Man Who Knew Too Much*," in *Music and Cinema*, ed. James Buhler, Caryl Flinn, and David Neumeyer (Hanover: Wesleyan University Press, 2000) 207–46.
72 Directed by Ray Ashley, *Little Fugitive* was a Hollywood film released in 1953 by the Morris Engel studio; the music was the work of Eddy Manson. *Genevieve* was a 1953 British film (J. Arthur Rank) directed by Henry Cornelius; the music was by Larry Adler, at the time a well-known harmonica virtuoso.
73 Philip K. Scheuer, "A Town Called Hollywood: Scorers Skip Classics, Seek New Approaches," *Los Angeles Times*, August 29, 1954, D2.
74 Leith Stevens, quoted in Scheuer, "A Town Called Hollywood: Scorers Skip Classics, Seek New Approaches." *The Wild One* (Paramount, 1945) was directed by Stanley Kramer; *Private Hell 36* (Filmmakers, 1954) was directed by Don Siegel. For more on the music of these two films, see Alfred W. Cochran, "Leith Stevens and the Jazz Film Score: *The Wild One and Private Hell 36*," *Jazz Research Papers* 10 (1990): 24–31.

75 See Philip K. Scheuer, "Movies and the Sound of Great Music," *Los Angeles Times*, January 26, 1964, A2, and "Hollywood and the Classics: An Uneasy Alliance," *Los Angeles Times*, October 7, 1973, 018.
76 Albert Goldberg, "The Sounding Board: Shostakovich's New 11th Symphony a Tragic Decline," *Los Angeles Times*, August 31, 1958, D5.
77 Ibid.
78 Philip K. Scheuer, "How Important Is Incidental Score?" *Los Angeles Times*, September 1, 1958, B33.
79 Walter H. Rubsamen, paraphrased in Scheuer, "How Important Is Incidental Score?"
80 Ernest Gold, quoted in Philip K. Scheuer, "Music in Movies Further Explored," *Los Angeles Times*, September 8, 1958, C9.
81 Ibid.
82 Ibid.
83 James C. Petrillo, quoted in "Petrillo Here Seeking Film Music Pact," *Los Angeles Times*, May 12, 1944, 1.
84 The AFM's ban on recording was instituted in August 1942 and ultimately lifted in the fall of 1944. For details, and for insights into how the ban affected jazz music in particular, see Scott DeVeaux, "Bebop and the Recording Industry: The 1942 AFM Recording Ban Reconsidered," *Journal of the American Musicological Society* 41, no. 1 (Spring 1988): 126–65.
85 Albert Goldberg, "The Sounding Board: Setting the Record Straight," *Los Angeles Times*, May 23, 1948, C7.
86 J.D. Spiro, "Hollywood Resume: Producers and Petrillo Face the Music," *New York Times*, August 15, 1948, X3.
87 Ibid.
88 "Petrillo Extends Film Agreement," *New York Times*, August 27, 1948, 12.
89 "5% Wage Rise Is Won by Movie Musicians," *New York Times*, January 28, 1954, 23.
90 "Musicians to Picket Two Films in 20 U.S. Cities," *Los Angeles Times*, June 24, 1958, B1.
91 "Goldwyn Inks Contract With Musicians," *Los Angeles Times*, April 10, 1958, 20.
92 Cecil F. Read, quoted in "Hollywood's Music Future Made Issue," *Los Angeles Times*, June 27, 1958, B1 and B28.
93 Thomas M. Pryor, "Musicians Guild Wins Coast Vote," *New York Times*, July 13, 1958, 16.
94 Herman D. Kenin, quoted in Pryor, "Musicians Guild Wins Coast Vote."
95 Eliot Daniel, quoted in Oscar Godbout, "A.F.M. Unit Hits Film Music Pact," *New York Times*, August 29, 1958, 17.
96 Cecil F. Read, quoted in Godbout, "A.F.M. Unit Hits Film Music Pact."
97 "Musicians Guild Wins 14% Hike in Studio Pay," *Los Angeles Times*, August 28, 1958, B3.
98 Godbout, "A.F.M. Unit Hits Film Music Pact," *New York Times*, August 29, 1958, 17.
99 "Musicians Guild Wins 14% Hike in Studio Pay."
100 "Musicians Get First Film Jobs Since Feb. 20," *Los Angeles Times*, September 4, 1958, B11.

Chapter 10

1 Jerry Goldsmith, quoted in Charles Champlin, "Sound and Fury Over Film Music," *Los Angeles Times*, March 12, 1967, C14.
2 In his 1998 *The Invisible Art of Film Music: A Comprehensive History* (Lanham, Md.: Ardsley House), for example, Laurence E. MacDonald uses the title "The Revival of the Symphonic Film Score" for his chapter on the period 1970–9. Similarly, Roger Hickman, in his 2005 *Reel Music: Exploring 100 Years of Film Music* (New York: W.W. Norton), calls his chapter on the period 1977–88 "The Classic Revival."
3 Gerald Mast, *A Short History of the Movies* (New York: Pegasus, 1971), 315.
4 Elmer Bernstein, "What Ever Happened to Great Movie Music?" *High Fidelity* (July 1972), 58. Directed by Raoul Walsh and released by Twentieth Century-Fox in 1956, *The Revolt*

of Mamie Stover starred Jane Russell as a saloon singer in Hawaii during the early years of World War II; the music, including the song "Walkin' Home with the Blues" (lyrics by Ned Washington) that played during the opening credits, was by Hugo Friedhofer.

5   Ibid. Emphasis original.

6   Ibid., 55.

7   Ibid., 58.

8   The music for *Easy Rider*, much of it heard extra-diegetically, was a compilation of generally hard-edged rock songs. All the music in *The Last Picture Show* was diegetic and consisted of recordings by such performers as Hank Williams, Bob Wills and His Texas Playboys, Eddy Arnold, Pee Wee King, Tony Bennett, Frankie Laine, Johnnie Ray, Kay Starr, and Jo Stafford. The music in *American Graffiti*, heard both diegetically and extra-diegetically, involved rock 'n' roll songs from the late 1950s and early '60s.

9   David Raksin, "Whatever Became of Movie Music?" *Film Music Notebook* 1, no. 1 (Autumn 1974), 23. The article was originally published as "Film Music: Beauty and the Beast? Raksin Raps State of Art" in *Variety* 275, no. 1 (May 1974), 59.

10 Ibid.

11 Ibid.

12 Vincent Canby, "Music Is Now Profit to the Ears of Filmmakers," *New York Times*, May 24, 1966, 52. John Sturges's *The Magnificent Seven* dates from 1960. Jules Dassin's *Never on Sunday* dates from 1959; although it was made by the Greek studio Lopert, by the mid 1960s the film—including the Oscar-winning title song by Manos Hadjidakes—was controlled by United Artists.

13 Herrmann's score was replaced with one by British composer John Addison.

14 See, for example, Steven C. Smith, *A Heart at Fire's Center: The Life and Music of Bernard Herrmann* (Berkeley: University of California Press, 1991), 257–74; and Jack Sullivan, *Hitchcock's Music* (New Haven: Yale University Press, 2006), 280–7.

15 Bernard Herrmann, quoted in Royal S. Brown, "An Interview with Bernard Herrmann," *High Fidelity* (September 1976), 65.

16 Bernard Herrmann, quoted in Kevin Thomas, "Film Composer Settles a Score," *Los Angeles Times*, February 4, 1968, D16 and D21.

17 William Axt, quoted in Philip K. Scheuer, "Musical Picture Quietly Undergoes Renaissance," *Los Angeles Times*, February 22, 1931, B9.

18 Martin Bernheimer, "Academy Scores: Fuzzy Recognition," *Los Angeles Times*, April 14, 1968, N32.

19 Elmer Bernstein, quoted in Bernheimer, "Academy Scores: Fuzzy Recognition."

20 The music for *The Last of Sheila*, which featured Bette Midler performing the song "Friends," was by Billy Goldenberg. The music for *The Way We Were*, including the Oscar-winning title song, was by Marvin Hamlisch. *The Graduate* is well known for its songs by Simon and Garfunkle, some of which were created for the film and some of which had already had popular success, but the score also involves original music by Dave Grusin.

21 Paul Gardner, "How to Make Sweet Music at the Box Office," *New York Times*, March 31, 1974, I11. Emphasis original.

22 Julie Hubbert, " 'Whatever Happened to Great Movie Music?': *Cinéma Vérité* and Hollywood Film Music of the Early 1970s," *American Music* 21, no. 2 (Summer 2003), 182.

23 Gerald Mast, *A Short History of the Movies* (New York: Pegasus, 1971), 416. In the first edition of Mast's book, the two sentences quoted here are separated by a sentence that reads: "This early principle of film scoring was a clear extension of the piano's function in the nickelodeon." Hubbert cites the first edition of Mast's book, but in fact her quotation comes from the third edition (Chicago: University of Chicago Press, 1981), 420.

24 Irwin Bazelon, *Knowing the Score: Notes on Film Music* (New York: Arco, 1975), 31–3.

25 Hubbert, " 'Whatever Happened to Great Movie Music?' " 182. The quotations are from Roy M. Prendergast, *Film Music: A Neglected Art* (New York: W.W. Norton, 1977), 167.

26 Ibid.

27 Ibid. In an endnote, Hubbert quotes Doty, who wrote: "By the early 1970s, Hollywood was committed to cultivating the youth market as perhaps the only secure share of an

otherwise unstable and unpredictable audience, and the industry lavished what was left of its pre-release publicity ideas and dollars on this sure thing market." Alexander Doty, "Music Sells Movies: (Re)New(ed) Conservatism in Film Marketing." *Wide Angle* 10, no. 2 (1988), 74.

28 Ibid.

29 "First Statement of The New American Cinema Group," *Film Culture* nos. 22–3 (Summer 1961). Quoted in *Film Culture Reader*, ed. P. Adams Sitney (New York: Praeger, 1970), 80–1.

30 Ibid. Quoted in *Film Culture Reader*, 82–3.

31 Alf Louvre, "The New Radicalism: The Politics of Culture in Britain, America and France, 1956–73," in *Cultural Revolution? The Challenge of the Arts in the 1960s*, ed. Bart Moore-Gilbert and John Seed (London and New York: Routledge, 1992), 57.

32 Andrew Sarris, quoted by Tom Gunning in " 'Loved Him, Hated It': An Interview with Andrew Sarris," in *To Free the Cinema: Jonas Mekas & the New York Underground*, ed. David E. James (Princeton: Princeton University Press, 1992), 74.

33 Richard Dyer, "Music, People and Reality: The Case of Italian Neo-realism," in *European Film Music*, ed. Miguel Mera and David Burnand (Aldershot: Ashgate, 2006), 28.

34 Jeffrey Richards, "New Waves and Old Myths: British Cinema in the 1960s," in *Cultural Revolution? The Challenge of the Arts in the 1960s*, ed. Bart Moore-Gilbert and John Seed (London and New York: Routledge, 1992), 218–19.

35 Ibid., 219–20.

36 Royal S. Brown, *Overtones and Undertones: Reading Film Music* (Berkeley: University of California Press, 1994), 188.

37 Craig Sinclair, "Audition: Making Sense of/in the Cinema," *The Velvet Light Trap* no. 51 (Spring 2003), 18–19.

38 Before *The Last Picture Show*, Bogdanovich directed two low-budget films (*Voyage to the Planet of the Prehistoric Women* and *Targets*, both 1968); after *The Last Picture Show* (1971), his big-budget Hollywood films included *What's Up, Doc?*, *Paper Moon*, *Daisy Miller*, *At Long Last Love*, *Nickelodeon*, and a half-dozen others.

39 Hubbert, "Whatever Happened to Great Movie Music?" 194. *Mean Streets* features a wide variety of music, ranging from rock 'n' roll to opera to vintage standards. Except for an Elton John song heard during the title credits, *Dog Day Afternoon* has no music at all.

40 Mast, *A Short History of the Movies*, 413–14. The European filmmakers whose influence has been especially significant, Mast writes, are Godard, Truffaut, and Antonioni. The influential American "underground" filmmakers include Andy Warhol, Robert Downey, Brian de Palma, Stan Brakhage, Kenneth Anger, Ron Rice, and Jonas Mekas.

41 Ibid., 415.

42 Ibid., 415–16.

43 Ibid., 416. The ellipsis represents the words quoted by Hubbert and referenced in note 23.

44 Prendergast, *Film Music: A Neglected Art*, 167.

45 Ibid.

46 Andrew Sarris, quoted by Tom Gunning in " 'Loved Him, Hated It': An Interview with Andrew Sarris," in *To Free the Cinema: Jonas Mekas & the New York Underground*, 74.

47 The first recording in the series was titled *The Seahawk: The Classic Film Scores of Erich Wolfgang Korgold* and the conductor was Charles A. Gerhardt. In existence from 1972 to 1978, and run primarily by George Korngold, the composer's son, the series included fourteen albums. See Jon Burlingame, *Sound and Vision: 60 Years of Motion Picture Soundtracks* (New York: Billboard Books, 2000), 14–16. The Varèse-Saraband label, which still produces recordings of film music, was founded in 1978.

48 John Heuther, "Musical Return to Hollywood's Golden Past," *Los Angeles Times*, May 1, 1977, Y22.

49 Tom Shales, "The Sound of (Movie) Music: Re-releases of Soundtracks Past," *Washington Post*, July 18, 1976, H1. Emphasis original.

50 Thomas Maremaa, "Movie Music Down Through the Decades," *Los Angeles Times*, April 25, 1976, Q1, Q34, and Q36.

51 In the case of *Nashville*, the country-western songs pre-existed the film; in the case of *Buffalo Bill and the Indians*, the "frontier" songs were for the most part created especially for the film. In both case, the music director/composer was Richard Baskin.
52 Thomas Maremaa, "The Sound of Movie Music," *New York Times*, March 28, 1976, I40.
53 Ibid., I45.
54 John Williams, quoted in Maremaa, "The Sound of Movie Music," I45.
55 *A Concert of Film Music*, RCA APL1–1379.
56 Shales, "The Sound of (Movie) Music," H6.
57 Meremaa, "The Sound of Movie Music," I45.
58 Williams composed the music for Clint Eastwood's *The Eiger Sanction* (Jennings Lang, 1975), Alfred Hitchcock's *Family Plot* (Universal, 1976), Arthur Penn's *The Missouri Breaks* (Devon/Bersky-Bright, 1976), and Jack Smight's *Midway* (Mirisch Corporation, 1976).
59 For Richard Lester's *Robin and Marian* (Columbia, 1976) and John Gullermin's remake of *King Kong* (De Laurentiis, 1976).
60 For John Huston's *The Man Who Would Be King* (Allied Artists, 1975) and Peter Hunt's *Shout at the Devil* (Tonav, 1976).
61 For Roman Polanski's *Chinatown* (Long Road, 1974), George P. Casmatos's *The Cassandra Crossing* (Associated General Films, 1976), and Richard Donner's *The Omen* (Twentieth Century-Fox, 1976).
62 Williams's first 1977 score was for John Frankenheimer's *Black Sunday* (Gelderse Maatschapii); his first 1978 score was for Brian de Palma's *The Fury* (Frank Yablans Presentations).
63 Robert Altman's *Nashville* (Paramount, 1975) had used the Dolby technology, but only in its final reel.
64 *THX 1138* (Warner Bros./American Zoetrope, 1971) and *American Graffiti* (Universal/Lucasfilm, 1973).
65 Peter Biskind, *Easy Riders, Raging Bulls: How the Sex-Drugs-and-Rock 'n' Roll Generation Saved Hollywood* (New York: Simon & Schuster, 1998), 335.
66 Walter Murch, quoted in Biskind, *Easy Riders, Raging Bulls*, 335. Murch had served as sound designer for Lucas's scoreless 1971 *THX 1138*; the sound designer for *Star Wars* was Ben Burtt.
67 Gianluca Sergi, *The Dolby Era: Film Sound in Contemporary Hollywood* (Manchester: Manchester University Press, 2004), 11.
68 Gianluca Sergi, "A Cry in the Dark: The Role of the Post-Classical Film Sound," in *The Film Cultures Reader*, ed. Graeme Turner (New York and London: Routledge, 2002), 108. Also see Gianluca Sergi, "The Hollywood Sonic Playground: The Spectator as Listener," in *Hollywood Spectatorship: Changing Perceptions of Cinema Audiences*, ed. Richard Maltby and Melvyn Stokes (London: British Film Institute, 2001): 121–31.
69 Ibid.
70 Ibid.
71 Charles Schreger, "Altman, Dolby, and the Second Sound Revolution," in *Film Sound: Theory and Practice*, ed. Elisabeth Weis and John Belton (New York: Columbia University Press, 1985), 349. The essay was originally titled "The Second Coming of Sound" and first appeared in *Film Comment*, 14, no. 5 (September–October 1978).
72 Harold C. Schonberg, "'The Music Lovers' Set Me Thinking . . .," *New York Times*, February 7, 1971, D15.
73 Charles Champlin, "Movie Music—Where Less May Be More," *Los Angeles Times*, February 1, 1979, F9.

Chapter 11

1 Danny Elfman, quoted in Larry Rohter, "Batman? Bartman? Darkman? Elfman," *New York Times*, December 9, 1990, H30.
2 George Antheil, "On the Hollywood Front," *Modern Music* 15, no. 4 (May–June 1938), 251–2.

3   Ibid., 252.
4   Named after George Lucas's debut film (*THX 1138*; Warner Bros./American Zoetrope, 1971), the THX specifications were developed by the Lucasfilm studio in 1982 to ensure high-quality reproduction of the soundtrack for *Return of the Jedi*, the third film in Lucas's "Star Wars" series. In order to be TXH-certified, a theater needed to be not only fitted with proper sound equipment but also needed to meet certain acoustical and architectural standards.
5   Elmer Bernstein, quoted in Steven Smith, "Movie Music: Is It Becoming Hit or Miss?" *Los Angeles Times*, January 5, 1986, S67.
6   For an account of how the *2001* score came to be, see Paul A. Merkley, "'Stanley Hates This But I Like It!': North vs. Kubrick on the Music for *2001: A Space Odyssey*," *Journal of Film Music* 2, no. 1 (Fall 2007): 1–33.
7   For more on the "back-up" scores that Selznick commissioned, or considered, for films directed by Alfred Hitchcock, see Jack Sullivan, *Hitchcock's Music* (New Haven: Yale University Press, 2006), 106–43.
8   Ridley Scott, quoted in Smith, "Movie Music: Is It Becoming Hit or Miss?"
9   Smith, "Movie Music: Is It Becoming Hit or Miss?"
10 Eliot Tiegel, "Pop and Rock Sounds Gain Movie Beachhead," *Los Angeles Times*, April 26, 1981, N55.
11 Pauline Reay, *Music in Film: Soundtracks and Synergy* (London: Wallflower Press, 2004), 21–2.
12 David T. Friendly, "Seeking the Groove in Movie Sound Tracks," *Los Angeles Times*, October 2, 1986, H1 and H6.
13 Ibid., H8.
14 Dave Anderle, quoted in Friendly, "Seeking the Groove," H8.
15 Jeff Smith, *The Sounds of Commerce: Marketing Popular Film Music* (New York: Columbia University Press, 1998), 209–10.
16 Reay, *Music in Film*, 22.
17 Stephen Holden, "How Rock Is Changing Hollywood's Tune," *New York Times*, July 16, 1989, H1.
18 Ibid.
19 Ibid., H18.
20 Ibid.
21 John Badham's *Saturday Night Fever* (Paramount, 1977) featured disco-oriented songs by the Australian pop group The Bee Gees.
22 Holden, "How Rock Is Changing Hollywood's Tune," H18–19.
23 In *Unheard Melodies: Narrative Film Music* (Bloomington: Indiana University Press, 1987), 73–91.
24 See, especially, her "Aesthetics and Rhetoric," *American Music* 22, no. 1 (Spring 2004), 14–26; and "Auteur Music," in *Beyond the Soundtrack: Representing Music in Cinema*, ed. Daniel Goldmark, Lawrence Kramer, and Richard Leppert (Berkeley: University of California Press, 2007), 149–62.
25 Ibid.
26 *Indiana Jones and the Temple of Doom* was the second installment in a series of action films featuring the eponymous archeologist/adventurer. The first film in the series was *Raiders of the Lost Ark* (1981) and the third was *Indiana Jones and the Last Crusade* (1989); to the surprise of audiences who might have thought that the title character, played by Harrison Ford, was quite old enough to retire, a fourth Indiana Jones film—*Indiana Jones and the Kingdom of the Crystal Skulls*—opened at the Cannes Film Festival on May 18, 2008. All four films feature scores by John Williams.
       The first sequel to *The Terminator* was *Terminator 2: Judgment Day* (1991), similarly directed by Cameron and featuring music by Brad Fiedel; the second sequel, *Terminator 3: The Rise of the Machines* (2003), was directed by Jonathan Mostow and featured music by Marco Beltrami. The sequels to *Back to the Future* were *Back to the Future II* (1989) and *Back to the Future III* (1990), both of them, like the original film, directed by Zemeckis and featuring, along with pop songs, original music by Alan Silvestri.

27 Vis-à-vis the introduction of the term into American culture, the two texts most often cited as seminal are Frederic Jameson, "Postmodernism, Or, the Cultural Logic of Late Capitalism," *New Left Review* 146 (July–August 1984): 59–92; and Jean-François Lyotard, *The Postmodern Condition: A Report on Knowledge*, trans. Geoff Bennington and Brian Massumi (Minneapolis: University of Minnesota Press, 1984). Lyotard's book originally appeared, in French, in 1979, and Jameson's essay was expanded into book form in 1991 (London: Verso; later Durham, N.C.: Duke University Press). Typically neglected in bibliographies is Hal Foster, ed., *The Anti-Aesthetic: Essays on Postmodern Culture* (Port Townsend, Wash.: Bay Press, 1983); the anthology includes the text of a lecture, titled "Postmodernism and Consumer Society," that Jameson delivered at the Whitney Museum in 1982.

28 Terry Eagleton, *The Illusions of Postmodernism* (Oxford: Blackwell, 1996), viii. Emphasis added.

29 Along with Jameson, Lyotard, Foster, and Eagleton, these writers include Steven Connor (*Postmodern Culture: An Introduction to Theories of the Contemporary* (Oxford: Blackwell, 1997) and, as editor, *The Cambridge Companion to Postmodernism* (Cambridge: Cambridge University Press, 2004)); David Harvey (*The Condition of Postmodernity: An Enquiry into the Origins of Cultural Change* (Oxford: Blackwell, 1990)); Brian McHale (*Constructing Postmodernism* (London: Routledge, 1992)); and Patricia Waugh (*Practicing Postmodernism: Reading Modernism* (London: Arnold, 1992)).

30 Frederic Jameson, "The Cultural Logic of Late Capitalism," in *Postmodernism, or, The Cultural Logic of Late Capitalism* (Durham, N.C.: Duke University Press, 1991), 18.

31 Ibid., 1.

32 Ibid., 18–19.

33 See Barbara Creed, "From Here to Modernity: Feminism and the Postmodern," in *A Postmodern Reader*, ed. Joseph Natoli and Linda Hutcheon (Albany, N.Y.: State University of New York Press, 1993), 398–418.

34 Michael Walsh, "Jameson and 'Global Aesthetics,'" in *Post-Theory: Reconstructing Film Studies*, ed. David Bordwell and Noël Carroll (Madison: University of Wisconsin Press, 1996), 485. Jameson's history is found in *Signatures of the Visible* (London and New York: Routledge, 1990), 148.

35 The most often-cited, although not uncontroversial, list of characteristics of so-called postmodern music is found in Jonathan Kramer's "The Nature and Origins of Musical Postmodernism," a 1999 essay that first appeared in the journal *Current Musicology* and which has been reprinted in *Postmodern Music/Postmodern Thought*, ed. Judy Lochhead and Joseph Auner (New York: Routledge, 2002), 13–26. An earlier version of the essay, titled "Postmodern Concepts of Musical Time," appeared in 1996 in *Indiana Theory Review*.

36 Anahid Kassabian, *Hearing Film: Tracking Identifications in Contemporary Hollywood Film Music* (New York and London: Routledge, 2001), 2.

37 Ibid., 2–3.

38 Ronald Rodman, "The Popular Song as Leitmotif in 1990s Film," in *Changing Tunes: The Use of Pre-existing Music in Film*, ed. Phil Powrie and Robynn J. Stilwell (Aldershot: Ashgate, 2006), 120.

39 Ibid., 120–1.

40 Hilary Lapedis, "Popping the Question: The Function and Effect of Popular Music in Cinema," *Popular Music* 18, no. 3 (October 1999), 367. Emphasis original.

41 Ibid., 370.

42 Reay, *Music in Film*, 116.

43 For comparable examples of intertextual referencing in scores for television programs, see Julie Brown, "*Ally McBeal*'s Postmodern Soundtrack," *Journal of the Royal Musical Association* 126, no. 2 (2001), 275–303.

44 For collections of essays that deal exclusively with the use of popular music in films, see, for example, *Celluloid Jukebox: Popular Music and the Movies since the 1950s*, ed. Jonathan Romney and Adrian Wooton (London: British Film Institute, 1995); *Soundtrack Available: Essays on Film and Popular Culture*, ed. Pamela Wojcik Robertson and Arthur

Knight (Durham: Duke University Press, 2001); *Popular Music and Film*, ed. Ian Inglis (London: Wallflower Press, 2003); and *Pop Fiction: The Song in Cinema*, ed. Steve Lannin and Matthew Caley (Bristol: Intellect Books, 2005).

45 *Changing Tunes: The Use of Pre-existing Music in Film*, ed. Phil Powrie and Robynn J. Stilwell (Aldershot: Ashgate, 2006).

46 "Introduction: Phonoplay—Recasting Film Music," *Beyond the Soundtrack: Representing Music in Cinema*, ed. Daniel Goldmark, Lawrence Kramer, and Richard Leppert (Berkeley: University of California Press, 2007), 8.

47 Among the books with provocative "doom and gloom" titles are Norman Lebrecht's *Who Killed Classical Music?: Maestros, Managers, and Corporate Politics* (London: Birch Lane Press, 1997), Joseph Horowitz's *Classical Music in America: A History of Its Rise and Fall* (New York: W.W. Norton, 2005), Sheldon Morgenstern's *No Vivaldi in the Garage: A Requiem for Classical Music in North America* (Boston: Northeastern University Press, 2005), and Lebrecht's *The Life and Death of Classical Music: Featuring the 100 Best and 20 Worst Recordings Ever Made* (London: Anchor Books, 2007).

48 Donal Henahan, "Film Music Has Two Masters," *New York Times*, July 19, 1987, H23.

49 Ibid., H1.

50 Ibid.

51 Alex North, quoted in Steven Smith, "The Tenacious Alex North," *Los Angeles Times*, March 23, 1986, X82.

52 Elmer Bernstein, quoted in Fintan O'Toole, "Elmer Bernstein Finds Himself in Tune With Movies," *New York Times*, October 28, 1990, H18 and H26. Emphasis original.

53 Steve Pond, "Scoring High on the Pop Charts," *New York Times*, August 20, 1995, H26.

54 Steve Pond, "The Soundtrack Boom Leaves Composers at a Loss," *New York Times*, August 20, 1995, H26.

55 Thomas Newman, quoted in Pond, "The Soundtrack Boom Leaves Composers at a Loss."

56 David Mermelstein, "In Hollywood, Discord on What Makes Music," *New York Times*, November 2, 1997, AR17.

57 Jerry Goldsmith, quoted in Mermelstein, "In Hollywood, Discord on What Makes Music."

58 Holden, "How Rock Is Changing Hollywood's Tune."

59 Stephen Holden, "The Image of Movie Music Is Changing Once Again," *New York Times*, January 28, 1990, H28.

60 David Schiff, "Taking Movie Music Seriously, Like It or Not," *New York Times*, April 22, 2001, AR1.

Chapter 12

1 Lipscomb, Scott D., and David E. Tolchinsky. "The Role of Music Communication in Cinema," *Musical Communication*, ed. Dorothy Miell, Raymond MacDonald, and David J. Hargreaves (Oxford: Oxford University Press, 2005), 384.

2 George Antheil, "On the Hollywood Front," *Modern Music* 15, no. 4 (May–June 1938), 251–2.

3 Chion introduced the term 'anempathetic' in his *Le Son au cinéma* (Paris: Cahiers du cinéma, 1985), 119–42. The term is explored further in *Audio-Vision: Sound on Screen*, trans. Claudia Gorbman (New York: Columbia University Press, 1994), 8–9.

4 Nicholas Cook, *Analyzing Musical Multimedia* (Oxford: Oxford University Press, 1998), 102–3.

5 Kay Dickinson, *Off Key: When Film and Music Won't Work Together* (Oxford: Oxford University Press, 2008), 19–22.

6 Louis le Sidaner, "L'importance de Cinématographe," *Mercure de France* (n.d.), quoted by Arthur Benjamin in "Film Music," *The Musical Times* 78 (July 1937), 595.

7 John Rockwell, *All American Music: Composition in the Late Twentieth Century* (New York: Alfred A. Knopf, 1983), 157.

8 James Wierzbicki, "Sound as Music in the Films of Terrence Malick," in *The Cinema of Terrence Malick: Poetic Visions of America*, ed. Hannah Patterson (London: Wallflower Press, 2003): 110–22. The composer for *Days of Heaven* was Ennio Morricone, and no

sound designer is credited; for *The Thin Red Line* the composer was Hans Zimmer and the sound designer was John Fasal.

9 John Cage, "The Future of Music: Credo," in *Silence* (Hanover, N.H.: Wesleyan University Press, 1961), 3. "The Future of Music: Credo" was originally a speech delivered to an arts group in Seattle in 1937; it was first printed in 1958 in the program booklet for a Cage retrospective concert in New York's Town Hall.

10 The composer for *The Cell* is Howard Shore; the sound designer, as was the case for Malick's *The Thin Red Line*, is John Fasal.

11 Anahid Kassabian, "The Sound of a New Film Form," in *Popular Music and Film*, ed. Ian Inglis (London: Wallflower Press, 2003), 93–4.

12 Ibid., 94.

13 For more on David Lynch's use of sound, see David Lynch, "Action and Reaction," in *Soundscape: The School of Sound Lectures, 1998–2001*, ed. Larry Sider, Diana Freeman, and Jerry Sider (London: Wallflower Press, 2003), 49–53; for more on sound in the "Matrix" films, see William Whittington, *Sound Design & Science Fiction* (Austin: University of Texas Press, 2007), 223–40.

14 William H. Rosar, "Film Music—What's in a Name?" *Journal of Film Music* 1, no. 1 (2002), 3–4. Emphasis original.

15 Ibid., 7, 1, Emphasis original.

16 Ibid., 14. The reference is to Helga de la Motte-Haber and Hans Emons, *Filmmusik: Eine systematische Beschreibung* (Munich: Karl Hanser Verlag, 1980).

17 Ibid.

18 Ibid., 15. Emphases original.

19 Carlo Ginzburg, in Keith Luria and Romulo Gandolfo, "Carlo Ginzburg: An Interview," *Radical History Review* 35 (1986), 99. Quoted in Rosar, "Film Music—What's in a Name?" 15.

20 Miguel Mera and David Burnand, "Introduction," in *European Film Music*, ed. Miguel Mera and David Burnand (Aldershot: Ashgate, 2006), 4. The reference is to David Morley and Kevin Robbins, "Space of Identity: Communication Technologies and the Reconfiguration of Europe," *Screen* 30, no. 4 (Autumn 1989), 21.

21 Stan Link, review of *European Film Music*, ed. Miguel Mera and David Burtnand, *Screen* 48, no. 2.

22 Annette Davison, *Hollywood Theory, Non-Hollywood Practice: Cinema Soundtracks in the 1980s and 1990s* (Aldershot: Ashgate, 2004), 55. Specifically, Davison offers close examinations of Jean-Luc Godard's *Prénom: Carmen* (1983), David Lynch's *Wild at Heart* (1990), Derek Jarman's *The Garden* (1990), and Wim Wenders's *Der Himmel über Berlin* ("Wings of Desire") (1987).

23 James Buhler, review of *Hollywood Theory, Non-Hollywood Practice: Cinema Soundtracks in the 1980s and 1990s* by Annette Davison, *twentieth-century music* 3, no. 1 (2007), 148.

24 Philip Brophy, *100 Modern Soundtracks* (London: British Film Institute, 2004), 1.

BIBLIOGRAPHY

Abel, Richard, and Rick Altman, eds. *The Sounds of Early Cinema*. Bloomington: Indiana University Press, 2001.

Ahern, Eugene A. *What and How to Play for Pictures*. Twin Falls, Idaho: Newsprint, 1913.

Aitken, Roy, with A.P. Nelson. *"The Birth of a Nation" Story*. Middleburg, Va.: Delinger, 1965.

Altman, Rick, ed. *Sound Theory/Sound Practice*. London: Routledge, 1992.

——. "The Silence of the Silents." *The Musical Quarterly* 80, no. 4 (Winter 1996): 648–718.

——. *Silent Film Sound*. New York: Columbia University Press, 2004.

Anderson, Gillian B. "The Presentation of Silent Films, or, Music as Anaesthesia." *The Journal of Musicology* 5, no. 2 (Spring 1987): 257–95.

——. "'Perfuming the Air with Music': The Need for Film Music Bibliography." *Music Reference Services Quarterly* 2, nos. 1–2 (1993): 59–103.

Anderson, Paul Allen. "The World Heard: *Casablanca* and the Music of War." *Critical Inquiry* 32, no. 3 (Spring 2006): 482–515.

Anderson, Tim. "'Buried Under the Fecundity of His Own Creations': Reconsidering the Recording Bans of the American Federation of Musicians, 1942–4 and 1948." *American Music* 22, no. 2 (Summer 2004): 231–69.

Andrew, Dudley. "Sound in France: The Origins of a Native School." *Yale French Studies* 60 (1980): 94–114.

Antheil, George. "Composers in Movieland." *Modern Music* 12, no. 2 (January–February 1935): 62–8.

——. "Good Russian Advice about Movie Music." *Modern Music* 13, no. 4 (May–June 1936): 53–6.

——. "On the Hollywood Front." *Modern Music* 14, no. 1 (November–December 1936): 46–9.

——. "Breaking into the Movies." *Modern Music* 14, no. 2 (January–February 1937): 82–6.

——. "On the Hollywood Front." *Modern Music* 15, no. 1 (November–December 1937): 48–51.

——. "On the Hollywood Front." *Modern Music* 15, no. 4 (May–June 1938): 251–4.

——. *Bad Boy of Music*. Garden City, N.Y.: Doubleday, 1945.

Arnoldy, Edouard. "The Event and the Series: The Decline of *Cafés-Concerts*, the Failure of Gaumont's Chronophone, and the Birth of Cinema as an Art." Translated by Franck Le Gac and Wendy Schubring. In *The Sounds of Early Cinema*, 57–65. Edited by Richard Abel and Rick Altman. Bloomington: Indiana University Press, 2001.

Atkins, Irene Kahn. *Source Music in Motion Pictures*. East Brunswick, N.J.: Associated University Presses, 1983.

Bakker, Gerben. "The Decline and Fall of the European Film Industry: Sunk Costs, Market Size, and Market Structure, 1890–1927." *Economic History Review* 58, no. 2 (May 2005): 310–51.

Balázs, Béla. *Theory of the Film: Character and Growth of a New Art*, trans. Edith Bone. London: Dennis Dobson Ltd., 1952.

Balio, Tino. *Grand Design: Hollywood as a Modern Business Enterprise, 1930–9*. Volume 5 of the History of the American Cinema series, Charles Harpole, general editor. Berkeley: University of California Press, 1993.

Bazelon, Irwin. *Knowing the Score: Notes on Film Music*. New York: Arco, 1975.

Bazin, André. *What Is Cinema?* Translated by Hugh Gray. Berkeley: University of California Press, 1967.

Belton, John. *American Cinema/American Culture*. New York: McGraw-Hill, Inc., 1994.

——. "Awkward Transitions: Hitchcock's *Blackmail* and the Dynamics of Early Film Sound." *The Musical Quarterly* 83, no. 2 (Summer 1999): 227–46.

Benjamin, Arthur. "Film Music." *The Musical Times* 78 (July 1937): 595–7.

Berg, A. Scott. *Goldwyn: A Biography*. New York: Knopf, 1989.

Berg, Charles Merrell. "The Human Voice and the Silent Cinema." *Journal of Popular Film* 4, no. 2 (1975): 165–77.

——. *An Investigation of the Motives for and Realization of Music to Accompany the American Silent Film, 1896–1927*. New York: Arno Press, 1976.

——. "Cinema Sings the Blues." *Cinema Journal* 17, no. 2 (Spring 1978): 1–12.

Bernstein, Elmer. "What Ever Happened to Great Movie Music?" *High Fidelity* (July 1972): 55–8.

Bick, Sally. "Political Ironies: Hanns Eisler in Hollywood and Behind the Iron Curtain." *Acta Musicologica* 75, no. 1 (2003): 65–84.

Biskind, Peter. *Easy Riders, Raging Bulls: How the Sex-Drugs-and-Rock 'n' Roll Generation Saved Hollywood*, New York: Simon & Schuster, 1998.

Blitzstein, Marc. "Theatre-Music in Paris." *Modern Music* 12, no. 3 (March–April 1935): 128–34.

Bordwell, David, Janet Staiger, and Kristin Thompson. *The Classical Hollywood Cinema: Film Style and Production to 1960*. London: Routledge & Kegan Paul, 1985.

——, and Kristin Thompson. "Technological Change and Classical Film Style." In *Grand Design: Hollywood as a Modern Business Enterprise, 1930–9*, 109–41. Edited by Tino Balio. Berkeley: University of California Press, 1995.

——, and Noël Carroll, eds. *Post-Theory: Reconstructing Film Studies*. Madison: University of Wisconsin Press, 1996.

Bottomore, Stephen. "An International Survey of Sound Effects in Early Cinema." *Film History* 11, no. 4 (1999): 485–98.

Brackett, David. "Banjos, Biopics, and Compilation Scores: The Movies Go Country." *American Music* 19, no. 3 (Autumn 2001): 247–90.

Brophy, Phillip. *100 Modern Soundtracks*. London: British Film Institute, 2004.

Brown, Julie. "*Ally McBeal*'s Postmodern Soundtrack." *Journal of the Royal Musical Association* 126, no. 2 (2001): 275–303.

——. "Listening to Ravel, Watching *Un coeur en hiver*: Cinematic Subjectivity and the Music-film." *twentieth-century music* 1, no. 2 (2004): 253–75.

Brown, Royal S. "An Interview with Bernard Herrmann." *High Fidelity* (September 1976): 64–6.

——. "Herrmann, Hitchcock, and the Music of the Irrational." *Cinema Journal* 21, no. 2 (Spring 1982): 14–49.

——. *Overtones and Undertones: Reading Film Music*. Berkeley: University of California Press, 1994.

——. *Film Musings: A Selected Anthology from* Fanfare *Magazine*. Lanham, Md.: Scarecrow Press, 2007.

Buhler, James, and David Neumeyer. Review of Caryl Flinn's *Strains of Utopia: Gender, Nostalgia, and Hollywood Film Music* and Kathryn Kalinak's *Settling the Score: Music and the Classical Hollywood Film*. *Journal of the American Musicological Society* 47, no. 2 (Summer 1994): 364–85.

——, Caryl Flinn, and David Neumeyer, eds. *Music and Cinema*. Hanover: Wesleyan University Press, 2000.

——. "*Star Wars*, Music, and Myth." In *Music and Cinema*, 33–57. Edited by James Buhler, Caryl Flinn, and David Neumeyer. Hanover: Wesleyan University Press, 2000.

——. "Enchantments of *Lord of the Rings*: Soundtrack, Myth, Language, and Modernity." In *From Hobbits to Hollywood: Essays on Peter Jackson's "Lord of the Rings,"* 231–48. Edited by Ernest Mathis and Murray Pomerance. Amsterdam and New York: Editions Rodopi, 2006.

——. Review of *Hollywood Theory, Non-Hollywood Practice: Cinema Soundtracks in the 1980s and 1990s* by Annette Davison, *twentieth-century music* 3, no. 1 (2007): 145–9.

Burch, Noel. "Qu-est-ce que la Nouvelle Vague?" *Film Quarterly* 13, no. 2 (Winter 1959): 16–30.

Burlingame, Jon. *Sound and Vision: 60 Years of Motion Picture Soundtracks*. New York: Billboard Books, 2000.

Burnand, David. "Reasons Why Film Music Is Held in Low Regard: A British Perspective." *Brio* 39, no. 1 (Spring–Summer 2002): 26–32.

Burt, George. *The Art of Film Music*. Boston: Northeastern Press, 1994.

Butler, David. *Jazz Noir: Listening to Music from 'Phantom Lady' to 'The Last Seduction.'* London: Praeger, 2002.

Butler, James. "The Days Do Not End: Film Music, Time, and Bernard Herrmann." *Film Studies* 9 (Winter 2006): 51–63.

Cage, John. "The Future of Music: Credo." In *Silence*, 3–4. Hanover, N.H.: Wesleyan University Press, 1961. (Orig. 1937).

Calvocoressi, M.D. "Music and the Film." *Sight and Sound* 4, no. 14 (Summer 1935): 57–9.

Carey, Melissa, and Michael Hannan. "Case Study 2: *The Big Chill*." In *Popular Music and Film*, 162–77. Edited by Ian Inglis. London: Wallflower Press, 2003.

Carroll, Noël. "*Entr'acte*, Paris and Dada." *Millennium Film Journal* 1, no. 1 (Winter 1977): 5–11.

——. "Lang, Pabst, and Sound." *Ciné-Tracts* 2, no. 1 (Fall 1978): 15–23.

Celeste, Reni. "The Sound of Silence: Film Music and Lament." *Quarterly Review of Film and Video* 22, no. 2 (2005): 113–23.

Chanan, Michael. *The Dream That Kicks: The Prehistory and Early Years of the Cinema in Britain*. London: Routledge and Kegan Paul, 1980.

Chion, Michel. *Le Son au cinéma*. Paris: Cahiers du cinéma, 1985.

——. *Audio-Vision: Sound on Screen*. Translated by Claudia Gorbman. New York: Columbia University Press, 1994. (Orig. *L'Audio-Vision*. Paris: Éditions Nathan, 1990).

——. *La musique au cinéma*. Paris: Fayard, 1995.

Citron, Marcia. Review of *Changing Tunes: The Use of Pre-existing Music in Film*, edited by Robynn J. Stilwell and Phil Powrie. *Music & Letters* 88, no. 4 (2007): 698–702.

Clague, Mark. "Playin in 'Toon: Walt Disney's *Fantasia* (1940) and the Imagineering of Classical Music." *American Music* 22, no. 1 (Spring 2004): 91–109.

Cochran, Alfred W. "Leith Stevens and the Jazz Film Score: *The Wild One* and *Private Hell 36*." *Jazz Research Papers* 10 (1990): 24–31.

Cohen, Annabel J. "Film Music: Perspectives from Cognitive Psychology." In *Music and Cinema*, 360–78. Edited by James Buhler, Caryl Flinn, and David Neumeyer. Hanover: Wesleyan University Press, 2000.

——. "Music as a Source of Emotion in Film." In *Music and Emotion: Theory and Research*, 249–72. Edited by Patrik N. Juslin and John A. Sloboda. Oxford: Oxford University Press, 2001.

——. "Music Cognition and the Cognitive Psychology of Film Structure." *Canadian Psychology* 43, no. 4 (November 2002): 215–32.

Collins, Karen. "'I'll be Back': Recurrent Sonic Motifs in James Cameron's *Terminator* Films." In *Off the Planet: Music, Sound and Science Fiction Cinema*, 165–75. Edited by Philip Hayward. Eastleigh, UK: John Libbey Publishing, 2004.

Conrich, Ian, and Estella Ticknell. *Film's Musical Moments*. Edinburgh: Edinburgh University Press, 2006.

Cook, Nicholas. *Analyzing Musical Multimedia*. Oxford: Oxford University Press, 1998.

Cooper, David. *Bernard Herrmann's "Vertigo" (A Film Score Guide)*. Westport, Conn.: Greenwood Press, 2001.

——. "Film Form and Musical Form in Bernard Herrmann's Score to *Vertigo*." *Journal of Film Music* 1, nos. 2–3 (Fall–Winter 2003): 239–48.

——. *Bernard Herrmann's "The Ghost and Mrs. Muir" (A Film Score Guide)*. Lanham, Md.: Scarecrow Press, 2005.

Copland, Aaron. *What to Listen for in Music*. New York: McGraw-Hill, 1939.

Coyle, Rebecca, ed. *Screen Scores: Studies in Contemporary Australian Film Music*. Sydney: Australian Film Television & Radio School, 1998.

——, ed. *Reel Tracks: Australian Feature Film Music and Cultural Identities*. Eastleigh, UK: John Libbey Publishing, 2005.

Crafton, Donald. *The Talkies: American Cinema's Transition to Sound, 1926–31*. Berkeley: University of California Press, 1997.

Darby, William, and Jack Du Bois. *American Film Music: Major Composers, Techniques, Trends, 1915–90*. Jefferson, N.C.: McFarland & Company, 1990.

Daubney, Kate. *Max Steiner's "Now, Voyager" (A Film Score Guide)*. Westport, Conn.: Greenwood Press, 2000.

Davison, Annette. *Hollywood Theory, Non-Hollywood Practice: Cinema Soundtracks in the 1980s and 1990s*. Aldershot: Ashgate, 2004.

de la Motte-Haber, Helga, and Hans Emons. *Filmmusik: Eine systematische Beschreibung*. Munich: Karl Hanser Verlag, 1980.

DesJardins, Christian. *Inside Film Music: Composers Speak*. Los Angeles: Silman-James, 2006.

De Vany, Arthur, and Henry McMillan. "Was the Antitrust Action that Broke Up the Movie Studios Good for the Movies? Evidence from the Stock Market." *American Law and Economics Review* 6, no. 1 (2004): 135–53.

DeVeaux, Scott. "Bebop and the Recording Industry: The 1942 AFM Recording Ban Reconsidered." *Journal of the American Musicological Society* 41, no. 1 (Spring 1988): 126–65.

Dickinson, Kay. *Off Key: When Film and Music Won't Work Together*. Oxford: Oxford University Press, 2008.

Donnelly, K.J., ed. *Film Music: Critical Approaches*. New York: Continuum, 2001.

——. *Pop Music in British Cinema*. London: British Film Institute, 2001.

——. *The Spectre of Sound: Music in Film and Television*. London: British Film Institute, 2005.

Doty, Alexander. "Music Sells Movies: (Re)New(ed) Conservatism in Film Marketing." *Wide Angle* 10, no. 2 (1988): 70–9.

Duncan, Dean. *Charms That Soothe: Classical Music and the Narrative Film*. New York: Fordham University Press, 2003.

Ďurovičová, Nataša. "Translating America: the Hollywood Multilinguals 1929–33." In *Sound Theory/Sound Practice*, 138–53. Edited by Rick Altman. London: Routledge, 1992.

Dyer, Richard. "Music, People and Reality: The Case of Italian Neo-realism." In *European Film Music*, 28–40. Edited by Miguel Mera and David Burnand. Aldershot: Ashgate, 2006.

Eagleton, Terry. *The Illusions of Postmodernism*. Oxford: Blackwell, 1996.

Egorova, Tatiana. *Soviet Film Music*. London: Routledge, 1997.

Eisler, Hanns [and Theodor Adorno]. *Composing for the Films*. New York: Oxford University Press, 1947. (Reprinted Freeport, N.Y.: Books for Libraries Press, 1971.)

Enticknap, Leo. *Moving Image Technology: From Zoetrope to Digital*. London: Wallflower Press, 2005.

——. "De Forest Phonofilms: A Reappraisal." *Early Popular Visual Culture* 4, no. 3 (November 2006): 273–84.

Evans, Mark. *Soundtrack: The Music of the Movies.* New York: Hopkinson and Blake, 1975.

Eyman, Scott. *The Speed of Sound: Hollywood and the Talkie Revolution, 1926–30.* New York: Simon & Schuster, 1997.

Faulkner, Robert R. *Hollywood Studio Musicians: Their Work and Careers in the Recording Industry.* Chicago: Aldine-Atherton, 1971.

——. *Music on Demand: Composers and Careers in the Hollywood Film Industry.* New Brunswick, N.J.: Transaction Publishers, 1983.

Feisst, Sabine M. "Arnold Schoenberg and the Cinematic Art." *The Musical Quarterly* 83, no. 1 (Spring 1999): 93–113.

Fell, John. "Dissolves by Gaslight: Antecedents to the Motion Picture in Nineteenth-Century Melodrama." *Film Quarterly* 23, no. 3 (Spring 1970): 22–34.

——. "Motive, Mischief and Melodrama: The State of Film Narrativity in 1907." *Film Quarterly* 33, no. 3 (Spring 1980): 30–7.

Fellini, Federico, with Tony Guerra. *Fellini on Fellini,* New York: Dalacorte, 1976.

Fischer, Lucy. "René Clair, *Le Million,* and the Coming of Sound." *Cinema Journal* 16, no. 2 (Spring 1977): 34–50.

Flinn, Caryl. "The Most Romantic Art of All: Music in the Classical Hollywood Cinema." *Cinema Journal* 29, no. 4 (Summer 1990): 35–50.

——. *Strains of Utopia: Gender, Nostalgia, and Hollywood Film Music.* Princeton: Princeton University Press, 1992.

Foster, Hal, ed. *The Anti-Aesthetic: Essays on Postmodern Culture.* Port Townsend, Wash.: Bay Press, 1983.

Franklin, Peter. "*King Kong* and Film on Music: Out of the Fog." In *Film Music: Critical Approaches,* 88–102. Edited by K.J. Donnelly. New York: Continuum, 2001.

——. "*Deception*'s Great Music. In *Film Music 2: History, Theory, Practice,* 27–41. Edited by Claudia Gorbman and Warren M. Sherk. Los Angeles: Film Music Society, 2004.

——. "The Boy on the Train, or Bad Symphonies and Good Movies: The Revealing Error of the 'Symphonic Score.'" In *Beyond the Soundtrack: Representing Music in Cinema.* Edited by Daniel Goldmark, Lawrence Kramer, and Richard Leppert, 13–26. Berkeley: University of California Press, 2007.

Frey, Hugh. "Louis Malle and the 1950s: Ambiguities, Friendships and Legacies." *South Central Review* 23, no. 2 (Summer 2006): 22–35.

Frith, Simon. "Mood Music: An Inquiry into Narrative Film Music." *Screen* 25, no. 3 (May–June 1984): 78–87.

Fukuyama, Francis. *The End of History and the Last Man.* New York: Free Press, 1992.

Gabbard, Krin. *Jammin' at the Margins: Jazz and the American Cinema.* Chicago: University of Chicago Press, 1996.

——. *Black Magic: White Hollywood and African American Culture.* Rutgers: Rutgers University Press, 2004.

Gallez, Douglas W. "Satie's *Entr'acte*: A Model of Film Music." *Cinema Journal* 16, no. 1 (Fall 1976): 36–50.

——. "The Prokofiev-Eisenstein Collaboration: *Nevsky* and *Ivan* Revisited." *Cinema Journal* 17, no. 2 (Spring 1978): 13–35.

Gish, Lillian, with Ann Pinchot. *The Movies, Mr. Griffith, and Me.* Englewood Cliffs, N.J.: Prentice-Hall, 1969.

Goldmark, Daniel, and Yuval Taylor, eds. *The Cartoon Music Book.* Chicago: A Cappella Books, 2002.

——. *Tunes for 'Toons: Music and the Hollywood Cartoon.* Berkeley: University of California Press, 2005.

——, Lawrence Kramer, and Richard Leppert, eds. *Beyond the Soundtrack: Representing Music in Cinema.* Berkeley: University of California Press, 2007.

Gomery, Douglas. "The Coming of Sound: Technological Changes in the American Film Industry." In *Film Sound: Theory and Practice*, 5–24. Edited by Elisabeth Weis and John Belton. New York: Columbia University Press, 1985. Originally in *Yale French Studies* 60 (1980): 80–93.

——. "Economic Struggle and Hollywood Imperialism: Europe Converts to Sound." In *Film Sound: Theory and Practice*, 25–36. Edited by Elisabeth Weis and John Belton. New York: Columbia University Press, 1985.

——. *The Coming of Sound*. New York and London: Routledge, 2005.

Gorbman, Claudia. *Unheard Melodies: Narrative Film Music*. Bloomington: Indiana University Press, 1987.

——. "Hanns Eisler in Hollywood." *Screen* 32 (1991): 272–85.

——. Review of *Overtones and Undertones: Reading Film Music* by Royal S. Brown. *Film Quarterly* 49, no. 4 (Summer 1996): 51–2.

——. "Aesthetics and Rhetoric." *American Music* 22, no. 1 (Spring 2004): 14–26.

——, and Warren M. Sherk, eds. *Film Music 2: History, Theory, Practice*. Los Angeles: Film Music Society, 2004.

——. "Auteur Music." In *Beyond the Soundtrack: Representing Music in Cinema*, 149–62. Edited by Daniel Goldmark, Lawrence Kramer, and Richard Leppert. Berkeley: University of California Press, 2007.

Greenspan, Charlotte. "Irving Berlin in Hollywood: The Art of Plugging a Song in Film." *American Music* 22, no. 1 (Spring 2004): 40–9.

Gunning, Tom. "The Cinema of Attraction: Early Film, Its Spectator and the Avant-Garde." *Wide Angle* 8, nos. 3–4 (1986): 63–70.

——. "'Loved Him, Hated It': An Interview with Andrew Sarris." In *To Free the Cinema: Jonas Mekas & the New York Underground*, 62–82. Edited by David E. James. Princeton: Princeton University Press, 1992.

——. "'Now You See It, Now You Don't': The Temporality of the Cinema of Attractions." *Velvet Light Trap* 32 (Fall 1993): 3–12.

——. "Doing for the Eye What the Phonograph Does for the Ear." In *The Sounds of Early Cinema*, 13–31. Edited by Richard Abel and Rick Altman. Bloomington: Indiana University Press, 2001.

Hagen, Earle. *Scoring for Films*. New York: E.D. Music, 1971.

Halfyard, Janet K. *Danny Elfman's "Batman" (A Film Score Guide)*. Lanham, Md.: Scarecrow Press, 2004.

Hall, Ben M. *The Best Remaining Seats: The Story of the Golden Age of the Movie Palace*. New York: Bramhall House, 1961.

Hammond, Richard. "Forecast and Review: Pioneers of Movie Music." *Modern Music* 8, no. 3 (March–April 1931): 35–8.

Hannan, Michael, and Melissa Carey. "Ambient Soundscapes in *Blade Runner*." In *Off the Planet: Music, Sound and Science Fiction Cinema*, 149–64. Edited by Philip Hayward. Eastleigh, UK: John Libbey Publishing, 2004.

Harmon, Robert B. *Perspectives on a Vanishing Species in Architecture: The Movie Palace, A Selected Bibliography*. Monticello, Ill.: Vance Bibliographies, 1981.

Harrell, Jean. G. "Phenomenology of Film Music." *Value Inquiry* 14 (1980): 23–34.

Hayward, Philip, ed. *Off the Planet: Music, Sound and Science Fiction Cinema*. Eastleigh, UK: John Libbey Publishing, 2004.

——, ed. *Terror Tracks: Music, Sound and Horror Cinema*. London: Equinox, 2008.

Hayward, Susan, ed. *Cinema Studies: The Key Concepts*. London: Routledge, 2000.

Heathcote, Edwin. *Cinema Builders*. Chichester: Academy Press, 2001.

Hepworth, Cecil. *Came the Dawn: Memories of a Film Pioneer*. London: Phoenix House, 1951.

Hickman, Roger. *Reel Music: Exploring 100 Years of Film Music*. New York: W.W. Norton, 2005.

Hillman, Roger. "Cultural Memory on Film Soundtracks." *Journal of European Studies* 33, nos. 3–4 (2003): 323–32.

——. *Unsettling Scores: German Film, Music, and Ideology.* Bloomington: Indiana University Press, 2005.

——. "Film and Music, or Instabilities of National Identity." In *Globalization, Cultural Identities, and Media Representations*, 143–52. Edited by Natascha Gentz and Stefan Kramer. Albany: State University of New York Press, 2006.

Hoffmann, Charles. *Sounds for Silents.* New York: DBS Publications, 1970.

Holbrook, Morris B. "A Book-review Essay on the Role of Ambi-diegetic Music in the Product Design of Hollywood Movies: Macromarketing in La-La-Land." *Consumption, Markets and Culture* 6, no. 3 (2003): 207–30.

Hubbard, Preston J. "Synchronized Sound and Movie-House Musicians, 1926–9." *American Music* 3, no. 4 (Winter 1985): 429–41.

Hubbert, Julie. "'Whatever Happened to Great Movie Music?': *Cinéma Vérité* and Hollywood Film Music of the Early 1970s." *American Music* 21, no. 2 (Summer 2003): 180–213.

——. "Modernism at the Movies: *The Cabinet of Dr. Caligari* and a Film Score Revisited." *The Musical Quarterly* 88, no. 1 (2005): 63–94.

——. "Eisenstein's Theory of Film Music Revisited: Silent and Early Sound Antecedents." In *Composing for the Screen in Germany and the USSR: Cultural Politics and Propaganda*, edited by Robynn J. Stilwell and Phil Powrie, 127–47. Bloomington: Indiana University Press, 2008.

Hunt, Martin. "Their Finest Hour? The Scoring of *Battle of Britain*." *Film History* 14, no. 1 (2002): 47–56.

Huntley, John. *British Film Music.* London: Skelton Robinson, 1947.

Hutchinson, Ron. "The Vitaphone Project: Answering Harry Warner's Question: 'Who the Hell Wants to Hear Actors Talk?'" *Film History* 14, no. 1 (2002): 40–6.

Inglis, Ian, ed. *Popular Music and Film.* London: Wallflower Press, 2003.

Irving, Ernest. "Music in Films." *Music & Letters*, 24, no. 4 (October 1943): 223–35.

Jablonski, Edward. *Gershwin.* New York: Doubleday, 1987.

Jameson, Frederic. "Postmodernism, Or, the Cultural Logic of Late Capitalism." *New Left Review* 146 (July–August 1984): 59–92. Reprinted in Frederic Jameson, "The Cultural Logic of Late Capitalism," in *Postmodernism, or, The Cultural Logic of Late Capitalism* (Durham, N.C.: Duke University Press, 1991): 1–54.

Jarrett, Michael. "Sound Doctrine: An Interview with Walter Murch." *Film Quarterly* 53, no. 3 (Spring 2000): 2–11.

Joe, Jeongwon, and Theresa Rose, eds. *Between Opera and Cinema.* London: Routledge, 2001.

Johnson, Ian. *William Alwyn: The Art of Film Music.* London: Boydell Press, 2005.

Johnson, William. "Face the Music." *Film Quarterly* 22, no. 4 (Summer 1969): 3–19.

Jones, Janna. *The Southern Movie Palace: Rise, Fall, and Resurrection.* Gainesville, Fla.: University Press of Florida, 2003.

Kallberg, Jeffrey. "Nocturnal Thoughts on *Impromptu*." *The Musical Quarterly* 81, no. 2 (Summer 1997): 199–203.

Kalinak, Kathryn. "The Text of Music: A Study of *The Magnificent Ambersons*." *Cinema Journal* 27, no. 4 (Summer 1988): 45–63.

——. *Settling the Score: Music and the Classical Hollywood Film.* Madison: University of Wisconsin Press, 1992.

——. "Max Steiner and the Classical Hollywood Film Score: An Analysis of *The Informer*." In *Film Music 1*, 123–42. Edited by Clifford McCarty. Los Angeles: Film Music Society, 1998.

——. *How the West Was Sung: Music in the Westerns of John Ford.* Berkeley: University of California Press, 2007.

Karlin, Fred, and Rayburn Wright. *On the Track: A Guide to Contemporary Film Scoring.* New York: Schirmer 1990.

——. *Listening to Movies: A Film Lover's Guide to Film Music.* New York: Schirmer, 1994.

Kassabian, Anahid. *Hearing Film: Tracking Identifications in Contemporary Hollywood Film Music.* London: Routledge, 2000.

——. "The Sound of a New Film Form." In *Popular Music and Film*, 91–101. Edited by Ian Inglis. London: Wallflower Press, 2003.

Keller, Hans. "Noisy Music and Musical Noise." *The Music Review* 13, no. 2 (May 1952): 138–40.

——. "World Review." *The Music Review* 13, no. 4 (November 1952): 310–12.

——. "*West of Zanzibar*: Some Problems of Film Music." *Musical Opinion* 77 (July 1954): 585–57.

——. "Alwyn—Benjamin—Black." *The Music Review* 17, no. 3 (August 1956): 254–5.

——. "No Music—Malcolm Arnold—Benjamin Frankel." *The Music Review* 17, no. 4 (November 1956): 337–40.

——. *Film Music and Beyond: Writings on Music and the Screen, 1946–59.* Edited by Christopher Wintle. London: Plumbago Books, 2006.

Knight, Arthur. *The Liveliest Art: A Panoramic History of the Movies.* New York: Macmillan, 1957.

Kraft, James P. "The 'Pit' Musicians: Mechanization in the Movie Theaters, 1926–34." *Labor History* 35, no. 1 (1994): 66–89.

——. "Musicians in Hollywood: Work and Technological Change in Entertainment Industries, 1926–40." *Technology and Culture* 35, no. 2 (April 1994): 289–314.

Kramer, Lawrence. "Melodic Trains: Music in Polanski's *The Pianist*." In *Beyond the Soundtrack: Representing Music in Cinema*, 66–85. Edited by Daniel Goldmark, Lawrence Kramer, and Richard Leppert. Berkeley: University of California Press, 2007.

Kreuzer, Anselm C. *Filmmusik: Geschichte und Analyse 2—Erweiterte und überarbeitete Auflage.* Berlin: Peter Lang, 2003.

Lack, Russell. *Twenty-Four Frames Under: A Buried History of Film Music.* London: Quartet Books, 1997.

Lacombe, Alain. *La musique de film.* Paris: F. Van de Velde, 1979.

Laing, Heather. *Gabriel Yared's "The English Patient" (A Film Score Guide).* Lanham, Md.: Scarecrow Press, 2004.

——. *The Gendered Score: Music in 1940s Melodrama and the Woman's Film.* Aldershot: Ashgate, 2007.

Lambert, Constant. *Music Ho! A Study of Music in Decline.* New York: Charles Scribner's Sons, 1934.

Lannin, Steve, and Matthew Caley, eds. *Pop Fiction: The Song in Cinema.* Bristol: Intellect Books, 2005.

Lapedis, Hilary. "Popping the Question: The Function and Effect of Popular Music in Cinema." *Popular Music* 18, no. 3 (October 1999): 367–79.

Larsen, Peter (trans. John Irons). *Film Music.* London: Reaktion Books, 2008.

Lastra, James. *Sound Technology and the American Cinema: Perception, Representation, Modernity.* New York: Columbia University Press, 2000.

Leinberger, Charles. *Ennio Morricone's "The Good, the Bad, and the Ugly" (A Film Score Guide).* Lanham, Md.: Scarecrow Press, 2004.

Lerner, Neil. "Copland's Music of Wide Open Spaces: Surveying the Pastoral Trope in Hollywood." *The Musical Quarterly* 85, no. 3 (Fall 2001): 477–515.

——. "The Politics of Polyphony in Selected Documentary Film Scores by Virgil Thomson and Aaron Copland." In *Film Music 2: History, Theory, Practice*, 1–25. Edited by Claudia Gorbman and Warren M. Sherk. Los Angeles: Film Music Society, 2004.

——. "Nostalgia, Masculinist Discourse, and Authoritarianism in John Williams's Scores for *Star Wars* and *Close Encounters of the Third Kind*." In *Off the Planet: Music, Sound and Science*

Fiction Cinema, 96–108. Edited by Philip Hayward. Eastleigh, UK: John Libbey Publishing, 2004.

———. "'Look at That Big Hand Move Along': Clocks, Containment, and Music in *High Noon*." *South Atlantic Quarterly* 104, no. 1 (2005): 151–73.

Levant, Oscar. *A Smattering of Ignorance*. New York: Doubleday, Doran & Co., 1940.

———. *The Memoirs of an Amnesiac*. New York: G.P. Putnam's Sons, 1965.

Leydon, Rebecca. "Hooked on Aetherophonics: *The Day the Earth Stood Still*." In *Off the Planet: Music, Sound and Science Fiction Cinema*, 30–41. Edited by Philip Hayward. Eastleigh, UK: John Libbey Publishing, 2004.

———. "*Forbidden Planet*: Effects and Affects in the Electro Avant Garde." In *Off the Planet: Music, Sound and Science Fiction Cinema*, 61–76. Edited by Philip Hayward. Eastleigh, UK: John Libbey Publishing, 2004.

Lev, Peter. *The Fifties: Transforming the Screen, 1950–9*. Volume 7 of the History of the American Cinema series, Charles Harpole, general editor. Berkeley: University of California Press, 2003.

Levy, Louis. *Music for the Movies*. London: Sampson Low, 1948.

Leyda, Jay. *Kino*. New York: Collier Books, 1973.

Limbacher, James L. *Film Music: From Violins to Video*. Metuchen, N.J.: Scarecrow Press, 1974.

———. *Keeping Score: Film Music 1972–9*. Metuchen, N.J.: Scarecrow Press, 1981.

Lindgren, Ernest. *The Art of the Film*. New York: Macmillan, 1963.

Link, Stan. Review of *European Film Music*, edited by Miguel Mera and David Burtnand. *Screen* 48, no. 2 (Summer 2007): 273–9.

Lipscomb, Scott D., and David E. Tolchinsky. "The Role of Music Communication in Cinema." In *Musical Communication*, 382–404. Edited by Dorothy Miell, Raymond MacDonald, and David J. Hargreaves. Oxford: Oxford University Press, 2005.

London, Justin. "Leitmotifs and Musical Reference in the Classical Film Score." In *Music and Cinema*, 85–96. Edited by James Buhler, Caryl Flinn, and David Neumeyer. Hanover: Wesleyan University Press, 2000.

London, Kurt. *Film Music: A Summary of the Characteristic Features of Its History, Aesthetics, Technique, and Possible Developments*. Translated by Eric S. Bensinger. London: Faber & Faber Ltd., 1936.

Loughney, Patrick. "Domitor Witnesses the First Complete Public Presentation of the [*Dickson Experimental Sound Film*] in the Twentieth Century." In *The Sounds of Early Cinema*, 215–19. Edited by Richard Abel and Rick Altman. Bloomington: Indiana University Press, 2001.

Louvre, Alf. "The New Radicalism: The Politics of Culture in Britain, America and France, 1956–73." In *Cultural Revolution? The Challenge of the Arts in the 1960s*, 45–71. Edited by Bart Moore-Gilbert and John Seed. London and New York: Routledge, 1992.

Lynch, David. "Action and Reaction." In *Soundscape: The School of Sound Lectures, 1998–2001*, 49–53. Edited by Larry Sider, Diana Freeman, and Jerry Sider. London: Wallflower Press, 2003.

Lyotard, Jean-François. *The Postmodern Condition: A Report on Knowledge*. Translated by Geoff Bennington and Brian Massumi. Minneapolis: University of Minnesota Press, 1984.

MacDonald, Laurence E. *The Invisible Art of Film Music: A Comprehensive History*. Lanham, Maryland: Ardsley House, 1998.

MacGowan, Kenneth. "The Coming of Sound to the Screen." *The Quarterly of Film, Radio and Television* 10, no. 2 (Winter 1955): 136–45.

———. "When the Talkies Came to Hollywood." *The Quarterly of Film, Radio and Television* 10, no. 3 (Spring 1956): 288–301.

Mancini, Henry. *Did They Mention the Music?* Chicago: Contemporary Books, 1989.

Manvell, Roger, and John Huntley. *The Technique of Film Music*. London: Focal Press, 1957.

Marks, Martin M. *Music and the Silent Film: Contexts and Case Studies, 1895–1924*. Oxford: Oxford University Press, 1997.

——. "Music, Drama, Warner Brothers: The Cases of *Casablanca* and *The Maltese Falcon*." In *Music and Cinema*, 161–86. Edited by James Buhler, Caryl Flinn, and David Neumeyer. Hanover: Wesleyan University Press, 2000.

Marmorstein, Gary. *Hollywood Rhapsody: Movie Music and Its Makers, 1900 to 1975*. New York: Schirmer, 1997.

Mast, Gerald. *A Short History of the Movies*. New York: Pegasus, 1971.

May, Lary. *Screening Out the Past: The Birth of Mass Culture and the Motion Picture Industry*. New York and Oxford: Oxford University Press, 1980.

Mayer, David, and Matthew Scott. *Four Bars of "Agit": Incidental Music for Victorian and Edwardian Melodrama*. London: Samuel French, 1983.

McAllister, Rita. "Sabaneyev, Leonid Leonidovich." In *The New Grove Dictionary of Music and Musicians*, volume XVI, 363–4. London and New York: Macmillan, 1980.

McCarty, Clifford. *Film Composers in America: A Checklist of Their Work*. Los Angeles: Valentine, 1953.

——, ed. *Film Music 1*. Los Angeles: Film Music Society, 1998.

——. *Film Composers in America: A Filmography, 1911–70*. Oxford: Oxford University Press, 2000.

McLean, Adrienne L. " 'It's Only That I Do What I Love and Love What I Do': Film Noir and the Musical Woman." *Cinema Journal* 33, no. 1 (Autumn 1993): 316.

Melnick, Ross, and Andreas Fuchs. *Cinema Treasures: a New Look at Classic Movie Theaters*. St. Paul, Minn.: Motorbooks International, 2004.

Mera, Miguel. "Is Funny Music Funny? Contexts and Case Studies of Film Music Humor." *Journal of Popular Music Studies* 14, no. 2 (September 2002): 91–113.

——, and David Burnand, eds. *European Film Music*. Aldershot: Ashgate, 2006.

——. *Mychael Danna's "The Ice Storm" (A Film Score Guide)*. Lanham, Md.: Scarecrow Press, 2007.

Merkley, Paul A. " 'Stanley Hates This But I Like It!': North vs. Kubrick on the Music for *2001: A Space Odyssey*." *Journal of Film Music* 2, no. 1 (Fall 2007): 1–33.

Milhaud, Darius. "Experimenting with Sound Films." *Modern Music* 7, no. 2 (February–March 1930): 11–14.

Moore-Gilbert, Bart, and John Seed, eds. *Cultural Revolution? The Challenge of the Arts in the 1960s*. London and New York: Routledge, 1992.

Morgan, David. *Knowing the Score: Film Composers Talk about the Art, Craft, Blood, Sweat, and Tears of Writing for Cinema*. New York: Harper, 2000.

Morrey, Douglas. "The Noise of Thoughts: The Turbulent (Sound-)Worlds of Jean-Luc Godard." *Culture, Theory & Critique* 46, no. 1 (2005): 61–74.

Morton, Lawrence. "Hanns Eisler: Composer and Critic." *Hollywood Review* 3, no. 2 (Winter 1947–8): 208–11.

——. "Film Music of the Quarter." *Hollywood Quarterly* 5, no. 3 (Spring 1951): 282–8.

——. "Composing, Orchestration, and Criticizing." *The Quarterly of Film, Radio and Television* 6, no. 2 (Winter 1951): 191–206.

Mundy, John. *Popular Music on Screen: From Hollywood Musical to Music Video*. Manchester: Manchester University Press, 1999.

Murphy, Robert. "Coming of Sound to the Cinema in Britain." *Historical Journal of Film, Radio and Television* 4, no. 2 (1984): 143–60.

Musser, Charles. *The Emergence of Cinema: The American Screen to 1907*. New York: Scribner's, 1990.

——. *Before the Nickelodeon: Edwin S. Porter and the Edison Manufacturing Company*. Berkeley: University of California Press, 1991.

Naremore, James. "American Film Noir: The History of an Idea." *Film Quarterly* 49, no. 2 (Winter 1995–6): 12–28.

Naylor, David. *American Picture Palaces: The Architecture of Fantasy*. New York: Van Nostrand Rheinhold, 1981.

Nelson, Robert U. "Film Music: Color or Line?" *Hollywood Quarterly* 2, no. 1 (October 1946): 57–65.

Ness, Richard R. "A Lotta Night Music: The Sound of *Film Noir*." *Cinema Journal* 47, no. 2 (Winter 2008): 52–73.

Nettelbeck, Colin. "A Cycle of Freedom—Louis Malle's Jazz Films." *Nottingham French Studies* 43, no. 1 (Spring 2004): 156–64.

Neumeyer, David. "Schoenberg at the Movies: Dodecaphony and Film." *Music Theory Online* 1, no. 1 (February 1993).

———. "Performances in Early Hollywood Sound Films: Source Music, Background Music, and the Integrated Sound Track." *Contemporary Music Review* 19, no. 1 (2000): 37–62.

———. "Merging Genres in the 1940s: The Musical and the Dramatic Feature Film." *American Music* 22, no. 1 (Spring 2004): 122–32.

Nisbett, Robert F. "Pare Lorentz, Louis Gruenberg, and *The Fight for Life*: The Making of a Film Score." *The Musical Quarterly* 79, no. 2 (Summer 1995): 231–55.

Niver, Kemp R. *Biograph Bulletins, 1896–1908*. Los Angeles: Locare Research Group, 1971.

———. *Klaw and Erlanger: Famous Plays in Pictures*. London: Renovare, 1985.

North, Joseph H. *The Early Development of the Motion Picture, 1887–1909*. New York: Arno Press, 1973.

O'Brien, Charles. *Cinema's Conversion to Sound: Technology and Film Style in France and the U.S.* Bloomington: Indiana University Press, 2005.

O'Rawe, Des. "The Great Secret: Silence, Cinema and Modernism." *Screen* 47, no. 4 (Winter 2006): 395–405.

Orledge, Robert. "Charles Koechlin and the Early Sound Film 1933–38." *Proceedings of the Royal Musical Association* 98 (1971–2): 1–16.

Palmer, Christopher. *The Composer in Hollywood*. New York and London: Marion Boyars, 1990.

———. *Dimitri Tiomkin: A Portrait*. London: T.E. Books, 1974.

Patterson, David. "Music, Structure and Metaphor in Stanley Kubrick's *2001: A Space Odyssey*." *American Music* 22, no. 3 (Fall 2004):

Pauli, Hanjörg. "Bernard Herrmanns Musik zu *Citizen Kane*." *Disssonance* 26 (November 1990): 12–18.

Paulin, Scott D. "Richard Wagner and the Fantasy of Cinematic Unity: The Idea of the *Gesamtkunstwerk* in the History and Theory of Film Music." In *Music and Cinema*, 58–84. Edited by James Buhler, Caryl Flinn, and David Neumeyer. Hanover: Wesleyan University Press, 2000.

Paulus, Irena. "Du role de la musique dans le cinema hollywoodien classique. Les functions de la musique dans le film *Casablanca* (1943) de Michael Curtiz." *International Review of the Aesthetics and Sociology of Music* 28, no. 1 (June 1997): 63–110.

———. "Music in Krzysztof Kieślowski's Film *Three Colors: Blue*. A Rhapsody in Shades of Blue: The Reflections of a Musician." *International Review of the Aesthetics and Sociology of Music* 30, no. 1 (June 1999): 65–91.

Paxman, Jon. "Preisner-Kieslowski: The Art of Synergetic Understatement in *Three Colours: Red*." In *European Film Music*, 145–62. Edited by Miguel Mera and David Burnand. Aldershot: Ashgate, 2006

Penn, William. "The Music for David O. Selznick's Production No. 103, *Duel in the Sun*." In *Perspectives on Music: Essays on Collections at the Humanities Research Center*. Edited by David Oliphant and Thomas Zigal. Austin: University of Texas Humanities Research Center, 1985.

Pomerance, Murray. "Finding Release: 'Storm Clouds' and *The Man Who Knew Too Much*." In *Music and Cinema*, 207–46. Edited by James Buhler, Caryl Flinn, and David Neumeyer. Hanover: Wesleyan University Press, 2000.

Potamkin, Harry Alan. "Music and the Movies." *The Musical Quarterly* 15, no. 2 (April 1929): 281–96.

Powrie, Phil, and Robynn J. Stilwell, eds. *Changing Tunes: The Use of Pre-Existing Music in Film*. Aldershot: Ashgate, 2006.

Prendergast, Roy M. *Film Music: A Neglected Art*. New York: W.W. Norton, 1977.

Previn, André. *No Minor Chords: My Days in Hollywood*. New York: Doubleday, 1991.

Putnam, Michael. *Silent Screens: The Decline and Transformation of the American Movie Theater*. Baltimore: Johns Hopkins University Press, 2000.

Rabb, Theodore K. "Preface." *The Journal of Interdisciplinary History* 36, no. 3 (2005): 319–20.

Raksin, David. "Whatever Became of Movie Music?" *Film Music Notebook* 1, no. 1 (Autumn 1974): 23–6. Orig. "Film Music: Beauty and the Beast? Raksin Raps State of Art," *Variety* 275, no. 1 (May 1974): 59.

Rapee, Erno. *Motion Picture Moods for Pianists and Organists: A Rapid Reference Collection of Selected Pieces, Adapted to 52 Moods and Situations*. New York: Belwin, 1924. (Reprinted New York: Arno Press, 1974.)

——. *Encyclopedia of Music for Pictures*. New York: Belwin, 1925. (Reprinted New York: Arno Press, 1970.)

Raybould, Clarence. "Music and the Synchronized Film." *Sight and Sound* 2, no. 7 (Autumn 1933): 80–1.

Reay, Pauline. *Music in Film: Soundtracks and Synergy*. London: Wallflower Press, 2004.

Richards, Jeffrey. "New Waves and Old Myths: British Cinema in the 1960s." In *Cultural Revolution? The Challenge of the Arts in the 1960s*, 218–35. Edited by Bart Moore-Gilbert and John Seed. London and New York: Routledge, 1992.

Robertson, Pamela Wojcik, and Arthur Knight, eds. *Soundtrack Available: Essays on Film and Popular Culture*. Durham: Duke University Press, 2001.

Rockwell, John. *All American Music: Composition in the Late Twentieth Century*. New York: Alfred A. Knopf, 1983.

Rodman, Ronald. "The Popular Song as Leitmotif in 1990s Film." In *Changing Tunes: The Use of Pre-existing Music in Film*, 119–36. Edited by Phil Powrie and Robynn J. Stilwell. Aldershot: Ashgate, 2006.

Rogoff, Rosalind. "Edison's Dream: A Brief History of the Kinetophone." *Cinema Journal* 15, no. 2 (Spring 1976): 58–68.

Romney, Jonathan, and Adrian Wooton, eds. *Celluloid Jukebox: Popular Music and the Movies since the 1950s*. London: British Film Institute, 1995.

Rosar, William H. "Music for the Monsters." *Quarterly Journal of the Library of Congress* 40, no. 3 (Fall 1983): 390–421.

——. "Stravinsky and MGM." In *Film Music I*, edited by Clifford McCarty, 109–22. Los Angeles: The Film Music Society, 1989.

——. "The *Dies Irae* in *Citizen Kane*: Musical Hermeneutics Applied to Film Music." In *Film Music: Critical Approaches*, 103–16. Edited by K.J. Donnelly. New York: Continuum, 2001.

——. "Film Music—What's in a Name?" *Journal of Film Music* 1, no. 1 (2002): 1–18.

——. "Music for Martians: Schillinger's Two Tonics and Harmony of Fourths in Leith Stevens's Score for *War of the Worlds* (1953)." *Journal of Film Music* 1, no. 4 (Winter 2006): 395–438.

Rossholm, Anna Sofia. *Reproducing Languages, Translating Bodies: Approaches to Speech, Translation and Cultural Identity in Early European Sound Film*. Stockholm: Almqvist & Wiksell International. 2006.

Rózsa, Miklós. *Double Life: The Autobiography of Miklós Rózsa*. New York: Hippocrene Books, 1982.

Sabaneev, Leonid. "Music and the Sound Film." Translated by S.W. *Music & Letters* 15, no. 2 (April 1934): 147–52.

———. *Music for the Films: A Handbook for Composer and Conductors.* Translated by S.W. Pring. London: Pitman, 1935.

Sadoff, Ronald H. "Composition by Corporate Committee: Recipe for Cliché." *American Music* 22, no. 1 (Spring 2004): 64–75.

———. "The Role of the Music Editor and the 'Temp Track' as Blueprint for the Score, Source Music, and Scource Music of Films." *Popular Music* 25, no. 2 (2006): 165–83.

Salt, Barry. "Film Style and Technology in the Thirties." In *Film Sound: Theory and Practice*, 37–43. Edited by Elisabeth Weis and John Belton. New York: Columbia University Press, 1985. Originally in *Film Quarterly* 30, no. 1 (Autumn 1976): 19–32.

Schelle, Michael. *The Score: Interviews with Film Composers.* Los Angeles: Silman-James, 1999.

Scheurer, Timothy E. "John Williams and Film Music since 1971." *Popular Music and Society* 21, no. 1 (Spring 1997): 59–72.

———. "Kubrick vs. North: The Score for *2001: A Space Odyssey.*" *Journal of Popular Film and Television* 25, no. 4 (Winter 1998):172–82.

———. "Musical Mythopoesis and Heroism in Film Scores of Recent Sports Movies." *Journal of Popular Film and Television* 32, no. 4 (Winter 2005): 157–66.

Schreger, Charles. "Altman, Dolby, and the Second Sound Revolution." In *Film Sound: Theory and Practice*, 348–55. Edited by Elisabeth Weis and John Belton. New York: Columbia University Press, 1985. Originally "The Second Coming of Sound," *Film Comment*, 14, no. 5 (September–October 1978).

Schwartz, Charles. *Gershwin: His Life & Music.* New York: Da Capo Press, 1973.

Schwartz-Bishir, Rebecca. "*Aleksandr Nevskiy*: Prokofiev's Successful Compromise with Socialist Realism." In *Composing for the Screen in Germany and the USSR: Cultural Politics and Propaganda*, edited by Robynn J. Stillwell and Phil Powrie, 148–60. Bloomington: Indiana University Press, 2008.

Sergi, Gianluca. "The Hollywood Sonic Playground: The Spectator as Listener." In *Hollywood Spectatorship: Changing Perceptions of Cinema Audiences*, 121–31. Edited by Richard Maltby and Melvyn Stokes. London: British Film Institute, 2001.

———. "A Cry in the Dark: The Role of the Post-Classical Film Sound." In *The Film Cultures Reader*, 107–14. Edited by Graeme Turner. New York and London: Routledge, 2002.

———. *The Dolby Era: Film Sound in Contemporary Hollywood.* Manchester: Manchester University Press, 2004.

Shapiro, Anne Dhu. "Action Music in American Pantomime and Melodrama, 1730–1913." *American Music* 2, no. 4 (Winter 1984): 49–72.

Sharp, Dennis. *The Picture Palace and Other Buildings for Movies.* London: Hugh Evelyn, 1969.

Sinclair, Craig. "Audition: Making Sense of/in the Cinema." *The Velvet Light Trap* no. 51 (Spring 2003): 17–28.

Singer, Ben. "Manhattan Nickelodeons: New Data on Audiences and Exhibitors." *Cinema Journal* 34, no. 3 (Spring 1995): 5–35.

Sitney, P. Adams, ed. *Film Culture Reader.* New York: Praeger, 1970.

Smith, Jeff. *The Sounds of Commerce: Marketing Popular Film Music.* New York: Columbia University Press, 1998.

Smith, Steven C. *A Heart at Fire's Center: The Life and Music of Bernard Herrmann.* Berkeley: University of California Press, 1991.

———. "Unheard Melodies? A Critique of Psychoanalytic Theories of Film Music." In *Post-Theory: Reconstructing Film Studies.* 230–47. Edited by David Bordwell and Noël Carroll. Madison: University of Wisconsin Press, 1996.

Sponable, E.I. "Historical Development of Sound Films." Paper presented at the annual meeting of the Society of Motion Picture Editors (SMPE) in Hollywood on October 22, 1946.

Stanfield, Peter. *Horse Opera: The Strange History of the 1930s Singing Cowboy*. Urbana: University of Illinois Press, 2002.

——. *Body and Soul: Jazz and Blues in American Film, 1927–63*. Urbana: University of Illinois Press, 2005.

Steiner, Fred. "What Were Musicians Saying about Movie Music during the First Decade of Sound? A Symposium of Selected Writings." In *Film Music I*, edited by Clifford McCarty, 81–107. Los Angeles: The Film Music Society, 1989.

Sternfeld, Frederick W. "Preliminary Report on Film Music." *Hollywood Quarterly* 2, no. 3 (April 1947): 299–302.

——. "Music and the Feature Films." *The Musical Quarterly* 33, no. 4 (October 1947): 517–32.

Stilwell, Robynn J. "'I Just Put a Drone Under Him . . .': Collage and Subversion in the Score of *Die Hard*." *Music & Letters* 78, no. 4 (1997): 551–80.

——. "*Sense & Sensibility*: Form, Genre and Function in the Film Score." *Acta Musicologica* 72, no. 2 (2000): 219–40.

——. "Music in Films: A Critical Review of Literature, 1980–96." *Journal of Film Music* 1, no. 1 (2002): 19–61.

——. "The Fantastical Gap between Diegetic and Nondiegetic." In *Beyond the Soundtrack: Representing Music in Cinema*, 184–202. Edited by Daniel Goldmark, Lawrence Kramer, and Richard Leppert. Berkeley: University of California Press, 2007.

——, and Phil Powrie, eds. *Composing for the Screen in Germany and the USSR: Cultural Politics and Propaganda*. Bloomington: Indiana University Press, 2008.

Strick, J.C. "The Economics of the Motion Picture Industry: A Survey." *Philosophy of the Social Sciences* 8, no. 4 (December 1978): 406–17.

Sullivan, Jack. *Hitchcock's Music*. New Haven: Yale University Press, 2006.

Sultanik, Aaron. *Film: A Modern Art*. Cranbury, N.J.: Cornwall Books, 1986.

Sundholm, John. "Listening to Film." *Review of Communication* 3, no. 1 (January 2003): 90–3.

Swynnoe, Jan G. *The Best Years of British Film Music, 1936–58*. London: Boydell Press, 2002.

Taruskin, Richard. "Speed Bumps" (review of *The Cambridge History of Nineteenth-Century Music*, edited by Jim Samson, and *The Cambridge History of Twentieth-Century Music*). *19th-Century Music* 29, no. 2 (2005):185–207.

Thiel, Wolfgang. *Filmmusik in Geschichte und Gegenwart*. Berlin: Henschelverlag, 1981.

Thomas, Tony. *Music for the Movies*. South Brunswick, N.J.: A.S. Barnes & Co, 1973.

——. *Film Score: A View from the Podium*. South Brunswick, N.J.: A.S. Barnes & Co., 1979.

Thompson, Emily. "Wiring the World: Acoustical Engineers and the Empire of Sound in the Motion Picture Industry, 1927–30." In *Hearing Cultures: Essays on Sound, Listening and Modernity*, edited by Veit Erlmann, 191–209. Oxford: Berg, 2004.

Thompson, Kristin. "Early Sound Counterpoint." *Yale French Studies* 60 (1980): 115–40.

——. *Exporting Entertainment: America in the World Film Market, 1907–34*. London: British Film Institute, 1985.

——, and David Bordwell. *Film History: An Introduction*. New York: McGraw-Hill, 1994.

Thomson, Virgil. "A Little About Movie Music." *Modern Music* 10, no. 4 (May–June 1933): 188–91.

——. *The State of Music*. New York: Morrow, 1939.

Timm, Larry M. *The Soul of Cinema: An Appreciation of Film Music*. Upper Saddle River, N.J.: Prentice Hall, 2003.

Tiomkin, Dimitri, with Prosper Buranelli. *Please Don't Hate Me*. New York: Doubleday and Company, 1959.

Toch, Ernst. "Sound-Film and Music Theatre." *Modern Music* 13, no. 2 (January–February 1936): 15–18.

Toulet, Emmanuelle. *Birth of the Motion Picture*. Translated by Susan Emanuel. New York: Harry N. Abrams, 1995.

Van der Lek, Robert. "Filmmusikgeschichte in systematischer Darstellung." Translated by Elicha Rensing. *Archiv für Musikwissenschaft* 44, no. 3 (1987): 216–39.

——. "Concert Music as Re-Used Film Music: E.-W. Korngold's Self-Arrangements." Translated by Mick Swithinbank. *Acta Msicologica* 66, no. 2 (July–December 1994): 78–112.

Van Vechten, Carl. *Music and Bad Manners*. New York: Alfred A. Knopf, 1916.

Vardac, A. Nicholas. *Stage to Screen*. New York: Benjamin Blom, 1968.

Vernallis, Carol. "Teaching Music Video: Aesthetics, Politics and Pedagogy." *Journal of Popular Music Studies* 9–10, no. 1 (September 1997): 93–9.

——. *Experiencing Music Video: Aesthetics and Cultural Context*. New York: Columbia University Press, 2004.

Walsh, Michael. "Jameson and 'Global Aesthetics.' " In *Post-Theory: Reconstructing Film Studies*. 481–500. Edited by David Bordwell and Noël Carroll. Madison: University of Wisconsin Press, 1996.

Weber, Horst. "Eisler as Hollywood Film Composer, 1942–8." *Historical Journal of Film, Radio and Television* 18, no. 4 (October 1998): 561–6.

Wefelmeyer, Bernd. "Musik zweiter Klasse? Musik zum Film: Eine Standortbestimmung" ("Second-class Music? Film Music: Where It Stands"). *Das Orchester* 51, no. 2 (February 2003): 16–21.

Weis, Elisabeth. *The Silent Scream: Alfred Hitchcock's Sound Track*. Rutherford, N.J.: Farleigh Dickinson University Press, 1982.

——, and John Belton, eds. *Film Sound: Theory and Practice*. New York: Columbia University Press, 1985.

Wescott, Steven D. "Miklós Rózsa's *Ben-Hur*: The Musical-Dramatic Function of the Hollywood Leitmotiv." In *Film Music 1*, 183–207. Edited by Clifford McCarty. Los Angeles: Film Music Society, 1998.

Whitesell, Lloyd. "Concerto Macabre." *The Musical Quarterly* 88, no. 2 (2005): 167–203.

Whittington, William. *Sound Design & Science Fiction*. Austin: University of Texas Press, 2007.

Wierzbicki, James. "Weird Vibrations: How the Theremin Gave Musical Voice to Hollywood's Extraterrestrial 'Others.' " *Journal of Popular Film and Television* 30 (2002): 125–35.

——. "Sound as Music in the Films of Terrence Malick." In *The Cinema of Terrence Malick: Poetic Visions of America*, 110–22. Edited by Hannah Patterson. London: Wallflower Press, 2003.

——. "Grand Illusion: The 'Storm Cloud' Music in Hitchcock's *The Man Who Knew Too Much*." *Journal of Film Music* 1, nos. 2–3 (Fall–Winter 2003): 217–38.

——. *Louis and Bebe Barron's "Forbidden Planet" (A Film Score Guide)*. Lanham, Md.: Scarecrow Press, 2005.

——. Review of *Hearing Film: Tracking Identifications in Contemporary Hollywood Film Music*, by Anahid Kassabian. *Journal of Film Music* 1, no. 4 (Winter 2006): 460–3.

——. "The Hollywood Career of Gershwin's Second Rhapsody." *Journal of the American Musicological Society* 60, no. 1 (Spring 2007): 133–86.

——. "Sour Notes: Hanns Eisler and the FBI." In *Modernism on File: Writers, Artists, and the FBI, 1920–50*, 197–219. Edited by Claire A. Culleton and Karen Leick. New York: Palgrave Macmillan, 2008.

——. "Shrieks, Flutters, and Vocal Curtains: Electronic Sound/Electronic Music in Hitchcock's *The Birds*." *Music and the Moving Image* 1, no. 2 (Summer 2008).

Williams, Alan. "Historical and Theoretical Issues in the Coming of Recorded Sound to the Cinema." In *Sound Theory/Sound Practice*, 126–37. Edited by Rick Altman. London: Routledge, 1992.

Williams, Martin. "Jazz at the Movies." In *Film Music: From Violins to Video*, 42–4. Edited by James Limbacher. Metuchen, N.J.: Scarecrow Press, 1974. Also anthologized in Williams, Martin, *Jazz in Its Time*, 17–21. Oxford: Oxford University Press, 1991.

Winkler, Max. *A Penney from Heaven.* New York: Appleton-Century-Crofts, 1951.

Winter, Marian Hannah. "The Functions of Music in Sound Films." *The Musical Quarterly* 27, no. 2 (April 1941): 146–64.

Winters, Ben. *Erich Wolfgang Korngold's "The Adventures of Robin Hood" (A Film Score Guide).* Lanham, Md.: Scarecrow Press, 2007.

———. "Catching Dreams: Editing Film Scores for Publication." *Journal of the Royal Musical Association* 132, no. 1 (2008): 115–40.

Zierer, Clifford M. "Hollywood—World Center of Motion Picture Production." *Annals of the American Academy of Political and Social Science*, 254 (November 1947): 12–17.

INDEX

CPSIA information can be obtained at www.ICGtesting.com
Printed in the USA
BVOW10s1821160813

328727BV00004B/10/P

9 780415 991995